The Life & Times of W.H. Arnold of Arkansas

Reconstructing the Southern Ideal

W.H. Arnold, 1861-1946

The Life & Times
of W.H. Arnold of Arkansas

Reconstructing the Southern Ideal

By

MARI SEREBROV

Copyright © 2005 by Mari Serebrov

All rights reserved. No part of this book shall be reproduced or transmitted in any form or by any means, electronic, mechanical, magnetic, photographic including photocopying, recording or by any information storage and retrieval system, without prior written permission of the publisher. No patent liability is assumed with respect to the use of the information contained herein. Although every precaution has been taken in the preparation of this book, the publisher and author assume no responsibility for errors or omissions. Neither is any liability assumed for damages resulting from the use of the information contained herein.

ISBN 0-7414-2549-1

Front cover design: Brett Murray

Published by:

INFINITY
PUBLISHING.COM

1094 New DeHaven Street, Suite 100
West Conshohocken, PA 19428-2713
Info@buybooksontheweb.com
www.buybooksontheweb.com
Toll-free (877) BUY BOOK
Local Phone (610) 941-9999
Fax (610) 941-9959

Printed in the United States of America
Printed on Recycled Paper
Published June 2005

In memory of
Richard Sheppard Arnold,
who fulfilled his grandfather's dream

Contents

Preface xi

Note About Sources xiii

Foreword xv

Introduction xix

1 Arkansas: A New Frontier 1
2 Shadows 11
3 In Search of El Dorado 20
4 Settling In 27
5 Road to Secession 39
6 Call to Arms 49
7 On the Homefront 58
8 A Discharge of Duty 67
9 Fall of Vicksburg 76
10 The War at Home 89
11 A State Divided 100
12 The End 109
13 Aftermath of War 119
14 Hard Lessons 132

15	Shadow of Reconstruction	139
16	Coming of Age	152
17	In Pursuit of the Law	161
18	Planting Roots	169
19	Upheaval	177
20	Politics, Texarkana Style	186
21	Progress and Problems	196
22	City of the Second Class	216
23	Modernity	224
24	Practicing Politics	233
25	Fear and Hatred	242
26	The Crusade	251
27	The Rule of Violence	259
28	North vs. South	269
29	Economic Divide	277
30	Year of Disaster	285
31	A Change of Times	294
32	Elections and Epidemics	303
33	Reconstructing the Ideal	310
34	A Civic Duty	319
35	In Search of Public Honor	328
36	The Arnolds in the 20th Century	336

Appendix A:
    Selected Arnold Genealogy 343
Appendix B:
    Selected Arnold Military Record 355
Appendix C:
    Selected Slave Records
    of the Arnold Family 361
Notes 364
Bibliography 406
Index of Place Names 413
Index of People 418
General Index 425

Preface

Sharecroppers looking for more opportunity, my grandparents migrated north during World War II, trading the cotton and tobacco fields of the South for a factory. But they didn't trade in their Southern culture. That they wore proudly – and passed on to their children and their children's children. That culture embodied a way of life – Sunday family dinners, a close connection to kin (many of whom had migrated with them), a sense of honor and duty, and a deep love for family history.

As a child growing up in the Midwest, I never tired of Grandma reciting poetry from her childhood, regaling me with stories from her youth, and poring over the family photo album. Sepia-toned tintypes of my ancestors staring unsmilingly into the camera lens shared the pages with the school pictures and black-and-white snapshots of my father, uncle, aunts, and cousins many times removed.

The faded photographs always sparked questions – especially the one of Grandma's grandfather, a bearded, ancient man clad in the remnants of his Confederate uniform. But Grandma's answers provoked even more questions. How had her family, once numbered among the planters of the South, been reduced to sharecroppers laboring on borrowed land? Those early questions indirectly gave rise to this book, which explores the effects of the Civil War and Reconstruction on the Arnolds, an emerging planter family, and the Arkansas communities they called home.

* * *

Many families have their share of oral traditions, of pride of lineage. But, frequently, when held up to the magnifying glass of research, some of these traditions may wilt, and the pride gets singed. Thus, it takes courage to open family records to an outsider. In freely releasing documents, suggesting sources, and granting interviews, Richard S. Arnold and Morris S. "Buzz" Arnold supported an honest portrayal of their family history as a representation of middle-class life in 19th-century Arkansas. This project could not have been completed without their openness, encouragement, and blessing. It was as if we were fellow explorers on an historical expedition. Having someone to share this with heightened the thrill of discovery as little shards of the past fell into place.

Thanks also are due to my advisers Dr. Nudie Williams and Dr. Jeannie Whayne. Their encouragement helped me overcome obstacles that could have prevented the completion of this project. Their professionalism and scholarship in this area set a standard for me to live up to. And their guidance was invaluable.

Two others deserve special recognition. Dr. Willard Gatewood, whom I will always consider a mentor, was the first to make me feel welcome as a nontraditional graduate student in the history department at the University of Arkansas. He gave me the confidence to pursue my studies and put forth my ideas. He understood the connection between my background as a journalist and the pursuit of a historian. To my husband, Job Serebrov, I owe the greatest debt. He introduced me to the Arnolds and, through his friendship with Buzz, developed the idea for this topic. He chased down research prospects, hunted for sources, endured too many monologues about my discoveries, and discussed various aspects of the topic with me.

Others who have had a hand in this project are Brett Murray, a fantastic graphic designer who created the cover art; Dr. Bruce Swaffield, my colleague at Regent University who offered a "second pair of eyes" at an opportune time; Frances Ross, who shared research notes; and the staff of the Torreyson Library Archives at the University of Central Arkansas. Thank you all.

My only regret is that Richard and Nudie did not live to see this project completed.

Note About Sources

This book relies heavily on *The Arnold Family*, a collection of correspondence, research notes, and reminiscences of William H. Arnold and various family members that Arnold had printed in 1935. Unless attributed to other sources, all factual information about the Arnold family and quotes attributed to William Arnold come from *The Arnold Family*.

Frequently used abbreviations:
ACA   *Autauga County, Alabama, Records*
AHQ   *Arkansas Historical Quarterly*
BHM   *Biographical and Historical Memoirs of Southern Arkansas*
CWA   *Confederate Women of Arkansas in the Civil War 1861-'65: Memorial Reminiscences*
DCA   *Dallas County, Alabama, Records*, vol. 90
DTD   *Daily Texarkana Democrat*
DTI   *Daily Texarkana Independent*
IMA   Morris S. Arnold, interview by author
IRA   Richard S. Arnold, interview by author
LH   *Louisiana History*
LHQ   *The Louisiana Historical Quarterly*
NYT   *New York Times*
19-F   "19th (Dockery's) Arkansas Infantry Regiment Confederate States of America, Company F"
19-SD   "19th (Smead's-Dockery's) Arkansas Infantry Regiment"
TDT   *The Daily Texarkanian*
VGD   "Life in Confederate Arkansas: The Diary of Virginia Davis Gray, 1863-1865," *AHQ* 42
WBT   *Widows by the Thousand: The Civil War Letters of Theophilus and Harriet Perry, 1862-1864*

Foreword

Having been called to the bar in Texarkana, Arkansas, in 1965, I am well acquainted with the breadth of the accomplishments of "those Arnold lawyers" over the past four decades; but until reading *Reconstructing the Southern Ideal: The Life and Times of W.H. Arnold of Arkansas*, I was only vaguely aware of the antecedents of the current generation of Arnolds.

The Arnolds came to Arkansas during its frontier days. All of them were, or soon became, upper middle class by the standards of the time. Ms. Serebrov's book gives the reader a special bonus. She includes an excellent portrayal of life in frontier Arkansas and the later years just before the Civil War years when Arkansas society was torn asunder. A judicious selection of contemporary sources carries the reader to those scenes of yesteryear.

And the discussion of the complicated Brooks-Baxter "war" is the most lucid summary of this imbroglio that I have seen.

W.H. (William Hendrick) Arnold, the centerpiece of this book, was born in 1861 and died in 1946 after a long and distinguished career. During his early years, his family struggled because the Civil War had virtually ruined them economically, as it had most of the people who had been upwardly mobile in the years just before the war. His father, David Arnold, prized education and was surely disappointed that his financial means would not permit him to provide classical educations for his children. Yet he insisted that they get the best education available to families in southern Arkansas during the lean years after the war.

W.H. (now "William"), who studied law in a law office and was admitted to the Arkansas Bar when he was 21 years old, wasted no time in commencing his practice in Prescott, Arkansas. But he soon moved to Texarkana where the opportunities were greater. Over the years, he built a flourishing law practice the old-fashioned way. The first few years, he – sometimes in partnership with another lawyer – struggled to build a practice. He drew deeds, closed alleys, and attended sessions of court in Texarkana and other southwest Arkansas towns. He attended church regularly (he was a lifelong Methodist), participated in civil affairs, and, early on, developed a love of politics and public life.

Those who suffer defeat in public affairs and who are tempted to withdraw from the field of battle ought to read this book. W.H. Arnold was shot through with ambition to succeed as a lawyer, to be elected to public office, and to be appointed to the federal bench. He wanted to serve. And, although he became a highly successful lawyer, his political defeats outnumbered his victories, and he was never able to secure a nomination to the federal bench. Nevertheless, he followed the admonition Winston Churchill was to give years later to the students at Harrow during his last appearance at his alma mater: "Never give in. Never give in. Never, never, never, never – in nothing, great or small, large or petty – never give in!"

Despite many setbacks, W.H. Arnold forged ahead and spent little time crying over spilt milk.

As the shadow of his career was falling far to the east, he developed the odd habit of dropping off his biography wherever he and his family stayed. But the building of his law practice and his law firm comports completely with the idea expressed by Chief Justice Charles Evan Hughes:

> The highest reward that can come to a lawyer is the esteem of his professional brethren. That esteem is won in unique conditions and proceeds from an impartial judgment of professional rivals. It cannot be purchased. It cannot be artificially created. It cannot be gained by artifice or contrivance to attract public attention. It is not measured by pecuniary gains. It is an esteem which is born in sharp contests and thrives despite conflicting interests. It is an esteem commanded solely by integrity of character and by brains and skill in the honorable per-

formance of professional duty.... In a world of imperfect humans, the faults of human clay are always manifest. The special temptations and tests of lawyers are obvious enough. But, considering trial and error, success and defeat, the bar slowly makes its estimate and the memory of the careers which it approves are at once its most precious heritage and an important safeguard of the interests of society so largely in the keeping of the profession of the law in its manifold services.

It seems as if W.H. Arnold passed on a lawyer gene to his children because the tradition of Arnolds becoming lawyers remains strong today. It makes one think of these words from Ecclesiasticus:

> All these were honoured in their generations
> And were the Glory of their times
> There be of them
> That have left a name behind them
> That their praises might be reported
> With their seed shalt continually remain
> A good inheritance
>
> And their children for their sakes
> Their seed shall remain forever
> And their glory shall not be blotted out
> Their bodies are buried in peace
> But their name liveth for evermore

I recommend, without reservation, this book to all Arkansawyers and others interested in 19th-century Southern history.

William Wilson
U.S. District Judge

Introduction

The Southern ideal.

The very concept unleashes a world of contradicting images and stereotypes rooted in fact and fiction, the distant past and the present, the Northern perception and the Southern reality. It also begs the question: Is there – or was there ever – a Southern ideal distinct from that of the rest of the nation?

To define the ideal, we must first understand the character of the South. The definitions of this character range from the simplistic to the complex, from the noble to the common. Historian Carl N. Degler, in one of the simpler definitions, equates the essence of Southern character with a deep-rootedness to place, family, and tradition; it is the embodiment of the Jeffersonian agrarian model. F.N. Boney describes the antebellum Southerner as a homegrown type with middle-class attitudes and a strong work ethic. He was "polite but not refined, intelligent but not intellectual," Boney writes. Wilbur J. Cash, himself a postwar Southerner, summed up the distinctive character of the South in terms of extravagance, gregariousness, boastfulness, and "the Southern love for high and noble and somewhat nebulous profession, and the Southern joy in the sense of participating in tremendous though indefinite enterprise and in mysterious bonds."[1]

Cash saw the dominant trait of the Southern character as an individualism spurred by both the long-lived frontier of the South and the self-sufficiency of plantation life and the hill country. While both the North and South valued individualism, the two regions had different ideas about this concept. In the North, Eugene D. Genovese explains, this concept applied strictly to individuals; while in the South, it was inextricably tied to family, community, civic responsibility, and a living history. In a region steeped in historical consciousness – a sense of the past in the present – the dignity of the individual was rooted in the community and the family, both past and present. Thornton Wilder noted these differences when he described the North's commitment to abstraction – an individualism with no tie to place, locality, or environment. But in the South, Wilder found that place was a door to the mind. "Place, environment, relationships, repetitions are the breath of their being," Wilder said of Southerners.[2]

Bertram Wyatt-Brown maintains that the distinctiveness of the Southern character stemmed from a unique code of honor. This honor united inner virtue with the natural order of reason and man's innate desire for good. While inner worthiness or virtue was crucial to honor, it alone did not make for honorable people. Instead, Wyatt-Brown explains, the evaluation of the community ultimately determined the honor of an individual. What others thought mattered. This emphasis on public scrutiny and evaluation resulted in intense devotion to family, commitment to community values, and dedication to tradition. Piety entered the equation in the late antebellum period when evangelical Christianity took hold, adding the element of accountability to God.[3]

The Southern code of honor was integrated more completely into the whole of culture than in the North. The very structure of Southern society rested upon it. This code affected the way Southerners judged themselves and others; it influenced how they viewed hierarchy and government; it dictated how they settled disputes and conflicts. Honor gave them structure in life and provided meaning to valor, values, and family. Allegiance to Southern honor produced order from chaos and made frontier life more predictable by establishing appropriate conduct. "It staved off the danger of self-love and vainglory and in the circles of the genteel, it elevated moderation and learnedness to virtues of self-disciplined community service," Wyatt-Brown writes. "Since honor gave meaning to lives, it existed not as a myth but as a vital code."[4]

Honor was woven into the lives of even the smallest children. "The determination of men to have power, prestige, and self-esteem and to immortalize these acquisitions through their progeny was the key to the South's development," according to Wyatt-Brown. This immortalized sense of honor, taught from infancy, took on a special intensity in the Southern family. It stressed lineage and an obligation to family reputation. What came close to veneration of forefathers, their traditions, and the genetic foundation served as both inspiration and a formidable duty to live up to ancestral heroes. Children of the South customarily knew their family tree and all of its branches. They were strengthened by the challenges their ancestors had faced and overcome. They breathed the essence of their forefathers passed on through tradition. These exercises in family history helped create solidarity among the generations and served as a guide for the young.[5]

Even a child's name connected him or her to the past. Southern naming patterns repeated family Christian names and often used the mother's maiden name as a first or middle name. "The relation of the dutiful child to ancestors and to community was made clear; one could not easily escape to pursue one's own hopes under such circumstances," Wyatt-Brown writes. In contrast, the North began changing its naming patterns by the early 1800s with fewer and fewer children named for family members. Some historians ascribe this change to a growing sense of individuality in the North, a freedom from the past and familial ties. The promise of the future for Northerners was for personal opportunity more so than family interests.[6]

The Southerners' early lessons in family roots grew into a structure that molded their sense of honor, class identification, and social status. Since class identification and status were so closely related to familial honor, kinship ties were valued over all others. It was common for Southern families to lace themselves closely together through marriages between cousins. In marrying a cousin, a young person was guaranteed a union of equals. The centrality of organic social relations – based on the kinship network – kept the South's cultural development intact while in the North, the traditional cultural development unraveled with the birth of new social relations more appropriate for an industrial society.[7]

The Southern sense of honor was not restricted to family duty. Its public face bore a sincere expression of responsibility to the community, especially for the genteel – the ideal of Southern society. This ideal, based more on attitude and upbringing than on accumulated property, embodied the best of Southern characteristics and stressed a life devoted to public honor. Southern gentility understood their great duty in life was to promote the happiness and welfare of their neighbors and, that in doing this duty, they would find true individualism and freedom. To prepare their children for this life of public duty, they valued education. Those with the economic means invested in their sons' future by sending them to English schools or to such Northern institutions as Princeton and Harvard to study law or medicine. Those who could not afford these schools – the gentility who made up the upper middle class – sent their sons to the newer schools springing up in the South. With an emphasis on classical education, they instilled in their sons a heroic, military tradition accompanied by a strong sense of obligation to their family and their state. (While the education of the sons was a top priority, those who could afford it also saw to it that their daughters received a proper education.)[8]

For many young men, a classical education was the entrée into the select fraternity of gentlemen in the 19th-century South. The ideal gentleman could be identified by his erudition. He could quote Latin mottoes, discuss what happened at Cannae, and understand allusions to classical history and mythology. He would have read the *Iliad* and could discourse on Socrates, Tacitus, Xenophon, Caesar, Polybius, Sophocles, Marcus Aurelius, Virgil, Hannibal, Lucretius. His learning did not stop with the ancient classics; he also could parade the thoughts of William Shakespeare, John Milton, Roger Bacon, John Locke, Isaac Newton. Such an education forged a common language among the genteel, providing reference points, identifiers, and a shared value system.[9]

It also provided a justification for their slave society. In his *Politics*, Aristotle defended slavery, saying, "He then is by nature formed a slave, who is fitted to become the chattel of another person, and on that account is so." The Greek philosopher further developed the concept of predestination to slavery: "It is the intention of nature to make the bodies of slaves and free men different from each other, that the one should be robust for their necessary purposes, but the other erect; useless indeed for such servile labors, but fit for civil life.... It is clear then that some men are free by nature, and others are slaves." With such reasoning, the Southern slaveholder could quiet his conscience and know that he was playing out the role that nature – or God – had intended.[10]

Unlike the European and Northern elites, the ranks of the Southern gentility were not strictly limited to the wealthy. That is not to say there was no aristocracy in the South. Distinguished bloodlines and wealth gave birth to a type of aristocracy that was like a "fine garment put on from the outside," Cash wrote. Although Southern aristocrats could wrap themselves in this elite garment with seeming ease and assurance and convince themselves that they had a right to wear it, "they nevertheless could not endow their subconscious with the aristocrat's experience – with the calm certainty, bred of that experience.... In their innermost being they carried nearly always ... an uneasy sensation of inadequacy for their role," Cash said of the Southern aristocrat.[11]

Southern aristocracy is not to be confused with gentility, which was not in itself a social rank; rather, it was a "specialized, refined form of honor, in which moral uprightness was coupled with high social position," Wyatt-Brown explains. This ideal rested more gently on the yeoman farmer than on the aristocrat as the middle-class Southerner did not have to put on false airs to convince himself or his neighbors of his personal self-worth. Instead, he developed a "kindly courtesy, a level-eyed pride, an easy quietness" that set him apart from his Northern peer. Living the ideal is what made a man a gentleman; a sizable wallet, without honor, meant nothing. Just as it was possible for a middle-class Southerner to be viewed as the pillar of his community and the embodiment of the cultural ideal, it was equally possible that an aristocratic planter, successful in financial terms and of the highest bloodlines, could be seen as a wastrel without honor.[12]

While the Southern ideal was not based on property holdings, there was an expectation that those people who exhibited true honor would be successful financially. Hard work would pay off; doing one's duty had its rewards. "Wealth was available to all, and honest labor produced it," Carl H. Moneyhan writes. So in theory, the idea of Southern aristocracy was not bound by rigid class lines or strata of nobility. Thus, in thought – if not always in practice – the Southern aristocracy belonged to a fluid class consisting of self-made, mobile entrepreneurs who diversified by speculating in land, establishing plantations, and functioning as merchants, doctors, and lawyers. In bettering themselves, they improved their communities and raised their family's status.[13]

The plain folk of the South assumed that their own ambitious and hard-working sons and daughters could enter the realm of the aristocratic planter, the top economic echelon – if they so desired. "... [I]t was considered a common occurrence outside the older states of Virginia and the Carolinas for the rank and file to move upward on the economic scale, and for individuals in every community to become well-to-do planters, political leaders, and members of a learned profession," Frank Lawrence Owsley wrote. However, Boney contends that "in practice only a tiny handful ever achieved this much success, and they were usually bourgeois types with business experience who carried on the progress of at least one previous generation."[14]

While only a relative few Southerners achieved the financial success associated with aristocracy, the ranks of the upper middle class swelled with the gentility whose lives were shaped by the ideal of honor. Many of them were doctors, lawyers, and preachers. They were the leaders of their churches, of civic organizations, of their communities. If given a choice between personal wealth and duty to others, they would choose the path of duty; it was their moral obligation, their tribute of honor to their ancestors. As often as not, this choice was not a selfless decision. Aspirations of serving as a judge, a senator, or a governor could be self-serving. But in choosing such aspirations, the Southern gentleman carried out his duties honorably and selflessly.[15]

Meanwhile, he clung to the possibility that, if not he, at least his children would reach the next economic rung while still holding fast to the family values and sense of duty. This success would reflect backward on the family that had produced such a child, imbuing that family with the public recognition necessary to Southern honor. It also would bind future generations to live up to and build upon the family honor. The Southern ideal survived on the fact that dedication to selfless duty achieved self-serving goals.

The ideal shaped the dreams and ambitions of Southerners. Its concept of honor as something inviolable and precious imposed standards of conduct that were handed down to every class and generation. Thus was born the image of the Southern gentleman to whom the community naturally turned for leadership in times of crisis. C. Vann Woodward describes this person as "a man of complete integrity, enlightened, gracious, and generous." Cash and Wyatt-Brown portray him as someone with a refined form of honor, in whom moral uprightness couples with social position, and as a man recognized for his learning, piety, and sociability – an attribute that includes wit and oratorical skills.[16]

Rather than creating envy in the hearts of the less successful, the gentleman became a symbol of hope. With a little luck and a lot of hard work, even the son of a poor hill family could achieve this ideal. While Southern society was not truly egalitarian, it rested upon equality of aspiration. "Regardless of class origins or position," Genovese explains, "every white man could aspire to be considered a gentleman by dint of his own effort and merit. In this respect, Southern society had a perpetually frontier quality, which democratized the aspiration to equality. In consequence, Southern republicanism recoiled against hereditary status but not against family and class." Such aspirations allowed those who equated the ideal with wealth – both the romantic dreamers and the more practical ones who peopled the region – to believe that the ideal was just a land deal away or another year's harvest. The South, with its abundant frontier offering a lifetime of opportunity, held out the promise of economic and social success to those who were willing to pursue its untapped riches.[17]

The opportunities of the region appealed to the individualistic nature of Southerners. Their ancestors had cut their ties to the Old World, had taken risks in an unknown land with unfamiliar crops, had fought against king and soldier to protect their rights to the promise of this frontier. Following the lead of their ancestors, Southerners of the late 18th and 19th centuries looked westward when their land played out or their sons needed more land. In the millions of virgin acres to the west rested the hopes of would-be planters. As they moved westward, they migrated as an entire congregation or community or moved to areas where their kin had already established a foothold. Along with their household goods and stock, they brought their dreams and aspirations, their commitment to honor, family, and community. They tamed the new areas in the likeness of their Southern culture, transplanting their sense of place to the frontier.[18]

Some historians argue that this distinctive Southern character with its honor-bound ideal died on the battlefields of the Civil War and was buried in the subsequent destruction of the Old South. The initial shock of losing what – in their minds – had seemed a just and glorious cause, coupled with the economic price of that defeat, was more than some Southerners could bear. "The revolution of our social fabric is too great, the entire upheaval and overthrow of all the foundations of our society too universal not to affect everybody and to place persons in an almost entirely new status," Dr. Richard D. Arnold, Savannah's wartime mayor, wrote upon the dawn of defeat.[19]

As if being the first Americans to suffer the shame of defeat were not enough, Southerners had to pay an even higher price to the Northern victors. In seeking both to punish and cleanse the South, the North tried to reshape the region in its own image. George W. Julian stood up in Congress January 28, 1867, to impress upon his peers his vision of congressional Reconstruction. He proposed a prolonged period of federal control so as to allow "loyal public opinion to sink deep roots and permit 'Northern capital and labor, Northern energy and enterprise' to venture South, there to establish 'a Christian civilization and a living democracy.'" Julian's words pushed open the door for congressional Reconstruction and military rule in the South.[20]

For years, traditional historians, following the lead of William Dunning and John W. Burgess, blamed Reconstruction for the demise of the Old South. Although they cast Reconstruction in a different light, revisionists such as W.E.B. Du Bois also saw it playing a crucial role in forever changing Southern life. There were the naysayers, though, who contended the distinctive South was, is, and always will be. "... [T]he extent of the change and of the break between the Old South that was and the South of our time has been vastly exaggerated," Cash wrote in 1941. "The South, one might say, is a tree with many age rings, with its limbs and trunk bent and twisted by all the winds of the years, but its tap root is the Old South." Because of this root, Cash insisted that the South marches from the present toward its past, and that both its present and future are determined by its past. More than a century after the Civil War, post-revisionists echoed Cash's philosophy as they began to question whether Reconstruction had truly changed anything. Were the war and Reconstruction merely part of the evolution of the South?[21]

Historians still debate whether the South evolved or was reconstructed. These academic inquiries are more than theoretical exercises. They provide modern historians a framework for digesting the economic, cultural, and political evolution of a region that had been torn apart by war and federal occupation. They help explain the rise of the glorious myths of the Old South in the stark reality of an encompassing and backward-pulling poverty. They give a context to continuing stereotypes and regional attitudes.

While these debates seek to shed light on the big picture of the Southern experience, they do little to tell the story of the people who lived through the war, through Reconstruction, through Redemption, and through the modernization of the South. While directly affected and shaped by such events, these people also were molded by their family values, their heroes, their sense of honor, and their debt to the past. In many instances, their vision of the Southern ideal was often strengthened by the war and its aftermath. After facing the initial shock of defeat, occupation, and total financial loss, they pulled up their sleeves and went back to work, relying on their families, their communities, their honor to overcome the setbacks of war and Reconstruction. For them, their sense of obligation to the past was intensified. The wartime sacrifices of their families and communities required of them a higher level of honor – an honor that demanded they erase the stigma of defeat and prove the righteousness of their culture.

The children born immediately before or during the war never experienced the "Old South." But they were its offspring. While sitting at their mother's knee, they learned its values, heard of its great leaders, dreamed of carrying on the family heritage. As they grew, they carried these lessons into makeshift classrooms and enlarged upon them as they listened to their fathers, uncles, and schoolmasters reminiscing about the Lost Cause and the battles they had fought. From these lessons, they learned how to judge the worth of a man, knew what was expected of true sons and daughters of the South, and understood their role in the continuum of their family's history. When they had families of their own, many of them handed the same lessons on to their children and their children's children.

Yes, they had to adjust their dreams in light of the harsh economic and political realities that followed the war. But through it all, they remained true to those Southern values that had been handed down from one generation to another. And, in the end, they formed the bridge from the Old South to the New. They provided the continuity that can still be sensed, even if much diluted, today. It is their lives that tell the true story – the human story – of the evolution of the South.

These children of the Old South instilled its historical consciousness in the next generation. But this fact is sometimes overlooked by a study of history that reduces the people of yesterday to one-dimensional caricatures or statistics to prove a hypothesis rather than recognizing them as complex human beings influenced not only by their circumstances but also by their families and communities. For instance, Charles Brough, the governor of Arkansas during World War I, has been widely accepted as a voice of the New South. Historians have described him as a "vanguard of southern reformers whose goal was to move their region into the mainstream of twentieth century American life." These historians, focusing on Brough's actions as the antithesis of traditional Southern politics and holding him up as a poster child for the New South, fail to see or purposely ignore the roots of his reforms. Looking deeper than the governor's actions, historian Charles Orson Cook discovered those roots are quite evident in Brough's writings. Cook says the governor's speeches and essays reveal "an important aspect of his thinking that was traditionally southern and rooted in the antebellum world of the nineteenth, not the twentieth, century.... [His] view of a new and progressive Dixie was based in part on his nostalgic conception of a pre-Civil War South characterized by hierarchy, stability, and order." Guided by these principles, Cook says, Brough "fashioned a view of a new southern society from the forge of historical experience."[22]

Brough is not an isolated example. All across the South, the children of the war years carried with them the ideals of Southern honor. The war, and even Reconstruction, could not change the ideals, the values, of Southern life. What they did change was the face of the frontier that had allowed the lowliest born to aim for the ranks of aristocracy. The frontier shifted, moving away from the tangibility of the land to an intangible concept carved out of pieces of opportunity, professionalism, and modernity. Strengthened by the principles of the Old South, its children, like their fathers before them, learned to tame and embrace this new frontier. In so doing, they quietly served their communities, invested in their children's education, performed their duty to God and man, and continued to bring honor to their family name.

History, in general, has ignored these children of the South. With its spotlight shining brightly on the famous, the infamous, the disenfranchised, and the marginalized, history seldom focuses on middle-class Americans, the true movers and shapers of our country. William Hendrick Arnold was such a man. He also was a child of the Old South.

Born in 1861 to an emerging planter family in southern Arkansas, William's first memories were not those of war and occupation. Rather, he remembered playing with the slave children in the smokehouse, being left atop a horse for what seemed an eternity, dangling his feet in the water as he crossed the Red River on a ferry, and being terrified the first night he camped under the stars. Although he was a war refugee, William's young life was the stuff of innocent childhood. War and its accompanying fears and tragedies were for adults.

The war, however, altered William's life in every way imaginable. It determined his upbringing, restricted his education, provided his childhood heroes, and shaped his future. Although it limited his options, the war, and its aftermath, also opened a new frontier with fresh possibilities. It gave William the chance to reconstruct the Southern ideal, to build upon his family honor, and to pass that responsibility to future generations of Arnolds. While this is William's story, it is the story of his ancestors, his descendants, and his community.

To understand William's life, we must see it painted against the bigger backdrop of Arkansas. There we will discover the events, the values, and the forces that molded his life. Thus, this is also the story of Arkansas.

1 Arkansas: A New Frontier

Like his father and grandfather before him, William Bideston Arnold was mesmerized by the call of the frontier. It beckoned him – almost taunted him – with the dust the wagon wheels spit up as they dug into the Alabama dirt on their way westward – always westward. It seduced him through the letters he received from relatives and neighbors who already had given in to its siren's call.[1]

A former sheriff of Chambers County, Alabama, who made his living from the land and served God as a lay minister with the Methodist Church, William thought of the many mouths he had to feed and silenced the urge to join those wagons headed toward a tantalizing promise of cultivating a new land with Southern values and hard work. But there were moments, long ones, in which his eyes settled musingly on the distant horizon. What waited for him beyond that skyline where the clouds gathered before descending on his patch of tired earth? Would life be better there?

A child tugging on his shirt or a knock at the door brought him back to the reality of his responsibilities. The frontier was for adventurers, for young men just making their way in the world, for those who could afford to take risks. He'd had his chance. Born in Logan County, Kentucky, in 1791, he had followed his parents to Autauga County, Alabama. He had been young then, about 27, and without the care of a family. The wilderness of Alabama had challenged the young man, who welcomed the chance to break in a country that was home to only a few settlers, to tame its wildness, to civilize it as only a Southerner could.[2]

He remembered when the first Methodist preachers came to hold services in his neck of the Alabama woods in 1821; they had used the untamed forest for a chapel and a wild river as a baptistry. It hadn't taken much arm-twisting to get the few whites in the area to attend the services. Most of them hadn't been in a church service for years, and they found any social event a rare treat. That had been quite an experience. Much as Jesus had preached to the multitudes along the shore of the Sea of Galilee, Rev. Thomas Griffin, the presiding elder, gathered the settlers at a small clearing near the river. As the settlers prayed and pondered the minister's words, they could hear the occasional splash of curious Indians fishing nearby in the river. William ignored the sounds of bears ravaging the cornfields and the wolves howling in the woods; God was speaking to him. His introduction to the pietism of Methodism was an intense experience that changed his life. Filled with an evangelical fervor that emphasized the need for individual spiritual conversion, William answered the call of God.[3]

William knew early on that the life of a Methodist preacher would not be easy. All of the ministers were circuit riders, which meant most of their time was spent traversing the dangers of the wilderness to preach and minister to isolated groups of settlers. It would be a hard life for a man with a family. Could he ask a woman to share that life with him? After weighing his choices, William chose to serve God as a lay preacher. His ministry began at home with his family, which included 10 slaves, and spread to the community.[4]

Armed with this missionary zeal, William served as a preacher in the growing frontier community when the circuit riders were not available. He performed marriages and exhorted both white and slave. Like many of the early Methodist preachers, William gave great attention to the religious interests of the slaves, who were numbered along with the whites as members of the local congregations. Among the early Methodists, slave and free frequently worshipped together, took the sacraments together, and prayed together. As a minister of the gospel and the head of his household, William could identify with Philemon, the New Testament slave owner who was challenged by the Apostle Paul to receive his runaway slave Onesimus as more than a slave – as a "dear brother" in the Lord. William understood that he had both a paternal and spiritual obligation to his slaves. Thus when the Methodist Church began licensing intelligent, trustworthy slaves to exhort and preach, William encouraged Sam, one of his slaves, to become a preacher. Sam became as popular with the white members of the church as with the black.[5]

William enjoyed attending and preaching at the slave services, which were so much freer and more passionate than the white worship. There was an innocence, a naturalness, about it that was almost inspiring. The slaves "were impulsive and demonstrative, and were easily moved," a Methodist minister wrote. "A certain sort of ecclesiastical outcry put them in a glow and set them in motion. Swinging and intoning were popular parts of their worship. There was a peculiar swaying of the body and there was a peculiar voicing of sounds the inhibition of which cooled their ardor and marred their happiness. The preacher who would be acceptable ... had to understand their desire to toss and intone during divine service, and grant them liberty and indulgence therein. There was among them in their worship a mixture of sighs, moans, and groans, which made a peculiar sound, and which were peculiar to them, and which it is impossible to embody in words. While they were not cultured in music, they were gifted in singing. Some of them were able in prayer and exhortation. They were 'fervent in spirit, serving the Lord.'"[6]

William and his family – both free and slave – rejoiced when revival swept through the area in the spring and summer of 1827. All of them put aside many of their routine chores so they could attend the services, which drew people from a 100-mile radius. As a result, some of William's nieces, nephews, children, and slaves were among the 350 converted that spring and summer. "The work of grace especially among the young people, was deep and Scriptural," J.G. Jones, a Methodist pastor in the Canebrake region of Alabama, wrote of the revival. "The awakenings were clear and well marked with true repentance and a saving faith in Christ, succeeded by a bright experience of love, peace, and joy." The revival continued at a camp meeting that fall when 50 to 60 more converts were baptized in the river.[7]

William smiled as he reflected on how God had worked in Alabama. Yes, life had been good for him here. He and his wife, Lucinda "Lucy" Powell Hardin, were well respected. Although not aristocrats in terms of property, they could count themselves among the upper middle class. And when it came to children, they were wealthy. Their eight children – the ninth was on the way – were growing up with their aging grandparents and plenty of aunts, uncles, and cousins to keep them from boredom and give them a sense of family continuity and responsibility. As he counted his blessings, William considered his slaves, who were healthy and living God-fearing lives. He would have been – could have been – content to spend the rest of his life in Alabama were it not for the call of the frontier. He missed that wilderness quality Alabama was quickly outgrowing.

The call had grown harder to ignore ever since his younger brother, Thomas Hendrick Arnold, had set off for the Arkansas wilderness. Thomas had bought 360 acres of government land August 1, 1837, in what was then Hempstead County, Arkansas. At about the same time, he had purchased a mill built several years earlier by John Jacobs at Terra Rouge in Hempstead County. Thomas was raising a large family, including triplet daughters, on his land that included Arnold's Mill. His letters to his family back in Alabama described the rugged beauty of the land, the possibilities waiting to happen on the western frontier.[8]

His stories were not the only ones tempting William. Several families from the area were moving west to Arkansas – some of them headed by men as old or older than he. Every letter and every story weakened William's resolve and Alabama's hold on him. His children deserved the same chances his father had given him when he had uprooted the family from Kentucky all those years ago. He owed them a chance to grow up in a new untamed country that they could mold as it, in turn, molded them. And he owed it to God and his fellow man to spread the gospel to the far-flung corners of the nation. Justifying the temptation, William filed on three sections of government land, totaling 160 acres, in Hempstead County November 1, 1839. With his ninth child, Temperance Lucinda Arnold, not even a year old, he packed up his family and began the arduous journey to Arkansas.[9]

As states go, Arkansas was an infant when the Arnolds arrived, having been admitted to the Union just three years earlier. Getting there from Alabama was not easy, especially with small children in tow. Rivers provided the most dependable transportation, and that was unpredictable at best. Most of the "roads" along the way were dim trails pressed down by adventurous feet. The trails cut through dense forests and led across malaria-infested swamps and streams. While William trusted in God to see them through, Lucy worried about the safety and health of her children. It was all too common for children to die at home from accidents or illness and disease. How much easier would it be for one of the little ones to succumb in this wilderness! Lucy could only imagine the horrors that lurked beneath the murky water as they trudged across the creeks and bayous. And at night as the family camped under the stars, she would lie awake, listening for wild animals. Only the exhaustion of the trail finally lulled her to sleep. The family traveled for hours – sometimes entire days – without meeting another soul. When they could, they traveled along the rough military roads cut through the forests and swamps. One of these roads, widened under President Andrew Jackson to 61 feet, cut from Little Rock to Fort Towson in Indian Territory, providing passage to Washington, the county seat of the vast Hempstead County.[10]

After days on the wilderness trail, the family, especially Lucy, welcomed any sign of civilization. Although more settled than much of the state, Hempstead County was anything but civilized. With a total population of 4,921 in 1840, Hempstead had fewer than seven residents per square mile. Many of these settlers were grouped by kinship in a few small villages and towns. By comparison, Arkansas as a state had only 1.9 residents per square mile in 1840, giving it wilderness status. (The U.S. Census Bureau defines wilderness in the 19th century as areas with fewer than two people per square mile and frontier as areas with two to six people per square mile.)[11]

Land, timber, game, and fresh fish were plentiful. So were the opportunities to minister. When the Arnolds arrived, the only place of public worship in the county was the Methodist Church in Washington. Circuit riders held camp meetings in brush arbors alongside the dirt roads to give the rest of the county a chance to repent. Although relatively small in size, Washington had become a major location in the state and was the natural business hub for the entire county. Abraham Block, the first Jewish settler in Arkansas, had opened a store in Washington by 1825 and then built a sturdy, two-story home for his family. By 1840, Block's store was the one-stop place to shop. With merchandise from New York and New Orleans, Block sold food, hardware, cutlery, saddles and tack, clothing, crockery, building materials – and slaves. The town also boasted a handful of other wooden shops, a few expensive homes, a fledgling Whig newspaper called *The Washington Telegraph*, several law offices, and a post office for its 400 residents. Four other post offices were scattered throughout the large county to service the farmers and tiny towns spread thinly across the rolling land. A few subscription schools provided the only education to be had.[12]

Although Washington offered the few amenities available to county residents, life throughout Hempstead was improving. The early settlers told tales of terror to remind newcomers how easy they had it compared with the "good old days" when the town was barely a thought. One of the tales concerned a minister, Parson Miller. An eccentric but devout Christian, the parson was preaching in the leafy grove where camp meetings were held in the earliest days of the county when he got so caught up in his sermon that he jumped from the pulpit to kneel with the repentant gathered at the mourners' bench. After praying fervently, he suddenly sprang to his feet and darted into the nearby woods. Another minister stepped to the pulpit, apologized for Brother Miller, and continued with the service. When the parson did not return, the faithful searched for him, but he was never seen again. Several years later, a skeleton, about his height, was found in the woods a few miles from Washington. The settlers figured the parson had lost his way and, overcome by fatigue, had lay down and died.[13]

Despite the dangers, William and Lucy discovered Thomas had been right about the opportunities that could be found in Arkansas. And the news about the state's potential had spread quickly. Within five years – from 1835 to 1840 – Arkansas' population had almost doubled to nearly 100,000. Little Rock, the state capital, was coming into its own as a city, complete with a mansion district, theater, a few churches, federal arsenal, horse racing, and occasional amusements such as visiting circuses and fireworks displays. Prominent residents of Little Rock sported fine beaver hats and silk dresses, drank quality wines, and read the latest books. Although Little Rock was acquiring the amenities of civilization, the rest of the state remained somewhat of an isolated wilderness – but a wilderness with hope. Those who endured the hardships were encouraged by the thought that someday the prosperity of Little Rock would spread.[14]

Such thoughts were spurred by generous land deals. The Arkansas Donation Law, passed in 1840, gave land that had been forfeited for nonpayment of taxes to any male head of family who would live on it, improve it – and pay his taxes. At first, a man could get only 160 acres under this law, but it was later modified, allowing a man to get an additional 160 acres for each member of his family. In 1841, the state offered 500,000 acres at $1.25 an acre with credit terms of six percent interest and a five-year payoff. Federal lands in Arkansas also were available at $1.25 an acre but on a cash-only basis. Two years later, Arkansas offered 930,000 acres that had been set aside for schools at $2 an acre with an option to pay off the land over a 10-year period.

Much of the land in Hempstead County became more attractive in the 1830s after workers cleared the "Great Raft" from the Red River. A tangled mass of stumps, logs, and debris, the Great Raft had blocked the river for 165 miles in northern Louisiana and southern Arkansas. It hindered river travel – and thus the marketing of crops to New Orleans – and the resulting trapped backwater rendered large areas of land unusable. With the raft cleared, several plantations flourished along the river by 1839.[15]

As pious Methodists, William and Lucy were not interested in the vices and frivolities associated with both the wilderness and civilization. They considered drinking a sin that subverted the family, weakened the church, and undermined the state. They also supported laws to keep the Sabbath holy and outlaw dueling and gambling.

But they were excited with the opportunities to expand both their ministry and their personal land holdings when they settled in the Missouri Township of Hempstead County (an area that later became part of Nevada County). They also expanded their family. Within a year, they had another child – a son, Robert – who rounded out their family to 10 children. Their farm, known as the McKillian plantation, prospered through the labor of the slaves. Like their neighbors, they grew corn, potatoes, and fruit and raised cattle and hogs.[16]

Besides tending to the plantation, William had ample social outlets through the church. He continued to preach, baptize, and officiate at weddings when no licensed minister was available and soon became known and respected as "Reverend William Arnold." As one of only 81 local Methodist preachers scattered throughout the state, William had plenty to keep him busy. He regularly attended church conferences and visited with the circuit preachers who ministered in Arkansas. If he had the time, he most likely helped John Henry – fondly called "Father Henry" – and William Stephenson build a church in the wilderness area of Mount Prairie. William would have been there in 1841 when Bishop Thomas A. Morris, while passing through the state, ordained Father Henry. And he would have helped the other church leaders plan and conduct brush arbor camp meetings throughout the county.[17]

Life was much lonelier for Lucy and her teen-age daughters. Raised in the traditional frontier society of the South, their choices of relationships – as women – were limited to neighborhood and kin. Their sense of identity stemmed from family and community. But on this new frontier, neighbors were a rarity, and they had left most of their kin in Alabama. The Arnold women had plenty to keep them busy – caring for the young children and the slaves, helping with the livestock and crops, and teaching Sunday school classes for both the slaves and their scattered neighbors. But they had little life outside their 650-square-foot, double-pen log house. Their world consisted primarily of the plantation and infrequent church services and camp meetings.[18]

The Arkansas frontier was home to few white women at the time. And the women who were there had their hands full raising an average of five to six children, the majority of whom were under 10. Besides tending to their families, they were expected to shoulder their share of the farm work. With little time or opportunity for visiting and socializing, frontier women lived a harsh life of duty with few rewards. The loneliness was even worse for teenagers and widows. Although the men outnumbered the women three to two, the oldest Arnold girls were hard pressed to find life partners who shared their pietism, tastes, likes, and dislikes. As they were considered gentility, they found it even more difficult to meet someone who would be considered their social equal. To fill the void, Lucy and the girls wrote long letters home to their relatives in Alabama.[19]

Some of those letters were addressed to William's oldest sister, Temperance Ross, who with her husband, Peter, and her younger children still lived by the family homestead on Mulberry Creek, near Burnsville, Dallas County, Alabama. The letters from Arkansas, coupled with the stories from Peter's relatives with Arkansas ties, proved too tempting for the Rosses, who also had the frontier emblazoned on their spirit. Leaving behind their oldest children who had married and started their own lives, Peter and Temperance packed up the remainder of their family, sold their home to her sister Ann "Nancy" Arnold Dunklin, and moved to Clark County, Arkansas, in 1843.[20]

Tagging along with the Rosses was the young Dr. Hendrick Howard Arnold. The son of William and Temperance's cousin Ira Arnold of South Carolina, Hendrick had moved to Pickens County, Alabama, in 1841, to start a medical practice near his kinfolk after getting a medical degree from Transylvania Medical College in Lexington, Kentucky. Equally seduced by the letters from Arkansas, Hendrick closed his fledgling practice in Alabama to join his relatives in Arkansas and hang out his shingle in Arkadelphia.

The move renewed family acquaintances and strengthened the valuable kinship network, creating a sense of familiarity and place in the Arkansas wilderness for both the Rosses and Arnolds. It also sparked romance as the Arnold girls found social equals in their Ross cousins. Caroline, William's third daughter, married her cousin Dr. David Carroll Ross August 11, 1842, in Hempstead County. Soon after their wedding, the young couple settled near Lisbon in Union County with its flat, rich soil ripe for plantations.[21]

2   Shadows

Life on the frontier was never happily ever after, a lesson that was driven home to everyone in Hempstead County in 1843 when the Red River, without warning, flooded its banks at unprecedented levels. People had gone to bed that night with no concerns about a flood. When the raging waters awakened them at midnight, they had to flee for their lives. Many of them heard the cries of neighbors drowning, but they were helpless in the dark of the night. Farms that had never before flooded were under water. The flood killed 100 people and destroyed everything in its path – houses, fences, stables, cotton presses, crops, and livestock. Although the Arnolds were not directly affected by the flood, they felt its economic impact. With no government programs to assist in such disasters, the county was devastated.[1]

Out of such tragedy, heroes always emerge. The community marveled over a farmer named Anderson who, when caught by the rising water, was forced to climb a tree and cling to it for dear life. With the water swirling below him and no one to answer his desperate cries for help, Anderson lashed himself to the top of the gum sapling with black jack vines – just in case he became too feeble to hang on. Four days later, another farmer was paddling about in a boat, looking for his stock. Seeing a turkey, he took aim and shot. The crack of the gun aroused the dazed Anderson who called out in a parched, feeble voice. Following the direction of the faint cry, the farmer came upon the starving man still lashed to the top of the tree.[2]

Another frontier hardship hit the Arnolds that December when they received word that William's father, Thomas, had died in Alabama. Given the distance and the difficulty in traveling through the wilderness, neither William nor his brother or sister could be at their father's deathbed. In his will, Thomas left the three children equal divisions of his land, but it was not enough to entice them to return to Alabama.[3]

On the heels of his father's death, William was faced with a spiritual dilemma of sorts that became a foreshadowing of what awaited the nation. The Methodist Church was tearing apart over slavery. There had been small rents in the past when individual clergy made an issue of slavery. Jesse Haile, for example, had created some division in Arkansas when he served as the presiding elder of the Arkansas Conference from 1825 to 1829. Vehemently opposed to slavery, Haile seized every opportunity to speak out against it. This offended most Arkansas Methodists who, like other Southern evangelicals, accepted slavery and encouraged the Christianization of individual slaves. Just as Methodist fathers considered themselves the spiritual leaders of their families, Methodist slaveholders saw themselves as the spiritual leaders of their slaves. They took seriously their responsibility for the souls of the slaves "entrusted" to them. Haile's harangues against slaveholders forced some Arkansans to leave the Methodist Church and join the Cumberland Presbyterians. Although Haile fomented divisions in the Arkansas church, those rifts began to heal when he was removed from the conference in 1829.[4]

Slavery was a serious issue in Hempstead County, which was very much a slave society by 1840 with 39 percent of its population slave. Although 20 percent of the taxpayers in the county owned slaves by 1840, the majority had one to four slaves. Only six percent of the slaveholders had at least 20 slaves. With 10 slaves, the Arnolds were in the upper echelons of Hempstead County society. Most of the slaveholders, including William, had long ago reconciled slavery with the teachings of the Bible. They would let no one, including a church hierarch, interfere with what they considered a sacred obligation to their slave families.[5]

After Haile left, Methodism thrived in Arkansas for more than a decade. Then slavery surfaced as a national issue for the church in the mid-1840s. This time, the rift could not be so easily mended. It began as a simple love story: Bishop James O. Andrew married a slave owner in Georgia. Because of state law, the bishop could not free his wife's slaves. Neither the bishop's marriage nor his ownership of slaves broke any church law, but his concession to slavery caused great excitement in the North where many Methodists had become outspoken abolitionists. Delegates from the Northern Conference raised the issue at the 1844 General Conference in New York, demanding that Andrew stop traveling as a bishop. "With the Northern Conference it was not a question of law and moral right, but of expediency," church historian Horace Jewell wrote. "The Southern delegates felt that Church membership was too sacred a right to be made to depend upon a question of expediency."[6]

As debate over the issue heated, tempers flared. Southern Methodists charged their Northern brethren with hypocrisy, pointing out that New Englanders had profited handsomely from the slave trade. They had made their fortunes using their ships to bring human cargo from Africa. In the opening days of the Revolution, slaves had been present in every New England colony; Massachusetts alone had had more than 6,000 slaves at the time of the war. The Southerners reminded their Northern brethren that all the larger colonial churches had accepted slavery without question and that many of the New England ministers had held slaves.[7]

The Northern Methodists refused to back down. Many of them believed the church would be better served if it split. The Southerners finally agreed and made plans to hold their own conference the next year in Louisville, Kentucky. The repercussions of the division were felt throughout the country. "It was impossible for such a large body of Christians so widely diffused over the whole territory of the United States, and occupying so commanding an influence in all the great centers of population to divide without creating a profound impression upon all classes of society," Jewell wrote. "Men of every religious creed, and those of no special faith, were profoundly moved with grave apprehensions for the safety of the country. It was felt that if so large and devoted a body of Christians, bound together by such ties ... could not resist the agitations of the slavery question, that other organizations and the country itself were in great peril."[8]

The division, seen by many as the opening wedge to divide other groups and the nation, shook the Methodist Church in Arkansas. Church membership dropped – the first decline in years. Nearly 1,000 Arkansans left the church in 1844 and another 336 left in 1845. Although the schism was discouraging, William remained steadfast in his faith and worked with other ministers to continue God's work. Their efforts eventually paid off. By 1847, the Methodist Church in Arkansas numbered 8,134 white members, 1,750 slave members, and 43 traveling preachers – up from the 1840 membership roll of 4,228 whites, 725 blacks, and 41 traveling preachers. The growth in membership, accompanied by the decline in circuit preachers, made lay ministers such as William more essential to the church. William dutifully fulfilled his role, baptizing converts, preaching at funerals, and performing marriages. One of those marriages was that of his nephew William B. Ross to Nancy P. Bozeman October 17, 1845.[9]

In the midst of these spiritual blessings, William and Lucy faced a personal test of faith in 1846 when their daughter Louiza Jane Arnold died at the age of 20. Until then, they had been spared the tragedy of burying a child, a common occurrence for most of their neighbors. William threw himself into a new project with the Methodist Church. A firm believer in the importance of education, William helped start church seminaries – one for young men and one for the women – in Washington, serving on the first board of directors for the school.

Modeled after similar Methodist efforts at LaGrange, Alabama, the school provided a classical education with an emphasis on godly living. The Female Seminary offered courses in music, foreign languages, art, and the traditional subjects of reading, writing, and arithmetic. It boasted "extensive chemical and philosophical apparatus" as well as several pianos and other musical instruments to assure the young ladies would be educated in "solid acquirements and in elegant accomplishments." The Male Seminary offered primary, preparatory, and collegiate programs. The collegiate courses enlightened students with classes that embraced "the advanced study of Mathematics,

Natural, Intellectual, and Moral Sciences and Ancient and Modern languages."[10]

While William devoted himself to ensuring that his children and others in the area could get a decent education, the United States was going to war with Mexico – ostensibly over the Texas boundary dispute. News of the war reached Arkansas in late spring. Gov. Thomas Drew, on May 27, 1846, called for the formation of a cavalry regiment to serve in Mexico and five companies of infantry to replace the federal soldiers who had served on the border of the Indian Territory until ordered south by Zachary Taylor. The response was so great that 10 companies formed and were supplied with arms from the arsenal in Little Rock. As the war fervor mounted, ladies embroidered the mottoes of the regiments onto flags and presented them in patriotic ceremonies replete with colorful drills and the sounds of brass bands. The itch to fight was so contagious that Archibald Yell of Fayetteville, a former governor and the state's leading Democratic congressman, resigned his seat and enlisted as a private in a company headed by Solon Borland.

The Arnolds, descended from Revolutionary patriots, were not immune to the fervor, but none of them answered the call to arms. Like many Whigs, they did not buy into the expansionist attitudes that gripped the nation. As a result, they opposed the Mexican War, which was the outgrowth of what had become almost a secular national religion – manifest destiny. Despite their political beliefs, the Arnolds could not help but get caught up in the pomp and ceremony as the Arkansas soldiers marched along the Military Road through Hempstead County on their way to Washington, their flags and colors flying high, the buttons of their uniforms glinting in the summer sun.

The county took on a festive atmosphere as the volunteers strutted the city streets in uniform, played to the press, and flirted with the young ladies. By July 10, all the Arkansas units had gathered in Washington, where they elected officers. The news spread quickly that the former congressman had been elected colonel, outranking the other Arkansas officers. After eight days of festivities in the Hempstead County seat, the Arkansas regiment marched through the rest of the county and on to Shreveport, Louisiana; San Antonio, Texas; and, eventually, the Rio Grande.[11]

With the departure of the soldiers, life returned to normal in Arkansas – but not for long. Utilizing the recent development of the telegraph, the nation's leading newspapers formed a forerunner of what was to become the Associated Press and sent correspondents to Mexico to provide first-hand accounts of the major battles and the military strategy involved. A 2,000-mile communication link – consisting of pony express, steamers, railroads, and telegraph – between New Orleans and New York provided speedy coverage in the major newspapers. These accounts were then picked up by smaller papers throughout the country. Thus, the local newspapers could regale their readers with stories about the war and reinforce the heroic images of Gens. Zachary Taylor and Winfield Scott. In Arkansas, the Whig and Democratic editors continued to debate the morality of the war while they cheered the local soldiers and feuded with each other over scandals stirred up by a rivalry between Yell, a Democrat, and Albert Pike, a leading Whig attorney and former newspaper editor, who was a volunteer in Mexico.[12]

The Arkansas regiment had been placed under Gen. John E. Wool, a Whig, in Texas. Wool took an almost instant dislike to Yell and ordered the Arkansas regiment to set up camp downstream from the other units. This position meant the Arkansans were forced to use the dirty water flowing down from the other camps. Used to making laws rather than obeying orders, Yell independently moved his men to a better location. Wool ordered Borland and another Arkansas officer to arrest the former congressman. When they refused, they were arrested, too. The politically ambitious Pike, who was disappointed when he was not elected to lead the Arkansas regiment, made sure the news of the arrests reached home.[13]

The Arkansas troops continued to disobey Wool's orders, saying he could "kiss their ass." One soldier went so far as to threaten to shoot the general. The disregard for orders added more fodder to the gossip back home when the regiment moved into Mexico. Borland led 34 Arkansas volunteers January 22, 1847, on a reconnaissance mission to Encanscion, a town 50 miles south of Saltillo, where they joined a small group of Kentucky volunteers. They set up camp and bedded down for the night, ignoring orders to post a guard. They woke up the next morning to find themselves surrounded by 3,000 Mexican cavalry. The volunteers quickly surrendered.[14]

A few weeks later, an Arkansas volunteer was killed near his company's camp at Agua Nueva, about 15 miles south of Saltillo. To revenge their comrade's death, men from two of the Arkansas companies rode into Cantana one night and indiscriminately killed an undetermined number of civilians. The incident appeared in headlines throughout the United States, bringing strong condemnation against the Arkansas regiment. Gen. Taylor demanded that the men involved in the murderous raid be identified and punished or else their companies were to be sent back home. Once again, Yell ignored the general's orders.[15]

This lack of discipline likely led to Yell's death at Buena Vista that spring. As the U.S. forces came under heavy fire at Buena Vista, Lt. Shover, who was commanding the defenses at Saltillo that day, saw a cloud of dust coming from Buena Vista. The cloud turned into "a considerable number of mounted volunteers ... rushing along the road," he reported. They identified themselves as members of the Arkansas calvary. Despite Shover's efforts to get them to join the defense at Saltillo, they continued to flee. The disgraceful behavior spread through Arkansas when Pike wrote a scathing account of the troops that was published in the *Arkansas Gazette* April 24, 1847.[16]

The detailed war coverage, with its colorful stories of heroes and scandals, was new to Americans, whether they lived in the cities of the Northeast or on the Arkansas frontier. The newspaper reports made the world a bit smaller as they brought the war vividly home. War became the topic of conversation and the focus of debate at the mercantiles, in churches, and at the dinner table. When the war ended in victory in 1848, newspapers across the country published the peace treaty, the terms of which justified the bloodshed for those who believed the United States was destined to rule from sea to sea.[17]

The victory went almost unnoticed by the Arnolds, who were mourning the death of William. Lucy, a widow at the age of 48 with seven children still at home, was left with few choices. Life in a more settled area would have been easier, but she had no place to go. Her land and family in Alabama were long gone; her family loyalties and sense of place had been transplanted to the Arkansas frontier. What she had left was her land, her slaves, her family obligations, and her dedication to fulfill William's legacy to his children.

Although it was a man's world in the more civilized areas of the country, the traditional society of the South was bound more by community and family than by gender. Lucy was not unfamiliar with running a plantation, and she had the frontier grit needed to generate an income sizable enough to support her large family and pay for her children's education. Two years after William's death, Lucy was managing a plantation valued at $3,800, overseeing six slaves (five men ranging in age from 18 to 52 and a 34-year-old woman), and providing for her children. When the value of her personal property was added to her real estate, Lucy was worth between $10,000 and $15,000, which placed her solidly in the upper middle class of Hempstead County.[18]

One of Lucy's biggest accomplishments was sending her children to the best schools in the area. When Bill, her third youngest, turned 13, Lucy sent him to live with Caroline and David Ross in Lisbon. While school was in session, Bill stayed with friends in Mount Holly in the northwest part of Union County so he could attend class at Mount Holly Academy. Run by the Rev. R.J.M. Hog, who also pastored the Presbyterian church in Mount Holly, the academy attracted students from all over southern Arkansas and northern Louisiana. As soon as he was old enough, Bill was sent to medical school. A few years later, Lucy's youngest son, Robert, followed in his footsteps.[19]

While most Northern families and Southern middle-class families invested their limited resources in educating their sons, Lucy made sure her youngest daughter, Temperance, also went to school, a privilege common to the daughters of the Southern aristocrats. The Southern ideal for women linked education with character building. Daughters refined by education and culture reflected the honor of the family; they became emblems of high social standing. As a result, the South led the nation in the founding of female colleges by the 1840s. As befit her family's upwardly moving status, Tempie attended the inaugural class of the Camden Female College, which was started by William P. Ratcliffe, a respected Methodist minister, in 1856. The subscription school offered a strong religious core with an array of other subjects, including literature, logic, science, ancient languages, mathematics, geography, and history. In short, Tempie was learning everything she needed to know to be a virtuous wife and helpmeet for the Southern gentleman who would someday be her husband.[20]

3   In Search of El Dorado

El Dorado.

The name rolled off the tongue with the taste of adventure and riches. It promised those struggling to survive on played-out land a chance at a better life. It smacked of opportunity to enter the ranks of the landed. It tickled the ears of the young men of South Carolina, encouraging them to head west toward a frontier begging to be tamed, a future waiting to unfold. Young David Saxon Arnold heard it often. As he watched the wagon trains with their human cargo of dreams and ambitions roll through Brewerton, South Carolina, he listened to the wistful banter of his neighbors. "They are headed for their El Dorado!" the townspeople said as the wagons rumbled past.[1]

David knew all about dreams and ambitions. His family had followed their dreams from England to the New World. His ancestors had risen to the ranks of the landed gentry through hard work and their willingness to conquer the frontier. His great-grandfather, Benjamin Arnold, and grandfather, Hendrick Arnold, had traced the frontier from Virginia to South Carolina. They had established themselves as gentlemen and leaders of the community. By the time he died, Benjamin had amassed considerable property, including 35 slaves, four of whom he had given to Hendrick to help him get started in life. David's father, Ira Arnold, was a respected farmer and justice of the peace. Together, the Arnolds and their kinsmen had created a legacy in Greenville and Laurens counties, South Carolina – a legacy of leadership, fairness, and prosperity.

Their prosperity included slaves at a time when few people in the area had them. In 1790, about 600 slaves lived in Greenville County. The 1790 Census for the county shows Hendrick had 13 slaves and Benjamin had eight. The Arnolds' character is revealed in their treatment of their slaves. While it was still legal, they occasionally freed their slaves, who then became their neighbors. A collection of slave records for the county shows that Ira, his brother William, and Benjamin, an uncle or a cousin,[2] helped each other emancipate slaves by selling them to freed men. For instance, when Ira wanted to free 17-year-old Moses in 1818, he informed Benjamin, a justice of the quarter section, of his intent. Following the requirements of the law, Benjamin summoned five slaveholders who, along with Moses himself, witnessed Ira answering questions under oath to the effect that Moses was of good character and capable of earning an honest living. The emancipation of Moses was not an isolated incident. The records show the Arnolds freed at least four other slaves. (The collection of 600 selected records involving black people in Greenville County reveals that all but one of the freed slaves, Samuel Taylor, were emancipated by the Arnolds.) They also show that Benjamin's secretary was a freed man.[3]

While many planters gave lip service to the idea that their slaves were part of their families, the Arnolds took this familial role to heart. A study of wills of 102 planters in the antebellum South reveals that only six of the planters made any effort to preserve their slaves as family units. Of those who made this consideration, the majority perceived the slave family as a mother and her children with little to no regard for the father. Benjamin Arnold, David's great-grandfather, distributed his 35 slaves as families as much as possible, and he went to great lengths to mention each slave by name – a rarity in planters' wills. For instance, Benjamin gave James and Hanna to his son William. To Hendrick, Ira's father, he gave Phebe and "her increase, Humphrey, Sarah and Phillip." Hugh Saxon, Ira's brother-in-law, stipulated in his will that his slaves were "to be sold as much in families and neighborhoods as possible, to prevent too great separation."[4]

Their sense of fairness and prosperity gave the Arnolds a leadership position in their community. As justices of the peace, the Arnolds held positions reserved for gentlemen. In this role, they helped their neighbors with land claims, business dealings, and estate settlements, but they frequently went beyond the call of duty. For example, Ira, with "esquire" after his name, proved the will of his neighbor, Hugh Goff, and served as the executor of Hugh's estate. In his 1823 will, Hugh expressed his gratitude to Ira for his friendship and left his estate to Ira on the condition that Ira build a five-foot high by 10-foot-square brick wall around his grave and care for a slave and his widow, Rebekah, until her death.[5]

From the time they were old enough to understand, David and his brothers were taught the Arnold catechism. They knew they were born to stalwart Southern stock that could trace its lineage to George Washington's family.[6] They were aware of relatives who were building the Arnold legacy in Kentucky and Alabama. And they understood their obligation to do the same. Surrounded by kin, they could not escape the concept that their future belonged to their family as much as it did to them. As part of their heritage, Ira encouraged his sons to be ambitious, to do their duty to family, God, and country by doing as well – if not better – than he had, even if it meant moving westward. But he gave them more than empty dreams and ambitions. He and his wife gave their sons the tools to fulfill their dreams and ambitions; they taught them the true test of a person was that he live an upright life favorable to God and man. They also sent Hendrick to medical school and David to Erskine for a classical education – the language of the Southern aristocracy.[7]

Like most Southerners, Ira peddled in dreams – for himself and his sons. These dreams, rooted in the land, built up lofty expectations. Because of their college education, David and Hendrick knew more was expected of them. It was their duty to break into the ranks of the Southern aristocracy. Their entry would open the door to the rest of the family – even the forefathers resting in their graves. To achieve their dreams, they needed more than a college degree; they needed land. Their father firmly believed true prosperity was always just one land deal away. Ira had started with the 184 acres on Horse Creek and the Cherokee Boundary that his father had left for his brother William and him to divide. William, who raised Ira after their father died, fostered the young boy's speculative nature when the two bought 300 acres for 120 pounds sterling in 1796.

Records show the two brothers engaged in several other joint purchases of both land and personal property. Ira also invested with other relatives. In 1821, he and Charles Saxon settled a debt with Hiram Sims by accepting a mortgage on Sims' grist mill, machines, tools, land, 18-year-old slave Larkin, and horses.[8]

Not all of Ira's investments paid off. Between 1840 and 1850, the family's prosperity faltered. In 1840, Ira had nearly reached planter status with 19 slaves. But as land prices increased, Ira's deals often left the family strapped – so much so that when his wife inherited from her mother and brother, their wills contained a clause or codicil placing Polly Saxon Arnold's share under a trustee other than her husband. Although it was rare, such protection was not unheard of in Southern society. The study of 102 planters' wills shows eight of them protected daughters or daughters-in-law from wayward spouses by putting their share in a trust or guardianship under another male relative. Polly's share of her mother's and brother's estates was put in the safekeeping of her son-in-law Samuel Barksdale and brother Joshua Saxon. By 1850, Ira had $1,200 in real estate and seven slaves. All but one daughter had left home, and he was still caring for 80-year-old Rebekah Goff. His wife had left him and was living with a young farm family. Their father's experience convinced David and Hendrick that they would have to leave home to find success.[9]

Hendrick, the oldest son, was the first to pursue his dreams by leaving South Carolina to eventually become a doctor and landowner in Arkadelphia, Arkansas. Hendrick's reports home had David, six years his junior, longing to start his own adventure. His imagination sparked by his father's tales of the frontier days of South Carolina, David wanted to experience a frontier for himself. Leaving home, though, was not an easy decision. Known for his good looks, violin playing, and dancing ability, David was a popular young man in Brewerton. He and his brother Thomas often matched their wits in oratorical competitions, providing welcome entertainment for the community. He also enjoyed the security that accompanies a sense of deep-rootedness stemming from nearly a century of family ties to the land.

Despite his reservations, by 1849, David, armed with a college degree, was ready to find his own El Dorado. Many planters in South Carolina, enticed by Arkansas' untapped resources, had sent squads of slaves supervised by a son or trusted overseer to squat on unoccupied land in the southern part of the state in the 1840s. Others were forced west by bankruptcies, worn-out land, and declining estates. Those who moved westward encouraged their kin to follow, sending them letters filled with hope. John Meek, who had recently settled in Union County, Arkansas, wrote home to his son-in-law in Laurens or Newberry County, South Carolina, boasting that "the poorest land in our country would beat in corn, cotton, wheat, oats or potatoes, any land" in South Carolina. Tempted by such stories, David said goodbye to his parents and joined a cousin, David Saxon, in the journey to Arkansas. Their first stop was the home of Hendrick – possibly in time for his July 19, 1849, marriage to Ann H.T. Ross, a cousin and the 14-year-old daughter of Peter and Temperance Ross.[10]

David and his cousin reached Arkansas at a time of phenomenal growth. In 1840, the state, with 98,000 residents, was seen as a wilderness emerging to frontier status. By 1850, the population had more than doubled – to 210,000 – with much of that growth occurring between 1848 and 1849. Still ranked a frontier state with four people per square mile, Arkansas saw steady signs of civilization. But some of the people flooding into the state were intent on passing through rather than staying put. The Mexican War had given a new generation a glimpse of the wilderness beyond the Arkansas border. And the California Gold Rush sent out a siren's call to those who spent their lifetime chasing rainbows. The Arkansas settlers and townspeople had become accustomed to tent cities pitched in a day and moved on toward California or Texas within a month. During the autumn of 1850, more than 1,500 wagons, ox-carts, and other vehicles traveled the tollgate bridge spanning Bayou Meto near Little Rock on their way westward. Similar traffic flows were found at many other river crossings throughout the state.[11]

Although a new frontier had opened up farther west, life in southern Arkansas still bore some of the hardships of the wilderness when David and his cousin arrived. Schools remained in short supply, as the state refused to spend a penny of tax revenue on education. The economy was affected by the absence of banks and the resulting lack of a fluid currency and reliable sources of credit. The vagaries of the waterways continued to dictate most travel. While newspapers were plentiful, the news they reported was often old, especially that traveling from other states and countries.[12]

Adding to the feeling of instability that naturally surrounds a frontier was talk of trouble over slavery. Prominent Arkansas politicians tried to stir up momentum for secession in 1850. The catalyst was the North's effort to make the territory gained in the Mexican War off limits to slaveholders. Early that year, Arkansas Congressman Bob Johnson, a leader of the "dynasty" that was to rule the state for most of its first century, issued two public letters through newspapers throughout the state to warn residents that their right to own slaves could be limited. He decried this move, saying Southern blood had been shed to gain that territory. Johnson's letters spurred a controversy that lasted nearly two years.[13]

While some of the planters rallied around the congressman, most Arkansans denounced his stance. The state, barely 14 years old, was not ready to sever its ties with the Union. People in the hill country were not willing to sacrifice their nation for a way of life they did not share. And those on the western border relied on federal troops to keep the lawlessness of the Indian Territory at bay. David, like his conservative neighbors, disagreed with the dictates hatched in the North, but he had no reason to leave the Union. He had a life to build, so he left politics to the politicians and concentrated on his future.

The Compromise of 1850, coupled with high cotton prices and a growing economy in the opening years of the decade, forced Arkansas politicians to tone down their secession rhetoric. Although some of them continued to seize every opportunity to preach disunion, their message, for the most part, fell on deaf ears. Optimism about a promising future, the opiate of the frontier, obliterated any lingering concerns about the stability of the nation – and the state – for a short time.[14]

Had it not been for family, David and his cousin might have moved farther west in search of their personal El Dorado. But they found the allure of family ties and the civilizing forces taking shape in southern Arkansas more attractive than the untamed frontier and unpredictable future of the West. Arkansas was wild enough for their tastes. Besides, David saw his brother was off to a good start. Hendrick filed on two 40-acre parcels of government land, valued at $1,500, in Clark County in 1850 and had plans to expand his land holdings soon. He also had four young slaves to help work the land. Hendrick's widowed mother-in-law, Temperance Ross, lived with him, along with her six slaves. Recognizing the opportunities and feeling the binding ties of family, David began his life in Arkansas as a much-needed teacher at a subscription school in Clark County. His cousin, David Saxon, considered practicing law. The two engaged in good-natured competition as they each reached toward a promising future.[15]

David Arnold's quick wit and eloquence, often associated with virtue and the marks of a gentleman in Southern society, quickly made him a popular figure in his new home. His violin playing put him in demand at community dances. And his brother made sure he met the right people. Most of those people were family. Many days were spent at the Ross farm near Lisbon in Union County. There he met Caroline Ross' brother, Bill Arnold, who visited when he was not in school or needed at home, and her youngest sister, Temperance Lucinda Arnold, who often stopped in during breaks from Dr. Hartwell's female seminary in Camden.[16]

4   Settling In

David was not content with remaining a schoolteacher or living off the meager pay it offered. That's not why he had left South Carolina. A son of the South, he felt an obligation to succeed – that is to become a planter and a benefactor of his community. "The planter status was more than the top of the social pyramid," historian Carl Degler writes, "it was the ideal to which other white Southerners aspired.... Mere wealth, if accumulated from trade, was not sufficient to bestow the final accolade of success. Nor was it simply enough to be a planter.... Those Southern planters who seemed to cherish money more than other social values were quickly stigmatized as 'Southern Yankees.'" This was the lesson David had been taught, and this was the lesson he intended to pass on to his sons.[1]

David and his cousin both chose to settle near the Rosses in Union County. First organized in 1829, the county saw an influx of emigrants in the 1840s from all the Southern states. "Most of the emigrants of that day were men of some means, with growing families," an anonymous settler near Lisbon wrote in the 1880s. "Union County filled rapidly with a class of men, take them all in all, that could not be surpassed in those sentiments that go to make up a reliable and trusty people." By the 1850s, the county was maturing into what could become a planter society. Besides its vast supply of farmland, the county was home to large tracts of valuable timberland. The Ouachita River connected it to the New Orleans market and seaport, a plus for cotton producers. South Carolina native John Meek boasted about this fact in a letter home to his son-in-law: "New Orleans is as it were at our Door."[2]

The majority of people in Union County at that time qualified as what historian Carl H. Moneyhon labels the upper middle class. These were mostly small planters and prosperous farmers who had personal property valued at $1,000 to $24,999 – or enough wealth to buy at least one slave. This signified the first step toward controlling the labor of others and the potential to step into the elite – the planter class or those who had property valued at $25,000 or more. In Arkansas, the elite included planters, doctors and lawyers; most of them were better educated than their neighbors, and they tended to be Episcopalians and Presbyterians. Few of the upper middle class had a college education, and they tended to be Methodists and Baptists.[3]

By 1860, Union County boasted 30 individuals – about two percent of the population – whom Moneyhon classifies as the elite. All of them owned slaves and land, averaging about 36 slaves and 2,300 acres each. The county also had 635 individuals – nearly 48 percent of its population – in the upper middle class. More than 80 percent of the upper middle class in Union County owned slaves and land, averaging about six slaves and 514 acres apiece. Most of the men in the upper middle class thought that, with hard work and ambition, they could turn the rich potential of the county to their advantage and enter the ranks of the elite. For the would-be planters who settled there, it seemed like El Dorado. Thus, when the county seat was established on the highest point in the county, it was named for the mythical city of gold.[4]

When David arrived in this county of promise, he heard of several newcomers turning their dreams and ambitions into a secure future. Harrison L. Dearing, for instance, was a carpenter and tenant farmer in Union County in 1850. Within 10 years, he owned 2,648 acres and 27 slaves, and his plantation averaged about 172 bales of cotton a year. Taking his cue from such success stories, David bought a few slaves and the old Hawthorne place, a 40-acre farm near Lisbon, a small village about 16 miles from El Dorado. Arkansas land prices varied wildly in the 1850s primarily because of government land grants to the state and to soldiers who had served in the War of 1812 and the Mexican War. While the government was selling land for $1.25 an acre, which was a bargain compared with South Carolina land prices, private individuals were selling land for as little as 12.5 cents an acre.⁵

As such opportunities arose, David expanded his farm. By 1860, his real property was valued at $5,000 and his personal property at $11,000, placing him solidly in the ranks of the upper middle class. His brother-in-law David Carroll Ross, by 1860, had $10,000 in real estate and $24,000 in personal property, which included 29 slaves. Both men fit the description Pattie Wright Hedges, who grew up in Lisbon in the 1850s, gave of her neighbors "as quite a goodly settlement of wealthy planters." Besides getting slaves to tend to his cotton, David, following the lead of many planters of the day, opened a mercantile business at the crossroads near his farm in 1856, depending on river transportation to send his cotton to New Orleans and bring back farming supplies, machinery, and merchandise for his store. As a man of education and property, David had a secure place in the ranks of the upper middle class and high hopes of eventually moving into the elite. Encouraged by his social position and a boom economy brought on by the high cotton prices, he decided it was time to start a family. Like his brother, he married a cousin – Temperance Lucinda Arnold.⁶

Although David was about 11 years older than Tempie, he was attracted by her education and the fact that she was related. In a sparsely populated area, suitable eligible women could be hard to find. By marrying a cousin, he was assured of marrying within his rank. So it was that the Union County records showed the marriage of "Mr. David S. Arnold, 30, to Miss T. A. [*sic*] Arnold, 18, on December 31, 1856." Although Tempie was a devout Methodist and David had been reared in the Baptist church, George N. Clampitt, the minister of the Cumberland Presbyterian Church in Ouachita County, performed the ceremony, reminding the young couple that their union signified "the mystical union that is between Christ and his Church." Later that day, according to custom, the newlyweds made their way to a relative's house where an "infare feast" awaited them.⁷

By this time, David was feeling pretty good about himself. He already was off to a better start than his cousin David Saxon, who was living with Frederick Reeves in Union County and still had no stake of his own. And the future seemed to promise only prosperity. Riverboat trade increased as several "floating palaces" brought a taste of luxury and sophistication to the area that had so recently been a wilderness. The amount of improved land in Arkansas almost tripled during the 1850s to nearly 2 million acres. Although slave owners made up only 18 percent of the state's population, more than half the population of Union County was slave. Despite a lack of banks and bank notes due to a banking scandal early in its history, Arkansas' economic development seemed to be following the patterns set by the older plantation societies, giving Union County planters and farmers a reason to be optimistic. With 16 slaves of their own, ranging in age from two to 34, and personal property valued at $11,000, David and Tempie counted themselves as part of the emerging planter society. They were on their way to the Southern dream.[8]

While disturbing warning signs had appeared on the horizon, the Arnolds forged ahead with their plans and their life as if nothing were threatening the stability of the nation. They quickly slipped into the routine of life in Union County, which was dictated largely by family and community duty. David gave one bale of cotton to secure Tempie a lifetime membership in the Methodist Church. In the early summer, after the cotton had been chopped, they and their slaves joined relatives and friends at the fervent camp meetings held in brush arbors along the roadside. Uncle Stephen, a slave Tempie's parents had bought in 1822, cooked meat for the family over the big fires. Uncle Sam, another slave of Tempie's parents, conducted sessions for the slaves and, upon special invitation, preached to appreciative white audiences at the meetings. Meanwhile, David and Tempie pitched their double log tent and set up rows of beds and a long table under the open shed of the tent. It was home for as long as the camp meeting lasted. They heartily joined in the singing and praying and watched as dozens of repentant sinners, dressed in white, solemnly marched to a nearby creek for baptism. They also caught up on the news of their brothers, sisters, and cousins. Camp meeting was the social and spiritual event of the season.[9]

In the fall, the entire household was involved with picking cotton and loading the ox-drawn wagons for the trip to the closest cotton gin. And a month or two later, David set out with his brother-in-law, cousin, and neighbors to tramp through the woodlands, loaded gun handy, as he followed the tracks of deer and wild turkeys. As the mistress of the plantation, Tempie was in charge of the smokehouse, dairy, poultry yard, garden, and household. Fall meant smoking meat for the winter and harvesting and preserving vegetables. Winter was the time for the men to fix fences and take care of the inside work that had been ignored during harvest. And for the women, it provided time to weave cloth and make garments for the slaves and the master's family. The cooler weather also gave David an opportunity to focus on his growing mercantile business. Spring brought planting season. And on those rainy days when it was too wet to go into the fields, he supervised his slaves as they shelled corn, cut potatoes for seed, ground corn, and cleaned out the corn crib. Before the long days of summer rolled around again, the slaves cleared new ground.[10]

In her spare time, Tempie nursed the sick in her slave and free family and tended to their religious education. Occasionally, she slipped away to visit her sister or other neighbors. David found his social outlet at the local Masonic lodge, Mount Moriah Lodge No. 18. Founded in 1852 or 1853 in Lisbon, the lodge attracted most of the gentlemen of the area. Secret societies were both a luxury and pleasure that appealed to the men of the day. "That part of one's nature which loves to lean upon others for aid, even in the social scale, finds its expression in some of the many forms of societies, clubs, organizations or institutions that now pervade nearly all the walks of life," an unidentified person wrote in explaining the popularity of such groups. "In everyday existence, in business, church, state, politics and pleasure, are societies and organizations everywhere – for the purpose of gain, charity and comfort – indeed for the sole purpose of finding something to do. . . ."[11]

Besides its mystical and social aspects, the Masonic fraternity offered an important network for young men aspiring to make the right business connections in their communities. It also served as a school of government, teaching its members the art of public speaking, the rules of a constitution, and the importance of being a good citizen. Many of the prominent political leaders, ministers, judges, and lawyers – even David's personal hero, Henry Clay – were Masons. While the Masons had long been established, scandals in the late 1820s and early 1830s had taken a toll on the fraternity's membership and its reputation. The fraternity started to make a comeback in the 1850s by distancing itself from the past and promoting its social good and charitable acts.[12]

Although he valued the connections he made through his lodge, David's first priority was to his family. Soon after the young couple gave birth to their first child, David Saxon "Sax" Arnold, Jr., in 1857, the looming troubles facing the nation became more difficult to ignore. The future David and Tempie had confidently envisioned became tenuous as the country rushed toward disintegration.

Rumors that abolitionists were trying to incite slave revolts led to demands that all free blacks and mulattoes be forced from the state. The demand gained so much impetus that Gov. Elias Conway signed a bill February 12, 1859, ordering them from the state by January 1, 1860. According to the new law, those who failed to leave would be arrested and hired out to the highest bidder for a year. That money was to be used to cover the expense of deporting the person at the end of the year. If the person still refused to leave, he was to be sold. The law forced free children between the ages of seven to 21 to be hired out until they reached 21, at which time they could leave the state. Those who refused were to be sold as slaves. Another part of the law made it illegal to emancipate slaves in Arkansas.[13]

The fear of a slave revolt intensified with John Brown's infamous raid on Harper's Ferry October 16, 1859. Newspapers throughout the South carried the story of the raid and continuously blasted the Northern abolitionists who pronounced Brown a heroic martyr. They also unveiled Brown's plans to infiltrate the South with abolitionist schoolteachers. As a warning to slave owners, many newspapers carried the text of a letter written by one of Brown's emissaries who used "Lawrence Thatcher" as an assumed name. The letter, written to Brown and found by Virginia authorities after the raid, told of Thatcher's "reconnaissance" of the Southern states a few weeks before the attack on Harper's Ferry. Throughout the South, Thatcher said he had found "an immense number of slaves ripe and ready at the very first intimation to strike a decided blow." After a "thorough scouring" of Arkansas, Thatcher was convinced that the slaves there were so primed for revolt that "a bold stroke of one day will overthrow the whole state."[14]

The newspaper accounts stirred up the white population in Arkansas, especially in Union County with its dominant slave society. The white population cracked down on free speech and would not tolerate the slightest criticism of slavery. Because of Thatcher's letter and Brown's promise to infiltrate their midst with abolitionist schoolteachers, white Arkansans became suspicious of any strangers. A schoolteacher who had taught for 10 years in Louisiana and Arkansas was given 36 hours to leave the state. A few months later, Arkansas newspapers reported on another incident that had occurred in Buchanan, Texas. A captured runaway slave claimed an abolitionist had given him a knife and encouraged him to cut his way to freedom. Local authorities arrested the abolitionist, who was then tarred and tied to a pole or tree. The slave was given a lighted torch and forced to ignite the faggots piled at the man's feet.[15]

Despite the growing tension and the fervor over slavery and states' rights, David and Tempie cautiously planned for the future. There was good news to celebrate. Work had begun in 1859 on the Memphis-Little Rock Railroad – the first for Arkansas – with 38 miles of track laid between Hopefield on the west bank of the Mississippi and Madison on the east bank of the St. Francis River. By 1860, engineers began working in the other direction with track being laid from Little Rock east to DeValls Bluff. That spring, telegraph lines ran from St. Louis to Fayetteville, Arkansas. Within a few months, the telegraph had stretched to Van Buren. Meanwhile, a gas company had opened in Little Rock, bringing gaslights to the capital. While all of this progress had yet to reach southern Arkansas, those living in Union County knew it would not be long before they, too, enjoyed such modern conveniences.[16]

As the nation prepared for the heated 1860 presidential election, Tempie gave birth to their second child, Mary Lucy – named for both her grandmothers. While Tempie cared for the children, the slaves, and the house, David tended the cotton fields and growing mercantile business, all the time keeping a wary eye on the political situation. Chance conversations at the post office, cotton gin, river landings, family gatherings, and his own store focused more often than not on the troubles plaguing the state and nation.

Although they, like their forefathers, relied on slave labor and probably took it for granted, David and many of his friends and relatives believed slavery would someday have to end. In view of more enlightened ideas of human rights, they were convinced that if the institution of slavery persisted too long, it would prove ruinous to the South. The quandary was how to free millions of uneducated slaves. The only result they could envision was anarchy and chaos. Despite their thoughts on slavery, they did not like Northerners telling them what to do and how to live their lives. As talk of secession and possible war increased, David, a Whig through and through, still mourned the loss of Henry Clay, the author of the Compromise of 1850. If only Henry were alive, he said on numerous occasions, the nation would not be in such a predicament. The Union could be saved.[17]

By 1860, the Union was unified in name only. The North's growing hostility toward slavery and its expansion had polarized the South, resulting in breeches in party politics and church hierarchies. Even in Arkansas, practically a one-party state since its birth, no unity could be found. But here the focus of the 1859-1860 winter campaign season was not on the issues ripping the nation apart. Instead, a rancorous battle over who controlled the state Democratic Party, and thus state politics, overshadowed the presidential election. Thomas Hindman, a young political upstart from Mississippi, took on the Sevier-Conway-Johnson family dynasty, which had ruled the state, in a war not of principles and political philosophy but of personal ambition. In their newspapers scattered throughout the state, both sides clung to the banner of states' and slaveholders' rights.

Throughout the verbally abusive campaign, the two factions came together only at the Democratic National Convention, held in Charleston in late April 1860. Although they had been given no instructions to do so, most of the Arkansas delegates walked out of the convention, along with other delegates from the Deep South, when the national party refused to adopt a platform endorsing Congressional protection of slavery in the Western territories. Recognizing that the walkout could lead to defeat in November, the Democrats adjourned the convention to reconvene in Baltimore in June. Despite a second walkout by the Southern delegates, including the same six from Arkansas, Stephen Douglas won the nomination. Still fighting each other, the two factions of the Arkansas party joined together at a rump convention in Richmond to give their support to a Southern Democrat platform and presidential candidate, John C. Breckinridge of Kentucky.[18]

The national election and issues were never far from their mind, but most Arkansans seemed preoccupied with the state elections that summer. The Arkansas press intensified the battle with innuendo and vicious editorializing. Since each paper represented one side, it was difficult for anyone to get an objective view unless he read more than one paper. David, although never exhibiting any personal political aspirations, closely followed the events of the day. He read several newspapers, especially those that had identified with the Whig cause, and was quick to discuss his opinions. What he felt about state affairs has been lost to history, but his dedication to slavery and Whig principles, which supported a strong union, are unquestionable.[19]

The state elections, held early in August 1860, brought an upset to the dynasty. For the first time, someone from outside the "family" would serve as governor, thanks to the backing of Hindman. Henry Massie Rector was to be sworn in as the new governor November 15, 1860, just nine days after the national election. Between the state election in August and the national election, the Arkansas press and most Arkansans turned their attention to what was shaping up as a national crisis.

Fear, once again, intensified the rhetoric of the political pundits pushing for their candidates on the pages of the state's newspapers. A terrible fire, causing about $400,000 in damage, broke out in Dallas in August 1860. Similar fires, thought to be the work of arsonists, were sparked in eight other Texas locations at about the same time. Arkansas newspapers ran with the story, fanning the flames by calling the fires an abolitionist raid and a slave insurrection. Headlines in a Van Buren newspaper reported: "Northern Texas to be Laid Waste. The Work Already Commenced." A month later, Fort Smith suffered the worst fire in its history, which destroyed property valued at $112,000. Again, arson was suspected. Coming on the heels of the Texas fires, the Fort Smith blaze convinced many Arkansans that their state was not safe from the treachery of abolitionists.[20]

Most Arkansans approached November 6, 1860, federal elections with apprehension. They had heard the rebellious threats from other Southerners. And they had seen the awkward upstart from Illinois vilified in the press. Even those who would be kind to Abraham Lincoln would have to wonder how this rough, self-taught frontiersman with no family connections could hope to bridge the growing gap between the Northern business interests and the agrarian Southern society. Judge John Brown of Camden wrote in his diary that day: "This is the most important day to the United States and, perhaps, to mankind since July 4, 1776." Men poured out in record numbers to cast their ballots. Besides voting for the next president of the United States, many of them feared they were voting for or against the continuation of the country as they knew it. When David went to the polls to vote that Tuesday, he had three choices of electors – those for the two Democrats, Douglas and Breckinridge, and those for John Bell, a former Whig senator from Tennessee put up by the new Constitutional Union party, which was made up of former Whigs and Know-Nothings. No electors for Lincoln appeared on any ballot in Arkansas or elsewhere in the South.[21]

Arkansans waited five days after the election to have the news confirmed – Lincoln, with less than 40 percent of the popular vote nationwide, would be sworn in as the 16th president March 4, 1961. "It was a great surprise to the people of Arkansas," Methodist historian Horace Jewell wrote. "No one dreamed of such a result." The election showed the South had lost its clout nationally, a frightening proposition to a society already planted on an eroding base. The election also revealed how politics was changing. Once the realm of respected, learned gentlemen, politics had now been thrown open to the masses. "As soon as it became known that Mr. Lincoln was elected the wildest excitement prevailed all over the country," Jewell added, "everything else was forgotten in the intense feeling that was produced by the talk of war and secession. It was the theme of conversation in every gathering of the people."[22]

Arkansans reacted with mixed emotions. Rabid secessionists demanded decisive and immediate action. Most of the Arkansas newspaper editors, however, urged a wait-and-see attitude. The new president might not actually be that bad – despite his lack of gentility. Gov. Rector optimistically stated upon taking office November 15 that he hoped the sectional differences could be resolved. But he added dark words of caution, saying that Arkansas might have to choose between "the Union without slavery or slavery without the Union." This would happen, he warned, if the states in the Deep South seceded and then federal troops tried to force them back. Hindman, who was largely responsible for putting the governor in office, threw optimism aside a few days later when he addressed the General Assembly. After a stirring speech in which Hindman demanded immediate secession, the legislators considered the issue and entertained several resolutions. But cooler heads prevailed, and the legislators postponed taking any action.[23]

As the year drew to a close, the secessionists intensified their arguments. Sen. Robert Johnson sent an open letter, dated December 1, to his constituents through the state's newspapers, urging secession. Since several states had seceded already, he argued, it would not be good for Arkansas to be a Southern minority in a nation dominated by the North. The governor added more weight to the issue when he sent a written address to the Arkansas General Assembly expressing his concern that the state would be in great peril should Mississippi and Louisiana secede. Besides severing Arkansas' economic lifeline to the

Gulf of Mexico, such an event would make it a border state and thus a haven for runaway slaves.[24]

The Arnolds, whose livelihood depended on river access to New Orleans, realized their plans, their dreams, all their hard work could be in danger. Yet all they could do was wait to see if the fears of the nation – their personal fears – would take shape and destroy the life and the country they had known.

5   Road to Secession

A dread anticipation greeted the arrival of 1861 in southern Arkansas. The usual wonderment about the new year and take-stock-of-life rituals took on deeper intensity as the possibility of secession and war became more than casual conversation. Only a month earlier, David's home state of South Carolina had brashly carried out its promise to secede from the Union if Lincoln were elected president. And several Arkansas politicians quickly jumped on the bandwagon, urging Arkansas to do likewise.

David and Tempie celebrated their fourth wedding anniversary that New Year's Eve. Anticipating the birth of their third child, they felt some apprehension as they faced the new year and what it was likely to bring to them personally and to the nation. A poor cotton crop added to the sense of uncertainty aroused by the constant talk of secession. That apprehension deepened within the first few weeks of 1861. With his parents and several other relatives and friends still living in South Carolina, David followed the news closely. His family had all opposed secession and did everything they could to avoid war. But when South Carolina cut loose from the Union, they went with her – right or wrong.

One by one in rapid succession, the states of the Deep South followed South Carolina's lead. Mississippi declared itself independent January 9, 1861; Florida left the Union the next day; and Alabama seceded the day after Florida. Georgia left January 19. One week later, Louisiana seceded. Texas ratified secession February 1. Despite some state leaders who loudly agitated for secession, Arkansas refused to be pushed into a hasty and, perhaps, regrettable decision.

Arkansas had reason to break the headlong rush to secession. A young state, it was just coming into its own culturally and economically. In the past decade, its white population had doubled and the value of its taxable property had increased four-and-a-half times. With a total population of 436,000 people in 1860 – or 8.3 people per square mile, Arkansas finally ranked as a civilized state. But it still lagged far behind its Southern neighbors – Louisiana with 15.6 people per square mile; Mississippi with 17.1; Missouri with 17.2; and Tennessee with 26.6. Leaving an established country for a fledgling experiment was risky; Arkansans realized they could sacrifice their growth and future prosperity by making the wrong decision.[1]

Although the state was witnessing the rise of an emerging planter society in its southern extremities, it was not a slave state in the same sense as its older neighbors. By 1860, fewer than 20 percent of Arkansans had slaves. Thus slavery was not as big of an issue in many parts of the state as it was throughout the Deep South. But the economic impact of slavery affected the entire state. Life was hard for slaves in Arkansas, who had a higher mortality rate and a lower birth rate than the white population. Because of the low increase in the slave population, the value of individual slaves was escalating. The average slave who would have sold for $380 in 1820 and $627 in 1850 would sell for $1,000 to $1,500 in 1860. Arkansas' emerging cotton culture, with its dependency on slaves, was attracting more and more newcomers by the late 1850s. Those who a few years earlier would have passed on to Texas were now making southern Arkansas their home. As a result, land prices in this region also escalated. A farm that had sold for $600 in 1856 sold for $2,500 five years later. Since the state raised revenue through a poll tax levied on white males 21 years and older based on their real and personal property, the state treasury benefited from the inflated value of slaves and land in the cotton south. Thus slaveholders, like the Arnolds, shouldered a disproportionate amount of the tax burden as most of their wealth was tied up in slaves. With the entire state dependent to some extent on the tax revenue raised by slavery and the southern part of the state dependent on the slave system as well as the New Orleans market, conflicting attitudes toward secession threatened to divide the state. The wiser course, for the moment at least, seemed to be to wait.²

But Arkansas was not allowed to remain neutral as the country split apart. As the pressure mounted for the state to join the rebellion, Arkansas' General Assembly passed a bill January 15, 1861, calling for an election February 18 to give Arkansans an opportunity to vote on holding a secession convention and select delegates to the convention. Many in Arkansas still held out hope for reconciliation – as did the majority of residents in a few other Southern states. Virginia sponsored a peace conference in Washington February 4 – two days before the Confederate States of America elected Jefferson Davis president. When the Tennessee Legislature met February 9, it refused to call for a state convention to consider secession.³

Meanwhile, the Arkansas governor was trying to avoid what could have been the opening shots of the Civil War. In late November 1860, Capt. James Totten and 65 federal troops had quietly slipped into Little Rock to garrison the previously unoccupied federal arsenal there. All was well until January when the telegraph lines to Memphis, Tennessee, and Helena, Arkansas, were completed. One of the first bits of news to travel the line was that of the federal occupation of the Little Rock arsenal. Angered, the people of Helena demanded that Gov. Henry M. Rector seize the arsenal. He refused but added that if the federal government tried to reinforce its troops there, he would consider it an act of war. His adjutant general (also his brother-in-law) sent a different message, saying the governor would welcome spontaneous action from the people. Secessionists in Pine Bluff watched the USS Tucker traveling upstream on the Arkansas River. Mistakenly convinced that it was carrying reinforcements to Little Rock, they fired on the ship.

By February, Little Rock was swarming with armed volunteers itching to take a shot at a Yankee. Yielding to pressure from the volunteers and concerned residents of Little Rock, the governor, on February 7, demanded the surrender of the arsenal to state control. Capt. Totten, outnumbered and with no orders from Washington, surrendered the next day. He and his troops marched, without incident, from Little Rock toward St. Louis, Missouri, February 9.[4]

The Arnolds helplessly followed the news accounts and listened to the rumors as the events of the day tore at their lives. They could not afford to dwell on the terrible possibilities the future might bring; they had to focus on more pressing personal matters. While David did his best to prepare their finances to weather the crisis, Tempie was making room in the small wood frame house for another child while preparing herself emotionally and spiritually for what childbirth could bring. Although she had already borne two children with no complications, she could not rid herself entirely of the natural fears with which mothers greeted childbirth. A hundred years earlier, Emelia Hunter of Gloucester had written, "I am now Every Day Expecting, Either to give Life or lose it – Whichsoever it pleases heaven." Not much had changed when it came to childbirth; the women of the antebellum South faced the birthing room with much the same trepidation. "[W]omen's fears of childbirth were not unfounded as they likely knew – or knew of – women who had died during delivery or shortly thereafter from the dreaded 'childhood fever'.... This was cause of untold apprehension that followed women throughout pregnancy," historian Ellen Plante writes. "The fear of dying as a result of childbirth 'far outweighed their dread of dying of any other manner.'"[5]

Using a midwife and chloroform to ease the pain, Tempie gave birth Friday, February 15. Following Southern family tradition, David and Tempie named their second son William Hendrick for David's grandfather and brother Hendrick and Tempie's father and brother Bill, who was just finishing his medical degree. Thankful for surviving her ordeal, Tempie's worries and prayers shifted to her young son. Too often forced to face the reality of burying a child, many parents learned early to treat their children as gifts from God. The slightest cold, complications brought on by teething, or reports of outbreaks of disease were reason for dire concern.[6]

While the Arnolds dealt with personal matters, the nation raced toward schism. Three days after "Willie" was born, Jefferson Davis was sworn in as president of the Confederacy, and

Arkansans voted two-to-one to call a convention to consider secession from the Union. However, Unionist delegates won the majority of the seats to the convention, which was to be held March 4 – Lincoln's Inauguration Day – in Little Rock. As Lincoln took the oath of office and offered words of reconciliation to the South, Arkansas delegates met to consider whether the state would remain part of the Union. The convention was marked by heated words of animosity and hostility that threatened to tear the state apart. Rumors of plans to split the state became the talk on the street.[7]

As the Arkansas delegates were meeting in Little Rock, Congress disbanded in Washington. But a small group of congressional delegates, including Arkansas Sen. Charles Mitchel, stayed in Washington to try to come up with a workable solution to keep the nation from splintering any further.

Meanwhile, public attention centered on two federally held forts located in seceded states – Fort Sumter in Charleston Harbor, South Carolina, and Fort Pickens in Pensacola, Florida. Those holding out for peace knew if the situation escalated at those forts, all hope would be lost. In mid-March, Mitchel telegraphed a report home from Washington that Lincoln planned to withdraw federal troops from both forts. Mitchel's report, which arrived at the Arkansas convention March 11, did little to help soothe the growing hostilities between the delegates. To forestall a possible schism in the state, the delegates endorsed an assembly of border states, of which it was now one, to be held in June in Frankfort, Kentucky; agreed to send proposals to Congress for consideration as constitutional amendments; and, at the last minute, approved putting a secession referendum on the August ballot. The Arkansas convention ended March 21. Mitchel and the other congressmen ended their session in Washington a few days later.[8]

The close of the state convention and the announcement of the August referendum gave rise to a political battle throughout Arkansas that rivaled any heated election campaign. Both the secessionists and the Unionists wasted no time in priming their loyal newspapers, forming clubs, and preparing their most prominent leaders for stumping tours. They had an election to win!

The campaign was short lived. In April, after weeks of vacillation and rampant rumors that he would relinquish the federal forts in South Carolina and Florida, Lincoln informed Confederate President Jefferson Davis that he would resupply, with nonmilitary provisions, the U.S. forces at Fort Sumter. Tired of the standoff and determined to exercise its right to secede and to claim government property within its borders, South Carolina demanded on April 11 that the fort be surrendered. Maj. Robert Anderson, the Union officer in charge of the fort, refused. At dawn the next day, South Carolina troops fired on the fort. Both sides shot off artillery throughout the day and into April 13, when Anderson agreed to terms of surrender. The federal soldiers packed up what they could, loaded a steamer, and evacuated the fort at noon April 14. The first battle of the Civil War was over, and the South had scored a major political victory. The scope of that victory grew the following day in the Southern states still straddling the secession issue when President Lincoln called for 75,000 90-day troops to quell the rebellion.[9] The uprising did not reach Arkansas until April 16 and then only in the form of rumors. But a day later, the rumors were confirmed by news reports in the newspapers. That same day, Virginia left the Union. In Arkansas, what had been a divided state became one voice clamoring for the secession convention to reconvene immediately. The people of Arkansas – most of whom could trace their roots to the Carolinas, Georgia, and Tennessee – wanted to secede, and they did not want to wait until August to vote on it. Yielding to public pressure, David Walker, a Unionist from Fayetteville and head of the convention, signed a proclamation April 20 calling for the delegates to reconvene Monday, May 6, in Little Rock.[10]

President Lincoln's request for troops to march on the rebels in South Carolina hit too close to home for the Arnolds and many other Arkansans. These "rebels" were their family and friends. The soil that had been bloodied by battle was their ancestral home. Even those with no roots in South Carolina saw the president's call to arms as an affront to the rights of every

American. Gov. Rector spoke for all Arkansans when he responded to Lincoln's request for 780 men from Arkansas. His written response, dated April 22, stated no troops would be sent. "The demand is only adding insult to injury," he warned. "The people of this commonwealth are free men, not slaves, and will defend to the last extremity their honor, lives and property against northern mendacity and usurpation." A day later, the governor declined a similar request from the Confederate States of America on the grounds that Arkansas had not formally seceded yet. However, he granted permission for the Confederates to establish a battery in Arkansas near Helena for defense of the Mississippi River. He also allowed the leaders of the state militia to independently raise a regiment for the Confederacy with the understanding that the soldiers would be armed and equipped from the state arsenal.[11]

Although Arkansas was not yet part of the Confederacy, it finally knew which side it would take. As the long months of indecision approached an end, Arkansans reveled in the anticipation of war and action. Brass bands formed; martial music and the beat of drums boomed through the streets of small towns and cities alike. Military companies began to form and drill. Prominent women and their slaves crafted regimental colors and uniforms.[12]

David and Tempie were caught up in the preparations as they pondered their role in the war they knew was inevitable. There was no soul-searching over which side they should take; their heart remained loyal to the land of their ancestors. The call to arms was a personal missile aimed at their families and the honored graves of their grandfathers and great-grandfathers who had risked their lives to create a new nation. Now the mantle was on them. It was their duty as Southerners – as Arnolds – to offer the same sacrifice to preserve the heritage of their forebears. But it was one thing to decide which side had their sympathies; it was another to make the commitment to don a uniform and march off to battle. While others could not wait to grab their guns in readiness of secession, David hesitated. It was hard to give up on a nation he had believed in. It was harder still to leave his family.

State officials did not hesitate. Neither did they wait for the convention before taking action. Gov. Rector quickly began seizing all the federal positions in the state. Placing the state militia under the command of Solon Borland, who had fought in the Mexican War, the governor ordered the troops to seize the U.S. outpost in Fort Smith, a garrison on the wild border of the Indian Territory. When the Arkansas militia arrived at the outpost April 23, it found the federal soldiers had fled the day before, taking with them the large supplies of arms and munitions that had been stored there. Word of the federal retreat spread throughout the state via the newspapers. Coupled with the quick surrender at Fort Sumter, the retreat portended a quick end to the war with a Southern victory – at least that is how it was viewed by many of the people angling for a full-fledged battle.[13]

When the secession convention finally opened at 10 a.m. May 6, the 70 Arkansas delegates were joined by observers from the Carolinas, Alabama, and Georgia in a room packed with spectators. Boys perched on the windowsills and squatted on the floor next to the chairs of the delegates. Almost immediately, a cry went up to have an ordinance of secession drafted that day. The delegates from the other Southern states listened anxiously as the draft was prepared and stirring expressions of the Southern cause sounded throughout the crowded hall. Until President Lincoln's call for troops, Arkansas had been a fairly staunch Unionist state – despite its sympathies with the Deep South. While the observers had reason to hope Arkansas would secede, they feared there could be enough no votes to postpone action or keep the state in the Union. A no vote in Arkansas would deliver a severe blow to the secessionist movement, which hoped to pull yet other border states away from the Union. Missouri had already said it was waiting on Arkansas to get out of its way so it could secede.

When it came time to vote on secession late that afternoon, various delegates prefaced their vote with eloquent speeches greeted with rounds of applause. The vote stood at 64 to five in favor of secession with David Walker yet to cast the final vote. The Unionist reversed his position, declaring that if it were "inevitable that Arkansas ... sccede ... let the wires carry the news to all the world that Arkansas stands as a unit...." Walker then asked the five men who had voted against secession to give unanimous support to leaving the Union. Silence filled the room as another roll call vote was taken. Four of the five dissenters agreed to change their vote, but they insisted they were voting for revolution and not secession as they did not believe a state had the right to secede. Only Isaac Murphy, a farmer from Madison County, stubbornly refused to vote for secession. Although he insisted his principles were Southern, Murphy said he could not "aid in bringing about the untold evils that would assuredly follow in the train of secession." His no vote was drowned out by the hissing and booing of the crowd. With a final vote of 69 to one, Arkansas seceded from the Union at 4:10 p.m. May 6, 1861. It was barely a month shy of its 25th anniversary as a state.[14]

The people of Arkansas had what they wanted. But the delegates were not done. Before the convention ended June 3, they had rewritten the state's constitution, committed the state to the Confederacy, chosen delegates to the Confederate Congress, set up a military board to oversee the state militia, selected generals to defend the state, and confiscated all public land and money in Arkansas. As of 1860, about a third of the land in the state was owned by the federal government. All of this was seized by the state. The group also used the convention to take care of some political business. The delegates established a much-needed yet controversial state bank, moved state elections from August to October, and slapped the Hindman-faction governor in the face by reducing his term, along with that of other state officials, to two years. One of the first official acts following secession was the creation of the State Troops, which were organized to serve from June through September 1861. Initially the state supplied enough men and equipment for seven regiments. Many of these men were mustered in without uniforms and with sticks to serve as guns.[15]

Arkansans needed nothing else to whip them into a state of frenzy. But news of a possible slave insurrection in Monroe County did just that. The Arkansas press reported on the incident that occurred 30 miles west of Helena. The revolt was put down before it could begin June 12 when the slaves were arrested and charged with attempted insurrection and plots to murder anyone who resisted.[16]

Although the war fever seemed contagious, David and Tempie tried to remain immune a while longer. They were resigned to the fact that there would be a war. But they hoped the opening chapters would prove quick and decisive. Maybe there would be no need for David to leave his family, his business interests, and his farm in exchange for a battlefield.

6   Call to Arms

As the first scenes of the war slowly unfolded, David and Tempie acted as interested observers. David ignored the state's pleas for 10,000 volunteers to serve for a year. While those first amateur troops drilled, there seemed to be little threat to hearth and home. David hoped he could serve his state by feeding the wartime economy. For the first few months, the action focused in Virginia, a stone's throw from the federal capital. David and Tempie, like others in both the North and South, expected the argument to be settled on the fields between Richmond and Washington. To help keep the battle far from home, Arkansas contributed a regiment to defend the Old Dominion, which was invaded by the North late in May.

Many of the Arnolds' neighbors and relatives hurried to Virginia to get in on the fighting before it ended. About 1,300 men and boys from Union County answered the call to arms between 1861-1865. Not to be outdone in their show of patriotism to their new nation, hundreds of the Union County recruits were among the first to muster in. Nearly all of the able-bodied men of the county took up arms in the early stages of the war, leaving the women, children, and elderly to face conditions that had never before existed.[1]

The soldiers and their families soon discovered there was more to war than honor and glory. Tempie's brother Bill, fresh out of the Atlanta Medical College, volunteered as a private in the First Arkansas Regiment, which served under Col. James F. Fagan with the Army of Virginia. Stationed in Evansport on the mosquito-infested Potomac for the remainder of 1861, he contracted malaria, which plagued him for the duration of the war. The volunteers, steeped in the rich military tradition of the

South, had expected wounds earned gloriously in battle, but they were not prepared for the illnesses that lurked in the camps.[2]

The first major battle, reported in biased, sensational accounts in Arkansas newspapers, occurred at Bull Run Creek near Manassas, Virginia, July 21. What appeared to be a rousing Southern victory boosted morale throughout the Confederacy and supported the optimistic view that this war would be short. Most likely, David and Tempie clung to this hope while at the same time teaching their children to pray for their friends and family members fighting for their country. Introspective by nature, David would have glimpsed the reality of battle as he read the one-sided accounts in the various newspapers to which he subscribed. His imagination would have pictured that pastoral landscape, in the space of a day, littered with the casualties of conflict. The Confederate force had lost nearly 12 percent of its soldiers. It was a cold statistic that translated into the very real deaths of 2,000 young men – young men his age, young men with wives, children, and a way to make in life. Along with that last breath went their dreams, their loves, their promise of a future.

The flush of optimism with which Arkansans greeted the news of Bull Run was renewed in August when the war struck closer to home, but some began to question the price. Three-thousand Arkansas state troops made up part of a larger Confederate force that repulsed the Union troops at Wilson's Creek near Oak Hills, Missouri. Poorly equipped and inadequately trained, the Arkansas volunteers were disillusioned by their first taste of battle. A few generations removed from the Revolutionary War, most of them had no concept of the grotesqueness of a battlefield. With only their imaginations – perhaps influenced by classic heroic prose or a woodcut or painting celebrating an acclaimed victory – to shape their vision of war, the young soldiers were unprepared for the gruesome reality. In a letter home to his mother in September 1861, Stephen Fair, a Benton County volunteer, described the aftermath of his first battle: "The ground strewed with the dead and dying – hundreds more than half dead all covered with fly-blows and creeping insects, uttering all manner of cries, lamentations, prayers and curses, stained of weltering in their own blood...." It was not surprising then that when given a choice of transferring to Confederate service or going home, many of these volunteers chose home. "They had driven the enemy away ..., had received no pay, and were 'naked and barefooted.'" Having done their duty, they wanted to return to the comforts of home.[3]

The Confederate victories strengthened the resolve of the North. Although no other major battles took place that first year, the war dragged on with no quick defeat in sight. By the end of 1861, Arkansas had fielded 21,000 soldiers – nearly half the number of men who had voted in the state election a year earlier. With that many men involved, talk of war and enlistment dominated daily conversation. It was more difficult to sit on the sidelines as the war spilled over the state's borders. A skirmish at Bushy Creek in northern Arkansas December 9 showed that the state was not to be saved from bloodshed.[4]

The new year brought a change in the news. Federal troops claimed victories, first at Mill Springs, Kentucky, in January and then a few weeks later with the capture of forts Henry and Donelson in Tennessee. With the action starting to pick up closer to home, Bill transferred to the Army of Tennessee and was sent to Memphis. The day after David and Tempie observed Willie's first birthday, the first real action took place on Arkansas soil at Sugar Creek in the northwestern corner of the state. The exchange lasted two days. Then another skirmish broke out in Bentonville February 18. It was time for David to enter the fray.[5]

The war's presence in their front yard had a lot of men in Union County considering enlistment or re-enlistment. It was a much-discussed subject at the Masonic meetings David attended. Patriotism went hand-in-hand with Masonry, which urged its members to be "true to your government and just to your country; you are not to countenance disloyalty or rebellion, but patiently submit to legal authority and conform with cheerfulness to the government of the country in which you live." While Masons in the North took this to mean loyalty to the federal government, Southern Masons interpreted this principle as loyalty to their state government. This sense of Southern patriotism increased membership in the fraternity throughout the war years and spurred many Masons to don a gray uniform. William Langford, a high-ranking Mason in David's neighborhood, recruited friends and neighbors to form Company F, an infantry unit, to serve in the Arkansas 19th Regiment, a part of Brig. Gen. Albert Rust's Brigade.[6]

Langford had no trouble raising 70 troops from Union County. An entry in the diary – in the form of a letter to his wife – of a Louisiana cavalryman shows that family honor, as well as personal honor, was at stake:

> Every male who possesses a spark of manliness should shoulder arms and march out to meet our foe. As for me, I am determined to strike for home, for wife and child as long as my arm is able to lift a weapon – and when the day comes to go back to the homes we have defended, I can look any one in the face and boldly say that I have tried to do my duty, and then my wife can look on her husband with pride, and when his name is mentioned feel a glow of pleasure instead of a blush of shame, and my daughter can truly feel a reverence for the name of her father, – but, if I should chance to fall in this holy cause it will be with the proud conviction that I have not altogether been unworthy of the love of my sweet wife ... and you will then know that you have not bestowed that priceless boon (your love) on an unworthy object, and my daughter will have that priceless heritage, the pure and unsullied name of her father.[7]

As a gentleman of the South, David knew his duty. Bidding a tearful goodbye to his wife and three young children, David, accompanied by his slave Joe, enlisted for 12 months as a third lieutenant with Langford's Company F in El Dorado March 1. At his side marched Capt. David Park Saxon. The cousins had faced the Arkansas frontier together; now they were facing the enemy together. Upon arriving in Little Rock, the company had little time to drill or train. The new recruits almost immediately crossed the Arkansas River to the ramshackle railroad station in Huntersville, a suburb of the capital city. First thing in the morning, they packed into several railroad cars to travel the 49 miles on the newly laid section of the Memphis and Little Rock Railroad that stretched from Little Rock to DeVall's Bluff.[8]

For many of the recruits, it was their first train ride, so they climbed aboard the belching, smoking contraption in a spirit of great adventure mingled with some apprehension. Stories of an accident that had recently occurred on the new railroad were all too vivid as they neared their destination three or four hours later. It was there – just outside of DeValls Bluff – that 10 soldiers had been seriously injured February 2 when one of the cars they were riding in somehow came uncoupled. The engineer in the lead locomotive realized what had happened and held up for the cars in the rear. But the engineer in the locomotive at the rear of the train was unaware of the problem and crashed into the detached cars at full speed. The men in David's unit were relieved to reach their camp at DeVall's Bluff without incident. The first order of business was to get organized and find guns and equipment. Langford was elected captain of Company F. As such, it was his duty to find weapons for his men at a time when supplies were scarce.[9]

While at DeVall's Bluff, the 19th rendezvoused with Gen. Earl Van Dorn's army that had just been soundly beaten at Elkhorn (Pea Ridge) in northwestern Arkansas. More than 1,000 Southern soldiers had died before the Confederate forces retreated in the face of the Union onslaught. In desperate need of supplies and reinforcements, Van Dorn had the 19th help his men forage for necessary provisions. But before the army was sufficiently resupplied, the general was forced to put the needs of the Confederacy above those of his men. With the Union strengthening its attack on the Mississippi and Tennessee rivers, the Confederate command ordered all units to withdraw from Arkansas and head to Tennessee to help protect the important waterways.[10]

Since the middle section of the Memphis & Little Rock Railroad, which eventually would cross several smaller rivers between the White and St. Francis rivers, was not yet completed, David and the rest of the soldiers of the 19th most likely boarded the new sidewheel steamer *Charm* for a six- to seven-hour boat ride down the White River to Clarendon. From there, they had their choice of several stage lines that made daily runs to Madison where the final stretch of the railroad began. After 45 miles – and 12-15 hours – of bumping over rough roads, the 19th traded the coach for the train at Madison for a three-hour ride to Hopefield, which was located on the western bank of the Mississippi.[11]

As the train rolled across the landscape, David wondered if he would live to see the bluffs and rivers again. It was one thing to read about battles and imagine what it would be like to have bullets whizzing by his head; it was another to be heading off to experience war first hand. On the west bank of the Mississippi, David saw signs of war everywhere. The new machine shop at the railroad station had been transformed into an armory that December. Here, many of the men had their guns repaired or the flintlocks on their muskets converted to a percussion lock system. The train depot was attached to the ferry landing by way of a long, inclined ramp. Several men rushed to unload cargo from the many steamers docked at the landing, pushing the trunks, crates, and barrels up the ramp where they would be loaded onto the train. The men of the 19th packed onto the steam ferries for the last leg of their journey to Memphis. A half hour later, they were at the foot of Poplar Street in Memphis.[12]

Their stay in the hustling river town was brief. Soon the 19th Arkansas Infantry was ordered to make its way 60 miles up the Mississippi River to Fort Pillow, a Confederate-built earthen fort with batteries of cannons overlooking the Mississippi from the Chicksaw Bluffs. The Arkansas soldiers joined Company B (the Claiborne Rangers) of the 12th Louisiana Volunteers that March in defending the Tennessee fort against a Union bombardment that lasted 60 days. The Union Navy had been seriously threatening the Southern hold on the Mississippi as everyone from Lincoln to Gen. Ulysses Grant saw the river as the "backbone of the Rebellion." If the North could wrest the river from Confederate control, it would split the rebellion in two. The fall of Island No. 10 on the Mississippi and other Union victories north and east of Fort Pillow made defense of the fort a priority for the Confederate forces.[13]

David's first weeks at the fort were spent acclimating to army life and getting used to the constant shelling from the gunboats. The situation intensified when the Union flotilla encountered the Confederate River Defense Fleet at Plum Point Bend. In his brief respites from duty, David watched the river battle from the batteries of the fort. Although the Confederate fleet was initially victorious, the Union Navy was able to focus its forces on the fort. Day after day it bombarded the fort from its mortar boats. The noise deafened the soldiers, and the shells exploding against the breastworks tore at their nerves.[14]

The Confederate defenders of the fort received much-needed reinforcements April 1 when Company G, which had organized in Homer, Louisiana, arrived as part of the 12th Louisiana Infantry. The new troops were immediately introduced to life at Fort Pillow. The day they arrived they "witnessed some of the realities of war, for on that day the Feds bombarded the fort," A.T. Nelson, who served with Company G, recalled. "The company not yet being properly armed, was sent about five miles down the river to guard the hospital, and to bury the dead; and being unaccustomed to the cruelties of war, this was the most painful duty we ever performed."[15]

The stress of war coupled with the poor sanitary conditions at the fort quickly led to disease. Company F lost two Lewisville, Arkansas, recruits – Thomas Mills and Frank Ward – to illness April 26; and the Claiborne Rangers lost four men. Other factors also began to reduce the ranks of the regiments defending the fort. The removal of all troops from Arkansas had left the state unprotected, a worrisome fact for the men of the 19th Arkansas.[16]

Political differences also came into play. A growing disillusionment – fed by the lengthening duration of the war, condition of the camps, and lack of provisions and pay – hindered recruitment and re-enlistment efforts at a time the Confederacy needed every man it could muster. As a result, the Confederate Congress that April passed the Conscription Act, which required three years' military service for men from 18 to 35. While conscription in itself was distasteful to a society that prided itself on volunteerism and commitment to duty, the act was further poisoned by an escape clause for wealthy slave owners. Such an exemption introduced an issue of class that had not existed before in the discussions of war. This further lowered morale, and many soldiers looked for reasons to return home. At Fort Pillow, two El Dorado volunteers were discharged after serving barely more than a month.[17]

While at Fort Pillow, David learned too well the demands of military life. When on the march, the soldiers generally slept out in the open and took whatever nature gave them. But when they were going to be in an area like Fort Pillow for at least several days, they set up tents and built shelters from anything they could find – leaves, bark, wood, dirt, blankets, or the occasional rubber tarp. With Joe as his valet, David had camp life a bit easier than most, including some of the higher-ranking officers who had no slaves. It was common for men from planter families to have a slave valet. These soldiers usually drew equal rations for their slaves and the slaves' horses. Joe took care of David's personal needs and tended to such domestic duties as cooking, washing, and mending. "A negro is invaluable in the army," one captain wrote home to his wife. "An officer has to live like a hog without one." But having a slave did not excuse David and the other slaveholders from camp duties. No matter how menial, they had to do their own camp duties as the other soldiers would not tolerate working as equals alongside a slave. In turn, the slaves, as noncombatants, were kept at the rear of the regiment and were expected to keep a safe distance from the firing line or any point of danger. They seldom accompanied their masters on picket duty or scouting expeditions. While they were not exposed to the front lines, the slaves endured all the hardships of camp life, and many succumbed to measles, whooping cough, and the other diseases that spread like a wildfire through the camps.[18]

Having Joe along gave David a little more spare time than some of the other soldiers enjoyed. When he was not drilling, reinforcing the extensive breastworks designed to protect the fort from a land attack, or skirmishing with enemy boats, David wrote letters home – letters sprinkled with news of the war, instructions on maintaining the farm, his needs, musings on the war, spiritual encouragement, and greetings to each of the children, neighbors, and slaves. He took advantage of opportunities to attend church services and prayer meetings conducted by Methodist preachers who had enlisted as soldiers or chaplains. Around the evening campfire, David read his Bible and discussed the fresh rumors about the war elsewhere and the progress of the main Union flotilla, which was headed downriver toward the fort.[19]

7   On the Homefront

Back at home, Tempie had little spare time. Like most of the women in Union County with husbands in the war, she had to run the plantation, oversee the slaves, and gather or make supplies for her family. Besides these daily tasks, she did her part for the war effort. She most likely was a member of one of the numerous women's organizations that sprang up throughout Arkansas to help supply the men.[1]

The women regularly met at courthouses, schools, churches, and private homes to make uniforms, tents, haversacks, wagonsheets, and care packages for the soldiers. These care packages included shoes, handkerchiefs, pin cushions, needles, thread, towels, salves, socks, underwear, writing paper, quills, ink, corncob pipes – all homemade. The women also put in balls of black beeswax so the men could color the white thread, scraps of soap for them to wash with and put in their socks to prevent blisters on long marches, and red pepper for their socks and boots to keep their feet warm. Young Sax, Mary, and Willie may have accompanied their mother to the regular meetings. While Willie played on the floor, Sax and Mary helped roll bandages from strips of old linen. Every bit of fabric was used. The pieces that were too thin to be scraped were unraveled and made into lint and carded until the threads were fluffy. This lint was sent to the hospitals where it was used as cotton is today.[2]

As the war progressed, Tempie and her friends sacrificed their woolen and silk gowns to make shirts for the men while they settled for scratchy homespun dresses. Some of them also gave up their woolen carpets so the soldiers could at least have a warm blanket to protect them from the elements. Whenever there was a chance to sit down and rest, Tempie picked up a pair of knitting needles, which were always nearby. A few minutes here and there added up to a good supply of socks – not only for her family but also for other needy soldiers.[3]

Like other women of the time, Tempie and her house slaves also made home remedies from herbs and weeds growing by the roadside. Just as necessary at home as they were on the front, such homegrown products sometimes were the only medicines available. As quinine became impossible to get, the women made substitute tonics from iron-weed and boneset. They extracted the oil from castor-bean and used sassafras tea to thin the blood in the spring. Some even raised poppies so they could harvest and dry the sap. They packaged the resulting powder and sent it to hospitals to be used as a potent pain reliever.[4]

As a religious woman, Tempie also took every opportunity to pray for the soldiers and the families they had left behind. Her prayers were fueled by concerns for her own husband and brothers. Heavy spring rains led to flooding, which stopped the mail from crossing the Mississippi in May. Dependent on the infrequent courier, Tempie received few letters from her loved ones who were fighting. When rumors of a battle – even a victorious one – arrived, her prayers grew more fervent and specific. Had her husband or brother been in the battle? Were they lying somewhere injured or dying? Or had they already been buried in an unmarked grave? With only rumors to serve as news, it was difficult to know where David or her brothers were at any given time.[5]

That spring, many of the rumors as well as much of the legitimate news centered around the large armies amassing near Corinth, Mississippi, under the Union's Gen. Grant and the Confederate Gen. Albert Johnston. Despite recent losses, the Confederates had reason to be optimistic of the outcome should the two armies engage. The anticipated battle was pitched near Shiloh Church in Tennessee, about 25 miles north of Corinth. Tempie's brother Bill was on the front lines at Shiloh, getting his first real taste of battle at a place designed for tranquility and worship.

The sights and sounds of battle, forever etched in Bill's memory, were juxtaposed against the steeple of the log church, a nearby peach orchard, an idyllic forest, two creeks swollen with the spring rains. The air he breathed reeked with the mingling of overwhelming odors. The pungent clamminess of rain-soaked earth. The stench of thousands of unwashed soldiers. The lingering smells of hastily dug latrines, of sweaty horse flesh, of spent gunpowder, of blood oozing from the wounded and dying.[6]

The disjointed, surrealistic images, caught in frozen glimpses, were the shades of nightmare unimaginable to someone who had not yet experienced war. A look of pure terror carved into the face of a fleeing soldier. Horses and men trampling the bodies of the fallen as if they were sacks of straw. Flashes of light as the artillery exploded their deadly loads. Fragile, white peach blossoms covering the maimed bodies of the dead like a mantle of snow.[7]

The air itself seemed to come alive with the sounds of battle. The spiteful, cat-like spit of the buckshot. The softer "pouf" of the antiquated musket ball. The "pee-ee-zing" of the minie bullet. The roar of the shells digging into the dirt. The "whoot-er-whoot-er" of the Whitworth "mortar-pestle." The hollow thud of a bullet connecting with bone. The shrieks of wounded men and horses. The pitiful pleas as the dying begged to be rescued.[8]

Still suffering from malaria, Bill stood in the heat of the battle, trying to ignore the horrific scene and focus on his duties. He steeled his nerves as a barrage of bullets cut through the cartridge box resting at his side. The cries of his wounded comrades were as piercing as the bullets. Trained to be a healer, he could do nothing for his injured friends except kill the enemy. At the end of that first day of battle, he and the other survivors stared in disbelief at the open field "so covered with dead that it would have been possible to walk across the clearing, in any direction, stepping on dead bodies, without a foot touching the ground," Grant wrote in his memoirs.[9]

Although he survived the battle, Bill's health broke due to exhaustion, stress, and the endless rain. To reach the battle, he had marched 25 miles through flooded fields and knee-deep muck. The night before the engagement, a fierce thunderstorm had robbed him of sleep as he huddled against the cold and wet. Lightning had seared his fitful dreams, while thunder mimicked the sounds of battle. Running on sheer adrenaline, he had faced the enemy. But after an exhausting day of battle, he could not retreat from the nightmare to sleep. To keep the Rebel soldiers unnerved, Grant ordered the Union gunboats to fire throughout the night following that first day of the battle; there would be no reprieve. Determined not to die on an army sick bed, Bill continued to fight the next day. But as soon as the Confederate forces retreated to Corinth at the end of the second day of battle, Bill traveled to Murfreesboro, Tennessee, where he went before the Confederate Medical Board and was subsequently made an assistant surgeon with the rank of captain. Now he could heal instead of kill.[10]

Shiloh was a turning point in the attitude toward the war – at least for the North. "Up to the battle of Shiloh I, as well as thousands of other citizens, believed that the rebellion against the Government would collapse suddenly and soon, if a decisive victory could be gained over any of its armies," Grant wrote. The severity of the battle – the worst one fought in the West during the war – made him give "up all idea of saving the Union except by complete conquest." The gloves were off. The Union soldiers buried any remaining ideas about chivalry and mercy. Their policy toward the "Seceshes" became one of burn and pillage.[11]

Meanwhile, the heavy bombardment at Fort Pillow and its growing vulnerability forced the South to rethink its priorities along the Mississippi. With the Union in possession of most of Tennessee, it was only a matter of time before Fort Pillow would be cut off from the rest of the Confederacy. The soldiers stationed there could serve their country better as reinforcements for the decimated Army of the Mississippi, which was still holding on at Corinth despite a daily threat from Grant's forces. As April gave way to May, David and Joe packed up their gear and quietly broke camp. The 19th Arkansas and parts of the 12th Louisiana evacuated Fort Pillow and headed to Corinth, where the Army of the Mississippi was now under the command of Gen. P.G.T. Beauregard. A few companies from the 12th Louisiana stayed behind to defend Fort Pillow a few more weeks, leaving it to the Union early in June.[12]

While David, Joe, and the rest of the 19th were glad to leave behind the bombardment that had become a daily occurrence at Fort Pillow, they soon found that life in the field wasn't much better. The grueling conditions of the march struck down more of their number as they trekked across Tennessee and into Mississippi. Nearly a week of rain had made the roads all but impassable, and heavy runoff had rendered the water in many of the streams undrinkable. The men ate and slept irregularly, sometimes getting only one scant meal a day. And with that barest of nutrition, they marched long hours – sometimes until nearly midnight and starting again a few hours later. Flux and dysentery plagued both the men in the camps and those headed there. Six of the men of Company F – J.C. Jackson, L.W. Jackson, John Knight, Liberty Rester, and S.A. Wilson, all from Union County – died before reaching Corinth. A few others were so sick they had to be discharged or sent to hospitals throughout Mississippi.[13]

When David and the rest of the 19th arrived in the strategic transportation center of Corinth, they found a small village-cum-military camp. The junction of the Memphis and Charleston Railroad and the Mobile and Ohio Railroad, Corinth had served as an important mobilization center for Confederate troops. Grant recognized it as "the most strategic position at the West between the Tennessee and the Mississippi rivers and between Nashville and Vicksburg." But following Shiloh, the town had become a place for the sick and dying. Its hotels and many of its houses served as hospitals for those wounded in battle. Large tent cities were filled with soldiers disabled by measles, malaria, dysentery, diphtheria, exhaustion, pneumonia, typhoid fever, scarlet fever, exposure to the elements, and lack of food and good water. A sickening odor – a disagreeable "kitchen" smell – pervaded the camps, tainting the taste of food, and clinging to the blankets and sheepskins the soldiers slept on.[14]

To avoid the diseases that swept through the camps, David fought a losing battle with cleanliness. "I change my clothes several times a week but am all the time dirty," a young officer wrote home to his wife. "A man gets indifferent to cleanliness very soon in camp. I try to keep my flesh clean, wash very often at night just before going to bed. I sit upon the foot of my pallet and poke my feet off to the tub; there wash one and draw it back on the pallet and then do likewise with the other...." The filth and the rain reduced the soldiers' clothes to rags, but new clothes were scarce and expensive. The demand for clothing fueled the spinning wheels, looms, and knitting needles of the women at home.[15]

Cleanliness was not David's only concern in the camps. Fresh food was increasingly hard to come by. Those soldiers with money could buy a limited amount of fruit to supplement the scant rations the army provided. In the camp economy that grew up, watermelons sold for $1.25 to $4 each and peaches went for $1.50 a bushel. But for the most part, David found little relief in camp from the stress of battle and the long marches he had endured. "The life of a soldier is a constant drag of existence through tedious, and trying hours," a young officer wrote to his father. "It subjects the body and spirits to all the pressure they are able to endure." The daily reality of death and his own mortality compelled David to seek comfort and strength in his Bible and prayer. He also participated in the impromptu Bible studies and preaching services that sprung up around the campfire. Such services provided opportunities to reflect and contemplate – on the war, his family, the future, and the meaning of life and death. "How can I do otherwise when the funeral procession and the funeral rites are daily seen and heard in our camps," a young officer mused as he tried to give his father a glimpse of his life and the man he was becoming. "Ten thousand things warn me of the uncertainties of life, and we ought all to be warned that to live is as solemn a thing as to die."[16]

The first order of business after the 19th arrived at Corinth was a reorganization and election of regimental officers. The men elected Col. Thomas P. Dockery as the new commander of their regiment May 12. The reinforcements raised morale in Corinth and once again soldiers had reason to hope for a Confederate victory. David and the other men still on their feet built breastworks on the perimeter of the village to defend against an anticipated attack from the north. They worked frantically, always with their guns at the ready, always listening for sounds that would signal the enemy was approaching. It was with a sigh of relief that David surveyed the finished project. Now all he had to do was wait for the enemy. "We now have a very large force here," William Edwards Paxton, a Louisiana soldier stationed at Corinth, wrote home to his wife that May, "and I am very hopeful of the result if they attack us – We have no notion giving up without a desperate struggle. What I fear most is that they will shun the attack here and strike at some point where we are not so prepared."[17]

The Union was not about to leave such a strategic position in the hands of the Confederacy. But it took its time traveling from Shiloh to the railroad center. All during May – while the Confederate soldiers waited anxiously and even some of the Union commanders grew impatient – the federal army advanced slowly toward Corinth. With each gain of a few miles, the Union soldiers would stop and entrench. The laborious digging of trenches in the rainy weather impeded their progress. Grant and his men had reason to complain about the ridiculous caution as it took them a full month to cover the 25 miles that separated them from the Confederates.[18]

The delay soon ended any optimism the Confederates had for a decisive victory at Corinth. By not attacking, the Union inadvertently let human nature and Mother Nature do its work. The defeat at Shiloh, the constant bickering among commanding officers, the senseless deaths of friends and comrades, the continuing blight of illness and disease had taken their toll on troop morale. The Army of the Mississippi was in a tight spot. It soon became clear that Dockery's 19th had traded one untenable position for another. After only a few weeks in Corinth, members of the 19th fell ill to the same maladies that had weakened the other units. Desertions were common. Food and water were in such short supply that David had to rely on the resourcefulness of Joe, who stole whatever meat he could find and then cooked it for David and his men.[19]

As May wore on, the Confederate officers acknowledged it was time to leave Corinth. With the large Yankee force encamped at the edge of the Confederate fortifications and no siege gun for protection, Beauregard gave the order to prepare to evacuate. David and the other men spent their last few days in Corinth destroying ammunition and crafting "Quaker guns" – logs, about the diameter of a cannon, mounted on wagon wheels. These faux guns were aimed at the advancing federal army. With everything packed up or destroyed, the Confederate soldiers slipped out of town under cover of darkness. In the midst of the retreat, David's company lost a few more men. J.B. Lassiter, a Louisiana recruit, died May 29 in Corinth just as his unit was leaving town. T.J. Parris of Union County was discharged that day. Two other soldiers, Cicero Burt of Louisiana and J.W. Durett of Union County, were on their deathbeds in nearby towns. [20]

When the Union soldiers marched into town May 30, they found, to their surprise, no sign of a Southerner fit to fight. "[E]verything had been destroyed or carried away," Grant wrote. "There was not a sick or wounded man left by the Confederates, nor stores of any kind. Some ammunition had been blown up – not removed – but the trophies of war were a few Quaker guns ... pointed in the most threatening manner towards us."[21]

The Southern evacuation of Corinth was a bitter event for both sides. The Confederate soldiers were tired of retreating. They had wanted revenge for the slaughter at Shiloh. The Union soldiers also thought they had something to prove after Shiloh, so just walking into Corinth without a battle was a hollow victory. "The possession of Corinth by the National troops was of strategic importance," Grant recalled, "but the victory was barren in every other particular. It was nearly bloodless. It is a question of whether the *morale* of the Confederate troops engaged at Corinth was not improved by the immunity with which they were permitted to remove all public property and then withdraw themselves. On our side I know officers and men of the Army of Tennessee ... were disappointed at the result. They could not see how the mere occupation of places was to close the war while large and effective rebel armies existed."[22]

What was left of the Army of the Mississippi moved south to Tupelo, Mississippi. Until this time, the losses of David's company were all due to illness and camp conditions. But two days after retreating toward Tupelo, J.W. Harden, who had signed on with David in El Dorado, was captured by Union soldiers. He was eventually sent to a military prison in Illinois. That same day, Durett died, and T.J. Primm, another El Dorado enlistee, was discharged. Tupelo also proved to be David's last camp with the 19th Arkansas. The lack of food and potable water, exposure to the elements, and exhaustion were more than his body could handle. He could go no further. On the point of collapse, David was relieved of duty June 3 along with Capt. Langford, who is said to have left the unit because of his disgust over the Conscription Act. With Joe nursing him every mile of the way, David made the slow journey home to Union County.[23]

8   A Discharge of Duty

The man Tempie joyously greeted was not the man she had waved off to war. That man had been full of fire and energy. But this man was a faint reflection of his former self. Tempie helped him into the house and reintroduced him to his growing children. Over the next few months, she slowly nursed her husband back to health while tending to all of the other demands of her family and plantation. After a long convalescence, David gradually took to the fields and what business he had left. It felt good to be back in his old life, to have a real roof over his head and a clean bed to sleep in.

While it was nice being home, David could not escape the war or the images he carried within. Nothing was as it had been. Few men remained in Union County. His neighbors lived in fear and want as essential foods were in short supply. As the planter society had taken root in southern Arkansas, landowners planted more and more acreage in cotton. The foodstuffs they had once produced themselves they now bought from farmers in northwest Arkansas, the breadbasket of the state. The first year of the war, 1861, had been marked by nearly complete crop failure in northwest Arkansas. The following year brought another crop failure, which was intensified by a hog cholera epidemic. As a result, essential foods were in short supply, and prices for the little food available skyrocketed; a barrel of flour sold for $35 to $40. With the shortage of flour, corn bread became the daily staple. Coffee, another essential, was diluted by mixing the precious grounds with parched corn. The lack of variety in the diet resulted in nutritional deficiencies, especially in the young and the elderly, that weakened the immune system, making people more susceptible to disease. In response to the food crisis, the Arkansas General Assembly imposed a cotton tax of $30 a bale to force farmers to plant food rather than their traditional cash crop. As further incentive, the General Assembly limited the number of acres that could be planted in cotton to no more than two acres per field hand. The penalty for violating the acreage restriction was a fine ranging from $500 to $5,000. This restriction, of course, benefited the wealthier planters who had more slaves, increasing the class resentment that had grown up around the escape clause of the Conscription Act.[1]

Another change was the very real threat of Union troops. By the time David returned home in the summer of 1862, the enemy had a secure foothold in the northern and eastern counties of the state. To protect their possessions from federal raids, many Arkansans buried or hid everything from cotton to silver to foodstuffs to wagon tires and iron axles. Reports spread throughout the state by word of mouth and in the newspapers that Yankee soldiers were torturing people by sticking their feet into fires to force them to reveal where they had hidden their valuables.[2]

Not all the news David heard was bad. That summer, Confederate loyalists cheered the exploits of the *Arkansas*, a steamer that gallantly, and successfully, challenged the Union boats on the Mississippi. The Confederate ram steamed out of the Yazoo River in northern Louisiana July 15, 1862, and fought its way through the federal fleet. Its daring victories, jubilantly reported by the Arkansas press, made it the state mascot that summer. By the time the steamer reached Vicksburg, Mississippi, it was so badly shot up that it could go no faster than one mile per hour. The Rebels waiting in Vicksburg did not care as they cheerfully welcomed the ship that had captured two Union gunboats and disabled several others. They were convinced that, with a few repairs, the *Arkansas* could single-handedly wipe out the entire federal fleet on the southern Mississippi. Mechanics and soldiers worked through the night to repair the ship's machinery and smokestack. But by dawn, they realized the *Arkansas* could fight no more. Its three-month odyssey ended when the crew blew it up so as not to give the Yankees that glory.[3]

By fall, the issue of concern was Lincoln's Emancipation Proclamation, which was to go into effect the next year. Who did Lincoln think he was freeing slaves in a country no longer under his jurisdiction? Where was the fairness in ending slavery in the Confederacy but preserving it in Missouri and Kentucky? While those loyal to the Confederacy disregarded Lincoln's proclamation, they worried about its effect. Would it spur slave revolts? Would it encourage slaves – their slaves – to run off and join the Yankees? And what would this mean to the South if it lost the war? The proclamation strengthened the resolve of many of the Southerners. There was too much at stake if the Confederacy were to go down in defeat.

Besides following the national news, David also tried to keep up on the news of his former unit. Whenever he walked into town or over to his neighbor's, he was sure to hear reports about Company F. With its predominance of soldiers from Union County, news of its whereabouts and actions was a major topic of local gossip. The unit fought under Gen. Sterling Price at Iuka, Mississippi, and in his costly attempt to retake Corinth that fall. Five soldiers from Company F fell at Corinth – Samuel D. Betts, J.B. Cowser of El Dorado, Levi Fanner, J.M. Johnson of Louisiana, and W.J. Myers of El Dorado. Another 10 were wounded, and most of those were taken prisoner. By the end of the year, only 28 of the 70 Union County men who had marched off to war together as part of Company F had not died, deserted, or been wounded, taken prisoner, discharged, hospitalized, or transferred to another unit.[4]

If the war pressing in on them were not enough, David and Tempie had family issues to face. A few months after David returned home, Tempie realized she was pregnant with their fourth child. Knowing he would have to enlist again, David worried about his family's safety. After considerable thought, they made plans to move to a farm on the Red River in Lafayette County (the part that later became Miller County). But first, David followed the example of his neighbors and hid one lot of cotton – 22 bales – in a field. The legislative restrictions together with the war made it impossible for him to sell the cotton then, and he figured it might be worth more after the war. In the meantime, he was afraid that if it were discovered, it would be stolen.[5]

David's fears were well founded. Cotton was a scarcity in the Northeast where the textile mills depended on the Southern staple to keep them running. By June 1, 1862, nearly 69 percent of the 4.7 million spindles in the Northeast sat motionless. A month later, 75 percent of the spindles were idle. The demand and the short supply made cotton a premium – so much so that many of the priorities of the federal government centered around this crop. The desire to get the Mississippi under Union control was partly fueled by the need to reopen the cotton trade routes and resupply the textile factories in the North.[6]

Cotton also spurred personal ambitions of U.S. generals such as Benjamin Butler and Nathaniel Banks and the rank and file of the U.S. Navy. Naval prize law awarded 45 percent of the value of captured property to the sailors who seized it and five percent to their admiral. The other half was paid into a fund for disabled seamen. Navy personnel foraged miles from their boats to claim cotton, seldom asking whether it belonged to planters loyal to the Union. When necessary, they took raw cotton to a nearby gin where they would gin and bale it themselves. They marked the 400-pound bales with "C.S.A." and then "U.S.N." to indicate that the U.S. Navy had fairly confiscated the cotton from Confederates. It became a joke that the letters actually stood for "Cotton Stealing Association of the United States Navy." The federal government also leased or seized plantations, using escaped slaves as laborers to bring in the cotton crop and produce food for the Union soldiers and growing number of runaway slaves.[7]

Such thievery and reports of Yankees killing loyal Confederates in cold blood had forced many Arkansans further west – away from the growing federal menace. While Tempie was still able to travel, the Arnolds packed up their household and moved to a 200-acre farm on the Red River near Garland City and the Wynne Plantation, where they joined Tempie's mother. What they found there was not encouraging. Although prosperous plantations could be found along the Red River, this part of Arkansas was one of the poorest regions by 1862. "The poor people live as poorly as Job's Turkey," a Texas soldier stationed in the area wrote. "What they have, the army has eat up." Determined to make the best of the situation, the Arnolds settled in to life as war refugees. David took comfort in the fact that Tempie would be with her mother and close to other kin while he was off fighting. Her brothers' families had retreated to nearby Hempstead County and Texas.[8]

As David's health improved, the pressure for him to re-enlist increased. At 34, he was still under the mandate of the Conscription Act. With the war stretching into its third year, there was talk that the Confederacy would soon begin impressing slaves and older men. The flagging nation needed every soldier it could muster, and Arkansas, especially, needed all of her sons if she were to remain a part of the Confederacy. There was no way David could sit out the rest of the war. By January 1863, rumors raged that Maj. Gen. Frederick Steele's Union Army was about to invade Little Rock. In response, Gov. Harris Flanagin, who had taken the oath of office November 15, 1862, issued an emergency proclamation calling for the citizens of Arkansas to come to her defense:

> The enemy has secured a position upon the Arkansas river, and the state calls on her sons to rise en masse and drive them from our borders. Choose ye. On the one hand the country is to be occupied by a foe who knows no pity, who claims your property as a right and who proclaims your deportation a duty; on the other hand you write your names on your country's history as its defenders, and retain the possession of your homes and firesides. A people determined to be free cannot be enslaved.... I hereby call upon the citizens of this state to appear FORTHWITH at LITTLE ROCK, with such arms and accoutrements as they possess, to engage in military service for SIXTY DAYS, in order to repulse the enemy.[9]

For reasons untold, David chose not to answer the governor's plea. Instead, he waited another month and then opted to enlist March 12, 1863 – along with others from Union County and some of the Louisiana soldiers he had served with at Fort Pillow – as a private in Company A of the 13th Louisiana Battalion, a partisan rangers unit. To be a part of this unit, David had to supply his own horse, arms, and military accoutrements and commit to keeping himself mounted and supplied for the duration of his service. Most of the men carried double-barreled shotguns and whatever sidearms they possessed as neither the Confederacy nor the state had guns to spare. David also had to equip his slave with a horse and camp essentials. With horses selling for $350 to as much as $800, uniforms costing about $175, and good sturdy boots going for $75, David had to invest much of his family's savings into outfitting himself for the cavalry. Whenever possible, he used Confederate money, reserving his gold and silver for the future. All the while he was buying supplies, David worried about any indebtedness he might be incurring. He, like many other soldiers, shared the thoughts of Theophilus Perry: "At the conclusion of this war the smallest indebtedness will brake [sic] a man.... Bankruptcy will prevail after this war I fear.... When the war closes Confederate money will depreciate & there will be no patriotism to sustain it. It will take several years for Commerce to introduce Specie & in the mean time wide spread ruin will overtake debtors."[10]

Riding with the rangers in northern Louisiana was a different experience from being in the trenches with the infantry. In Louisiana, regular cavalry units were the domain of gentlemen – the best citizens of the region, planters who were used to the saddle. In these units, chivalry rode right along with honor. When Louisiana's cavalry units and other defenses were commandeered by the Confederacy to fight outside the state's borders, Gov. Thomas Moore in 1862 began organizing the state's forces into companies known as partisan rangers. The rangers were irregular cavalrymen who, along with the scouting and picket duties of the regular cavalry, would make sudden dashes on the rear and flanks of the enemy, ambush small groups of Yankees, disrupt communication lines, and generally harass Union outposts and supply trains.[11]

David's company "was in several skirmishes, but in no regular battle or general engagement," Lt. J.R. Monk of the 13th recalled years later. Although the 13th Louisiana never endured a Shiloh, Monk said, "it certainly had its share of suffering, hardships and privations incident to a soldier's life; after marching day and night through heat, rain and cold, stopping only when the imperious command of nature demanded resting, lying down supperless upon the wet earth for a bed, with saddles for pillows and wet blankets for covering...."[12]

With supplies often non-existent, the partisans did their best to feed their comrades with the enemy's provisions and stole uniforms that were then dyed brown or black to replace the threadbare clothing of the Rebel soldiers. Overcoats, which shed water like feathers, were a prize in high demand, especially in the wet regions of Louisiana. The state's many waterways, threatened by Union gunboats, offered another tactic for the rangers. The rangers often tramped through the water as they felled and spiked trees and then sunk them in the rivers, shallow swamps, and bayous to snag and disable the enemy boats. In exchange for their services, the rangers got to stay in Louisiana. Joining the rangers assured David he would remain in the northern part of the state, which was close to home.[13]

The 13th Louisiana, under Lt. Col. Samuel Chambliss, was in a state of reorganization when David joined. Formed the previous summer in Monroe, Louisiana, the battalion raided Union supply trains in the northeastern corner of the state of Louisiana and performed picket duty and destroyed crops on federally leased plantations in East Carroll Parish near Lake Providence. Just to the west of the Mississippi River, Lake Providence was one of the Rebel defenses against Grant's quest to take Vicksburg, about 35 miles downriver. In November 1862, the 13th Battalion had been consolidated with four independent companies to create the Third Louisiana Cavalry. When Col. Frank Pargoud was commissioned to command the new regiment over Chambliss, many of the officers and enlisted men protested. This consolidation of units created such confusion that Union troops were able to raid nearby Delhi and Dallas Station in Louisiana with no opposition from the Confederate forces. The raid on Delhi, just 40 miles west of the Mississippi River, showed how vulnerable the road to Vicksburg was. As a result, the 13th was restored and returned to Lake Providence shortly before David enlisted.[14]

En route to join the new unit, David and Joe passed through the war-scarred Louisiana countryside. Considering all the rumors and reports David had heard, he was surprised to find some parts of the state almost untouched by battle – at least visibly. In Alexandria, no houses had been burned. And although Gen. Banks had been ordered to destroy the corn crop, "he found that too tedious, and the crop had only been destroyed in the neighborhood of his encampments," a fellow cavalryman wrote. "There they (Union forces) burned the fences for convenience & foraged their horses in the cornfields. The[y] carried off a great number of horses, mules & wagons." While the planters in this area were spared the horrors experienced elsewhere, they knew the theft of their livestock and farm implements would lead to considerable loss as they would not be able to harvest the coming crop. Reflecting on such scenes, David whispered a prayer for his family – their safety and their future.[15]

When he arrived at Lake Providence, David was greeted by men worn down by the drudgery of camp life and guerilla-style warfare. With army tents a luxury, most of the men were forced to sleep under the open sky, waking to find their hair and clothes soaked with the heavy Louisiana dew. Such living conditions, coupled with the pestilence of the swamps, weakened the men's health. Colds became a way of life. Poor health increased their sense of helplessness and frustration over the progress of the war, whittling away at the men's morale and, subsequently, their values. Driven by necessity, many of them resorted to stealing from each other – taking cooking utensils, blankets, anything they needed that another solider had. The lack of tents and a sense of personal space increased the opportunity for theft within the camps.[16]

David's first few months with the 13th were spent riding picket at Lake Providence and trying to foil Grant's advances on Vicksburg. When David and his men rode out on a mission, they left all their supplies on the supply train, taking with them only a change of underclothes and a bed roll. Anything they needed along the way they had to forage. Occasionally when the rangers rode through a town or village, they were met by small crowds of women at the crossroads or public places. The women, living in daily fear of the rumors and reality of Yankees pillaging the area, were encouraged by the sight of Confederate cavalry. They greeted David and his unit with cheers, throwing flowers in their path and giving them slices of cake and bread. Knowing how valuable flour had become, David all the more appreciated the women's efforts. Such sacrifices were a reminder of why he was fighting. He needed that reminder to keep going. It fueled his determination to halt Grant's resolute push toward Vicksburg.[17]

9   Fall of Vicksburg

It was no secret that Grant wanted Vicksburg, the heavily fortified city that gave the Confederacy control of the middle stretch of the Mississippi. "To dispossess them of this became a matter of the first importance," Grant said in his memoirs. "The possession of the Mississippi by us from Memphis to Baton Rouge was ... a most important object. It would be equal to the amputation of a limb in its weakening efforts upon the enemy." Rumors of Grant's movements spread through the Rebel camps where officers plotted new ways to cut off the enemy's communication and destroy his supplies.[1]

Vicksburg's perch atop high, unscalable bluffs allowed its batteries to dominate the river below and promised destruction to any Union gunboat that attempted to pass. This seemingly impregnable city was protected to the north by the vast Yazoo Delta, which was impassable to a large army. In his analysis of the situation, Grant said this area was "cut up by bayous filled from the river in high water – many of them navigable for steamers. All of them would be, except for overhanging trees, narrowness and tortuous course, making it impossible to turn the bends with vessels of any considerable length. Marching across the country in the face of the enemy was impossible; navigating it proved equally impracticable." The situation was not much better south of Vicksburg in Louisiana where Port Hudson had, thus far, prevented Union boats from moving upstream. Seasonal floods, combined with the terrain of Louisiana's bayous and swamps, had repeatedly stymied Grant's ambitious plans to conquer Vicksburg and thus gain ultimate control of the Mississippi.[2]

Despite the Confederate efforts, Grant, focusing on naval strategies, gradually closed in on his target. Encouraged when two gunboats managed to run the gauntlet of batteries at Port Hudson that spring, Grant decided to try the same tactics at Vicksburg. Taking advantage of a dark, moonless night, Union ships stole past the Vicksburg guns April 16, 1863. Although one transport ship was lost, there were no casualties among the Union soldiers. By the end of April, Grant had managed to get his army across the Mississippi just south of his target. The resulting siege of Vicksburg effectively cut the Confederacy in two, giving the Union control of the entire Mississippi.[3]

As Grant's troops were crossing the Mississippi, David's regiment, the 13th Louisiana Cavalry, was undergoing more command changes that started with Chambliss' April 30 resignation as lieutenant colonel. Maj. Richard Capers was promoted to lieutenant colonel and James H. Capers, the commanding officer of Company A, was promoted to major of the battalion. The promotions signaled new duties for David, who had been serving in Company A. He now found himself with the rank of captain and as the commanding officer of Company G, a unit of about 100 men from Union County, Arkansas, and Claiborne Parish, Louisiana. As captain, it was his responsibility to ensure his men were fed, outfitted, and prepared for battle. He also had to be more concerned about his own appearance; officers were expected to dress well as a way to command the respect of their men. As a symbol of honor and valor, officers had to dress the part.[4]

Grant's move on Vicksburg increased the frequency and intensity of skirmishes in the area and had Confederate soldiers preparing for what they saw as an inevitable battle for the city. A newspaper account, printed years later, described how individual soldiers prepared to fight – regardless of whether they were facing a skirmish or a major battle: One soldier reads from his New Testament. "[I]t takes his mind from what is going on around him – from what is before him." The captain is sitting a little apart from the others. He "is saying nothing; but is apparently thinking deeply, and is industriously whittling twigs, which he puts in his mouth as if they were toothpicks, throwing one away every moment to put in a new one." Another soldier also sits quietly. "He is busy picking up twigs and breaking them into bits. Like the captain, he is keeping his fingers busy as a relief to his thoughts – as a balm for nervousness." Another has a face as white as a sheet. "He is afraid, but not greater so than those around him. He knows that he may be killed at any moment...." Yet another soldier shows no sign of anxiety or fear. He had been sick at the thought of the approaching fight "but is now ready for any duty. The excitement or the dread was too much for him at first, and 'went to his stomach,' but that is over.... Another comrade is reading a letter – the last one received – and he is well aware that it may be the last one he will receive."[5]

In the desperate days before the fall of Vicksburg, David most likely scratched out his thoughts to Tempie on scraps of coarse paper. His words home probably echoed those of Theophilus Perry – whose life, education, religious views, and future goals closely mirrored David's:

[Y]ou must know that I will soon be exposed to the fatalities of War. I am hopeful. You must be so too. We do not know what Fate has decreed for us to undergo & suffer. The uncertainty is calculated to alarm us. It should also keep us hopeful. For why should we mourn before it is our time? Why take upon ourselves the suffering of tomorrow? We are always in the Hands of our Maker. He sustains in Battle as well as in peace. When his upholding hand is withdrawn, we sink into our graves. We live and die according to God's appointed (time). Let us await then with a uniform silence that he watches with the tender eye of a parent over us; and will at last conduct his children into fields of Bliss, forever prepared for them. I feel awfully solemn. You know, my dear Wife I have always felt so [about] battles and wars. But for all this, I bless my Maker for the hope he yet permits to light my pathway, that these eyes are to see & these arms again embrace my [wife] and her children.[6]

Despite the rumors and anticipation, David's regiment was not sent in to attack Grant. Instead, the men engaged in a few skirmishes in May that resulted in artillery exchanges between Rebel batteries and Yankee gunboats. Such fights might last an hour or so with 30 to 40 shots being fired, and they often proved deadly to a few of the men. Engaging in a skirmish required the same courage, the same willingness to accept death, as needed in a major battle. But those who fell in the hit-and-run exercises along the Mississippi had no monuments erected to memorialize their last breath, no glorious accounts written of their bravery. They had only their comrades and families to mourn their passing, to celebrate their life and courage.[7]

While denied a glorious role in actively pursuing Grant himself, the 13th Louisiana and other units in the area were encouraged by reports supposedly coming out of Vicksburg. "The news from Vicksburg to day [sic] is glowing," a soldier reported. "Gen. Grant made a great effort to withdraw his forces by way of Sniders Bluff and was cut off by Gen. Johnson.... He then made two efforts to escape by Yazoo Pass, and failed in each. It is understood that he is now preparing for a desperate attack upon Vicksburg again. There he will sacrifice his men by the thousands and expire in agony."[8]

David and the other men of the 13th waited eagerly for news of a Confederate victory. But as the hot, steamy Louisiana summer set in, the waiting became unbearable. Camp conditions reflected the war-inflicted poverty of the area. Since the Yankees had destroyed all of the cisterns, often poisoning them with the carcasses of dead animals, the soldiers were forced to drink the bayou water, which was "intolerable but necessity forces us to drink," one of the men wrote. "It preserves life but does not quench thirst." Yet hope prevailed. Although the men had been falsely encouraged by rumors in the past, they grasped at anything that promised the slightest possibility of victory, that offered them a reason to go on and an assurance that their sacrifices were not in vain. As the situation in Vicksburg worsened, David and his men took comfort from news that the Confederate forces under Lee were beating the Yankees back in the East. They also found cause for hope in the renewed rumblings that the British would intervene on behalf of the South. "I think our affairs are more promising than they have ever been before," a soldier wrote, summing up the feelings in the camps. "Our hopes are bright...."[9]

Still looking for ways to weaken Grant's position outside of Vicksburg, Col. Frank Bartlett led David's battalion and a Texas cavalry unit in a June 9 attack on a Union garrison in the town of Lake Providence. The attack led to more skirmishes and what seemed like endless and pointless exercises of riding and marching in circles in the swamps as the Confederate officers searched for a way to stop Grant. Gens. Henry E. McCulloch and James Morrison Hawes came up with a partial answer – a two-pronged attack on Union gunboats protecting Young's Point near where the public road leading to Vicksburg first touched the Mississippi River. The Confederate forces, which included Texas and Louisiana rangers, pushed back the federal pickets but the full-scale attack was canceled when Hawes became convinced that his men, overpowered by the heat, would be enfiladed by the gunboats. The general wanted no part in a "useless sacrifice of life."[10]

Even without the stress of battle, such exercises took their toll on the men. Swamp sickness increased daily in the camps, worsened by the lack of potable water. Many of the regiments had been separated from their supply trains, which meant some of the men had not had a change of clothes in four weeks. To relieve the chafing and stench of their soiled garments, they stripped naked as they washed their only suit of clothes in the bayou. Those who had been reduced to bare feet were restricted to the camps, while others shuffled over the soggy earth in scraps of leather that bore little resemblance to their earlier life as shoes and boots. Their forages for food had turned to scavenger hunts as the scorched earth policy on both sides of the war left little for nourishment. The needs were even greater for cavalry units like David's as it took 500 bushels of meal to feed the horses in a cavalry brigade each week. The hope that had encouraged them quickly ebbed as they were treated to the constant reminder of the imminent fall of Vicksburg. "We are under the sound of the cannon at Vicksburg. It is ceaseless day & night, with short intermission rarely," an officer wrote.[11]

Driven by desperation and a growing sense of helplessness, the men welcomed any chance for action. While they had given up hope of attacking Grant at Vicksburg, they looked for other targets – such as the Union fort at Goodrich's Landing on Lake Providence. Manned by 113 soldiers of the First Arkansas Infantry, African Descent, the stout fort, constructed on a large Indian mound, provided protection to several federally leased plantations being worked by former slaves. Besides protecting the Union plantations, the black soldiers raided and destroyed everything in the vicinity that could be used for the Southern cause.[12]

When the Rebel forces arrived June 29, they demanded the unconditional surrender of the fort. The three white officers of the African infantry agreed to trade their position in exchange for a promise of proper treatment for themselves along with an unconditional surrender of their black troops. But later that day, the Union's First Kansas Mounted Infantry clashed with the Rebel soldiers. The confrontation gave the Southern soldiers an excuse to vent their frustration and, perhaps, their hatred as they retaliated by burning and destroying the plantations in the area, especially those leased by the Yankees. The battle escalated the next day, resulting in a minor setback for the Union and desperately needed supplies of food and weapons for the Confederates. But the Rebels were not satisfied with supplies; they wanted blood. One of the Union officers was accused of murdering Capt. Charlie Collins of the Fourth Louisiana Cavalry. In what was presumed an act of vengeance, he and another of the white officers disappeared; a Confederate major later was charged with their murder. Meanwhile, the third Union officer, Lt. John East, was taken as a prisoner to Camp Ford, where he was held until the end of the war. While the rout of the fort did little to shift the direction of the war, it distracted the rangers from the looming fate of Vicksburg while boosting their confidence in the Southern cause.[13]

Independence Day, which once had been a great day for all Americans, became a day of irony for the South in 1863. Playing on the symbolism of the day, Grant decided the Fourth of July would live in infamy throughout the Confederacy as that would be the day he would end his merciless siege on Vicksburg and march in to claim what was left of it for the Union. David and his comrades on the west side of the Mississippi accepted the news with mixed reactions. Some were outraged by the defeatist sentiments they heard from home. "It appears to the first view that the fall of Vicksburg must prolong the war very much," a young officer wrote. "But from what I can hear of the sentiment amongst many of the people ... our cause will be surrendered by them and our guns put away. I have great contempt for noisy men ... who once violently talked of whipping the reluctant youths of the land off to war, and who themselves have ignobly speculated upon the necessities of the soldier and his family, accumulated fortunes out of the sacrifice of those that have bared their bosoms to the bayonet, and yet sculked [sic] away from danger themselves."[14]

Such sentiments, coupled with the loss of Vicksburg, discouraged many of the soldiers. But others had prepared themselves and tried to downplay the importance of Vicksburg. As a captain, it was David's mission to cheer those who were low-spirited, reminding them that the Confederate "armies are yet in the field and they are the hopes of the country. They may be able to overturn the pride and boast of the enemy yet." The pep talks worked. Within a few days, the soldiers were joking and laughing in the camps just west of Vicksburg as they waited for new orders. "It is good that the soldiers can laugh," an officer wrote as he pondered the scene of a crowd of his men laughing as they discussed the war. "It is his only source of pleasure. He laughs at the queer ideas of his fellow soldiers."[15]

There was not much else to laugh about. Vicksburg, under siege for nearly three months, had become a disaster zone. Everywhere were scenes of destruction and want. Women and children, ravaged by starvation, now found themselves homeless in a country that was no longer theirs. Fatherless families, elderly couples, and isolated individuals streamed westward out of the city, trying to find refuge and welcome in a land destroyed by war. David's men and other units in the area were ordered to help the fleeing refugees. The sight of a young mother, her tattered dress too big for her bony body, struggling to keep her small children walking moved David to compassion. This could have been his wife, his children. "God, keep them safe," he prayed as he helped the mother with her children. "How bad for the people to be driven from their homes," another officer wrote. "How soon we may be left homeless ourselves. Those that live away from the scenes of war, can form no ideas of its Horrors."[16]

Wherever possible, the rangers also were asked to reinforce the regular Confederate army. Those orders resulted in the relocation of the 13th Louisiana west to Delhi, where it was to become part of Col. Isaac Harrison's cavalry brigade. As the 13th rode toward Delhi, the men burned everything in their path to keep the crops from falling into Northern hands. Having witnessed so much destruction, David had to wrestle with himself over the Louisiana governor's policy to torch the fields of fellow Southerners. Hadn't they suffered enough? But orders were orders; David instructed his men to burn the fields.[17]

Once they got to Delhi, David's men continued to harass Grant's army – only from a safer distance than before. The Union general wrote that his troops, following the fall of Vicksburg, were "very busily and unpleasantly employed in making expeditions against guerilla bands and small detachments of cavalry which infested the interior, and in destroying mills, bridges and rolling stock on the railroads. The guerillas and cavalry were not there to fight but to annoy, and therefore disappeared on the first approach of our troops."[18]

Besides annoying the enemy, the units that made up Harrison's Brigade built bridges, foraged for food, and loaded wagons in the sultry summer heat of the swamps. Again, the stress of camp life and the extreme weather conditions, combined with disease-carrying mosquitoes, did more than the enemy to weaken the soldiers. Chills and fever swept through the camps, debilitating the men. Most of them were not sick enough to be sent to the army hospitals, but they were not well enough to work. By mid-July, some of the units in Harrison's Brigade had fewer than a third of their men fit for duty. Meanwhile, the Yankees increased their activity and control in northeastern Louisiana. Badly outnumbered and weakened by illness, the brigade was in a bad condition and in desperate need of recruits. But the only option it had was to retreat toward Monroe late in July. There the rangers continued harassing Union forces, destroying crops, attacking enemy gunboats, and doing their part to keep Gen. Banks from advancing any farther up the Red River.[19]

News of Lee's defeat at Gettysburg and the desperate condition of Confederate forces heightened the need for recruits. If the South had any hope of winning this war, she needed her sons – all of them – to come to her aid. Throughout the Confederacy, generals and governors pressured men to enlist. Two days before Gettysburg, Gen. John Bankhead Magruder had issued a proclamation calling upon all citizens – without regard to their age – to come to the rescue of their wives and children. Gen. E.K. Smith required slaveholders to send their slaves between the ages of 17 and 45 to work on public projects so as to free the white workers for battle. The proclamations were cause for concern and celebration in the camps. On the one hand, many of the soldiers worried about their fathers, who would be forced to enlist. At the same time, they welcomed the pressure this would place on vocal politicians who had pushed for secession but shielded themselves from military service. Men like David who had not wanted secession but felt obliged to fight for the South felt a growing resentment and contempt toward the "rabid violent secessionist who denounced all persons that differed from him, [and who] ought to have shouldered his gun at the beginning of the war." While deploring the necessity of a draft, David felt some satisfaction in knowing that some of these hypocrites would be forced to back their words with their life.[20]

As summer turned to autumn, few new men had joined the Confederate defense of the Red River area in Louisiana. Dejectedly, David listened to the accounts of the bloodiest battle of the war at Chickamauga, Tennessee, and the fall of Little Rock. Again, he prayed for the safety of his family as his sense of helplessness increased. His orders were to harry the enemy as much as possible between the Ouachita (Black) and Mississippi rivers. How could such tactics help when the South was losing thousands of men – her future – in Tennessee and elsewhere? Wouldn't he be of more use at home? But he couldn't even go home to check on his family. Orders were that only men too sick to remain in camp would be granted furloughs. And those men, upon returning home, faced undeserved scorn from the politicians who had never shouldered a gun. "We hear that when a soldier goes home on sick furlough, that such miserable dogs express their suspicions, and say that the soldier looks to them like he is in good health. They have a holy horror to the soldier going home," an officer wrote.[21]

David, resigned to fulfilling his duty honorably, kept his thoughts to himself. His job was to lead his men, to lift their spirits, to assure them that victory was still possible. His brigade spent the remainder of 1863 in northern Louisiana. As the weather turned cold, the men burrowed into winter quarters in a thick pine forest. They used their free time to build wooden huts and shelters for the winter and spent the nights huddled around the campfire. While food was scarce, wood, at least, was plentiful. Aside from an occasional skirmish, they spent most of their time marching or riding through the mud and water, often searching for food. Some men, overcome by exhaustion and hunger, would fall into the mud and die. Others died in the camps of starvation and illness. By now, death had become commonplace, and the hardships of camp life served as a constant reminder that eternity might be just a moment away for each of them. To cope with the death of their comrades and prepare themselves for the inevitable, David and other devout men attended nightly prayer meetings conducted by the many preachers in their ranks. Sundays were filled with preaching and biblical exhortation. Capt. Smith, a chaplain in the brigade, frequently preached in the evenings. As a result, something of a revival swept through the camps that winter. A number of mourners answered the chaplain's call every evening, and 130 soldiers were baptized in the icy bayou.[22]

The talk around the campfire turned from religion to politics early in 1864 when the pleas and demands for recruits gave way to a conscription law that, in effect, drafted all men from ages 15 to 55. The new Conscription Act, which could commit nearly 100,000 more men to Confederate service, meant that those who had evaded the draft before by sending a substitute would now have to serve. It also impressed slaves. While grateful for the new recruits this would bring, David worried about the impact it would have on his family. How would Tempie survive without their trusted slaves? Who would tend the fields? There was no way she and the other women could bring in a crop by themselves. And who would protect her and the children? David remembered the dire predictions of how the Yankees would starve them out. Those predictions could easily come true now. David was not alone in his dark thoughts. "Our prospects darken every day I fear," a wife wrote to her husband. "I wish the war would end and I reckon it will soon but not in our favor I am afraid."[23]

Reinforced by the recruitment of several new companies, David's battalion was reorganized as the Fifth Louisiana Calvary Regiment as Harrison's Brigade became part of the Sub-District of North Louisiana early in 1864. David retained his command of Company G as the regiment prepared to do its part to push the Yankees from the Red River area. To keep in shape and train the new men, individual units within the regiment held drill competitions, offering a flag and a few furloughs as prizes. Such competitions weren't enough to break the boredom that was becoming a major problem. With too much time on their hands, some of the men whipped themselves into a frenzy over the Confederate cotton trade with the Yankees, which was benefiting a handful of wealthy planters who had sat the war out. And the men from cavalry units that had been dismounted complained that they were still owed cavalry pay and that they should have been remounted before any new cavalry units were raised. These complaints gave rise to mutiny and a two-day work stoppage in some of the units. The mutiny ended with the arrest of several of the men and the threat that the leaders of the insurrection would face a firing squad.[24]

As winter gave way to spring, David's regiment followed the progress of Adm. David Porter's Union gunboats and transports upriver from Alexandria to Shreveport. Their objective was to slow the progress of the navy by taking out as many ships as possible and hindering its foraging efforts. If they were successful, they would keep the navy from its scheduled rendezvous with Banks' land troops. For once, nature was on the side of the Confederates as low water kept the Union boats from moving freely, making them somewhat easy targets for the Rebels who would appear out of the dense forests along the banks of the river.

As Confederate Gen. Dick Taylor was halting Banks' march north at Sabine Crossroads, other Confederate troops (possibly including Harrison's Brigade) halted Porter's advance upriver above Loggy Bayou. "It was the smartest thing I ever knew the rebels to do," Porter wrote later. "They had gotten that huge steamer, *New Falls City*, across Red River, 1 mile above Loggy Bayou, 15 feet of her on shore on each side, the boat broken down in the middle, and a sand bar making below her." While trying to cut through the debris blocking the river, Porter and A.J. Smith, on loan to Banks from Gen. Sherman, learned of Banks' defeat. They had little choice but to turn their fleet around and head back down the river. The retreat was hazardous at best, and the Rebel cavalry, following Porter's progress from the woods and fields flanking the river, made it even more dangerous. On the first afternoon of the retreat, the *Chillicothe*, Porter's armored steamer, got stuck on a submerged stump. It took most of the afternoon to free it. The next afternoon, the Rebels opened their muskets on one of Porter's river monitors and two of Smith's transports. The gunboats responded by shelling the banks.[25]

In mid-April while the large Union flotilla eased its way downriver amid snags, accidents, and skirmishes, some of the soldiers with Harrison's Brigade were camped at Campti, Louisiana, along the banks of the Red River. As the straggling members of the flotilla floated past Campti, Harrison's men opened fire, only to be silenced by the great guns on one of Porter's river monitors. Hearing the exchange 12 miles downstream in Grand Ecore, two Union brigades marched toward Campti, reaching it after nightfall. They fell on the Confederate camp, routing the Rebels. A few days later, several regiments of Harrison's Brigade were camping at Bayou Des Cedars, near St. Maurice, Louisiana, when Yankees attacked them. This time the surprised Confederates managed to force the enemy back.[26]

Harrison's hit-and-run campaign continued as his cavalry regiments followed the Union's demoralized retreat to Alexandria. When David and his men were not skirmishing with the enemy, they blocked the roads by felling trees. Their actions, along with a lack of drinking water, made the forced march for the Yankee land troops almost unendurable. In retaliation, Smith, who had learned the "art" of war under Sherman's tutelage, ordered his retreating men to lay waste the Louisiana countryside. "From Mansfield to the Mississippi River the track of the spoiler was one scene of desolation.... You can travel for miles, in many portions of Louisiana, through a once thickly-settled country, and not see a man, nor a woman, nor a child, nor a four-footed beast," Confederate Louisiana Gov. Henry Allen wrote. "The farmhouses have been burned. The plantations deserted.... A painful melancholy, a death-like silence, broods over the land, and desolation reigns supreme."[27]

As David rode with Harrison's Brigade, he could not escape the horror of war. Everywhere he looked were the ashes of houses, barns, cotton gins. Even the slave cabins, chicken houses, and corncribs had not been spared. The rotting carcasses of livestock littered the roadside. Black smoke hazed the sky, marking the trail of the fleeing enemy. In those first days of brass bands and flamboyant patriotism, who could have thought it would come to this? How could so much hatred spew from people who prided themselves on their civilization and modernity? David could find no answers. Instead, there was only fear for his family and the future. Were Tempie and the children wandering homeless in Arkansas? Was his farm a smoldering pile of debris? What hope – what dreams – remained for his sons?[28]

Driven by their need for revenge, the regiments under Harrison's command took the initiative and raided Pineville where the Yankees were camped April 24. Following this small victory, they defeated a sizable Union force in a skirmish at nearby Hadnot's plantation. While the war was far from over, David had had enough. Camp Hadnot was his last stop with Harrison's Brigade. Once again, his health had given out, and he was forced to resign. While his regiment spent the rest of the year fighting in the last chapters of the war, David headed home to Arkansas.[29]

10 The War at Home

The days following David's departure were torture for Tempie. Her fourth child was due any day. The usual fear of birthing took on horrific proportions as she faced the ordeal without David. Her sleep was riddled with bad dreams as she relived her previous experiences in childbirth. Although she dreaded the evil day, as many women considered it, she also longed for it as she found herself almost helpless in the last days of her pregnancy. There were times when she believed death might be preferable. And on those days, she hoped and prayed she would never be in this condition again. In those anguished hours, she prayed for deliverance and protection – for both her and the unborn child. She was grateful for her mother's presence, but she longed to have David there to calm her fears and terrors.[1]

Nearly a fortnight after David had gone off to war for the second time, Tempie gave birth to a healthy baby girl, Sally Temperance Arnold. As she held the tiny baby, she prayed that Heaven would grant David the opportunity to meet his daughter this side of eternity. She salvaged whatever paper she could find to write lengthy letters to David, telling him of the children's antics, describing the baby, and spilling out her thoughts and fears. She would then unglue an old envelope and turn it inside out so she could reuse it. With mail disrupted, she sent most of her letters by soldiers returning to the camps.[2]

During the day, Tempie busied herself with taking care of her family and the plantation. With four children to care for and several slaves to supervise and provide for, she had plenty to distract her thoughts from the war. But conversations with neighbors and relatives or a letter from David or one of her brothers brought the reality of war crashing in on her private little world. Concern that the Yankees would invade the Red River area had several women talking of pulling up stakes and moving off to a place of safety – if such a place could be found. Tempie tried to be optimistic. If the Yankees took her land, she'd do what her parents had done – find a new frontier. Surely, there was room in the West for her family.[3]

To her children, Tempie presented a calm face as she read to them from the family Bible and taught them to recite their prayers. With David gone, she was both mother and father to the four children. She was the center of their life. Knowing she had to create a cocoon of security for her family, Tempie discovered within herself reservoirs of competence and courage that she had not known existed. And in those few weak moments when she might have faltered, Tempie leaned on the strength of her mother who had carved out a home in the wilderness and knew too well the ache of loneliness.[4]

For two-year-old Willie, life was about change – not loneliness. In a few short months, he had moved to a new home, lost his status as the baby of the family, and learned that grandmothers like to spoil little boys. Although he was a war refugee, his father a soldier, and his home threatened by an invading enemy, Willie's first memories were those of innocent childhood in southwestern Arkansas.

Living on a farm beside the Red River provided the toddler with endless delights, not the least of which was watching the field hands set out trout lines on the river or a nearby lake. Willie loved to go fishing with the slaves. He enjoyed watching the young slaves, dressed in their baggy cotton clothes, teasing each other about how big their fish were or how many each of them had caught. He liked it even more when they would help him cast his line. He watched in wonder as circles of water rippled from the baited hook. And when he saw the line pull taut, he puffed his chest in pride as the slaves helped him land his catch. Just wait till Mother and Grandmother saw what he had caught.

One fishing trip stood out from all the others. Willie had been playing with the other boys along the river bank, perhaps searching for a smooth, rounded skipping stone, when one of the slaves gave an excited shout. Willie looked up to see the young angler, on the edge of the river, tugging on the fishing pole that curved like a rainbow toward the water. The other slaves echoed the excited shouts and rushed to help their comrade keep hold of his prize. It was man against fish as the slaves struggled to conquer whatever was at the working end of the line. The excitement grew as the fish neared the shore. Every flop, every tug assured the anglers that this was a worthy adversary. When they finally dragged it ashore, they found the largest catfish any of them had ever seen. It must weigh 90 pounds, they boasted. Numbers meant nothing to a little boy. All Willie knew was that was one giant of a fish. All the way back to the house, he cast awed but cautious glances at the huge fish the slaves so proudly carried.[5]

Despite its abundance, fish was not the mainstay of their daily diet. The Arnolds owned a great many cows – or so it seemed to the small child. He spent long hours watching the cows get milked. He also was fascinated by the smokehouse with its large hunks of meat suspended from a pole above a pit dug in the middle of the dirt floor. The slaves gathered chips from the woodpile and placed them in the pit, creating a dense smoke that curled and danced around the hanging meat – and inspired the imagination of children. Sax and Mary Lucy had devised a game – of sorts – in which the children would all run into the smokehouse and see how long they could stand the smoky air before they would run out, choking and gasping for fresh air. Willie, who had not quite mastered the art of holding his breath, would run in with his brother and sister and their slave playmates. Within seconds, the sting of the smoke had his eyes watering and his throat burning. Being the youngest, Willie was usually the first to surrender, running outside for a breath of fresh air. Any hurt pride turned to laughter when he got to watch the older children run blindly out a few seconds later, choking and sputtering. At least no one had seen his indignity.

In a time of scarcity, the smokehouse served many purposes. Besides preserving meat and entertaining children, it also provided salt when there was no other source. Willie watched in amazement as the slave women carted bucket after bucket of water from a nearby spring to the now empty smokehouse. Soon, the floor of the smokehouse was transformed into a shallow pond. How the children begged to splash through the water, but the women would have none of it. They had work to do. Hours later, they took up the water and boiled it down, leaving the salt that had dripped from the meat. After being flooded, the smokehouse was off limits until the muddy floor dried out.[6]

Another area that was off limits was the thick forest behind the house. Tempie and the slaves constantly warned the children not to wander into the woods because of the wild hogs that roamed the area. When Willie heard the warnings, his imagination turned the creatures into fierce monsters with great teeth waiting to eat little children. It was with curiosity and excitement that he ran out to meet the slaves returning from a boar-hunting trip. He could hardly take his eyes off the large beast they carried between them. He marveled at the long tusks, running his chubby fingers along the smooth length of the protruding teeth. As he patted the skin of the boar, he was struck by the coarseness of the bristles on its back. So this was what the monster looked like.

Watching out for boar attacks was not the only worry on the farm. The slaves always were keeping an eye on the domestic hogs as they could go wild if they came in contact with their untamed cousins. Another concern was mosquitoes and the deadly diseases they spread. The insects were so bad that whenever the children played outside, the slaves built fires with woodchips to create clouds of smoke in the yard to keep the mosquitoes away. It was almost as bad as playing in the smokehouse. "The smoke in my eyes seemed worse than mosquitoes," Willie recalled later.

Life on the farm provided lessons the small boy found painful. On one occasion, a slave set the toddler on the back of the family's large horse and left him there untended. Willie's short legs could barely straddle the broad back of the horse. Clinging to the horse's mane for dear life, the little boy ventured a quick, guarded glance downward; from where he sat, the ground appeared to be a long, long ways down. Alarmed, Willie sat rigid – afraid to make a sound – waiting for someone to lift him off the animal and end his torture. But no one seemed to remember the little boy on the horse or made any effort to rescue him. Despite his determination to sit perfectly still, Willie just had to wiggle as the heat of the sun sent trickles of sweat tickling down his neck and the short hairs of the horse pushed like cockleburs against his bare legs. Suddenly, he felt himself slipping; his frantic grab at the horse's neck unsettled him further. The next thing he felt was the hard ground slapping against his chest and stomach. A tight, strangling sensation gripped him as he tried to breathe. It felt as if something heavy was pushing against his chest, forcing the last bit of air from his lungs. In too much pain to cry out, Willie could only lie on the ground, waiting, it seemed, for death. Having the wind knocked out of him was an experience he would remember the rest of his life and the gauge for all other pain.

As one of the younger children, Willie always seemed to be in the way of the older people. Without a strong father figure to guide him, he became extremely shy and introverted. Traditionally in the South, parents encouraged their sons to be aggressive. Young boys also had several male role models in addition to their fathers. These figures – grandfathers, uncles, and older cousins – and the emphasis on self-assertiveness were important in the formation of a boy's character and social demeanor. Such role models helped a son learn his place as a member of a community of men, not just of a parental or sibling group. The ideal of aggressiveness, displayed by these role models in physical and intellectual contests, kept a boy from becoming effeminate – a taboo in Southern culture. But for Willie and other youngsters growing up in the war years, these role models did not exist outside of letters home and the recollections of their mothers and grandmothers. Both of Willie's grandfathers were dead, and his father and most of his uncles and male neighbors were off fighting in the war. His was a world of women and slaves.[7]

At his young age, Willie was unaware that he was being cheated of his Southern birthright. The biggest hardships he knew in those days were the itch of a mosquito bite, the ouch of a skinned knee, and the frustration of being one of the youngest. Otherwise, his world was secure – filled with what to him was the everyday stuff of childhood. He lived in ignorance of the war that consumed the thoughts of the grownups and threatened the lives of his own relatives. He paid no attention to the torn and faded hand-me-downs that he and his siblings wore. Going barefoot was a joy that allowed him to squish mud between his toes, to feel the coolness of the grass, to splash through every puddle he could find. With everyone dressed in rags, he saw nothing unusual about his tattered clothing. And while he went to bed every night with his belly full of meat, cornbread, and the simple food that could be grown on the farm, he had no memory of the delicacies that had been his family's fare before the war. As he played in the evening by the light of pine knots or candles made from beef tallow, he could not remember a time when his mother did not have to squint as she knitted in the dim light. What others saw as sacrifices and hardships he saw as adventures or accepted as part of the routine of life.[8]

Willie's first brush with the war was pleasant. One day a tall stranger in a gray uniform with a sword sheathed at his side rode up to the front of the house. With a shout of joy, Tempie swept the children out onto the piazza to greet him. Shyly, Willie hid behind his mother as she tried to introduce him to his father. "Of course, I did not know him as I never had an opportunity to see him while he was in the army," he later wrote. Curious about all of the commotion this stranger was causing, Willie pulled at his mother's dress, peeping through the holes of the tattered fabric to get a better look at the soldier. His eyes were drawn to the hilt of the glistening sword. "My father thought it was evidence of remarkable brightness and laughed inordinately," he said.[9]

When David mounted his horse to rejoin the cavalry after his three-day visit, he was still little more than a stranger to his young son. While Willie returned to the secure routine of his life, his father rode back to his regiment with a heavy heart. Those few days at home had intensified his concern for his family and his country. He knew that Grant, having secured Vicksburg, had turned his attention to Arkansas and Louisiana. But what bothered him most was the lack of news about the war and the overwhelming despair gripping the homefront. Accustomed to reading several newspapers regularly, David had a hard time finding any reliable account of what was going on during his brief visit. Regular mail had ceased, and shortages of labor and paper had forced most of the newspapers in the state to shut down. By the summer of 1863, *The Arkansas True Democrat* and *The Arkansas State Gazette*, the leading newspapers in Little Rock, were publishing irregularly. *The Washington Telegraph*, although still publishing on its normal schedule, had to refuse all new subscriptions because of the paper shortage. The newspapers with their accounts of the war and rallying editorials had helped cheer people. But the absence of a newspaper resulted in no news, and no news was considered bad news.[10]

Morale had been low even before Vicksburg, but now some Arkansans were giving up hope. Many businesses had closed because there was no merchandise to sell, and doctors and lawyers could not open accounts because of a lack of such basic supplies as account books. Towns were desolate and unnaturally quiet. Virginia Gray, a Confederate woman who kept a diary of these trying times, described a lonely visit to what had been a busy town near Arkadelphia, where David's brother lived. The town had once teemed "with busy brains, planning happy futures, never dreaming that God could send them such days as these. Many a form, quick and active once, is cold and still where no friend can find its resting place ... [and] has learned the long unknown mystery of eternity.... We all sit knitting and reading tonight, only listening to the clock as the hours go by. Must another winter, the third of this dismal war go by, and we still wait? Will neither prayers or tears bring peace? Alas, they do not."[11]

As hope gave way, some people, once loyal to the Confederacy, began trading with the Yankees, ignoring the sacrifices of their neighbors to seize personal opportunity. Deaf to the desperate pleas for recruits to keep Confederate hopes alive, these men cared for nothing but money and their own position. Such attitudes filled David and the other soldiers with contempt. They saw these opportunists as flouting the Southern code of honor by putting their desire for wealth above their duty to community. There was no honor in sitting safely at home, making money off the war, as neighbors died in service to their country. There was no honor in valuing self over others when that value was not founded on true duty. "The people will (not) volunteer to fight anymore, I mean those now at home," a soldier's father wrote of the situation, "nor will they render any material voluntary assistance(.) they seem absorbed in money making and in devising the best means of escape when the enemy approaches(.) I am disgusted and ashamed(.)" It was enough to make David question the justification for the war. He was fighting for the South, but this country that was emerging was not one he recognized.[12]

While riding back to camp, David also reflected on the other stories he had heard – stories about those living in fear for their very life. He had heard of the fate of towns abandoned to the federal troops who took whatever they wanted from the residents. Of old men sympathetic to the Confederate cause forced to flee or face possible death at the hands of the occupying army. Of women housing their animals inside shelters to keep them from being stolen or senselessly slaughtered. Of Yankees raiding poultry yards, killing the chickens and effectively ending the egg supply. Of enemy soldiers littering yards with the heads, hooves, and entrails of animals they had killed just for the sake of killing.[13]

David also had heard tales of bushwhackers and disheartened Confederates who took out their frustrations on neighbors thought to be loyal to the Union. Of Unionists who were just as ruthless toward their Confederate neighbors in those parts of the state now controlled by the North. Of the savagery practiced by the federal soldiers who blamed the Seceshes for the war, the death of their comrades, and their long enforced separation from their loved ones. The wealth of the planters angered and enticed them. They wanted to teach the Southerners a lesson they would not soon forget. The lessons, forced on women and old men, were cruel and inhuman.

One of the stories of such atrocities involved five or six federal soldiers who took it upon themselves to "instruct" the people living at S.J. and Lutetia Howells' plantation in Clarksville. S.J., an elderly man in fear of his life, had taken most of the slaves to Texas, leaving his wife with her widowed sister and some of the house slaves to look after things in Arkansas and protect their possessions. Even the Yankees would not molest elderly ladies, he had thought. But when the soldiers arrived at the plantation and found the women alone, two of them dragged the sister, Mrs. John W. Willis, outside and held her prisoner while the others tried to force Lutetia to tell them where the family's money was buried. Getting nothing but denials of buried treasure, they forcibly stripped her shoes and stockings and dragged her across the floor to the large open fireplace where they pushed her naked right leg down on the red hot coals. Convinced by her screams that she was ready to confess, they removed her leg briefly from the coals and demanded the money again. When she insisted there was no money or other valuables, they thrust her leg back on the coals, threatening to burn her to death unless she gave them the money. The soldiers finally ended the torture when "the flesh was cooked until it fell off from the knee to the toe," her daughter, Sallie E. Jordan, wrote later.[14]

Realizing they would get nothing from Lutetia, the soldiers had her sister brought in and did the same thing to her but not quite so severely. Disappointed in their quest for riches, the men dragged the crippled sisters to the slaves' quarters and locked them in, threatening to shoot the women's heads off if they came out before sun up. The soldiers then slaughtered all the livestock on the place, leaving most of it to rot. The terrified sisters spent the night in excruciating pain, their only relief some linseed oil and linen they found in the room. Early the next morning, three slave women, despite their fear of the soldiers, came to help them.[15]

Having done all they could to nurse the burns, the slaves left the sisters and took the laundry to a spring about a quarter mile from the house. As one of them turned to go back, she saw flames bursting from the roof of the house. Frightened for their mistress, the slaves left the laundry at the spring and ran back to the house. They found Lutetia and her sister hiding beside the woodpile; they had crawled to safety. From the safety of the woodpile, they watched as the house burned to the ground and as federal officers brought an ambulance to fill with the furnishings they had removed from the house before they torched it. When the officers saw the condition of the women, they were compelled to take them into Clarksville for treatment. Lutetia's leg was amputated, and she lingered on the edge of death for several weeks. She finally was released to the care of her widowed daughter. Two years later, her painful existence ended.[16]

Such incidents created a reign of terror that either demoralized people or strengthened their resolve and hatred against all things Northern. Despite the growing number of Arkansans who had abandoned the cause and were siding with the Union – even in the staunchly Confederate southwestern part of the state, many still prayed for a miracle. "The poor confederacy, for the time has struck upon a reef – God helping she may ride out safely once more," Mrs. Gray wrote in her diary. "Everyone is sad, not *knowing* what to look for in the future – even what to *hope* for is questionable."[17]

As David rode back to his regiment, he had plenty of time to think about the state of the Confederacy – and Arkansas in particular. He was not encouraged by his thoughts. One of the biggest fears for loyalist Arkansans had been the Yankees taking Little Rock. This fear had many state officials moving their offices to Washington as early as May 1863. Albert Pike, a state Supreme Court justice, set up four tents for himself and three slaves just outside of Washington. The state archives ended up in a big store in Washington that was owned by a Col. Abrams. The store, like many others throughout the state, had closed at the beginning of the war.[18]

A year earlier when Union Gen. Samuel Curtis had invaded the state, angry Arkansans hounded his flanks and cut off his supplies. But when Gen. Steele marched toward Little Rock in August 1863, no one opposed him. By this time, most of the state's soldiers had been called to defend the Confederacy elsewhere, and only a few units, under the command of Gen. Price, were left to protect Arkansas and its capital. The residents of Little Rock seemed resigned to the inevitable. Gov. Flanagin and what remained of the state government fled the city September 5 to establish the loyalist capital in Washington. With Steele right across the river, Price spared his troops and the city the fate of a siege. At 11 a.m. September 10, he ordered his infantry to cross a pontoon bridge at the foot of Main Street and head out of the city. The Union army marched in on the heels of the retreating Rebels and established a state government in Little Rock loyal to its cause. Dual images of Arkansas officially existed in both the Confederacy and the Union – each with its own government and capital.[19]

It was enough to make a weary soldier want to surrender his gun. Instead, David rode on, his thoughts weighed down with worry for his family. He once again saw his young son shyly peering out at him through the holes in Tempie's gown. Would that be the only glimpse Willie would have of the grandeur, the honor, that once had defined the South – a glimpse seen through the tatters of war? Wincing at the thought, David whispered a prayer for the salvation of his country.

11   A State Divided

With the Union firmly in control of the Mississippi and establishing uncontested control of large portions of Arkansas and other Southern states, the Confederate government had little reason for hope. Morale was low. Supplies of every type were scarce. The situation worsened as 1863 drew to a close and even Mother Nature aligned herself against the Southern cause. An extremely harsh winter froze all of Arkansas. River transportation halted as entire rivers froze over and large floating cakes of ice clogged the Mississippi. The Arnolds, along with the rest of the state's residents, shivered in their rags while huddling close to the hearth. Everyone was anxious for good news. But all *The Washington Telegraph*, the only Confederate newspaper still in regular production in Arkansas, had to offer that Christmas was a call to Southerners to work harder so they could once again enjoy the comforts of home "before Northern greed and fanaticism forget the doctrines of Christ."[1]

But in a world gripped with hopelessness and desperation, it was all too easy to forget the doctrines of Christ and the binding code of Southern honor. The madness of greed brought out the worst in many people. With their structured society dismantled, those who had adhered to the Southern code of duty and honor out of a sense of mere propriety or as a vehicle to get ahead let slip their façade of decency and respectability. Mastered by avarice, vengeance, and opportunism, such people forgot their obligations to their community and indulged their baser nature in justifying what would under other circumstances be seen as criminal and intolerable. Politicians who had pushed for war so long as it was other men making the sacrifices found new ways to profit from the conflict. The state treasurer had fled to Washington along with the governor and other Arkansas officials, taking with him the important documents of his office and the entire state treasury, which consisted of gold. As the Union army pressed closer to the last Confederate stronghold in the state, the treasurer suggested to another official that they personally appropriate the state's gold as it would be taken by the Yankees otherwise. When the other official refused, the treasurer hightailed it to Texas – along with all the gold. Neither he nor the treasury ever returned to Arkansas.[2]

The dawning of 1864 drove home the realization that this war had dragged on for nearly three years and victory was nowhere in sight. People on both sides of the issue were weary of the hardships and deprivations. No matter how hard it was, life before the war had been better than what they faced. Their only source of strength was a sense of the rightness of their cause. But some had given up on that. Secret Unionist organizations that had sprung up throughout Arkansas with the passage of the Conscription Act continued to expand – even in the southwestern portion of the state. A large band operated near Arkadelphia in Clark County where David's brother Hendrick practiced medicine and had a prosperous farm. These armed groups attacked or harassed Southern loyalists. In retaliation, Confederate officials captured and publicly hanged several of the leaders and members of these groups.[3]

Hangings, once reserved for the worst of the criminal lot, now occurred frequently on both sides of the battle. But one in particular drew the wrath of loyal Arkansans and served as a rallying cry and demonstration of the atrocities of the North. The hanging of 17-year-old David Owen Dodd in Little Rock was, literally, the talk of the state in January. The boy, who was too young to serve in the military, was leaving Little Rock to visit his father in Washington when a Union soldier destroyed his travel pass. Further down the road, another Union soldier stopped the teenager and asked for his papers. When Dodd could not produce a pass, he was taken prisoner. A search revealed some notes in Morse code; the youth had worked for a time at a telegraph office. A Union soldier insisted the code revealed military information about the federal forces in Little Rock. Dodd was tried before a military tribunal, convicted of espionage, and hanged. His gravesite soon became a Southern memorial.[4]

One note of optimism occurred early in January when rumors circulated throughout the army camps and in the towns that Lincoln had died. These rumors apparently stemmed from the fact that the Union president had suffered from smallpox in November and into December. The antagonist of the war (at least in the Southern mind), Lincoln personified the enemy. He was the one who had called for troops to quell the rebellion at Fort Sumter, issued the Emancipation Proclamation, kept this cursed war going by refusing to recognize a state's right to secede. With him out of the way, there was hope that peace – without defeat – could be restored. When rumors of Lincoln's death proved untrue, the soldiers looked for new sources of hope to lift their flagging spirits. Their talk turned to the Union election that would be held that fall. A rising peace movement in the North might just cause enough of a groundswell to sweep Lincoln from office. If the faltering Confederacy could hang on until fall, there might be a chance for its survival.[5]

To strengthen its chances, the Confederate Congress in February 1864 once again authorized the Secretary of War to employ slaves – 20,000 of them. He was instructed to take volunteers first and then impress others as needed. Each slave owner was allowed to keep at least one male slave at home. David and Tempie had several slaves before the war, including Joe who had accompanied David when he enlisted. With David off fighting, Tempie relied on the slaves to tend to the farm, hunt for food, and protect her family. With most of the able-bodied white men fighting, there was no one else who could help her or defend her property and children. The possibility of losing the slaves – the last vestige of life as she had known it – added to the stress of waking up every morning to a world that was falling apart.[6]

"Few people living now have any idea what heroism it required to be a Confederate mother," Mrs. A.A. Tufts wrote in a memorial to her own Confederate mother. "They lived in a state of constant apprehension, fear of death or wounds to their soldier boys [or husbands and brothers] at the front and fear of starvation and rags for the little ones at home.... Eagerly they listened for news from the front, though at the same time dreading to hear what was often bad news than good. They toiled and slaved and comforted each other during the day, but at night while their little ones slept, their pillows were wet with tears as they wept and prayed with none but the great God to listen to their sobbing."[7]

While her children snuggled together in bed to dream of laughter and play, Tempie found no escape from the nightmarish reality of life. Her dreams were the horrors of war. In her sleep, her worst fears took shape. When she awoke, it was to the realization that today the dreams could become reality. And in those long dark hours when her worries kept sleep at bay, she thought of David and what he must be suffering. If only she could do something to make his lot easier. Her heart ached with love for him as she prayed that God, in his mercy, would spare David's life. As sleep evaded her, Tempie's prayers expanded to embrace all the women and children affected by this cursed war and all the sick and wounded soldiers – be they friend or foe.[8]

The worst was yet to come. The desperate times of early 1864 brought out the beast in that class of society that thrived in a wilderness untouched by the stamp of civilization and its accompanying laws. These were the men who would obey the law not out of respect but out of fear of the consequences of breaking it. Adding to the lawlessness were those who felt betrayed – by their country, their neighbors, even God. Their crimes were justified and encouraged by secret organizations and, depending on whose property they were threatening, by military officials. By this time, law and order had disintegrated. With war refugees flocking to populate southwestern Arkansas with makeshift tent cities, what was left of the infrastructure was overtaxed, opening the door to a reign of terror.

Even in Washington, which protected what was left of the Confederate state government, crime had become a way of life. The small town had mushroomed to between 30,000 to 40,000 residents in 1864. (The population of the entire county had been just under 14,000 four years earlier.) Thieves and burglars infested the area, breaking into stores and even into occupied houses. To remedy the situation, authorities suggested that anyone caught in such an act be shot on sight. While crime was not as bad in the Garland City area, Tempie lived with the daily threat that these roving bands of thieves who had lost any respect for the plight of women and children would visit her farm. She also worried about Gen. Banks' army, which everyone knew was trying to make its way up the Red River. Along the way, the Yankees were looting and destroying Southern farms in a wide swathe on both sides of the river and confiscating cotton wherever they could find it. With her farm close to the river, Tempie doubted it would be spared should Banks or the Union gunboats make it that far. "I don't know what is to become of us – we are sorely scourged if any people ever were," a soldier's wife wrote, sharing feelings that were common to the women of the day. "I feel so low spirited I don't know what to do – I can't sleep or take any pleasure or interest in any thing in the world – trouble is making me old fast."[9]

Adding to Tempie's general malaise was the constant specter of death. Too many of her friends had received word of the death of a husband, a brother, or a son. So far, none of the Arnold men had been killed or seriously wounded. But Tempie, despite her steadfast faith in God, could not dare hope her family would remain so blessed while others all around were struck down. Not all the death occurred on the battlefield. Illness decimated families and towns. Too many children were left orphans, too many women were made childless widows, too many people mourned as they buried yet another loved one beside the fresh graves in the family cemetery.[10]

Trouble seemed to rain on Arkansas in 1864. From the beginning of the year to mid-March, 44 skirmishes were fought throughout the state along with two operations, one affair, and six expeditions. By the end of March, the action hit a little too close to home for the Arnolds' comfort. In the scant two weeks between March 20 and April 1, there were four skirmishes in Arkadelphia and one in Camden. Gen. Steele began his expedition from Little Rock toward Camden March 23. David's older brother, Hendrick, who at 39 was semi-retired from his medical practice when the war started and exempt from conscription, had stayed on his small plantation near Arkadelphia. But with the war coming to him, he enlisted early in 1864 under Capt. R.E. Reeds as an army surgeon for troops stationed on the home front.[11]

The first action Hendrick saw did much to raise the morale of the Arkansas Confederates after it had been devastated April 15 by Steele's conquest of Camden, considered to be one of the strongest Rebel points in southern Arkansas. But Steele's occupancy of Camden came with considerable risks. The shortage of food and supplies was critical due partially to loyal Southerners destroying anything they thought the Yankees might take. The town – deep in Confederate territory – was a long way from Union supply trains. When two federal steamers carrying provisions for Steele's army collided with each other en route to Little Rock and starvation became a very real probability, the general knew he could not wait for more supplies to be sent his way. He sent an escorted wagon train – of about 200 wagons – on a foraging expedition.

Hendrick was with the Confederate army that attacked the Union foragers April 18 near Poison Spring. Surprised, surrounded, and outnumbered nearly three to one, the Union army did not have much of a chance. When the guns stopped firing, 301 Union soldiers lay dead or wounded or were listed as missing. The Confederates lost 114 men but captured four pieces of artillery and, perhaps more importantly, the wagons loaded with thousands of bushels of corn. The Confederate victory, the first of that campaign, increased the optimism of soldier and civilian alike. While others celebrated the victory, Hendrick dealt with the losses. Like most field hospitals, his resembled a butcher's shamble "with maimed and bloody men lying on all sides; – some with their arms off; some with their legs off, some awaiting their time, while the doctors, with upturned cuffs and bloody hands, are flourishing their knives and saws, and piles of bloody-looking limbs are strewn around them."[12]

The loss of the corn – not the men – dealt a devastating blow to Steele. Although a lightly guarded supply train made it through to Camden from Pine Bluff April 20 with enough half rations for his soldiers for 10 days, Steele worried that the continuing scarcity of food could lead to further complications. Despite the news that Gen. Banks had been forced to retreat down the Red River, Steele's orders to march on Shreveport stood. Before that march could begin, he had to get more provisions. Once the supply train that had just arrived in Camden was unloaded, Steele made arrangements for it, along with nearly 100 additional wagons, to be sent back to Pine Bluff for more supplies. Comprised of 240 wagons and guarded by about 2,000 soldiers, the train headed out April 22 for the 150-mile round trip. Accompanying the train were a large number of private citizens, cotton speculators, Arkansas refugees, sutlers, army followers, and about 300 former slaves. Along the way, the Union soldiers took whatever food they could find and "robbed every household of its silverware, jewelry, bedding, and fine clothing, in fact every article of family stores of any value, besides taking every horse in sight."[13]

Confederate soldiers stationed in Arkansas, several of whom were from the area, were outraged by the crimes being committed against their families and neighbors. Under the command of Gen. James F. Fagan, about 4,000 Rebel soldiers attacked the supply train April 25 near Marks' Mill. In the ensuing battle, 41 Confederates were killed, 108 wounded, and 144 reported as missing. The numbers were much worse for the Union, which had about 100 men killed and nearly 1,400 wounded and/or captured. The Union also lost another supply train and the much-needed provisions. Hendrick saw action again once the guns were silenced. As the army surgeon, he was responsible for moving the wounded into makeshift hospitals set up in the homes of Wat Smith, Bill Davis, and Warren Crane, who all lived in the vicinity of the Marks plantation and the gristmill that lent the battle its name.[14]

The dual victories at Poison Spring and Marks' Mill and Banks' retreat were welcome news in Arkansas that spring. Once again, Arkansans had hope that they might be able to win the war. The Arnold family received more good news when David came home for good. But the good news was mingled with bad. On the heels of David's homecoming came word that Tempie's younger brother, Robert Arnold, had been seriously injured at the Battle of Spotsylvania Courthouse in Virginia. The family prayers focused on the well-being of Robert and the other relatives still in the thick of battle. When they weren't praying, Tempie and her mother waited for news. Had Robert survived? Or had he already been welcomed to heaven by his father and sister? Information was scarce, and the wait interminable. When news finally came, they received small comfort. Either a bullet or shrapnel had hit his windpipe, confining him to an army hospital until he was well enough to go home – that is, if infection didn't set in.[15]

Willie did not understand the concern for uncles he had never met; all he knew was that for the first time since he was old enough to remember, he had a father. But David's illness rendered him a marginal part of the toddler's life. The boy continued to feel he was in the way and that no one paid any attention to him. His father did not appear in any of his childhood memories of these years. Willie's life still revolved around his mother and grandmother. It took the Battle of Atlanta to produce a male hero for the little boy.

Tempie's brother Bill had been serving as an army surgeon ever since Shiloh. He had endured many battles mostly unscathed and, perhaps more miraculously, had survived his early bout with malaria as well as the pestilence and filth that pervaded the army camps and hospitals. At Atlanta, the battle-hardened surgeon was in the center rear of the fighting troops, tending to the growing number of wounded. As he bandaged a fallen soldier, he ignored the bullets buzzing by his head and the deafening thuds of shells detonating around him. But a shell hitting the earth right in front of him caught his attention. The exploding pieces "looked like a drove of partridges as they flew around," he recalled later. One of the pieces tore through his arm, causing more pain than he had ever experienced in his life. Bill was carried to the field hospital, where he lay among the more seriously wounded, waiting his turn. With one surgeon down, the wait was agonizingly long. His chief concern was keeping his arm.

After being treated in a hospital for a month, the wounded doctor was sent home to recuperate. "Home" to him was where his mother was, and that was David and Tempie's farm near Garland City. Once home, the young man took an instant liking to his timid but curious little nephew and namesake. The youngster was a welcome diversion from the pain and the boredom of being cooped up inside. For his part, Willie reveled in the attention, spending as much time as he could in his uncle's room. He didn't mind it when Bill teased him or ruffled his hair. At least he wasn't being shooed out of the way. And Uncle Bill had promised to take him hunting. He kept his promise. As soon as he was well enough, Bill mounted the family mule and pulled his three-year-old nephew up behind him for an adventure in the woods, which were full of deer, fowl, and boar. From then on, whenever Bill ventured into the woods, he took Willie with him. That attention earned Bill a special place in the small boy's heart and created a bond that would last a lifetime. "I seemed to be a favorite with him, but with no one else," Willie wrote in his senior years.

Soon after Willie had latched onto his new role model, Uncle Bill received a letter from his major, requesting him to return to duty as surgeons were desperately needed. Although his arm had not totally healed, Bill said goodbye to the family and headed to Franklin, Tennessee, where his regiment was serving under Gen. John B. Hood. Willie tried not to cry as his uncle left. Once again the timid little boy found himself alone with no one special to turn to.[16]

12   The End

The Arnolds tried to return to normal family life. For Tempie, that meant stepping back from the decision-making to submit to David's authority. It was good to have someone to share the responsibility with, and she felt much safer with David home. But it was difficult, at times, to relinquish the independence and strength that had helped her through the hardest times. It also was difficult to gracefully accept the changes in their lifestyle. Things Tempie had taken for granted just a few years earlier were now unheard of luxuries – things like cotton cards, paper, even coffee. And there still was no escaping the war. Too many neighbors, too many friends, too many relatives had lost a part of themselves for the Southern cause. Even in those conversations that did not revolve around the war, it was there – in a sigh, an expression, or a shared glance.[1]

Tempie had to remind herself that she was much more fortunate than most people in Arkansas. With David home to manage the farm, they could provide their own necessities. They would not go hungry. The same was not true elsewhere. Although crops were good throughout the state that fall, the presence of federal soldiers and the scarcity of manpower kept most crops from being harvested. The resulting shortages in animal feed forced many people to butcher their hogs and livestock. While corn rotted in the fields in the Arkansas River valley, people in other parts of the state were starving to death or scrounging for anything barely edible.[2]

By the fall of 1864, only the most optimistic could continue to predict the Confederacy would stand. Many no longer prayed for victory; instead, they prayed for the strength to repel the Yankee assault that day. And a few still clung to that last hope that Lincoln would be defeated November 8 at the Union polls, but even they did not really believe he would lose. On election day, Mrs. Gray wrote in her diary: "This is the great election day in the U.S. We have no doubt but Lincoln will be again elected. I do not know as it makes much difference to us but I do not wish him that gratification. There are many in Camden who believe that today every man's head will be raised – may they strike elsewhere than at us."[3]

With telegraph lines frequently severed and mail service stopped, it took several days for news of the Union election results to reach Arkansas. When it came, Arkansans couldn't believe it. Gen. George B. McClellan, a Democrat, had won the election! Since the North's Democrat Party had adopted a peace plank as part of its national platform, the South welcomed the news of McClellan's victory and the chance for peace without defeat. But their hopes were crushed November 23 when the real election results reached the state. Lincoln's re-election meant the war – and its hardships – would drag on. How much more could they suffer?[4]

The election, accompanied by one Union victory after another, bled the Confederate morale and stifled any hope. Four years of enduring sacrifice and deprivation – of seeing the worst characteristics of mankind come to life – had taken their toll on the spirit of the South. With the final scenes an almost foregone conclusion, the last year of the war was a sad but somewhat uneventful time for the Arnolds. They paid little heed to the rumors that the countries of Europe would recognize the Confederacy once Lincoln was inaugurated in March 1865. Spurred by the belief that Lincoln would have no legal claim to jurisdiction over the South, which had not been represented in the Union's presidential election, these rumors ignored how much England and France abhorred slavery. Inauguration day dawned with no new support from Europe. Again, false hope was dashed.[5]

While the Arnolds resigned themselves to the inevitable, they could count their blessings. The terrors of bushwhackers and renegade bands that ravaged much of the state did not reach their home. The only hardships they encountered were the privations that resulted from inflation, the scarcity of goods, and the closure of practically all businesses and services. These hardships were very real; Confederate and state warrants were almost valueless, yet prices for necessities continued to escalate. A subscription to *The Washington Telegraph*, for example, could be had for $1.50 in gold or silver. But that same subscription would cost $25 in state warrants. While cotton was valuable, Union restrictions on the trade of Confederate cotton and unethical cotton factors made it nearly impossible for the smaller planters to realize any profit from their crop. The resulting economy allowed the Arnolds to eke out merely an existence from the land, but they could not put anything aside for the future.[6]

The end came slowly. Isaac Murphy, who had cast the lone vote against secession in Arkansas, had been installed as the state's Union governor in Little Rock. Under his direction, the Unionist legislature had passed a law requiring each voter to swear an oath that he had not voluntarily taken up arms against the United States and had not aided the Confederacy, either directly or indirectly, since April 1864. With this law in place, those Arkansans loyal to the Union elected two U.S. senators, one of whom was Elisha Baxter. But when the two went to Washington, the Senate refused to seat them. It did not recognize Arkansas as a state. Congress also promptly tabled a January 27, 1865, resolution that declared Arkansas restored to the Union.[7]

Despite such ominous warnings, Arkansas Unionists had become more ardent as the conflict wore on. They were joined by a growing number of fair-weather Confederates and opportunists, who, seeing defeat on the horizon, had switched to the winning side as early as 1863 to position themselves in places of power when the victory was secure. Edward W. Gantt, an outspoken secessionist and Arkansas congressman before the war, was one of many who endured the charges of turncoat when he started talking reunification in 1863. He got his payoff in March 1865 when he was named to head the Freedman's Bureau in southwest Arkansas. Lincoln's Emancipation Proclamation, delivered at Gettysburg two years earlier, had resulted in many slaves throwing off their bondage. But the establishment of the bureau in the heart of Confederate Arkansas made the proclamation a reality to those slaves still in servitude – even though the Confederates were not yet ready to bow to the law of the Union.[8]

Meanwhile, Arkansas' Confederate governor, in Washington, still claimed to be in control of the state. With the war turning against the South, Gov. Flanagin thought, a bit naively, he might be able to negotiate acceptable terms for Arkansas to rejoin the Union. When A.H. Garland, the state's senator to the Confederate Congress, returned home that March, Flanagin asked him to meet with U.S. Gen. J.J. Reynolds to restore peace and order in Arkansas. Flanagin's terms included convening the Confederate legislature to repeal all laws hostile to the Union. He also was willing to cooperate with Murphy's Unionist government in calling for a convention to establish a state government Congress would recognize.[9]

The governor's efforts were too little too late. He had not reckoned with the bitterness the North harbored toward the South or its intense desire to punish all those who had sided with the Confederacy. Reynolds refused to receive Garland. He also refused to recognize any duly elected county official in Arkansas, prohibited anyone from running for election until that person had been pardoned by the president, and killed any idea of a convention in which the loyal and disloyal would be seated on equal terms. When his efforts for peace failed, Flanagin had no choice but to let the war continue to impoverish his state.[10]

While the war headed toward its final battles, Arkansans also had to fight with nature. Throughout March 1865, the state was deluged with heavy rains. Rivers flooded, washing out roads and swamping unharvested fields. Living near the river, the Arnolds faced the natural threat to their property. With a new enemy to guard against, they were, for a while at least, able to escape the omnipresence of war. Fresh news became nonexistent as the flooding cut Arkansas off from outside communication and transportation.[11]

Some of the first news to make it through to the rain-soaked state in late April and early May was of Gen. Robert E. Lee's surrender at Appomattox April 9. No one knew what to think. Was this rumor or fact? "It is said and believed that Lee's army has surrendered.... We are all much troubled about it," an Arkansas woman wrote May 2. It had been a long four years, and most people were tired of war, of futile sacrifice, of fear. But it was hard to accept that all the hardships had been for nothing. This couldn't be the end. In Arkansas, and other parts of the Confederacy, the war continued. The *Telegraph*, which published the entire correspondence between Grant and Lee in a special issue, returned to wartime coverage two days later. Throughout the month of May, the *Telegraph* encouraged the South to stand strong. In many minds, Lee's surrender was the loss of a battle – not the war. It still was being fought west of the Mississippi. "It is evident that all East of the river has surrendered," an Arkansas woman wrote May 20. "Lincoln is killed and we know not what else. I am sorry that assassination should be added to make things worse than they are." While the North mourned its fallen president, the South began to mourn its fallen cause.[12]

With their friends and relatives still in the action, the Arnolds had no peace until they received news that Gen. Joseph E. Johnston had surrendered his army April 26 near Greensboro, North Carolina. Bill, the last of their family still fighting, would be coming home. After the surrender, Bill and the other Arkansas soldiers in his regiment boarded a train from North Carolina for the long journey home. They got as far as Knoxville, Tennessee, when the train ran off a bridge that had been damaged and then improperly repaired during the war. The train plunged into the French Broad River, killing eight soldiers and wounding 50 others. After assisting the wounded, Bill hopped a boxcar from Knoxville to Memphis where he switched to river transportation. He was forced to walk from the river to Little Rock. After a short rest, he walked 18 hours from Little Rock to visit his family in Arkadelphia for a few days. Late that May or early June, he made it home to the farm near Garland City. The reunion had the tenor of a funeral that follows a lingering, debilitating illness – a somber sadness tinged with relief.[13]

Although the war was over, the lessons of defeat had yet to be learned. "When the last Confederate force had surrendered ... the Arkansawyers, or most of them, were probably relieved at last," John Gould Fletcher wrote 80 years later. "Few of them suspected that it would require their utmost strength, courage, cunning, and determination to survive for the next ten years." Although there had been a few hints of the vengeance to come, the first real evidence was when the military occupation of Arkansas began June 21, 1865.[14]

With the political situation so unsettled, David and Tempie hesitated to take their family home to Union County. It was too late to plant a crop there. Besides, the extreme southwestern part of the state was still the safest place to be in Arkansas for former Confederates. And Tempie was expecting their fifth child late that summer. The family, which included Tempie's mother and Bill, spent the remainder of the summer in Garland tending their livestock, taking care of the crops, planning the next move – and wondering how their farm near Lisbon had survived the war.[15]

They also worried about the future of their former slaves. The South's defeat had given the slaves their freedom, but some of the freed workers were not quite sure what to do. Many left the countryside, flocking to towns and causing a labor shortage on the farms. Under the Freedman's Bureau, planters could sign contracts with their former slaves, paying them $15 to $20 a month. Farmers who could not afford to pay the workers in cash were allowed to pay them in food, shelter and clothes – along with a share of the proceeds of the crop. For the time being, several of the Arnolds' former slaves remained with them, most likely being paid with room and board and a share of the crop.[16]

Despite the military occupation, the Arnolds and their neighbors were determined to put the war behind them and plan for the future. By this time even the most passionate of Confederates realized there was no sense in prolonging the inevitable. John Eakin, editor of *The Washington Telegraph*, urged his readers in the July 19, 1865, issue to take the Oath of Allegiance as soon as possible. Only by taking the oath could life return to a sense of normalcy, he wrote. Such sentiment was widespread. Some Arkansans, like the Arnolds, had been spared much of the destruction and vengeance visited upon the Deep South, so they did not share the extreme bitterness of the rest of the Confederacy. They had fought well and lost; now they were resigned to get on with life. "Well, all that is over now," one Arkansas cavalryman said upon returning from the war. "I don't intend ever again to talk or think about it."[17]

David and Tempie shared those intentions. Just as they had buried their cotton, they tried to bury their memories and mementos of the war. The sword David had so proudly worn into battle disappeared, and his commission papers and letters to his wife were packed away in a trunk, all but forgotten. "I remember the old papers with the seals, worn and broken where they were folded," Tempie wrote to her son nearly 50 years later. "They were such sad old relics, funereal in every respect. We never talked of them, and looking back now it seems to me we laid it all down and tried to forget all its horrors."[18]

The Arnold men, intent on doing their duty to God and country – regardless of which country it was – took the oath. But the war had made its mark on all of them. Hendrick had seen enough of death and illness in his year as an army surgeon. When he returned home, he retired from his medical practice and focused on farming his 700-acre property. Bill and Robert, who had both come close to death, were grateful to be alive; they devoted themselves to caring for the sick. Robert, suffering intensely from his wound the rest of his life, died an early death. David returned to the only life he knew – farming and merchandising. Gone was the carefree violinist who had been the life of a party; in his place was a taciturn man trying to make sense of it all as he watched his dreams fade away. Looking back as a mature man, William Arnold wrote that his father and uncles "were all men of education, large property interests, extensive influence, and high character, patriotic, and stood for the traditions of the land in which they lived; and after the arbitrament of the sword, they accepted the results and devoted their protracted lives to the restoration of the country from the ruins of war...."

The Civil War had extracted a heavy price from the entire nation. Years later, the *New York Sun* reported that the North had lost 350,000 men and the South had lost 150,000. The *Sun* estimated the cost of the war to the North at $8.5 billion. Since the Southern states were valued at about $5 billion in 1860, the *Sun* reported, it had cost the North more to keep the region than what it was worth. The cost of the war in the South was even greater as, for the most part, it had been the battlefield. Entire cities lay in smoldering ruins; farms and plantations were little more than scars on the landscape. It was as if the entire South had become a disaster area – but there was no national aid to help the stricken families reclaim their lives and property.[19]

Sometime after the September 4 birth of Carrie Ella Arnold and the fall harvest, David and Tempie packed up their belongings and said goodbye to their Garland City neighbors. It was time for them to face what was left of their farm in Union County and restore their life. They also bid farewell to Bill, who was headed to Prescott to make his future with nothing but his skills as a doctor as starting capital. David tried to get Bill to take something as payment for his summer labor. But Bill knew David and Tempie, with five small children to raise, had nothing to spare. All he would consent to take was the hide of a large bull that had taken a great many shots to kill. He said he could sell the hide to get some money to live off of until he established his practice.

As Bill headed north, the rest of the family turned eastward to cross the Red River. It was a motley caravan – although a familiar sight – that approached the ferry at the local landing. David and Tempie, with the help of her mother and a few of their former slaves, maneuvered their five children, a herd of cattle, other livestock, and all of their possessions onto the ferry. Excited about crossing the river and riding on a boat, Willie slipped away and found a precarious seat on the edge of the boat. He dangled his bare feet into the cool water and let his imagination roam. A quick headcount ended his reverie. When the grownups discovered him sitting with his feet in the water, they scolded him and pulled him to the center of the ferry. The spiked tree trunks, placed in the river by Confederate troops to stop the advance of Union ships, still littered the river and made it quite dangerous.[20]

That night brought more adventures to the young boy when the family camped on the far side of the river. Watching the food cook over the open fire and then playing around the fire were part of the excitement for the child. But when the beds were made up on the ground and he realized he was expected to sleep outside with nothing between him and the darkness of the great outdoors, Willie became frightened. Sensing his trauma, his grandmother tucked him into his makeshift bed. But as he lay there looking up into the immense, star-studded sky, he was sure he was going to die that night. The tales of battles, ambushes, and renegades that he had overheard sparked his imagination and took shape in the blackness. His grandmother helped him say his prayers and told him to shut his eyes. His fear shut out behind closed eyes, Willie quickly went to sleep.

The rest of the trip was not quite as eventful – although there were a few more rivers to cross and a lot of miles to cover. As they neared the Hawthorne place, David left the cattle to water at a nearby stream and continued with the family toward the farm, which was several hundred yards from the public road. When the family arrived at the turnoff, David stopped. He spent a long while deliberating with Tempie whether it might not be better to move on to Texas instead. This was not the first time he had had this thought, but the reality of having to make a decision that would affect their future weighed heavily that afternoon.

David was not alone in making this decision. Of the 1,300 men from Union County who actively fought, only 400 returned to make their home there after the war. A lot of refugees – from Arkansas and other parts of the defeated South – moved on to Texas, lured by the advertisements in the Arkansas newspapers of cheap farms for sale in the Lone Star State. For some, especially those demoralized by their losses, it seemed easier to start over than to have to rebuild. For others, that old allure of the frontier beckoned. But after weighing his options as well as his responsibilities, David ignored the call of the frontier. His kinship ties to Arkansas were stronger than his economic considerations. The stability of that close kinship network had helped his family survive the war. Instinctively, David knew they would need that network if they were to survive the next few years. Besides, rebuilding offered a new challenge, a new frontier. He and Tempie, buffered by family, would, in a sense, begin again to create social and economic order out of chaos.[21]

The Arnolds took the turnoff and were relieved to find the house and the nearby kitchen, smokehouse, and slave cabins much as they had left them. Large white oaks stood guard over the big front yard, and a tangle of weeds spread over the side garden. The house – an old-time Southern dwelling typical of the upper middle class – had two large rooms separated by a hall, two shed rooms on the back of the main rooms, and a long gallery stretching across the front. Leaving his family to settle in, David returned to the river to get the cattle.[22]

13   Aftermath of War

The destruction and collapse of the economy left many Southerners dazed as their world seemed to spin out of control. "Southern planters emerged from the Civil War in a state of shock," historian Eric Foner says. "Their class had been devastated – physically, economically, psychologically." Those whose wealth had been invested in slaves saw their net worth plummet to a small fraction of what it had been before the war. The inheritance built up over generations had disappeared in a few short years. Faced with this desolate frontier begotten on the battlefield, Southerners had a choice – they could live as broken, defeated people or they could reclaim their lives, remaining faithful to their Southern ideals.[1]

While the tools and resources necessary to rebuild their homes and fortunes were scarce, the foundations of their society were still intact. The old social order – based on strong family ties, Southern values, and Christian principles – brought a stability that allowed men, women, and children to slip back into their traditional roles despite the upheaval around them. They discovered solidarity in knowing that their neighbors and relatives shared their suffering and hardship. They found it easier to mourn when everyone else was mourning. They looked to their families for comfort, to their communities for purpose, and to God for strength. The familiar social order allowed them to cope with the unfamiliar and gave them the will to go on living.[2]

As the old roles resurfaced, they took on newer, broader meaning. For instance, David's paternal relationship with his slaves survived the war as the freed slaves continued to look upon the Arnolds as family. With money in short supply, David could not provide for all the former slaves, so he helped them find jobs elsewhere. Soon after returning home, David placed

Clark Arnold, one of the former slaves, with his brother-in-law, Dr. Carroll Ross, who lived a few miles down the road. Clark frequently visited David and Tempie. Whenever he showed up, Tempie would feed him as much as he could eat. Each time he left to go home, Clark vowed that next time he would bring "Miss Tempy" some vegetables. The promise became a good-natured family joke as the vegetables never appeared.

Although it was not unique, the Arnolds' relationship with their former slaves also was not typical. There were those who would rather shoot a freedman than talk with him. Bands of desperadoes rode through the countryside killing freed slaves – hunting them down as they would a rabbit. As a result, one of the Arnolds' former slaves, Elbert, was shot through the head and left for dead. When he was found, Elbert was carried home to the Arnolds to die. Although no one held out any hope for his recovery, Tempie called for a doctor she couldn't afford. When the doctor had made Elbert as comfortable as possible, he left him to die in peace. But Elbert lingered on in one of the cabins behind the house, while Tempie nursed him through the long months of what was thought to be a death watch. True to her Southern roots, she lived her piety not in reforming society or working with charities but in ministering to her household, which still included her former slaves. The Arnolds didn't have much at the time, but what they had they shared with the injured man. The children also shared this responsibility; Willie and Sax carried food out to Elbert every day until he finally recovered. After his long convalescence, Elbert moved on to Texas but kept in touch with "his" family.[3]

Paternalism expanded its role after the war as former soldiers looked to their old officers for guidance and advice. The elected officers had earned their rank because of their antebellum status or their leadership qualities. They had been respected before the war and still commanded respect after. Many soldiers owed their lives to their captains. As for David, he found it hard to shrug aside that burden of leadership and responsibility for his men that he had shouldered so long in the Louisiana swamps. A number of those men were his neighbors, and he still felt duty-bound to help them.[4]

The familiar roles defined by the antebellum social structure helped the Arnolds and their neighbors cope with the drastic economic and political changes wrought by the war. El Dorado, less than 20 miles from Lisbon, had been an industrious city with at least two hotels and several thriving businesses before the war. By 1865, all the businesses had closed, giving the county seat the feel of a ghost town. When the Arnolds returned to Union County, only two businesses had opened their doors in El Dorado. Thomas Marrable brought a small stock of fabric to town, selling it for 75 cents a yard. Ingram & Bussey also opened as a small store dealing in such family supplies as could be obtained from area farmers. Occasionally the store had a small stock of groceries, which was brought overland from the Mississippi River.[5]

Although broken in health, David was not yet broken in spirit. The pioneer blood of his ancestors ran through his veins. He saw the war as a temporary setback; there were still plenty of opportunities to get ahead – as well as to fail. But first, he needed to sell the buried cotton. While provisions were starting to become available again, everything was costly. (Flour was selling for $17 a barrel and salt for $50 a barrel.) Although low in comparison to other costs, cotton was bringing in 25 cents to $1.20 per pound, depending on where it was sold. The first bale of cotton brought in to Washington following the war sold for about 53 cents a pound. The scarcity of the crop in 1865 further increased the price. The wartime destruction of tools and animals, labor shortages, and the use of old, infertile seed resulted in a poor crop that year. Those who had managed to put away some bales were able to demand decent prices. A woman who had hidden her cotton under layers of fodder in an outbuilding sold it for $70 in gold that fall. David did the calculations; with the money he could get for the cotton, he would be back on his feet financially. His first task was to check on the cotton. To his relief, it was still there. Thus David had high hopes when he made arrangements to ship his cotton to New Orleans.[6]

David's biggest obstacle was getting the cotton to market. "[F]ollowing the war there was no protection, it seemed, to the property of those who fought for the Southern cause," his son later recalled, "and there were many thousand outrages perpetrated upon the lives of the people.... The depredations after the war were greater and more frightful than during the war, hordes of murderers and cutthroats and plunderers were turned loose on the south and we were put under the jurisdiction of the military officers, and there was no appeal from their decision except in capital cases when the President of the United States would have a right to pass upon the subject. It is easy to see how such power could be abused, even by honest men, but when it was turned over to bands of cutthroats and thieves we, at this day, cannot realize the terror that brooded over the country during this period."

David was very much aware of the terror that stalked the countryside. He also knew his cotton was worth thousands of dollars – money his family desperately needed. Getting the cotton from its hiding place to market could be a risky, even life-threatening, endeavor. After careful thought, he devised a plan and enlisted the help of his brother-in-law Carroll. Under cover of the night, the two men each hitched a team of horses and slipped into the field where David had hidden the bales. In the darkness, an accident occurred – perhaps one of the animals stumbled – that spooked the horses. One of the teams ran off amid a great deal of clamor. David was forced to postpone his mission that night. Word quickly spread that the Arnolds had cotton. Before David could retrieve it, the cotton disappeared. Despite evidence that his cotton was stolen by the federal officials who controlled the county, he could do nothing to reclaim it.

Before the war, David had been in a good financial situation, being thrifty and successful in both his farming and merchandizing. The loss of 8,800 pounds of cotton – which could have brought in nearly $9,000 – was a great blow. With it went his dreams, his chance at success, and his trust in the government. Although he could feed and shelter his family, he was never again able to regain his financial footing.

While the Arnolds had been spared many of the ravages of war, they were not to be spared the humilities and atrocities forced on the defeated. Besides raiding the countryside, the federal troops stationed in Union County took up quarters wherever they desired on their patrols. A cavalcade of federal soldiers arrived in the Arnolds' front yard late one autumn afternoon when David was not home. The officers ordered Tempie, along with her five children, out of the house. It was to be their camp for the night. That evening the family stayed in the yard, listening to and wondering at the noises coming from within the house and kitchen. Soon the smell of cooking food wafted from the detached kitchen. Willie, not yet five years old, could hardly wait for supper. It had been a long time since lunch. As the evening stretched into night, the growling of his stomach grew louder as did his complaints to his mother. He was hungry; he wanted to eat. Tempie had her hands full trying to keep the children quiet as the soldiers ransacked her larder and smokehouse.

The next morning brought no relief as the soldiers showed no sign of quitting the house. Once again, their cook commandeered the kitchen to prepare breakfast for the men. And then it was dinner. By this time, Willie's mouth was watering and his stomach hurting from hunger. The smell of fresh-baked biscuits and roasting meat was almost torture. After dinner, the soldiers packed up and left. As soon as they were out of sight, Tempie and the children rushed into the house – she to see what remained intact and they to fill their empty stomachs. The dirty plates and remnants of the meal sat on the table for Tempie to clear. Willie's eyes lit on a biscuit as large as a saucer; it was the only one left. He made a quick grab for it before anyone else could get it. But just as his little fingers were about to close around it, his mother seized him, pulling him away from the table. "Don't touch that," she told him sternly. "That's a Yankee biscuit." She almost spat the word "Yankee," filling it with all the vengeance and hatred she could muster. Hungrier than he had ever been in his life, Willie watched his mother throw the biscuit away.

Such incidents created great hostility toward the Union forces. Much of it was vented on the freed slaves still living in the county, who many feared or blamed for the war. The situation worsened early that November when Jerry Atkins, a former slave, wanted revenge on Mrs. H.M. Simpson for some wrong she had done to him. Knowing the family's habits well, Atkins targeted Mrs. Simpson's youngest children. On the morning of November 7, 1865, he slowly walked along the path the children usually took to school about three miles north of El Dorado. When he saw 13-year-old Sarah and eight-year-old Jesse, Atkins brutally murdered them. Everyone in the county, including the Arnolds, was in an uproar as a massive manhunt began. Mothers kept their children close by as the men formed posses. The freed community joined in the search. They did not want to be branded with the sin of this man. They, of all people, had too much to lose should he not be brought to justice.[7]

A few days later, Ed Tatum, a freedman, captured Atkins in Ashley County and returned him to El Dorado to stand trial. Atkins confessed, admitting he had murdered the children out of anger toward their mother. He was put in jail to await trial. News of the murder and confession spread quickly, fanning hatred and resentment. The crime gave many of the residents of Union County a focal point for their frustration and anger. They came together as a bloodthirsty mob justified with self-righteousness and fueled with the need for revenge. The murderer had confessed. Why go to the expense of taking the case to court? He was guilty. He deserved to die. All the people in the El Dorado area – both black and white – went to the jail November 21 to pass their sentence on Atkins. They dragged the frightened man out of town and chained him to an old tree. There the crowd – including women, children, and a small squad of U.S. soldiers – watched as he was burned to death.[8]

Strong supporters of law and order – as opposed to mob violence – the Arnolds could not escape the boastful gossip and gleeful eyewitness accounts that followed the burning. David could only wonder at the lawlessness taking over the country he had fought for. The burning was further proof of a world gone amuck.

Surrounded by such moral upheaval, David and Tempie clung to their old values to survive in this new world. While they could not control the actions of others, they believed they could control their own destiny through hard work. Disheartened with farming, David focused most of his energies on rebuilding his merchandizing business. Many times he may have regretted his decision to stay in Union County. But it was too late to move on. Not only was his cotton gone, but his land was almost valueless in what had become a buyer's market. A farm that had sold for $600 in the county in 1856 when David first started out was selling for $2,500 on the eve of the war. After the war, land prices fell sharply. Union County had once again become a passageway to the West, and many of its early settlers chose this time to relocate to Texas. Fifty-three percent of the people who had been on the tax rolls in the county in 1860 were gone by 1866. Farms that could not be sold were abandoned. With no nest egg and very little likelihood of selling the farm, the Arnolds were stuck in Union County.[9]

In groping for a solution, David saw some people turning the situation to their advantage – and making a lot of money. Many Southerners gave up or supplemented farming by setting up shop on a credit system with Northern suppliers. These shops, which sprang up at country crossroads and in villages, provided necessities to the residents in that vicinity. The owners, in a sense, became banker-merchants as they extended credit to their customers, many of whom were struggling to survive. It was no business for a person with a soft heart or who had grown up steeped in the code of Southern honor. To turn a profit, these entrepreneurs had to be able to take the last ear of corn from a family in payment of their debt. While some men made their fortunes in merchandizing, many more failed, and others merely survived. David, who had done well in merchandizing before the war, now just barely hung on. He found it difficult to live his Southern values and be ruthless in business.[10]

Despite all the changes that defeat had brought, the Arnolds slipped into a rhythm, which, like before, flowed with the cycle of nature. They had crops to plant in the spring, wooded land to clear in the summer, and crops to harvest in the fall. But nothing was quite normal. The seed for cotton, the primary cash crop, was scarce and defective. And nature had vowed not to cooperate with the designs of man. Once all the crops were planted in the spring of 1866, it began to rain in southern Arkansas. The rain continued steadily into early summer, causing the major rivers to overflow and wash out fields. The resulting mud and floods prevented farmers from working their fields. As the rains washed away the topsoil, Union County farmers complained that the ground beneath had packed so firmly the cotton could not come up. And in the fields where the topsoil had not washed away or compacted, an abundance of grass and weeds choked out the cotton.[11]

The floods of the early summer were followed by a parching drought that forced what little cotton had pushed its way through to drop its blossoms before they could mature into cotton bolls. In what seemed to be a series of plagues intended to punish the Southerners, army worms arrived in force in September to strip what little remained of the cotton. Most of the planters and farmers in Arkansas had emerged from the war buried in debt. They were relying on the high cotton prices of 1866, which were three times higher than they had been in 1860, to bail them out. Instead, many of them lost their entire crop. One Union County farmer, who counted himself among the upper middle class before the war, lost everything. He put his family up in a slave cabin with instructions to collect any money owed him while he went off to Texas to teach school. His was not an isolated failure.[12]

Throughout the weather problems, economic downturns, and uncertainty about the future, the Arnolds spent time with their friends and family, made the occasional trip into town, and tended to church obligations. For young Willie and Sax, there were chores to do around the farm. Occasionally, their father trusted them to travel to the post office, which was located about a mile away in the impressive white mansion of Col. Coulter. By this time, Willie often found himself the oldest child at home as Sax and Lucy attended school whenever it was in session near Bear Creek. When his older brother and sister were at school, Willie turned to Pincher, a four-legged playmate who was about as feisty as dogs came. A shy boy, Willie confided in Pincher. The boy and the dog were almost inseparable, going on great adventures together. It got to the point that Willie thought more of his dog than he did of any member of his family.

On Sundays, Willie had to leave Pincher to attend Bear Creek Church, which was located next to the log schoolhouse. Getting to church meant riding behind Sax and Lucy on the family's gray mule. Dressed in what passed as his Sunday best, Willie squirmed and scratched at his bare legs as the hair on the mule's back stung his skin unmercifully. Once inside the church, he timidly followed his family to their pew, wishing the floor would open up and swallow him from the gaze of the people already seated. The sermons and the singing passed by unnoticed, but one parishioner made a lasting impression on the boy. A young lady, who always arrived long after the service had begun, dressed "fantastically" in clothes that looked uncomfortably tight. She would writhe and twist all the way down the aisle to take a seat in the front pew, her gown rustling loudly in the stillness of the church. After the final prayer, she made a big to-do in apologizing to everyone for arriving so late. The timid boy could not understand why anyone would want to draw so much attention to herself.

Another part of Willie's routine was visiting the neighbors with his mother and little sisters. Hardly a day went by that Tempie did not see Mrs. Yarbrough, a widow who lived less than a half mile away with her son, Will, and an elderly kinsman, Dr. Manning. Willie played quietly as his mother visited or his father discussed the events of the day with the doctor, who Willie later remembered as old and eccentric but nevertheless a "true Southern gentleman whose delight was reading newspapers and looking over the farm."

David's conversations often dealt with politics. Former Confederates still chafed under what they considered Murphy's vindictive rule as governor. They had welcomed an Arkansas Supreme Court ruling in December 1865 that had declared the governor's voting restrictions unconstitutional. The overthrow of the law meant that all those who had taken the oath – regardless of whether they had fought for the Confederacy – could vote in the 1866 state elections. But the state's status as part of the United States was still questionable. Congress adopted a resolution in February 1866 that no U.S. senator or representative would be admitted from any of the rebellious states until

Congress itself declared the states ready for readmission. This had people throughout the South shaking their heads and wondering just what it would take to appease the North. Forebodings increased that June when the Committee on Reconstruction reported that the South would not be ready to be brought back into the Union until it had been properly chastised by its conquerors.[13]

While they could do nothing about the federal situation, Arkansans thought they could take back their state government with the Supreme Court protecting their voice. The voters elected a legislature hostile to Murphy. Fearing their loss of power and position, prominent Unionists appealed to Congress, seeking intervention. While in Washington, Edward Gantt, once an eager advocate for secession, publicly said the state election showed that Arkansans had not accepted the results of the war. Gov. Murphy added his voice, saying Arkansans had become "venomous and disloyal." When the newly elected legislature assembled in November, it rejected the 14th Amendment and overrode the governor's veto to approve pensions for Confederate soldiers. The legislators' actions were cheered by David and his neighbors. They considered themselves free men in a democracy. They believed they had every right to participate in the form of government they and their forefathers had fought for.[14]

Congress, goaded by the fears of Arkansas Unionists, thought otherwise. George W. Julian stood up in Congress January 28, 1867, to pave the way for a reconstruction to mold the South in the image of the victorious North. His vindictive words, calling for a lengthy period of punishment, produced the first Reconstruction Act, which was introduced by Thaddeus Stevens of Pennsylvania in March. The act made it clear that the former Confederates were excluded from participating in the democracy, that they had no voice in how they were to be governed. Declaring that no legal state government existed anywhere in the South, the act divided the region into five military districts, with Arkansas and Mississippi making up the fourth district under Maj. Gen. E.O.C. Ord. Civil courts were to be disbanded with military commissions set up in their place. To be readmitted to the Union, each Southern state had to adopt a new constitution, which had to meet with the approval of Congress, ratify the 14th Amendment, and extend suffrage to all males 21 or older – except those who had fought for the Confederacy.[15]

Ord refused to let the Arkansas General Assembly convene in July 1867 and, instead, ordered a November election on holding a state constitutional convention. At the mercy of the victors, Arkansans had no choice but to acquiesce. The convention was approved and held, and the delegates dutifully produced a document Congress would accept. The eligible men of the state, under military supervision, went to the polls March 13, 1868, to vote on the new constitution and elect a governor. Rather than vote for a document so odiously contrived, a majority of the eligible voters stayed home. And those who went to the polls were never sure their vote counted. Joseph Brooks, a former Methodist minister and a Republican carpetbagger from Missouri, controlled the election commission that oversaw the election. Brooks kept the polls open in the Republican-controlled areas of the state until after the results were in from the Democrat areas. He then adjusted the vote in the Republican areas to ensure that the constitution would pass and Gen. Powell Clayton, a fellow carpetbagger and former Union officer, would be governor. The outcome of the election was announced more than a month later. The new constitution had passed by slightly more than 1,000 votes. Arkansas became a state again June 20, 1868, but there was little cause to celebrate – Reconstruction was far from over. David and the other men who had led their communities before the war, who had been respected citizens, were barred from office because of their allegiance to the South. That left political offices wide open to carpetbaggers and scalawags.[16]

The new constitution gave the governor power over the state's finances, contract awards, state jobs, militia, and the election machinery. With such absolute power, a governor could literally rape the state's taxpayers while assuring himself re-election and support through his grants of patronage. The Northern carpetbaggers who seized control of Arkansas used their office to get rich – at the expense of the people. "The politicians here, as a class, are formed of the worst elements of society, the stragglers of both armies who settled here after the war for the Union," a correspondent for the *New York Times* reported. They seemed to have no compunction about adding to the burden of those who had lost nearly everything. They were the victors, and they had the right to profit from the defeat of the South. Firmly ensconced, Gov. Clayton and his team systematically took everything they could from the state by issuing state bonds for railroad projects that benefited them, awarding inflated state contracts so they and their friends would profit. Between 1868-1871, Clayton's administration had run up a state debt of $10 million in construction projects only valued at $100,000.[17]

Meanwhile, farmers and planters were still trying to reconstruct their personal prosperity. Those who had salvaged some cotton from their fields in the disaster of 1866 managed to get credit and hang on for the next planting season. With everything they owned mortgaged on the 1867 crop, they went into the planting season with the desperate optimism of a losing gambler. Once again, nature refused to cooperate. A cool spring and heavy rains that persisted into early summer threatened the cotton. Rivers flooded, swamping many recently planted fields. Farmers frantically replanted their fields as soon as they dried out – only to have them flood and wash out again. Another drought followed the rain, scorching the land throughout July and August. Then caterpillars invaded the fields, eating what little nature had left for them.[18]

Many of the Arnolds' neighbors were wiped out. Like most merchandisers, David had stocked his store and what remained of his farm on credit and then had extended credit to his customers. Realizing how bad the situation was, he and other businessmen in the area stopped extending credit in June. All sales were cash only. When cotton prices dropped to 17 cents a pound that fall, the businessmen were left with bills of their own and numerous outstanding accounts they could not collect. Even land, which often served as collateral on accounts, had sunk to new lows with farms in Union County leasing for 35 cents an acre. For the rest of the year and into the next, David had to stave off his own creditors while trying to collect the debts owed him.[19]

It was hard to collect from people who had nothing. Between 1860 and 1870, the upper middle class in Union County suffered a 77.3 percent drop in the overall value of their real property. The biggest drop – 93.7 percent – in personal property could be attributed to the emancipation of the slaves. Overall, David's losses were greater than the average. The value of his total estate dropped 90 percent in that decade. His land value went from $5,000 in 1860 to $400 10 years later; his personal property, most of which had been tied up in slaves, dropped from $11,000 to $1,200. Despite his losses, David was one of the wealthiest people, in terms of personal property, in his township in 1870. In comparison, his brother Hendrick, who lived in Caddo, suffered an 87.5 percent loss in his estate. While his land values dropped a third – from $3,000 to $2,000 – his personal property dropped from $15,000 in 1860 to $250 a decade later.[20]

At 41, David was past his peak. He resigned himself to the status quo. Accepting reality, he knew he would not be able to improve his family's position. He still had dreams, but he recognized them for what they were. And he still had hope, faint though it was, that his children's world would be one of progress and opportunity. His duty was to prepare them for it.[21]

14 Hard Lessons

Unaware of the problems plaguing his family, Willie, at age 7, was starting to learn of his own obligations in life. And he hated it. Going to school on a perfectly good summer day was the worst torture that could be imposed on a shy boy who made the fields his fortress and his dog his only confidant. But every morning, his mother forced him to get up behind Sax and Lucy on the big gray mule for the two-mile ride to the log school located next to Bear Creek Church. And almost every morning, just as the mule started up the long hill leading to the schoolhouse, Willie would fall off into the sand, pulling Sax and Lucy with him. This did not endear him to his older brother and sister, who would brush off the sand and march after the mule while all the time scolding him for being so careless.

Life was no better once he got to school. Being among the youngest in the one-room school made him a target for the older children. And his natural timidity did not help him make any friends or allies. He despised school and couldn't wait to go home each afternoon. One day was particularly rough, and Willie could bear the ordeal no longer. He asked the teacher, Mary Strain, for permission to go down to the nearby spring for a drink of water. With her consent, he headed outside. It felt good to be free, to be out of that stuffy, crowded classroom. There was no way he was going back there today. He cautiously looked around to see if anyone was watching. Seeing no one, he lit out for home, taking a shortcut through an old field where a herd of cattle was browsing.

Although he had grown up around cattle, his imagination transformed these unfamiliar animals into dangerous beasts. When the curious cows turned to stare at him, Willie was sure they would charge him. He frantically glanced around for an escape, finding it in a dusty ditch a few feet away. Willie slipped into the ditch and held his breath. He couldn't make a sound or the cows would find him. After a few minutes, he peeped out to see if any cows were near. A soft moo or a twitch of a tail had him ducking for cover. After awhile, the cows forgot about the boy and wandered to the other side of the field. When Willie thought they were a safe enough distance from him, he climbed out and slowly walked across the field. Whenever one of the animals turned toward him, he froze, hoping it would think he was a tree stump. Hot, tired, and very much afraid, he finally made it out of the field.

The relief of escape was short-lived, though. As he hurried the rest of the way home, he thought about the switching he was sure to get from his mother for skipping school. When he got close to the house, Willie was greeted loudly by Pincher. The dog's joyful barks brought Tempie running out to see what was causing the commotion. Before she could launch into a lecture, Willie told her about his terrifying ordeal with the cows. She held back the laughter as he finished his tale. To his surprise, she was sympathetic and did not even threaten a switching.

While he did not get punished, Willie was forced to go to school the next day with strict orders that he was to stay there all day and return with Sax and Lucy. Both of his parents lectured him on the importance of getting an education. And they reminded him of how hard his father worked so he could go to school. It was a privilege relatively few children received in post-war Arkansas. Never a state to spend money on education, Arkansas had even less money to spend after the war – especially when the state officials were more concerned about their own pocketbooks than the welfare of the people. With no free public schools available, parents who wanted their children to get some education had to pay for it while the children of the poor were condemned to ignorance. Field schools, also known as subscription schools, sprang up wherever there was a building, enough interest, and a teacher. The parents paid the teacher directly for each child enrolled. Pre-war subscription charges ran from $1 for a six-week summer session to $2.50 per student for a five- or six-month term. The education the children received was sketchy, usually focusing on the basest fundamentals of the three R's.[1]

The poor education his children were receiving bothered David. A college graduate himself, he valued education and saw it as the path to the future both financially and intellectually. Education had always been important in the South. It was the foundation of the traditional pattern of upward social mobility for those who would move into the planter class. Historian Frank Lawrence Owsley described this pattern: "First, the parents, though often very poor, usually possessed education beyond the limits of mere literacy and had great respect for education as a means of attaining success. Then, too, they had a certain refinement, which their robust neighbors did not usually have. Not that they were ... prideful in their bearing; only they nursed a spark in their bosoms which they were able to pass on to some of their children. Next the son, or sons, who felt this spark of pride and ambition, utilized all possible opportunities at home and at school to acquire education."[2]

David possessed this spark and hoped to pass it on to his sons. Before the war, he had every reason to believe he would be able to give his children – both his sons and his daughters – a college education. The antebellum South had boasted one college student per every 247 white residents whereas the North had one college student per every 703 residents. In the South, these students had included women, as many planters and upper middle-class families sent their daughters to academies and boarding schools. Although the education in frontier states such as Arkansas had not been on a par with that in the more established areas of the South, settlers had reason to hope that their schools would soon catch up to the norm. For many, those hopes were destroyed by the war. State universities went begging for students while academies and private colleges closed their doors. Illiteracy increased drastically as even an elementary education was hard to get. "Many of the men whose fathers had boasted degrees or academy training had now, in this moneyless, passion-engrossed world, to content themselves with such sketchy knowledge of the three R's as could be snatched in a few months in an occasional 'old field' school," Southern historian Wilbur Cash wrote. The situation hit the girls even harder as families with limited resources would educate their sons before their daughters.[3]

"[W]e never had any schools in those days other than for a few months in the year at uncertain intervals," William Arnold wrote years later of his education. "Teachers could not be had and the people were all very poor on account of the ravages of the civil war. In the days of reconstruction especially it was impossible to maintain any certain or definite system of school, and what schools we had amounted to little. The main thing to the success and merit of the teachers depended upon how many of the pupils he would whip each day...."

Such circumstances bothered David, who valued education as more than a door to opportunity. A classical education created the foundation of Southern honor; it was essential for those who would strive to live the Southern ideal. This focus on the classics, which had died off years earlier in the North, reflected the continuing relevance of the Stoic traditions of honor and virtue in the South. Like the people of the ancient world, Southerners believed that pursuit of the just, the beautiful, and the true was more important than the acquisition of valor. The resulting worldview was demonstrated through a sense of high-mindedness, greatness, openness of heart, along with pride in one's self-worth and achievements. To achieve this worldview, the educated men of the South encouraged their sons and nephews to study the classics well. This course of study was so common among the gentility that it came to be expected that a true Southern gentleman would have easy reference to Homer, Plato, Horace, and Livy.[4]

While this emphasis on classics produced some intellectuals, it also created a gulf between the masses, those with some education, and the few true thinkers of the day – especially in Arkansas. Yes, gentlemen were expected to be educated. But Southern society stressed sociability and manliness as the highest measures of honor, thus restricting a truly free pursuit of the life of the mind. Before the war, "oratory was cultivated to the extreme, and often to the neglect apparently of all else of intellectual pursuits," according to a history of Arkansas. Students focused on literature that glorified fierce battles, detailed political debate, and memorialized great speeches. Thus, the Southern sons attending Northern schools before the war were known for their good-naturedness, their manly prowess, their manners, their commitment to duty – but not generally for their intellectual inquiry of the theoretical or philosophical. The few who were thinkers were men apart; they were separated from the masses and even the elite by their own attitudes. They disliked vulgarity and ignorance so much that they remained aloof from the politics and antics of their neighbors.[5]

David had seen another benefit of a classical education during the war; it had offered him an intellectual escape from physical hardship. "[T]he greatest blessing of Education is the ability it confers of abstracting the mind from troublesome thoughts, by engaging all of its powers in some other pursuits," an officer, who, like David, was schooled in the classics, wrote. "This cannot be purchased by wealth or commanded by power. It is an exemption from trouble that the Educated alone are able to enjoy. Amongst the advantages and blessings of Education this may be the greatest." David wanted his children to enjoy the same advantages of a classical education; it was their birthright.[6]

It saddened David to compare his own schooling – which included instruction in spelling, reading, writing, arithmetic, English grammar, geography, chemistry, logic, ethics or moral philosophy, intellectual science, physics, astronomy, algebra, geometry, trigonometry, analytical geometry, calculus, political economics, composition, rhetoric, Greek, Latin, and French – with the meager offerings his children received in the field schools. How would they ever succeed with such rudimentary knowledge, he wondered. Whatever else happened, he could not fail in his efforts to provide them with a decent education. To this end, he supplemented their learning at home and became a community leader in making sure field schools were available on a somewhat regular basis. Even if his family had to go without in other areas, he was determined that his children would not be deprived of at least a basic education. So Willie continued to attend the Bear Creek School. There he was introduced to *Webster's* blue speller and *McGuffey's Eclectic Reader* with its collection of stories and poems that emphasized the importance of loving God, being a good citizen, and having a strong work ethic.[7]

With school only in session during the summer growing season, the children were home to help with harvest. And they had the winter months for uninterrupted play and chores. Willie was far happier at home than he was at school, so he looked forward to winter all summer long. The winter of 1868 was extra special for the young boy. He was going to get to see his Uncle Bill! Ever since the family had parted after the war, Willie had pestered his mother with questions about his favorite uncle. Where was he? When would he visit again? He could not understand the distance between them or that his uncle's medical practice made it impossible for him to live with them.

Finally in December 1868, Tempie answered his queries with the news that they were going to spend Christmas with Uncle Bill and attend his wedding. Tempie packed their things for the trip and loaded all the children in the two-horse wagon. At the last minute, she gave in to Willie's demands to take Pincher along. With the children and dog loaded, Tempie said goodbye to David and took the reins for the two-day trip to Bill's house near the Artesian Church in what was soon to become Nevada County. Two days after celebrating Christmas with their relatives, they attended Bill's wedding to Mary "Mollie" McCollum of Hempstead County and met Mollie's family, which included her brother James, who was about Willie's age. On the trip home, Pincher somehow got lost and no manner of searching found him. It was a tough loss for the seven-year-old boy. "This caused the greatest grief I had ever experienced," he recalled.[8]

Going to his uncle's wedding and losing his dog were among the biggest events of Willie's childhood. But for his parents, those events paled in comparison with the hard economic times and the continuing difficulties of Reconstruction. Cotton prices remained low, and many people were barely able to survive. Visitors from the North were appalled by the still visible effects of the war. "The South has been devastated by the war," Mrs. John A. Logan wrote in a letter to the editor of *The New York Herald* following a visit to the war-ravaged region in 1868.

"Everywhere signs of privation and devastation were constantly presenting themselves to us." But no one stepped forward to offer assistance. Instead, Northerners and Southern opportunists continued to rape the land and its people.[9]

15 Shadow of Reconstruction

The financial straits of the Arnold family were worsened by increasing local taxes – as well as the mounting state taxes. In the first few years following the Civil War, Union County tried to live within its means. But by 1868, the county had a small indebtedness of $1,600. Over the next seven years as Reconstruction policies took hold, the county's spending soared to $128,892 – most of which went for salaries as it made no public improvements during that time. As the Reconstruction officials increased their spending, they raised personal and property taxes, but the tax revenue couldn't keep up with their spending habits. By 1874, the county's indebtedness hit $35,000. The tax burden financially crippled people who needed every dime to survive. Nearly every acre in the county was mortgaged at a high rate of interest.[1]

Meanwhile, cotton was selling for 12 cents to 18 cents a pound, with local farmers often getting 25 percent less than the market price when they dealt with area merchants. The plagues of nature continued to cut into the crop and the farmers' profit as flood or droughts wiped out entire fields and reduced the yield in others. The farmers could not afford their own debt – let alone the debt of their county and state. Realizing that Reconstruction would strangle them if it went on indefinitely, the Democrats began reorganizing on the local level. In collusion with the Brindletail Republicans, who had organized in response to the tax-and-spend policies of the regular Republicans, the Democrats in 1872 took eight Senate seats – six short of a majority – and 38 House seats, four short of control of that chamber.[2]

It was an election steeped in corruption – mainly due to the gubernatorial race between Clayton's hand-picked candidate, Elisha Baxter, a homegrown scalawag who had barely escaped the death penalty for treason during the war, and carpetbagger Joseph Brooks, who had split the Arkansas Republican Party. The Minstrel Republicans, who represented the Clayton machine, supported Baxter. Brooks' supporters came to be known as Brindletail Republicans because Brooks bellowed as loud as a brindletail bull. Both candidates promised to give the franchise back to Confederate veterans. The get-out-the-vote campaigns were intense on both sides because the stakes of patronage were so high. Clayton, now serving as a U.S. senator, perhaps had the most to lose. He needed a governor he could trust to continue the railroad payola with which he lined his pockets.[3]

Election laws meant nothing that Election Day. Eligible men were encouraged to vote – often. Even the dead rose from their graves to cast a ballot or two. The "wrong" voters were banished from polling places at gunpoint. At some places, ballots were destroyed; at others, they were created. But with Clayton's people controlling the election commission and overseeing most of the polling places, the result was decided before the first vote was cast. Baxter was declared the winner by 3,200 votes. Brooks, who had been disappointed by Clayton's refusal to give him a position in return for his work at the ballot box in 1868, was not about to lose to Clayton again. Claiming he had won by 8,000 votes, Brooks took his case to the U.S. District Court, which said it had no jurisdiction in the state matter and suggested Brooks try a state court.[4]

Brooks then appealed to the Arkansas Supreme Court. He later claimed that Baxter had stationed an officer in the courtroom with orders to arrest the justices if they decided for Brooks. When the Supreme Court denied his motion, Brooks filed against Baxter in circuit court in Pulaski County. There the case sat, virtually ignored. While Brooks was looking to the courts for victory, Baxter appealed to the General Assembly, which upheld his win. He was sworn in January 6, 1873. Brooks claimed Baxter had bought the Legislature by promising 30 to 40 legislators higher-paying jobs with his administration.[5]

Once in office, Baxter silenced those who had voted against him as he sounded the death knell for Reconstruction in Arkansas. He quickly proved he was no one's puppet by appointing both Republicans and Democrats to the election commission and placing control of the militia back in the state's hands. He also paved the way for the March 3 election to rid Arkansas of the last vestiges of Reconstruction. Few people turned out, and the measure to do away with the disenfranchisement of Civil War veterans passed 10 to one. With that odious obstacle out of the way, the Democrats finally had the ability to regain control of the state. Recognizing the threat, the Republicans, still in the majority in the Legislature, struggled to hang onto their power. They pushed a bill to strengthen their control of elections, which would negate the effects of the franchise legislation, and another bill that would allow Northern-owned railroads to pay off their state debt using their stock as tender. Gov. Baxter vetoed both bills – over the protests of Sen. Clayton.[6]

To the Minstrel Republicans, it looked as if Baxter had switched parties. With the governor working against them, they became more concerned about losing control of the state. Their fears were realized November 8, 1873, when a special election was held to fill the vacancies left by 88 legislators who had resigned to take higher-paying state jobs. David and other Confederate veterans flocked to the polls to vote for the first time since Reconstruction began. Their votes enabled the Democrats to sweep the election and gain control of both houses with a small majority for the first time since the war. Hendrick Arnold, David's older brother, was elected to serve in the House from Arkadelphia, and his cousin, David Saxon, was elected from Union County. The politics of the state had become a family matter to the Arnolds.[7]

Now that the Democrats had the Legislature and at least a sympathetic ear in the governor, the Republicans worried about the inevitable constitutional convention that could reapportion electoral districts and revamp the election machinery in favor of the Democrats. If that should happen, Sens. Clayton and Steven Dorsey were sure to lose their seats and would be forced to take their hand out of the public till. And it would be impossible for the Republicans to reclaim the governor's office with its rich rewards of patronage. Their only hope of securing their position was to get rid of Baxter. Brooks, starving for power, was more than willing to help his former opponents.[8]

Baxter's attorneys unwittingly gave the Republicans the opening they needed. Trying to tie up loose ends, the attorneys in April 1874 requested that Brooks' case against Baxter, which was buried in the Pulaski County Circuit Court, be taken up on demurrer so it could be dismissed. They were given a court date in two weeks. But Brooks' attorney showed up in court the following Monday and told Judge John Whytock, a Republican who had originally upheld Baxter's election, that he and Baxter's attorneys had agreed that a demurrer to the jurisdiction of the court should be submitted immediately. Taking Brooks' at his word, Whytock took up the case without notifying Baxter's attorneys, who were out of town. Presiding over a nearly empty courtroom, the judge overruled the demurrer April 15 and called for Baxter's ouster. Chief Justice John "Poker Jack" McClure, who also had upheld Baxter's election, swore Brooks in as governor on the spot. Brooks – along with his general, R.F. Catterson, former commander of the state militia, and about 20 armed men – wasted no time in bursting into Baxter's office at the Statehouse. When Baxter refused their demand to give up the office, they forcibly dragged the stout man through the Statehouse and threw him into the street.[9]

As soon as Brooks had secured the Statehouse, he sent Catterson to seize the state arsenal. Baxter's Adj. Gen. Strong, who was in charge of the arsenal, was surprised to find himself surrounded by a band of determined, armed men. Refusing to be intimidated by their threats and show of force, Strong would not surrender the keys to the arsenal. Brooks' men shoved him aside and broke down the door. They seized 100 guns. By mid-afternoon, Brooks and 300 armed men, mostly African Americans led by white officers, occupied the Capitol. Baxter, not about to relinquish his post, set up an office in the Anthony House about three blocks from the Capitol. As soon as the word got out, his supporters rallied to his cause.[10]

Neither side was willing to try diplomacy, but both appealed to President Grant to legitimize their claim to the gubernatorial throne. Three of the five Supreme Court justices were the first to wire a message to Grant stating that Brooks was now governor of Arkansas. Every state constitutional officer, except the secretary of state, signed off on another telegram to the president giving their support to Brooks. While these messages were ones of fact, Brooks' telegram to Grant was an appeal – for recognition and access to the federal arsenal in Little Rock and its supply of weapons. Baxter sent his own telegram to Grant, referring to Brooks' actions as a "revolutionary movement." In its coverage of the crisis, *The New York Times* stated, "The general sentiment of the people is favorable to Baxter."[11]

Grant, who had recently been accused by the press of being a caesar and a despot, was reluctant to intervene – even though the Republican cause would be strengthened should Brooks be named governor. The president denied both men access to the federal arsenal and ordered the U.S. army detachment stationed in Little Rock to intervene only to prevent an armed struggle; the soldiers were not to take sides in the affair. Grant also referred the matter to the state courts. Neither claimant was deterred by the president's neutrality. Brooks proclaimed himself governor April 16 and imposed what in effect was martial law on Little Rock. Baxter also proclaimed himself governor and placed all of Pulaski County under martial law.[12]

The would-be governors prepared for war. Baxter ordered his men to seize all the guns from the shops in Little Rock and sent purchasing agents to Texas. Brooks ordered his men to seize the weapons from the arsenal in Fayetteville and sent purchasing agents to St. Louis. Along with the guns, Baxter's men seized a cannon, which they named "Lady Baxter," and aimed it at the Capitol. Brooks' men built breastworks around the Capitol yard. And in the middle of the two factions, Col. Rose, in command of the U.S. army detachment, ordered his men to erect barricades – formed of the city's hook and ladder vehicles – along Main Street. Soon each side had about 600 armed men jamming the city streets, separated only by the U.S. army and Main Street. Meanwhile, downtown merchants boarded up their windows.[13]

While Baxter and Brooks readied their troops, Sens. Clayton and Dorsey and three of the state's four congressmen met with

Grant and U.S. Attorney General George H. Williams April 18, urging them to support Brooks. (Congressman David Wilshire of the Third Congressional District stood firm for Baxter.) After the meeting, Clayton wired Brooks assurances that the president would back him. The senator told Brooks to take care of things in Arkansas while promising to take care of everything in Washington. The following day, Brooks issued an edict calling on those who supported the "pretender" to lay down their weapons. Baxter's response was a second telegram to Grant.[14]

Their fortifications ready, both sides were temporarily content with parading their men up and down the streets of their turf and trying to outblast each other with loud martial music. But after a few days of parades and music, they grew restless of what appeared to be a stalemate. The break came when Col. H. King White, a flamboyant former Confederate cavalry officer from Pine Bluff, arrived by flatboat April 21 with 800 black troops pledged to Baxter. As the men marched through the city toward Baxter's stronghold, they chanted a ditty in honor of the beleaguered governor. When the men approached the Anthony House, Baxter stepped out on a second-floor balcony to greet them. After a brief ceremony, White turned his men toward Main Street to march them to their barracks. Thinking White was beginning an assault on Brooks and the Capitol, Rose mounted his horse and hurriedly rode among White's men, ordering them to keep the peace. The former Confederate accused Rose of trying to ride down his men, and a scuffle ensued. Rose's gun discharged. At the sound of the shot, both sides started firing. Brooks' sharpshooters took aim at the balcony where Baxter had stood a few minutes earlier. Within five minutes, Rose had restored order. The only casualty was an innocent bystander who had been watching the action from a window in the Anthony House. The next day, Baxter called for a special session of the Legislature to convene May 11. Knowing Brooks would seek recourse in the courts, Baxter's men kidnapped two justices so the Supreme Court would not be able to hear the case.[15]

Fighting broke out again April 30 when word reached White that 200 of Brooks' men would be marching toward his hometown of Pine Bluff. This was getting personal. Angered by the affront, the tall red-head led his black troops to New Gascony where they ambushed Brooks' men, killing nine and wounding 29. The next battle in what was becoming known as the Arkansas Civil War took place May 8 when Baxter's men learned that a flatboat loaded with guns from the Fayetteville arsenal was heading downriver from Fort Smith. Baxter sent 40 men on a gunboat to intercept the weapons. But they were ambushed by 200 of Brooks' men at a bend in the river near Palarm. When Sam Houston, captain of the boat, refused to halt, the ambushers fired at point blank range, killing Houston and his pilot and disabling the boat. After drifting aimlessly for half an hour, the boat's crew – what was left of it – surrendered.[16]

The antics of the Arkansans were trying the patience of the nation. Just as Grant was criticized before for intervening too much in other states, now he was being criticized for his lack of action in Arkansas. Knowing the General Assembly was to convene in a few days, Grant called on the legislators to resolve the issue. He also asked both sides to disband and requested that Brooks vacate the Capitol. Brooks refused the president's requests and denied the Legislature's authority in the matter. He maintained that only the Arkansas courts, made up of Republican carpetbaggers who sided with him, could decide the issue. With Brooks still holed up in the Capitol behind hundreds of armed men, Baxter also refused to disband. Rather than working toward a solution, both sides seemed intent on slipping away from the surveillance of the U.S. army so they could fight it out with no interference.[17]

Amid all the upheaval and despite possible bodily harm from Brooks' men, Hendrick Arnold and David Saxon made their way to Little Rock for the special session May 11. They were joined by several other legislators loyal to Baxter, but by May 12, there was not a quorum as the Republican legislators refused to convene. Hendrick, David, and the other legislators who showed up sent the sergeant-at-arms "out into the highways and byways to collect the unwilling representatives of the people," the newspapers reported. This matter needed to be resolved quickly as it was killing what was left of the state's economy and making Arkansas a national laughingstock.[18]

The New York Times lamented the message this affair was sending other Southerners: It was "instilling into the public mind the dangerous notion that there is no power in the National Government to decide contests for the possession of a State Government, however lawless and violent they may become." This message was especially dangerous, the paper added, because "[t]here are in all the Southern States large numbers of half-unoccupied men, with lawless passions and little regard for the rights of others, who are restrained from violence in the prosecution of their political controversies by the feeling that there is in the General Government a latent power for regulation that cannot be provoked with impunity." Unless the federal government used this power, the paper argued, such men would be freed from their restraints, and violence would rule.[19]

While the legislators loyal to Baxter tried to secure a quorum May 12, Brooks' men ambushed a train bringing new recruits to join Baxter. Brooks, whose forces had not grown appreciably above the original 600 men, desperately needed to halt the flood of men joining the other side. In the sporadic fighting that followed the ambush, two of Baxter's men were wounded and eight of Brooks' men were killed or wounded. Both sides sent reinforcements, and the fighting, which resulted in several deaths, spilled into the city streets. Rose's soldiers enforced a ceasefire just in time to avoid a major battle. Brooks, meanwhile, sent an insolent message to Grant, in which he lectured the president on his duties and practically defied him to interfere. Such tactics did not garner Brooks any favor in the North. With the situation deteriorating, *The New York Times* suggested the only solution was to send "General Sherman with troops to Arkansas, with instructions to restore order, and not to quit the State until we know who *is* Governor, and until that Governor and the State Legislature are properly obeyed."[20]

Kept apprised of the situation by his brother and cousin, David worried about the impact of another round of federal occupation. Arkansas was sinking deeper into debt every day; it did not need more Northerners coming in to drain the economy and enforce their version of law and order. His own business, already faltering, could not weather such a storm. David's concerns were shared by other Arkansans, who viewed Clayton and Brooks as outsiders and usurpers driven by their personal greed. Although Baxter had been seen as a traitor to the South, he at least was a true Arkansan and was showing that he wanted what was best for the state.

Shaken by threats of federal occupation, pressure from their neighbors, and the realization of how close the state had come to an all-out war, several recalcitrant legislators finally appeared for the special session. With a quorum present, the General Assembly declared Baxter the governor May 14. The following day, U.S. Attorney General Williams wired Brooks, ordering him to disband and surrender the Capitol. Brooks refused. In Washington, Clayton and Dorsey were in a rage and "breathing forth threats" as they faced public accusations of corruption. They could see their empire was about to crumble. Pointing out that Arkansas' entire congressional delegation had supported Baxter when he was first elected, conservative newspapers across the country questioned why most of them had turned on him. "There must be some explanation of their action besides honesty," *The New York Times* mused.[21]

Within a few days, Brooks – now under U.S. guard in the Statehouse – began to disband his troops. Two boats, each loaded with 100 of Brooks' men, left Little Rock for northwest Arkansas the night of May 18. Another 225 set off by boat toward Fort Smith early the next morning. The boats sailed under white flags, and each group had been allowed to keep a few muskets for protection as the boats would have to pass through Pope County, a Baxter stronghold still up in arms over Brooks' actions. Since Brooks was finally disbanding, Baxter sent some of his 2,000 men home. A company of his men marched out of town the afternoon of May 19, firing their guns indiscriminately as they went; two men were seriously wounded by stray bullets. As the men from both sides returned home, they burned houses and barns in areas thought to be loyal to their enemy. Several people were murdered, and others were threatened. Little Rock remained under military rule with armed men parading the streets and standing picket on every corner. Despite the precautions, numerous fights broke out on the streets. Murphy, the leader of Brooks' black forces, had been ordered to leave the state. Instead, he visited several black communities, trying to incite more rebellion against Baxter. The violence led to reports in Washington that the governor's men were murdering Brooks' black supporters in cold blood.[22]

That same day, Baxter received his first report of the state of the Capitol. His secretary of state, escorted by U.S. soldiers, was allowed to visit the Statehouse. His first concern was his office. He found the safe intact and all the state seals accounted for. But the rest of the building hadn't fared so well. Home to 600 men for a month, it was pretty much trashed. The halls and stairways were covered with bits of mortar, empty whiskey bottles, discarded clothing, and decaying meat and vegetables. The courtroom used by the Supreme Court was in shambles. He estimated it would take $20,000 to restore the building. Amid all the refuse and damage, Brooks remained defiantly holed up in the governor's office. He had received a telegram that day from Clayton and Dorsey, assuring him that Congress would intervene on his behalf. But later that day, the U.S. House voted down a resolution calling for a congressional investigation.[23]

By now, Baxter had had more than enough. He publicly reminded Brooks and the state officials who had sided with him that they were guilty of treason – a crime punishable by death. His advice to Brooks: "Get out of Arkansas while you still can." As Baxter waited impatiently to move back into the governor's office, the General Assembly, now controlled by Democrats, continued its special session. But now, Hendrick, David Saxon, and the other Democrat legislators focused their attention on Clayton and Dorsey. Allegations of corruption flew in both chambers. Dorsey was accused of bribing potential opponents to keep them from running against him. He also was accused of bribing legislators and other officials. As a reaction to the charges, the House voted to change the name of Clayton County to Anthony County and promised to change the name of Dorsey County the next day.[24]

The next morning dawned with more acts of violence. Someone tried to burn downtown Little Rock by setting three fires in a centrally located building. The hook and ladder crews fought desperately to keep the flames from spreading. Gunfights and knife fights continued on the city streets. Although the violence raged throughout Arkansas that day, the Brooks-Baxter War officially ended May 20. Still defiant, Brooks quietly left the Statehouse at noon. As soon as he was gone, the U.S. detachment disassembled its barricades on Main Street, and both Brooks and Baxter withdrew their pickets. Storeowners began tearing down the heavy planks they had nailed to their windows as protection from looting and stray gunfire.[25]

An hour after Brooks had withdrawn, Baxter left his rooms in the Anthony House and rode triumphantly to the Capitol. His supporters and city residents lined the streets to cheer him on his way. As soon as Baxter took his seat behind the massive desk in the governor's office, a 100-gun salute sounded through the city. The war was over. The governor was back – with a vengeance. Baxter promised a thorough investigation of the books and papers of all state officials who participated in the rebellion. He vowed that if Clayton set foot in Arkansas, he would be arrested on charges of conspiracy to overthrow the state government. And he reiterated his advice to Brooks to leave the state. Meanwhile, several of Brooks' friends and supporters, afraid they would be brought up on charges of treason, hurriedly left the state. And Baxter's men arrested Murphy while he was trying to incite the black residents of Pine Bluff.[26]

As life returned to normal, the Arnolds and their neighbors took stock of the situation. The war for the governor's office had cost the taxpayers $300,000. It was a bill no one could afford. Newspapers gave the final cost in lives: Baxter lost eight men and had 13 wounded; Brooks lost 30 men, mostly black supporters, and had 40 wounded. In the aftermath of the uprising, Baxter called on the General Assembly to investigate acts of treason by state officials and strongly recommended that, at the least, they be removed from office. He also asked the legislators to prohibit the future issue of scrip by the state, counties, and cities as it is "one of the most fruitful sources of fraud and distrust." The General Assembly had been considering a bill that would give full pardon to all those who had participated in the rebellion – except Brooks and his general officers. "[A]fter a long and disgraceful discussion, during which the vilest personalities were indulged in, the bill passed the House," *The New York Times* correspondent in Little Rock reported. Attached to the bill was an amendment extending the pardon to Brooks and his officers. The only people not covered by the pardon were the state officials who had participated in the coup d'etat.[27]

If nothing else, the Brooks-Baxter War served to shine the national spotlight on the evils of Reconstruction. It also demonstrated, once again, the great divide between the North and South. *The New York Times*, which reminded its readers that it had always deplored Congress' ill-advised Reconstruction policies, called the conflict "a legacy of the rebellion and reconstruction" and blamed it in part on the ignorance of the Arkansas people. Using racist and elitist overtones, the *Times* said this is what comes of giving suffrage to ignorant people, including poorly educated whites. "[T]he great masses of people (in Arkansas) are so ignorant," the paper commented, "and living as they do, in remote districts, without the means of receiving information from, or communicating with, the outside world, are so easily led...."[28]

The fallout continued a few more months. The state treasurer, fearing the investigation of his books and his involvement with Brooks, resigned. The Democrats, now firmly back in control, called a constitutional convention in July to get rid of the federally mandated Reconstruction constitution. Each article of the new constitution repudiated the old one. The passage of the new constitution marked the end of a despised era for the state and a new beginning for the Democrats. With the restoration of the vote and the new constitution, the Democrats were ensconced in Arkansas. They looked toward the fall election with confidence, assured that they would reclaim every state office. When the Democrat Party held its state convention in September, the delegates ignored Baxter's affiliation with the Republicans and twice offered him the nomination. He refused both times. He had had enough of public office.[29]

That October, Agustus H. Garland was the first Democrat to be elected governor since the war. The Democrats were back in business. They "ceased to be a party in the South and became a party of the South, a kind of confraternity having in its keeping the whole corpus of Southern loyalties," historian Wilbur Cash wrote, "and so irresistibly commanding the allegiance of faithful whites that to doubt it, to question it in any detail, was ipso facto to stand branded as a renegade to race, to country, to God, and to Southern Womanhood."[30]

16 Coming of Age

While his brother Hendrick and cousin David Saxon were being citizen politicians and paving a fresh direction for the state, David was looking for a new course for his family. He was not alone. Nearly 15 years had passed since the war, but the South was still a mess. Destruction of the factorage system – which was dependent on the plantation, cotton, and slavery – and the vacuum it left had crippled the agricultural economy. What the war hadn't destroyed, nature had taken as it mocked the farmers' struggle to survive year after year. There began "to emerge the feeling, nebulous at first but waxing always clearer, that another line must be found, that somehow some way must be hit upon, at once vastly to widen the chance for the individual to achieve security and success, and to bring the necessary wealth and power and strength to the South in general," Wilbur Cash wrote a generation later.[1]

Those working the poor, tired lands of the older states resorted to the traditional solution – they headed west to Arkansas and Texas, both of which had mounted mammoth campaigns boasting about their natural resources in hopes of attracting new settlers. Like his countrymen, David had spent years looking for a new way. His farm and store near Lisbon had not provided the income he needed for his growing family. And the lack of good schools was a major concern. After careful thought, David moved the family to Marysville – about 10 miles from Lisbon and six miles from Mount Holly. There he gave up farming and concentrated on running a store. At the time, Marysville had little else but a sawmill and Pleasant Grove Church. But Mount Holly looked to be an up-and-coming community that boasted a brand new cotton gin.[2]

Life did not get any easier for Willie in Marysville. If anything, school was worse. Charlie Gordon, his teacher, was impressed with his own education, acquired at a school in Alabama, and with the reputation of his father, a well-respected educator. "That education is about to kill him," the students said of the young teacher. Charlie came across as vain and fastidious with a mean streak that revealed itself daily. It was a common practice that summer for Charlie to call as many as half a dozen boys at a time to stand before his desk. Knowing what was coming, they shuffled forward as Charlie took out his long hazelwood switch and flexed it. When the boys were in place, he whipped them across their backs, the switch cutting into their thin cotton shirts. The older ones and the stubborn ones resolutely forced the tears from their eyes as the switch dug in time after time. Unable to make them cry, Charlie would not let up until blood mingled with the sweat on their backs. Willie was not spared this "discipline." Nearly every day the 12-year-old was called to the front along with the other boys for his beating. One day, Charlie was particularly brutal with the switch and "came very near wearing the life out of me," Willie recalled, "and that is another thing I shall never forget." Along with several other boys in the school, Willie vowed that if he ever had a chance when he was a grown man, he would whip Charlie Gordon.[3]

As he matured, the focus of Willie's life gradually shifted from his mother to his father. Approaching manhood, he needed his father's approval more than his mother's comfort. But his shyness often kept him from measuring up to David's high standards. One Sunday morning, David asked Willie to ride over to get the mail, which they still received at the post office located in Col. Coulter's mansion near Lisbon. This was a first for the adolescent as he usually accompanied Sax on the mail run. Butterflies churned in his stomach as he saddled up the family mule, but he knew better than to whine or complain. His father expected him to behave like a man. Willie made the long trek to the Lisbon area uneventfully. But when he arrived at the gate in front of the large white house, he was too intimidated to get off the mule and go to the door. Instead, he remained mounted, hollering "hello" repeatedly from the dirt road.

Finally his shouts were heard, and a young man came out onto the grand gallery and hollered back: "What do you want?"

Willie asked him if there was any mail for the Arnolds.

"No!" the young man shouted.

With that, Willie turned his mule around and headed home, traveling the final miles in the dark. When he arrived, he was tired and hungry, having had no dinner. His father's eagerness to get the mail quickly turned to frustration. David knew there were several newspapers and letters waiting for the family at the post office. He had been looking forward to catching up on what was going on in Little Rock and elsewhere. He told Willie that he should have gone to the door and asked for the colonel. Failing that, he should have had sense enough to go to Dr. Manning's house to get his used newspapers. Willie, who wanted nothing more than to please his father and fill his empty stomach, bristled at once again being a disappointment to his father. "Hardships and disappointments of this kind are rarely ever forgotten," he wrote years later.

The family's stay in Marysville was short-lived. As the Brooks-Baxter War was being waged in Little Rock, David decided to take up farming again, this time in Nevada County. Formed in 1871 from part of old Hempstead County, Nevada represented a new type of frontier. Towns, such as Prescott, were forming, and, with the railroad coming in, the county seemed to offer plenty of opportunity to hard-working, enterprising people. David bought a farm about two miles from Prescott, which had been laid out and settled in 1873, and moved his family, now consisting of seven children, back to the area where Tempie's family had started their life in Arkansas. It was a good move for Willie. Although it meant a lot of hard work for him on the farm, he was closer to Uncle Bill and a better school.[4]

In Prescott, David met John Ansley, who also hailed from South Carolina and had graduated from Erskine College several years after David. When the Arnolds moved, John was finishing a term in the Legislature, where he had met David's brother and been a part of the Brooks-Baxter War. David and John became friends, and David encouraged John to open an academy in Prescott. Sax, and possibly Lucy, attended this school when David could spare them from home. By the time Willie, now going by the grownup nickname of Dick, was ready for the academy, John had moved the academy to Artesian near Uncle Bill's place, which was four miles west of Prescott. That suited Dick just fine as he got to stay with Uncle Bill while attending school. His classmates included Uncle Bill's brother-in-law, Jim McCollum, several Ross cousins, and Carrie Arnold and John H. Arnold, Jr., the daughter and son of his Uncle John.[5]

When his studies were done for the day, Dick returned to Uncle Bill's house, which was also home to Jim as well as Uncle Robert and Bill's family, which included five children. In the evenings, Dick and Jim studied together and planned illustrious futures for themselves. When they put away their schoolbooks, they spent long, enjoyable hours joking and playing cards with Uncle Bill, who took every opportunity to encourage them to pursue their dreams. Dick didn't feel like he had to prove himself with Uncle Bill, who seemed to understand him and accept him for who he was. "It is not surprising that we thought he was the greatest man in the world," Dick said of his uncle. In every aspect of his life, Uncle Bill modeled the Southern ideal for his nephew. An extremely busy physician, he provided not only medical care to his needy patients, he also gave them food to keep them from starving. Blossoming under Uncle Bill's approval, Dick began to take more interest in school.

"I enjoyed very much my work as a student at Ansley Academy," William Arnold wrote, "and the only regret I had was that I could not be a constant attendant, as it was necessary for me to make crops." Putting the children in the academy was a sacrifice for David and Tempie as most academies of the day charged $15 to $25 per student for a 10-month term in the elementary grades and $25 to $35 for the high school level. This didn't include room and board. David was willing to pay the price, but he couldn't afford to send the boys to school when he needed them in the fields.[6]

Instead of doing sums and long division, Dick often found himself plowing up new ground laced with the roots of giant elm trees. "I made some marvelous escapes and sometimes the plow would strike a stump or root and the handles would be thrust against me, other times the roots would fly back and strike my knees and shins," he recalled. "I pursued this work with so much energy that one of my knees swelled up for six weeks, and while I was in bed I continued my studies." Dick also missed school when he was laid up with a slow fever for several weeks. To convalesce, he needed the constant care and oversight of a doctor. Uncle Bill came to the rescue. He put a mattress in his two-horse wagon and drove the team to the farm to get Dick, who stayed at the doctor's house until he fully recovered. While there, Uncle Bill teased him, telling him he was so emaciated and thin that his bones rattled when he walked.

As Dick continued his studies, he discovered a fondness for Davies arithmetic and Bourdon's algebra. He also developed a liking for reading. David had a good library and gave Dick the run of it. He enjoyed reading histories, biographies of great men, and exploits of great generals, especially Napoleon. Other popular military heroes of the time were George Washington and Francis Marion, the "Swamp Fox" of Revolutionary fame. Added to the stories he read were the family tales of his ancestors who had fought in the Revolutionary War and the Civil War escapades of the Confederate heroes, his uncles, his father, and even his teacher. "Every boy growing up in this land now had continually before his eyes the vision, and heard always in his ears the clamorous hoofbeats of a glorious swashbuckler, compounded of Jeb Stuart, the golden-locked [George] Pickett, and the sudden and terrible [Nathan Bedford] Forrest ... forever charging the cannon's mouth with the Southern battle flag," Cash wrote.[7]

For Dick, it was more than hero worship. "I ... had it in my mind that I possessed great military genius, and resolved to be a general in war, and a lawyer in time of peace," he wrote later of his childhood dreams.

David encouraged his son's interest in books and his ambitions. His father's approval was the impetus Dick needed. "He took notice of my reading and told me one day that if I kept my reading up I would some day make a great man. I at once made up my mind to pursue the study of history to ascertain whether his prediction would prove true. I cultivated the habit of frowning heavily, as I believed that was evidence of deep thought and distinction. As a matter of fact, my ambition ran high and I could not see why I should not become a wonderful character in the annals of the race," he recalled.

Before Dick could be a leader of men, he needed to overcome his weaknesses. His shyness remained a considerable problem. Once when school was not it session, Tempie gave Dick two chickens to sell at the hotel in town. When he arrived in Prescott, he timidly walked up to the front entrance of the hotel where a number of people were sitting. Convinced they were all watching him, Dick nervously shifted from one foot to another, holding the chickens tightly and looking as purposeful as he could. His eyes darted from the road to the door to a buzzing fly as he tried to ignore the people gathered on the gallery. Finally a man with a glass eye came out of the hotel, silently took the chickens, and, just as silently, went back into the hotel. Dick continued to stand there, waiting and trying to act nonchalant. Several long minutes ticked by before the man with the glass eye came to the door and, without a word, handed Dick a slick 20-cent piece. Relieved, Dick put it in his pocket and went on his way. "I have no recollection of any word having been said between us," he wrote. "I was literally scared to death and glad to get away."

Dick experienced other coming-of-age lessons. Although most people still did not have much, appearances were important. Clothes said a lot about the man who wore them. After the war, those devoted to thoughts of gentility "were marked out by the long-tailed coat – a sort of uniform of the class at the time," Cash wrote. As an awkward teenager desperately wanting to be seen as a gentleman, Dick was very conscious of how he appeared to others. One Christmas Day, Tempie asked him to go into town to get some more squill at the drugstore. Since it was a holiday, Dick was sure everyone would be dressed to the nines. Not to be outdone, he donned an old broadcloth swallow-tail coat, which had belonged to his Uncle Robert in his younger days, and headed into Prescott with the empty squill bottle in his pocket. Confident he looked every part the gentleman in that long-tail coat, Dick swaggered into the drugstore. Once he had the bottle filled with the pungent dried flakes of sea onion, he put it in his pocket. His errand accomplished, he marched around town a bit to show off his finery, smiling smugly when he saw someone he knew. Stepping proudly through the snow and slush, he suddenly noticed no one else seemed to be on dress parade. His newfound confidence vanished, and he felt "perfectly miserable," convinced he looked more a fool than a gentleman. To make matters worse, the squill bottle came uncorked in his pocket and the spilt expectorant had him sneezing all the way home.[8]

Such incidents made Dick, who felt the spark of pride and ambition, all the more determined to succeed. Since his dreams to become a military genius depended on a war occurring, he focused instead on becoming a lawyer. While still attending Ansley Academy, he borrowed a law book to study. His chosen course was the path to success many of the elite had walked prior to the war. Historian Frank Owsley described the next step for those Southern sons who felt this spark: "After he had acquired sufficient education and age he would teach school ... or find other employment which would enable him to save enough money to attend the academy or even college.... The third step was the preparation for his profession, usually the law, medicine, or the ministry." With almost everything else in shambles, this path of upward social mobility had survived the war. In the decades following the war and Reconstruction, the men who possessed the people's confidence were doctors, lawyers, teachers, planters, and clergymen.[9]

In preparing for a law career, Dick chose a profession that provided the easiest entrance into the ranks of the elite. To be a doctor, he would need to attend medical school – something his family could not afford. To be a planter, he would have to inherit a large farm or have the funding to purchase one. That door was closed to him. While clergy were respected, they were not always well-heeled. That left the law, which did not require a large purse to get started as most lawyers were self-taught or they apprenticed under respected lawyers in their communities.

The law created a broad opportunity to carve out wealth and honor in even the older, more settled communities. Success in the law rested on ambition and ability rather than class and money.[10]

Law was not a profession for opportunists, though. Lawyers of 19th-century Arkansas were respected for their gentility, their civic-mindedness, their sense of fair play. They were seen as composing an important class in the community and were known for their "vigorous minds ... lofty ideals of personal honor, and an energy of integrity admirably fitted to the tasks set before them." Any complaints leveled against them were far from the stereotypes that the profession earned in the closing decades of the 20th century. Rather, the criticism of that era focused on a blind adherence to precedent or a love for the abstruse technicalities of the practice. Such a passion could create a "learned judge" whose usefulness to his fellow man was apt to be permanently impaired.[11]

These very dangers, especially adherence to precedent, made the practice of law one of continuity, of building upon the past. The war and Reconstruction may have disrupted other facets of Southern life, but they did not change the essential practice of law, which flowed back to the founding fathers and the colonial powers. "The school of the lawyer is to accept precedent, the same as it is a common human instinct to accept what comes to him from the fathers – assuming everything in its favor and combating everything that would dispute the 'old order.'" This tie to the past, to the code of Southern honor, resulted in post-war lawyers noted for their "wise, conservative and noble efforts on behalf of [their] race as ever distinguished patriot or sage."[12]

There was a practical side to the law that attracted shrewd, energetic young men of the late 19th century. Young lawyers were assured of rising quickly to a prominent position in a firm or having a successful private practice if they were ambitious and possessed the essential skills and qualities – a practical knowledge of the law, an understanding of country jurors, some oratorical talent, and cleverness in debate and repartee. In the years following Reconstruction, legal business was in abundance in the rural South, so even lawyers of modest talent could make a comfortable living. Successful lawyers often became the leaders of their communities, going on to serve as U.S. senators, governors, or judges. Besides these practicalities, the glamour of the law appealed to impressionable young men such as Dick who imagined the battles played out in the courtroom, the fight for justice, the astounding displays of logic and rhetoric that would immortalize their name.[13]

17   In Pursuit of the Law

Before he could seek immortality, Dick had to deal with the realities of mortal life. After finishing at Ansley's Academy, Dick began introducing himself as "William." He was a man now; he needed to present himself as one. Encouraged by his teacher, he applied for a job teaching a five-month public school near Hollywood in Clark County in 1879. It was the course his father had pursued, and it was a path common to many successful Southerners. As part of his application, William had to pass an oral examination given by J.W. Wilson, the county examiner. Nervous as usual, William studied hard for the exam. But when he appeared before Wilson, he discovered he had studied the wrong subjects. Wilson's questions focused on oratorical skills – diphthongs, the vocal organs, use of the tongue – all things William had never studied.

Thinking Wilson's questions were foolish for a teaching exam, William summoned the courage to stand up for himself. He informed the examiner that he could answer questions about grammar, arithmetic, or algebra – the subjects he would be teaching in the classroom. But Wilson said he could not give the young man a first-grade teaching certificate. "I do not think I was ever hurt so badly before," William remembered.[1]

When the would-be teacher asked for a reason, Wilson said it was because he had never taught before. All that reading of the law came to the fore as William argued this proposition with the examiner. How could someone get the teaching experience necessary for a certificate if he couldn't teach without the certificate?

Finally the two men reached an agreement: William would be allowed to teach for two weeks without the certificate. With that experience, he could return to get his certificate. William promptly returned November 24, 1879 – the end of the two-week period – to receive his Grade No. One Department of Public Instruction Teachers License, the highest teaching certificate Arkansas offered. The certificate stated that he had presented "satisfactory testimonials of good moral character" and was qualified to teach orthography, reading, writing, mental and written arithmetic, English grammar, modern geography, and U.S. history.

Hollywood, a small village about 12 miles west of Arkadelphia, was home to about 100 people, a post office, two general stores, a drugstore, a steam-operated cotton gin, the school house, and Methodist and Baptist churches. Instead of living in Hollywood, William boarded with his Uncle Hendrick and Aunt Ann, who lived on a 700-acre farm near Arkadelphia. He got up at 4 each morning and saddled up his horse for the cold, dark ride to get to school on time and would not arrive home until late each evening. William didn't mind making the long ride as it gave him a chance to connect more closely with his father's side of the family. Also living with Hendrick and Ann was "Cousin Lewis" Saxon. While William wasn't sure of his exact relationship with the elderly man, he enjoyed his company and his humorous tales drawn from the family history. Driven from his home in Cass County, Georgia, by Gen. Sherman's army, Cousin Lewis was a kind, meticulous man. Standing more than six feet tall with an impressive build, Lewis, now in his 70s, "was most particular about the neatness of his clothes, and took especial care of his shoes and hat," William remembered. "His precepts were so high and true that I bless his memory."[2]

While William enjoyed his time with his relatives, he found teaching school a challenge. Several of the pupils were larger and older than the 18-year-old teacher. He was "specially shy of the big girls, and they told funny stories on me which I should not care to be repeated," he wrote. Some of those stories were passed on to family members as several of the students were his Ross cousins. When the five-month session ended, William thankfully headed home to the farm near Prescott with $103 in his pocket. Within no time, the various members of his family had borrowed most of his earnings.[3]

Late the next summer, William received a second teaching certificate – this one from T.W. Hays, the examiner for Nevada County – and began teaching at a three-month public school for white children near Emmett. Located along the Iron Mountain Railroad, Emmett was a booming little town close enough to his family's farm that William was able to live at home with his parents while teaching there. Although private academies and colleges thrived for the upper grades, segregated public schools were replacing the irregular subscription field schools for elementary education. While children from poorer families now had access to education, many of them still did not take advantage of it. By the mid to late 1880s, 67 percent of the white children in Nevada County attended school while only 52 percent of the black children attended.[4]

After school ended in Emmett, William taught three months at Bluff City, a "post-hamlet" located at a rural crossroad. Since Bluff City was too long of a daily ride from home, he boarded with Bill Jones. When he was not teaching, William read law books morning and evening. The two bachelors had but one lamp – a brass one that smoked copiously. William claimed it every evening after supper so he could pore over *Blackstone's Commentaries*, *Chitty's Pleadings,* or *Rules of Evidence*.[5]

Bluff City was William's last stint as a schoolteacher. Soon after the three-month session ended, David and Tempie gave up the farm and moved into Prescott proper. Made the county seat a few years earlier, Prescott was becoming a shipping center for cotton, lumber, and livestock – thanks to its location on the Iron Mountain Railroad. Several shops, hotels, mills, and churches had sprung up, and a new two-story brick courthouse was in the works. Prescott, like the other railroad towns scattered throughout the state, had plenty of opportunities for those tired of scratching for a living from the land.[6]

With no farm chores to distract him, William took advantage of the opportunities Prescott offered to devote all of his energies to studying law. He lived at home while reading law for a few months in the office of Warren & Mitchel, a prominent law firm in town. C.E. Mitchel had just finished a term as state senator for Hempstead and Nevada counties and was running for

Congress. Preoccupied with politics, Mitchel spent little time in the law office with William. Col. E.A. Warren, the other partner, practiced little law as most of his energy was focused on editing the Prescott newspaper. That meant the young law student had the office pretty much to himself. William described both men as "jovial whole-souled men, [who] took life easy and enjoyed politics, always kind hearted and generous to young fellows coming on in their profession."[7]

While William admired his mentors, "like most nineteenth-century legal apprentices, he did not think very highly of the tutelage that he received," his grandson Morris S. "Buzz" Arnold writes. For the most part, legal apprentices were self-instructed. In his experience, William explained, "the old lawyers seldom ask any questions of the students with reference to books, and the conversation seems to relate to practical matters or incidents of the present time and in detailing their own experiences and successes, their failures never mentioned." William did get some practical experience during his apprenticeship by working briefly with George Christopher, the clerk of the court at Prescott.[8]

After his brief apprenticeship, William applied to be admitted to the bar. At the age of 21, he went before the examining committee, which included George P. Smoote, a noted lawyer and poet who had been appointed by the governor on several occasions as a special state Supreme Court justice. Smoote quizzed William at length on points of law and then recommended him to the court for admission to the Arkansas Bar. "The young man had stood a brilliant examination," Smoote told the court.[9]

Nevada County was part of the Ninth Judicial District in Arkansas. Its circuit court terms began on the first Monday of May and November and lasted two weeks each time. It was easy to tell when court was in session in Prescott, as lawyers and judges from the surrounding counties booked rooms in the hotels, and people from town and the outlying areas packed the courtroom to take in the more interesting cases. Attending court was an entertaining experience that gave people a chance to hear great oratory and juicy gossip. It also gave young lawyers a chance to observe the techniques of the great attorneys and size up any potential legal opponents.[10]

William wasted no time in setting up practice – or as he put it, offering to practice – in Prescott. Immediately upon his admission, he was appointed by the court to defend a freedman. His opponent was Col. John Cook of Texarkana, "a very forceful character and a vigorous and aggressive prosecutor" who frequently attended court at Prescott, where he had once lived. William's memories of that trial revolved around the prosecutor. "I remember Colonel Cook's eyes when he fixed them upon me and called me 'Colonel,'" he wrote. Cook died a few months later with no idea of how his family would become entwined with the young lawyer he had stared down that day in court.[11]

When William's practice did not take off in Prescott, he headed south to Texarkana, Arkansas, in March 1883. The booming, rough-and-tumble railroad town marked a new kind of frontier for the young, optimistic lawyer and others like him who were searching for a beginning, a chance for greatness. By the 1880s, the upstart town in the southwest corner of Arkansas seemed to promise all that and more. Platted by the railroad in 1873, the town was not incorporated until August 10, 1880 – and then over the wishes of a lot of its residents. Col. Cook had represented those petitioning for incorporation. By 1881, the town had become a railroad center attracting hundreds of railroad workers, businesses, entrepreneurs, and professionals. Between 1882 and 1888, it experienced phenomenal growth. Along with the growth came the crime, graft, and opportunity that so often inhabit a boom town.[12]

The city straddled the Arkansas-Texas state line, with businesses multiplying on both sides of the line. Broad Street and State Line Avenue, both 100 feet wide, formed the central business district. The Arkansas side, known as the "East Side," was the county seat for Miller County. It boasted a two-story brick courthouse with a four-cell jail on the ground floor and the courtroom on the upper floor. The East Side also had its own public school system with separate frame school buildings for the black and white students. The growing population included whites, blacks, German immigrants, and immigrants from Eastern Europe. In the early 1880s, the various groups got along relatively well. Black leaders served on the city council along with whites and held positions as law officers. And Texarkana's Jewish community regularly celebrated the High Holy Days with Rev. Charles Goldberg, pastor of the Cumberland Presbyterian Church, serving as rabbi.[13]

Like the Southerners of old, Texarkanians thrived on the individualism and frontier outlook that had settled and civilized other parts of the South. Progress, in itself representing a new frontier to be conquered and tamed, had come to Texarkana in the form of railroads and the accompanying industry. Its promise of prosperity was as seductive as the siren's call of the old frontier. The East Side's population grew from 1,000 in 1877 to more than 2,500 10 years later as people from all over the country gave in to this seduction. With most of the migration coming from the South and Arkansas itself, the new frontier was built on the old foundation. "[T]here was no revolution of basic ideology and no intention of relinquishing the central Southern positions and surrendering bodily to Yankee civilization.... So far from representing a deliberate break with the past, the turn to Progress clearly flowed straight out of that past and constituted in a real sense an emanation from the will to maintain the South in its essential integrity," Cash wrote.[14]

Still struggling with the legacy of the war and Reconstruction, Southerners were on the move in the 1880s. Those who were older had tired of the struggle and were ready to trade their plows for city life. And the children of the war, having come of age, wanted more than the land could provide. They looked to progress for their El Dorado. The Arnold family mirrored this migration. Some of those who had stayed behind in South Carolina followed the new frontier to Arkansas. William's brother Sax moved to Sweetwater, Texas. His Uncle John gave up the farm to move to Texarkana. Even his law tutors, Mitchel and Warren, left Prescott for Texarkana. Thus, no one was surprised when William bought a train ticket for a one-way trip to the border town.[15]

When William arrived with 15 second-hand books, a little old tin or zinc trunk, and $40 in cash, Texarkana still had all the rawness of a frontier – and plenty of business for aspiring lawyers. Besides the criminal fare to occupy the courts, there were numerous disputes between the railroads and individuals as to who owned large parcels of land. William was confident he would have all the business he could handle within a few months. But before he could dive into practice, he had to find an office. "I went around looking up the various stairways, went in and chatted with one or two lawyers and finally came to the office of W.J. Smithers, Justice of Peace, told him I was a lawyer and would like to have an office and a room," William wrote. Smithers took him up the stairs in his ramshackle wooden building and led him down a long, narrow hall lined with several small rooms. When William opened the creaky door to the last room on the left, he noticed holes in the floor and a thick layer of dirt and tobacco juice coating every surface. It wasn't much, but it was a room, and it was available. William rented it for $2.50 a month, a price he considered high at the time. He brought his single bed and mattress, which he had shipped by freight, to his new home and settled in.[16]

The first few nights were unnerving. As soon as William put out the lights and retired for the evening, the other residents of the room emerged from every hole in the floor and walls. "[R]ats, large and small, ran back and forth all the live long night ... but I slept securely in that old building, although one would not have thought it very secure as there were fires in Texarkana at that time nearly every night, and nearly everything in the town was burnt up first and last except that old building," he recalled. Although Judge Smithers charged William for the room, he admitted the young man to his office without charge.

With his living and working space arranged, William explored his home. Everything was new to him — from the hustle of the railroad yards to the tramps walking the rails. Every morning he watched as large gangs of workers passed through town on the Texas and St. Louis Railroad, heading for points in Texas where they were widening the rail bed to standard gauge. Occasionally, he would see a company of black soldiers passing through to the Wild West or a Native American walking along the dusty street, leading his pony and followed by his wife carrying a papoose. He watched in wonder as the brass band from the Monarch Theatre noisily paraded the streets, getting in the way of pedestrians and carriages. The novelty quickly wore off as he had to dodge a tuba once too often. William also saw his share of street fights, of hooligans gambling on the dirt sidewalk, of people begging for money or food. The poorhouse built on the edge of town was an uncomfortable reminder that not everyone who came to Texarkana prospered. But William was young, and the town was young. With the confidence of youth, he looked forward to a bright future in his new home.[17]

William got a taste of what the future would hold when he was introduced to law and order Texarkana style at his first circuit court term in March 1883. What started out as a routine day in the crowded courtroom turned to chaos when Sheriff C.E. Dixon pulled out his gun and shot a Mississippi gambler by the name of Johnston. The sheriff, a prominent Democrat who had an interest in the gambling houses of Texarkana, reportedly had killed or had ordered the killing of six men in and around town. Although the *code duello* had supposedly been banned from the South, violence was still a way of life. Expressed in gunplay, fisticuffs, and knifings, it cut across class lines. Violence had been present in times past, but after the war it became an endemic ugliness that scarred society. Intensified by the shame of defeat, it provided a way to deal with pent-up frustration, a way to demonstrate that the men of the South still had what it took to defend their honor, family, and home. "Guns blazed in banks, courtrooms, and schoolhouses as well as in bars and ginhouses," Southern historian C. Vann Woodward writes.[18]

Although Dixon's killing ways had been overlooked before, he was charged with murder this time. Claiming he shot the man for "traducing the good name" of his wife, the sheriff was acquitted by a jury of his peers – all Southern white men who would brook no insult to womanhood. Dixon was replaced as sheriff in 1884 but re-elected two years later.[19]

18 Planting Roots

Despite this introduction to Texarkana justice, William quickly adjusted to his new life. He hired a carpenter to put in a shelf for his books in Smithers' office and slipped into a routine of continuing his studies, observing other lawyers, and looking for clients. Much of that routine in those early days was reading – even on Sundays. Most afternoons when the sun was not too bright, he could be found on top of an inclined plank awning overlooking Broad Street with a law book in hand. He did his best to ignore the sports who were always up for an impromptu horse race on the dusty street, the men noisily going in and out of the saloons, the people shopping at the stores that were open from 7 a.m. to 10 p.m. seven days a week, the trains pulling into what served as a depot, depositing curious passengers and taking on new ones. Sitting there with a law book in hand while other young lawyers were enjoying their leisure time, William thought he was a living advertisement for his services. His studious habits had him convinced that he could solve any difficult legal question. When potential clients, seeing his public display of scholarship, did not come running to his office, he was astonished that they had not reached this same conclusion.

Starting a practice, even in a town where legal arguments abounded, was not as easy as the idealistic young man had imagined. William blamed his slow start on his retiring personality: "In those early days of study I did not cultivate acquaintances, nor did I mix around with the business interest. I was naturally shrinking and timid and therefore my business was not very extensive for a long time, and another result was that I was unable to pay my board promptly," he wrote. Despite his frugality, the initial $40 he had brought to Texarkana did not last long. Judge Smithers was understanding, but, being a Southern gentleman, William did not like to be in arrears. Thus, when he received a gift of $20 by express mail from Uncle Bill, he was surprised and grateful. He never found out how his uncle knew he needed that exact amount at that time.

William may have been too hard on himself. He recognized years later that it takes most young lawyers a long time to get a start. When he began practicing in Texarkana, he was one of several young attorneys trying to make a name for themselves in a boom town. Many of them stayed a year or two and, not having much success, moved on – frequently to a prosperous career elsewhere. One of his early associates, A.H. Carrigan, left Texarkana to become a district judge in Texas. Another one became a district attorney in Texas. Many of the lawyers, district attorneys, and judges in the Lone Star State in the early 20th century got their start in Arkansas in the late 19th century.

While William did not cultivate clients at first, he did make some connections that assured the occasional work. "Being in Judge Smithers' office brought me some Justice of Peace practice, and lawyers who would be on the other side of a case with me, pending before Judge Smithers would not hesitate to urge before the Judge that he should not decide the case with me because I was in his office," he recalled. "This was extremely mortifying to me, and as a rule he decided against me on that argument, which finally resulted in my calling for a jury in all cases, and by this means I was relieved of the mortification of sure defeat and he was relieved of the embarrassment incident thereto."

The first case William had in Texarkana may have been a result of this arrangement with Smithers. The case was an emotional one involving a young man, a young woman, and a child. "The whole town was stirred up about it," William wrote. "I was on the right side and all the sentiment was in my favor." When he won the case, he earned quite a reputation and made considerable acquaintances. He said the case was still being discussed 30 years later.[1]

William was not as fortunate with his second case – a civil suit against a pawnbroker. A woman had convinced him that Mr. Samuels was trying to sell her stolen wash-pot in his pawnshop. In court, William passionately established that someone had stolen this poor woman's wash-pot and that the pot in the pawnshop was identical to her pot. He went on to argue that not only was it identical, it *was* the stolen pot. Then it was the defense attorney's turn. He called to the stand a hardware man who testified that there were a great many black pots in the world identical to the woman's pot, thus it was doubtful whether one could be identified from another. "I had that sinking feeling inwardly which comes but few times in life.... [T]he loss of the wash-pot case hurt my conscience very much," William wrote, "and I thought that there was no justice in the law." But rather than becoming disillusioned, William grew more passionate in his desire to be a tool in the hand of justice.

Soon after moving into Smithers' office, William found a compatriot in Joe Cook. A few months younger than William, Joe had received a university education – first at the University of Arkansas in Fayetteville and then at Poughkeepsie in New York. After attending the Little Rock Law Class, Joe was admitted to the Arkansas Bar in 1883. As the son of Col. John Cook, Joe had connections with some of the top attorneys in southwest Arkansas. But choosing to go it alone, he rented space from Judge Smithers. The two young lawyers quickly became friends; that friendship led to a partnership with Joe's outgoing, fun-loving personality balancing William's reserve. When business was slow, which it usually was in their first years together, they sat around with their law books in hand. Although they took the law seriously, they enjoyed their partnership. "Both were great tobacco chewers and instead of throwing the quids away, we would throw them upon the roof and they would stick there, and finally it was full," William wrote of those early days. "Judge Smithers would get very angry when he would look up, and would say 'Who in the hell did that.' We would tell him a petit jury did it, and then when Judge would turn his back we would throw another big wad up to hit the ceiling and then look at our books again."[2]

In their more serious moments, the young men sat in on Justice of Peace court proceedings while reading their books. Paul Jones, a brilliant young lawyer of the day, appeared often in the court, facing off against older worthies. "They would speak for hours at a time in the trial of J. P. cases, we would sit back and read or make a pretense of reading part of the time," William wrote, "but there was a deep feeling that some of this business ought to be brought to us...." The lawyers called their firm Arnold & Cook, but during those first years, they acted as partners only when they felt like it. At other times, they took opposing sides of the same case. One of their friends, who served as sheriff after Dixon was ousted, asked them, "What sort of double-barrelled [sic] concern have you got that you sometimes appear as partners and other times on the opposite sides?" Although their loose partnership may have been confusing, it enabled them to get more business.[3]

William and Joe had a lot of competition as Texarkana seemed to be a magnet to the law profession. With so many lawyers in town, the profession was hardly lucrative. When a burglar entered the house of prosecuting attorney Webber to relieve him of his "cash capital," all he got for his troubles was a nickel, three postal cards, half a plug of navy tobacco, and two old copper pennies. In reporting the burglary, newspaper editor E.A. Warren (William's mentor who had moved to Texarkana from Prescott) quipped, "The burglar was doubtless a stranger here or he never would have tackled a Texarkana lawyer." The next day, Webber announced he would recoup his loss by selling vegetables from his market garden.[4]

Although several of the law firms advertised in the local papers, Arnold & Cook did not. Instead, the partners relied on referrals, word of mouth, and what they could pick up by attending court. William also got involved in the community. He joined the Democratic Party, the Fourth Street Methodist Church, and the local Masonic lodge. All three organizations symbolized his ambition and his pursuit of the Southern ideal. And all three completed the circle his father, uncles, and grandfathers had begun. In joining the party, William identified with the Southern cause. In joining the church, he showed his devotion to God and Southern values. In joining the Masonic lodge, he identified with a fraternity of men of the upper classes. "It was what you did in that time if you were 'a prominent Texarkanian,'" William's grandson Richard Arnold said. There was no other path open to William. He had to be a prominent member of his community; he owed it to his ancestors as well as to his descendants.[5]

With his mentor editing the *Daily Texarkana Independent* and the *Weekly Texarkana Independent*, William received plenty of free press identifying him as a future community leader. Looking out for his protégé, Warren frequently included little tidbits about William in his "Local News" column. Sometimes the editor referred to William as a "bright young lawyer;" other times, he ribbed him with comments such as "Dick Arnold feels mighty lonely now" or "Dick Arnold has a new hat. It is of the latest style, and Dick will get a patent for it." The comments showed that William "Dick" Arnold was on the right course.[6]

While such publicity was good, it wasn't building the law practice fast enough for William. He didn't have far to look for inspiration. His father, who had always talked politics but never gotten involved, was elected as city alderman in Prescott in 1883 to complete the term of an alderman who had resigned. David used the position to step into the mayor's office in 1884. David's involvement in city government demonstrated the networking possibilities. While his father was running for mayor in Prescott, William launched his own campaign to become city attorney in Texarkana. Although he had been in town only a year, William thought the campaign was worth a shot. If he won, he'd be able to pay the bills, demonstrate his abilities, and build a clientele. And if he lost, he would have built name recognition, which would help him get clients and position him for a future office. William did not advertise, but he attended party meetings and welcomed opportunities to present his candidacy to the public at political rallies in town. He was defeated by H.L. Grigsby, a jovial person who had lived in Texarkana for a number of years and who had paid his dues to the local Democratic Party. After the election, the two men became good friends, and Grigsby, who also had a private practice, asked William to handle several of his cases.[7]

Although he could have used the money that came with being the city attorney, William remained optimistic about the future. He turned his attention to the state and national elections that fall, attending the Democratic speakings held throughout the county and encouraging the residents to vote the Democratic ticket. Even though Reconstruction had officially ended 10 years earlier, the South needed a Democratic president to do away with its remaining vestiges. The tariffs supported by Northern industrialists hurt farmers and laborers, blocking their path to advancement. And the South feared the passage of the so-called Force Bill, which Congress had threatened to pass several times. Designed to federalize elections in the South, the Force Bill would ensure ongoing Republican control of the old Confederacy. To stop it, the Democrats had to capture the White House. They also wouldn't mind all the patronage that went with the presidency. They were tired of Republican carpetbaggers getting the federal jobs, which included the local postmaster and judiciary appointments.

When they learned Grover Cleveland had won the presidency, the Democrats of Texarkana pulled out all the stops for a celebration that would be unparalleled for years to come. For the first time since the Civil War, the Democrats would occupy the White House. Joe and William saddled up their horses to join hundreds of men in a torchlight horseback procession that paraded through Texarkana the night after the election. Anvils were fired and guns shot as the townspeople gathered to celebrate. For them, it was the final, bittersweet victory of a long war. No one minded the number or length of the speeches as orator after orator tried to outdo the ones before. The local saloons stayed open into the wee hours to allow plenty of time for joyful toasts. "The election of a democrat to the presidency was considered one of the most hopeful and glorious events of modern times so far as the South was concerned," William wrote in a newspaper article commemorating the event. "In the election of Cleveland, the majority of voters of the United States laid aside those questions which related to the Civil War of 1861 and the outrages of Reconstruction times, and the threats which had been hanging over the South for a long time to enact what was known as the force bill in Congress, which authorized federal control of the elections, passed away...."[8]

Encouraged by Democratic victories on the local, state, and national levels, William ran for city recorder in 1885 and won. The position paid him a monthly salary to record the proceedings of city council meetings and serve as the mayor's assistant. "This did not interfere with my practice," he recalled, "in fact, my practice amounted to but very little during those years." As recorder, William assisted Mayors Forster and Schicker, filling in for them when necessary in dispensing justice in the mayor's court, which handled violations of city ordinances. William also found himself dealing with sanitation and nuisance issues, handling residents' complaints, and growing a thick skin as all the ills of the town were blamed on city officials. The position gave him an extensive education in city government while spotlighting the numerous problems facing his adopted home.[9]

Although somewhat on the edge, William had become a part of Texarkana society. During the Christmas holidays, he visited with relatives and joined the other young adults in surrendering themselves "to the bustling joyous influence of St. Nicholas and his crew." The holiday season was filled with evenings of dances, dinners, and receptions, which often featured "candy stew," a favorite concoction. Christmas Day took on a military air as "all day long, the small and the large boys, in double phalanx, kept up, with their Christmas guns, a continued bombardment of everything resembling sadness. Then at night the glittering Christmas trees, on which, both rich and poor, were remembered, [threw] their halo of gladness over the expectant throng, gathered to watch their distribution." William joined the crowds heading to church as "Sunday morning broke amid the peals of the Sabbath bells, and the carols sent up by joyous choirs...." The week between Christmas and New Year's was a continual social whirl as the young people were determined to keep the Yule log burning the entire week so the holiday fun would continue. New Year's ended the holiday spectacle with a round of visitations. The young ladies held "at-homes" for their New Year's Day visitors who went from one house to another for music and refreshments. William most likely joined Joe in the social calls as such calls were a great way to make connections.

And by now, he had several friends who expected visits from the good-looking city recorder.[10]

The holidays were the peak of Texarkana's social season as most social events came to a halt in the spring when all the Christians in town – Catholics, Presbyterians, Baptists, and Methodists – observed Lent. During the 40-day observance, they held no dances, galas, or dinners. Few entertainments came to town, and only the Jewish societies held any celebrations. While social life, for the most part, was at a standstill during the spring, the political life of Texarkana was pulsing as the Democrats prepared for the local elections in early April. William easily won re-election for another year as city recorder. Two other city officers – Grigsby and Treasurer James – also were re-elected. "They had made prompt and excellent officers, and their re-election was a just tribute to most worthy gentlemen," the newspaper said of the three men. A few days after the election, William headed to Hot Springs for a much-needed two-week rest. "[W]e trust he may find perfect relief for his rheumatism," the newspaper said in announcing his departure.[11]

19 Upheaval

William's involvement in city government gave him a front-row view of the danger that results when personal and civic discipline breaks down. Despite its proliferation of lawyers, Texarkana in the 1880s was not known as a city ruled by law and order. With its reputation as a boom town, mild climate, and an abundance of manual labor jobs with the railroads, Texarkana attracted more than its share of transients and troublemakers. People with no stake in the community and no desire to establish ties were not bound by the traditional code of honor that for so long had provided structure to Southern life.

Thus, when the Knights of Labor declared a nationwide war on railroad tycoon Jay Gould, a celebrity of sorts in Texarkana, the city government knew it wouldn't take much to spark violence among the strikers at the Texarkana rail yards. By March 1886, the battlefield had spread to rail yards throughout the Midwest and South as rail workers went on strike, sabotaging trains and tracks. The strikes and the resulting mob violence threatened the routine calm of life across the nation. Since it was a railroad center, Texarkana was affected by whatever affected the railroads.

Hearing rumors that strikers would sabotage the trains in Texarkana, the railroads hesitated to keep their schedules in and out of the town. They couldn't afford to send trains to the Texarkana yards only to have them destroyed. But if no trains came, none of the city's products or resources would get to market. Concerned about the economic impact as well as the safety of the townspeople, city officials, business leaders, and worried citizens met with the Knights of Labor March 22 to discuss the situation. Some of the local leaders of the Knights were respected men in the community. Recognizing that they had as much to lose as their neighbors if things got out of hand, they pledged that the local strike would not interfere with the running of the trains. The citizen group telegraphed the news to the railroads – along with the message, "Send on the trains." But not everyone believed the union leaders could enforce their pledge as the rank-and-file union member had little, if any, sense of loyalty to Texarkana.[1]

The next day, Miller County Sheriff W.T. Hamilton, a member of the Knights' executive committee, summoned a posse of 20 men and stationed them about half a mile from town to protect any trains rolling in. As the 1 p.m. freight train pulled in, about 700 strikers rushed out of the woods and swarmed the tracks. They pulled the switch to sidetrack the train and then killed the engine and separated the cars. When the small posse tried to intervene, several of the deputies were forcibly carried off into the woods. The mob, unchecked, proceeded to the yard where it killed all but one engine and literally took control of the yard. J.H. Trigg, captain of the Gate City Guards, the local militia, telegraphed Arkansas Gov. Simon P. Hughes, who ordered the state militia to Texarkana.[2]

Rather than wait for the state troops to arrive, Trigg summoned the Guards and made plans to march on the mob the next morning. Learning of the plan, a delegation of union members met with Triggs to dissuade him. "I said I had taken an oath to support the constitution and he (a spokesman for the Knights) replied that the Knights would protect me against the authorities, and if necessary keep me out of jail if I disregarded the governor's orders and refused to go out," Triggs told a reporter. Undaunted, Triggs led the Guards into the rail yards at 10 a.m. March 24 and dispersed the mob. While his action took care of the immediate threat, it did not eliminate random acts of sabotage against the railroads. Desperate to protect their property and keep the trains rolling, Iron Mountain officials promised a reward for the capture of anyone interfering with the tracks and trains during the strike. The Gate City Guards, a self-funded local militia, offered its services in exchange for the reward. But when the Guards asked the railroad for the $6,000 reward money, the Iron Mountain refused to pay, saying the militia was just doing its job so it wasn't entitled to the reward. The Guards took the railroad to court for what became a lengthy battle.[3]

Meanwhile the rail strikes continued everywhere, and the nation's focus turned from Texarkana to East St. Louis April 9 as the strikes there grew deadly. A crowd of strikers met at the relay depot that afternoon to march on the railroad yards in an effort to stop newly hired scabs from working and to keep the trains stalled. The strikers were met by railroad guards, who ordered them to disperse. The strikers refused. Instead, they rushed the yard, running en masse into a barrage of gunfire as the guards started shooting. Within minutes, six strikers lay dead.[4]

Meanwhile, a crowd of 300 strikers had gathered at the nearby Louisville and Nashville yards to jeer at the scabs and railroad officials. Fearing the worst, several armed deputies for the railroad opened fire on the screaming mob, killing three men and a woman. As the frightened strikers ran from the yards, the deputies continued shooting at their backs. Shouts of "To arms! To Arms!" rang out as women and children rushed out of their houses to join the excitement. As the crowd calmed a bit, several leading strikers rallied support and drew their revolvers, swearing they would drive all the deputies out of the city. The eight deputies involved in the shootings surrendered to the police, claiming they were fired upon first.[5]

Early the next morning, devastating fires were set at three or four locations in East St. Louis, destroying $100,000 in property. "It looks as if the entire town will be burned," the *Daily Texarkana Independent* reported on the situation. The fires were blamed on the strikers, and the violence spread from East St. Louis throughout the country. In Argenta, a small town close to Texarkana, strikers shot it out with deputies at the railroad yards. More than 100 shots were exchanged, and two strikers were reportedly killed. Deputy Sheriff Ham Williams was seriously injured. An investigation into the shootout revealed both sides may have been drunk at the time.[6]

The tension eased a bit across the country when the Illinois militia, armed with artillery and heavy machines, moved into the East St. Louis railroad grounds to disperse the mobs and restore peace. The arrival of the militia dampened the spirit of strikers all along the Missouri-Pacific line from East St. Louis to Deniston, Texas. Many of the strikers disbanded and headed home; others remained peacefully on the picket line. But the labor unrest spread from the railroad to other industries, giving rise to new warnings throughout the South that echoed the antebellum fears of slave revolts. "[Northern] adventurers and meddlers are at work organizing some kind of secret societies amongst the colored men in the country.... [A]bout the time the crops need attention, they will create discord and strife among the hands and induce them to quit work," the Texarkana newspaper warned local farmers. While such rumors, sown at opportune times, rarely proved true, they fueled the increasing racism and paranoia of the South.[7]

The people of Texarkana had reason to fear an agricultural strike, but they had to deal with the more imminent rail strikes, which were still disruptive despite the lack of violence. Pamphlets calling for more strikes were circulating in the Iron Mountain yards in Texarkana. The strikers published a "manifesto" addressed to the traveling public "in the interest of humanity, and those who may become the innocent victims of corporate cupidity." The manifesto proclaimed that since most of the experienced railroad workers had been replaced with the "bungling work of unskilled men," those who traveled by rail would be risking life and limb. "[W]e feel it a duty to warn the traveling public against the condition of the Missouri Pacific, Iron Mountain and Missouri, Kansas and Texas railways, which are running with a fourth of their necessary force and those they have are a class who can never get employment save when good and experienced men are on strike."[8]

The stoppage of freight trains across the nation depressed the lumber business, which was one of Texarkana's leading industries. "[I]t looked for a time as if all the mills would be forced to close," the local paper reported. Strikers in Chicago were so determined that no freight trains would move from the Lake Shore yards that the railroad had to threaten to send in 150 or more sheriff's deputies and 50 Pinkerton detectives to restore its control over its own property.[9]

To further the workers' cause, the Knights of Labor tried to raise $10,000 to $20,000 to help the strikers. It also called for a national boycott of Western Union and any company that did business with it. News of the boycott was accompanied by reports that strikers had been arrested for tampering with telegraph wires. The Texarkana strike grew violent once again when a gang of about 25 men slipped into the Iron Mountain yards at 11 p.m. April 21 and shot into some of the cars sitting in the yard. The bullets barely missed the switchman. The gang fled into the woods when the sheriff's men arrived.[10]

The next day, Texarkana was hit again – but this time with an economic blow. Nearly 500 employees of the Missouri Car Foundry joined the Missouri-Pacific strike that morning. The company had been the sole provider of cars for both the Missouri-Pacific and Iron Mountain roads since the strike began. With the foundry on strike, the railroads could hardly keep trains moving on the track, let alone on schedule. The nation had become dependent on the railroads to move its crops, resources, and manufactured products. With trains idled by the strikes, business was paralyzed.[11]

Strikes were contagious that spring. The newsboys struck against the *Detroit Evening News*; 450 billiard table makers walked off the job; schoolboys across the country struck for shorter hours or longer recesses. In Texarkana, "the colored cooks and washerwomen ... formed an association and will make a demand for higher wages and shorter hours of labor," the local newspaper reported. "Housewives would do well to be ready for the 'strike' and with their accustomed promptness and cheerfulness prepare to invade the kitchen. Like other strikes it will prove disastrous to the strikers...."[12]

While strikes of all kinds continued to disrupt daily life, Congress appointed a committee to investigate the railroad strike, which was beginning to wind down. Texarkana Mayor C.C. Dorrian, Capt. Trigg, and businessman J.H. Wooten went to Washington to testify before a congressional committee April 27 about the violence in Texarkana. A politician who knew many Knights had voted to put him in office, Dorrian told the committee that "the objectives and aims of the Knights of Labor in its organization might be good, but the conduct of many of them during the strike has been socialistic."[13]

During the final days of the strike, William was recuperating from the latest city elections in Hot Springs. The day after he returned from his rest, the Knights of Labor called off its nationwide strike and ordered its members to return to work. But when the men reported to work May 4 in Texarkana and at rail yards throughout the country, they were told their jobs had been given to others and that their services were no longer required. Meanwhile, the congressional committee took its investigation on the road to towns hardest hit by the strike. The committee held a three-hour hearing at Conductors Hall in Texarkana May 11 before traveling to Little Rock to examine witnesses there. The people of Texarkana thought the hearing was a waste of time as the primary focus seemed to be on the impact the strike had on business. "That the strike paralyzed business was a known fact before the investigation began," the *Texarkana Independent* reported, "hence we can see no good sense in spending time and money in an effort to obtain that which everybody already knows."[14]

The aftermath of the strikes lasted more than a year in Texarkana as the Gate City Guards battled it out in court with the Iron Mountain Railroad over the reward the militia thought was its due for apprehending railroad vandals. Certain it would not get a fair hearing in Miller County, the railroad was granted a change of venue to Nevada County. Like William, many Texarkanians had ties to the Prescott area. So when the case was to be tried May 10, 1887, in Prescott, several community leaders went up for the trial. William, who was one of the most faithful city officials, missed a city council meeting to attend the court session. After a one-day trial, the Nevada County jury awarded the Gate City Guards $6,000. Ignoring the community outcry, the railroad refused to yield and appealed the decision to the state Supreme Court two weeks later.[15]

The disregard for law and order had been a problem in Texarkana before the strikes, but it seemed to escalate that spring. Almost nightly, thieves and burglars took what they wanted from Texarkana businesses and homes, sometimes using arson to cover their deeds. Some of the burglars were so brazen that they boldly rifled through houses while the owners slept. This disrespect for the law and the rights of others bothered the respectable citizens of Texarkana who hoped to build a future there for themselves and their children. While the strikes may have provided the initial justification for this rash of crime, the laxity of Texarkana's law enforcement provided the opportunity. Editor Warren went so far as to blame the thefts and burglaries on the indifference of the police, claiming in the pages of his paper that some deputies "are seen gambling at night when they should be in the streets." Soon after the strikes, the *Independent* began receiving several anonymous letters threatening to burn down the office. At first Warren treated the letters as a joke, but then he started to take them a little more seriously. Rather than trust the local law enforcement, Warren turned the letters over to private detectives.[16]

Another incident that month seemed to prove the editor's case against local law enforcement when West Side City Marshal George Edwards physically attacked a minister at an open air meeting. Traveling evangelist Wolfe had come to Texarkana in May 1886 to hold a series of revivals, jointly sponsored by several of the local churches. Clad in his ministerial cloak, Wolfe, accompanied by several church leaders, was standing next to a large red wagon parked on the Texas side of Broad Street the evening of May 11. A large crowd had gathered around the wagon to hear Wolfe's sermon. When Edwards saw the gathering, he interrupted Wolfe, demanding to see his license or authority for the meeting. Wolfe told Edwards he didn't need a license as he was a minister. Infuriated by what he considered Wolfe's arrogance and unwarranted contempt, Edwards flew into a rage and knocked the minister down. "My act was in hasty retaliation for what I, at the time, thought to be an open insult, directed at me," Edwards said later. Several prominent citizens attending the meeting denounced Edwards and asked Wolfe to continue preaching. Overwhelmed by the cheers offered at the conclusion of his sermon, Wolfe promised to preach at the same place two nights later.[17]

Outraged by Edwards' conduct, a large number of prominent citizens, mostly from the East Side, met the next day at the law office of Henry and Estes to discuss the proper way to handle this affront. They called for a mass meeting to be held that afternoon at the Bowie County Courthouse on the Texas side. Word of the meeting spread quickly through town, and Edwards was asked to represent himself. When the appointed time arrived, an immense crowd had gathered at the courthouse, but Edwards, who knew the ways of mob justice, wasn't to be found. The group elected Joe Cook secretary and then listened as several community leaders – including Cook, C.E. Mitchel, and E.A. Warren – spoke out against Edwards. They denounced him as an atheist who hated Christians and called for his dismissal as city marshal. The group calmed down after appointing a committee of five to draw up resolutions. The resolution that was adopted required Texarkana, Texas, "to denounce an outrage of a character so unwarranted and unnecessary."[18]

Knowing his job was at stake, Edwards published an apology addressed to the citizens of Texarkana in the *Independent* the next day. "[H]ad I known that the meeting called yesterday would have been as conservative as it proved to be, I would have taken the occasion to explain my position and apologized for my seemingly inexcusable action," he wrote. He admitted he had been "a little hasty" in his dealings with Wolfe and acknowledged that while he was not a Christian himself, he was "the friend of all good people."[19]

Despite his apology, Edwards was charged with official misconduct. When the West Side City Council convened May 24 to hear the case, Edwards' attorney moved to quash the complaint on the ground that it was made by a Texarkana, Arkansas, resident. After a lengthy debate, the city attorney and city council declared the attorney's objection was valid and dropped the charge against Edwards. The people on the East Side – many of whom were instrumental in denouncing Edwards – took great offense at what they saw as corruption of the law. Warren used his paper to take the West Side to task. "It is a nice law that will permit offenders to go 'scot free' simply because they may outrage some non-resident," he wrote. Warren's attack led West

Side Mayor Henderson, who disagreed with the council's action, to clarify the issue, saying the case against Edwards was an impeachment – not a criminal prosecution. As such, the city council thought the case should have been brought by a Texarkana, Texas, resident. Warren insisted on having the final word, stating that it was still a "devil of a law."[20]

20   Politics, Texarkana Style

Official misconduct was not limited to Texarkana law enforcement. Statewide, corruption had been a problem ever since the war. In many places, it had become a joke. When the state Speaker of the House asked if there was a member on the floor who would pretend to deny that nine ballot boxes were stolen from the clerk's office in Pulaski County, a Pulaski legislator quickly denied the charge. "Only six were stolen," he said. In Texarkana, corruption wore a different guise. While there were those officials who took bribes, looked the other way, or pocketed public funds and votes, corruption had become a political tool.[1]

By charging an official with corruption, a political party could hope to unseat him. Such was the case with William's mentor C.E. Mitchel, who had been elected as circuit judge in Texarkana. Although the Democrats had regained control of the General Assembly and most state and local offices by this time, federal judicial appointments, made by Republican presidents, went mostly to Republicans. Mitchel, an ambitious man with his sights on a federal position, had quit the Miller County Democrats and joined the Republicans after being elected circuit judge. While some Democrats continued to support him, most of them hated him, seeing him as a traitor who catered to the freedmen and the few scalawags left from the days of Reconstruction.

Mitchel's party switch led to allegations of misconduct. Local Democrats started rumors alleging that Mitchel was incompetent in handling court affairs. As a result, the Arkansas General Assembly appointed a committee in May 1886 to investigate all the accords and proceedings of Miller County, specifically the December 1885 term of the Miller Circuit Court over which Mitchel had presided. The investigating committee, realizing early on that the charges were part of a political ploy, didn't want to play games. In advertising its hearing in Texarkana, the committee asked "all persons interested, and especially those who are trying to manufacture a little cheap capital to be used in their own interest, to come forward and by specific charges assist the committee in the work, or their assertions ... will be branded as prevarications from the truth."[2]

William had always thought a great deal of the judge and didn't want to see him unfairly maligned. That was not the purpose of politics. Although an ardent Democrat, William often found himself disagreeing with a strong faction of the county party, which was controlled by Dixon and other established Democrats known as "the colonels." This group tried to strong-arm the party in an effort to preserve the status quo, which benefited them. The other faction, known as "the kids," stood for law and order and progress. Made up of young, ambitious lawyers and businessmen, "the kids" saw politics as a way to create a better future rather than as a power grab. Despite these disagreements, the Miller County Democrats were united in wanting one of their own as circuit judge, and they thought William stood a good chance of unseating Mitchel.[3]

Thus, the *Little Rock Gazette* announced May 22, 1886, that Miller County would support William H. Arnold for circuit judge. The announcement put William in a bind. He wanted to be a judge someday, so he couldn't offend the Democrats and ruin future prospects. But he wasn't ready to take on his mentor. As soon as the *Gazette* hit the streets of Texarkana, William spoke to *Independent* editor Warren, Mitchel's former law partner. William went on the record to deny that he would seek the post. His excuse? His promise to be best man at a friend's wedding had "necessitated such a large expenditure of cash for clothes that it [would] be impossible for him to raise funds sufficient to enter the contest for judicial honors."[4]

Although he declined the potential judicial nomination, William continued to pay his dues to the Democratic Party, working along with Joe behind the scenes and speaking at public rallies. More than a month before candidates would announce their intentions to run that spring, the county and state campaigns took on a military feel as the Democrats evoked grand visions of Southern patriotism as a way to bring turncoats back to the fold. "Democrats, look to your laurels! Wake up and get to business," the *Independent* challenged. "The time is short. Take the old democratic banner and throw her to the breeze again. You have work to do. A hard battle is anticipated. Follow the old banner and fear not. Your leaders are true and tried veterans ... and like Longstreet at Fredericksburg, are ready for the fight. Some of the soldier democrats have wavered and fallen back. Encourage them, rally them and bring them back."[5]

With their involvement in the Democratic Party and William's position as city recorder, William and Joe eventually got their practice firmly established. Once business started coming their way, they got nearly all of the Justice of Peace cases in Texarkana. As their cases multiplied, they dispensed with the double-barreled feature. They had some remarkable trials in Smithers' court, which naturally brought them cases in other courts. Within a decade, their firm had the second largest practice in the city. But their growing prosperity didn't affect their frugality. While the firm still refused to advertise in the newspaper, William paid for a small ad in 1886 to announce that he had "a fine lot of second hand shoes" that he would dispose of cheap. And Joe joined his brother John Cook and a few other men in advertising that they would be peddling watermelons on College Hill one afternoon.[6]

His position and increasing success mandated that William become more social. Recognizing that he was now a "local dignitary," William rose to the occasion and overcame what natural shyness he had left. Thus, he allowed Joe to shut down the office on a fine May afternoon so the two of them could join a picnic excursion. They walked to the State Line Depot where they joined about 100 other young people who crowded onto the special train for the 20-minute ride to Clear Lake station. From there they walked about 300 yards to the picnic grounds, which included a large pavilion surrounded by beautiful shade trees on the banks of the "finest lake in the vicinity of Texarkana." As soon as the lake was in sight, the picnickers rushed to secure boats for the afternoon. Joe rented a boat for the two of them and, most likely, their dates. As the boat drifted on the water, they listened to the strains of a local string band playing in the pavilion. It was the final event of the spring season as many of the wealthier residents would be leaving for cooler climes. "[A]lthough the void created here by so many precious absentees will be cruel and sad, we can manage to stand it, by the help of Ben Foreman's ice cream parlor, Mr. Dick Arnold and other refrigerating influences," the society columnist wrote. William took such ribbing in stride. It was a sign that he was recognized as a part of Texarkana life.[7]

For those who stayed in town, the highlight of summer was the semi-annual Miller County circuit court session. Like most of the attorneys in town (and the townspeople, for that matter), William and Joe lived for the court sessions that provided entertainment as well as a continuing legal education and an opportunity to publicly demonstrate their growing talents. The day before a session was to begin, lawyers from all over the region would arrive in town – by train, stagecoach, and horseback. And people, black and white, from the surrounding countryside came in for the spectacle. Some of the older visiting lawyers had attained almost celebrity status, so their comings and goings were duly noted in the local papers. The sessions were accompanied by much wining and dining and organized social events.

During the June 1886 court session, a daylong picnic had been arranged at Old River. The court recessed for the entire Tuesday so all the lawyers could enjoy the festivities. The picnickers, many of them packing their customary guns, arrived at the depot first thing Tuesday morning where they were greeted by the Texarkana cornet band. As the train backed up to the round house for a 10-minute delay, the band entertained the riders with a short concert. All along the way to the picnic grounds, the train stopped to pick up more revelers. Once at Old River, the picnickers got "drunk" on ice cream while the band performed again. Dinner followed a target-shooting competition. All the while, trains continued to drop off more picnickers. The event turned serious after dinner when Joe introduced several dignitaries, who delivered political speeches. Once the speeches ended, the band began to play and the picnic turned into an outdoor dance.[8]

The next day was not quite business as usual when court resumed. The session was disrupted almost before it began when a black man, finding no seat in the packed courtroom, "seated himself in the lap of [a] white man, who earnestly protested but the colored man refused to get up, when very properly the white man gave him a 'chuck' under the ear," the *Independent* reported. Judge Lawrence Byrne, who was filling in for Judge Mitchel, fined both men and ordered them to jail. The judge later relented and remitted the punishment.[9]

The incident created more than a few laughs in both the white and black communities. Racism, while definitely present in Texarkana, had not yet become a widespread institution of intense hatred. Feelings of white superiority led to two distinct communities – each with its own schools, neighborhoods, and churches – on both sides of the state line. But respectable African Americans in Texarkana had more opportunities and earned more esteem from their white neighbors than they would in the future. African Americans were elected – by black and white voters – to serve as aldermen and hired as police on the East Side into the late 1880s. During the June court session, the black community held large Emancipation Day celebrations. Not only did the white community contribute financially to the festivities, many whites attended the barbecues and speeches. Two barbecue dinners were held – one at the city skating rink and one at Proctor Springs. Speakers included S.J. Hollingsworth, a black attorney from Pine Bluff, and several local black dignitaries.[10]

Another event that occurred that court session boosted the stature of the Arnold & Cook law firm. By this time, Joe was building a name for himself in criminal law and was frequently appointed to serve as one of several defense attorneys in serious cases. While circuit court was in session, Joe received word that Gov. Hughes had commuted the death sentence of one of his clients. Jerry Lewis, who had been convicted of rape in Miller County, "owes his life to the faithful work of his attorneys," the local paper commented. That kind of success and publicity helped Joe establish his reputation as a top-notch criminal attorney and build the law firm.[11]

Although William often helped Joe with his cases, he wasn't that interested in criminal law. An advocate of law and order, he wanted to help develop Texarkana, to make it a modern city that self-respecting citizens would be proud to call home. Both his legal and social interests were directed at developing legitimate business interests in the city. Recognizing that the city needed to be business friendly and aggressive in pursuing new companies and industries, William was convinced that conventions were the way to bring businessmen to Texarkana to see first hand what it had to offer. One of his first efforts was to land the regional lumbermen's convention. Throughout the convention, William represented the city with pride and enthusiasm. And even though he wasn't a dancer, he stood out in his finery – a diamond-cut parliamentary swallowtail coat and a semi-stovepipe hat – at the Lumberman's Ball. "It became him very nicely," the society columnist for the *Independent* wrote of William's attire.[12]

Many of the visiting lumbermen were pleasantly surprised by what they found in Texarkana. It was not a quiet sleepy little town that went to bed at sundown. A variety of businesses – besides the saloons, gambling houses, and brothels – remained open until 10 p.m. or later. A favorite late night stop was the ice cream parlor, where the newly introduced milkshake was marketed as a healthy tonic for the summer heat. By 1886, the city also boasted limited telephone service, electric lights, and a water system.[13]

But many of the bugs had yet to be worked out of these innovations, and the city was plagued with nuisances from its past – problems common in many small towns of the day. Abandoned wells were left open throughout the city, creating traps for livestock and people. Soon after the lumbermen left, a horse fell into an old well behind the new Benefield Hotel and was crippled. "This is the second horse that has fallen into this well," the *Independent* complained as it called on the city to force property owners to be responsible for the old wells. A few days later, a cow wandered into a downtown business, resulting in complaints about the increasing number of cows in the streets. Many townspeople had milkpens next to their houses with gates facing the streets rather than the alleys. The cows would get out and stand in the sidewalks, forcing frightened women and children to walk in the dusty or muddy roads.[14]

All the modern conveniences the city boasted about weren't quite so convenient – yet. The city's waste disposal service consisted of a scavenger crew and wagon that rolled through the streets at night, picking up whatever waste was lying around. By the time the wagon rolled past the ice cream parlor on State Line Avenue, it was loaded with decaying food and animal carcasses and waste. The crowd of ladies enjoying their ice cream virtually gagged at the awful stench. Editor Warren called on the city to delay the scavenger wagon until after midnight when all the businesses had closed for the day.[15]

The utilities, all privately owned, also had their share of problems. Lightning hit the telephone office July 6, 1886, burning out all the instruments and frightening the operators. A week later, the city was left without electric lights when someone broke the circuit. The incident prompted the Texarkana Ice Company, which owned the electric system, to place the following notice in the local papers: "Consumers of electric lights should see that no one touches or handles the lamps, wire or anything connected therewith, as to do so at one place throws off all the lights in the city.... Parties interfering with anything connected with the lights will certainly be prosecuted and may also be killed or seriously hurt in fingering with them."[16]

As city recorder, William often was called upon to respond to complaints or to serve on committees appointed to investigate such problems, which always seemed to get worse in the heat of the summer. But in 1886, he earned a brief reprieve from city problem-solving when he got to attend the Democratic 21st District Senatorial Convention in Lewisville. The convention began at 10 a.m. July 8 with a full delegation present from Miller, Lafayette, and Columbia counties – the three counties in the district. The delegates quickly deadlocked as they strictly adhered to the instructions they had received from their county committees, leaving each candidate with four votes. After 276 ballots, the convention adjourned at 5 p.m. As the delegates left the room, they expressed little hope for a resolution the next day as they all vowed they had come to stay. To ease the tension, Judge Webber entertained the tired delegates after dinner that night with violin music while a fresh keg of beer was brought in.[17]

When William returned to Texarkana two days later, he reported the convention was still deadlocked after 825 ballots. Even though the delegates were meeting through the weekend, William saw little prospect for a nomination. Each county was insistent on nominating its favorite son. A break came the next week when the delegates from Columbia County, tired of the game, left the convention in a huff. More than 2,100 ballots had been taken with no nominee. With the Columbia delegates gone, one of the Lafayette delegates joined those from Miller County to nominate Judge Byrne for state senate.[18]

Flush with their victory, the Miller County delegation returned home where the summer campaign season for county and state races was in full swing. Although a few Republicans still went through the motion of running for county office, everyone knew that whoever won the Democratic nomination would be elected. And Democrats knew better than to buck their party leadership. Thus, when Democrats put their name out for consideration, they included the line: "subject to the action of the democratic party." Even those running for re-election – such as Sheriff Hamilton – knew they needed the party's approval to run. But this year there was a question of who was speaking for the party. The "colonels" of the party liked to nominate by convention rather than by primary as they had more control over the outcome at a convention. They saw the party as their private property; it was their right to control the issues, the candidates, and the platform. As early as May, the colonels had floated four names for the top county positions, calling on all Democrats to support these four leaders.[19]

In the past, the colonels had been able to get by with such tactics. All political aspirants or hopeful lawyers in Miller County had recognized that they needed to reach an understanding with the colonels or they would be condemned to almost certain failure. But "the kids" were growing up. Infuriated by the unwarranted power grab, they condemned the colonels for naming candidates before the county nominating convention was held at the end of July. The delegates to the convention wouldn't even be selected until mid-July. Tired of the control of the colonels, the kids saw the township conventions as a way to stack the county nominating convention in their favor.[20]

But even the township conventions were contentious. William and Joe attended the Garland Township Democratic Convention July 17. After a spirited contest, William was elected secretary of the convention. He and Joe also were elected as delegates to the county convention and given strict instructions on which candidates to vote for. When the county convention was held more than a week later, four townships refused to participate. They wanted to select candidates through primaries rather than a nominating convention. William was appointed to serve on a committee that would confer with the delegates from those townships and find a way to resolve the issue.[21]

Meanwhile, delegates from the other townships began to nominate candidates. When one of the colonels nominated Judge E.F. Friedell for county and probate judge, the kids balked. Friedell was one of the candidates the colonels had pushed back in May. Joe and William were so vocal in their opposition to the colonels that editor Warren remarked, "Jo Cook and Dick Arnold are no sardines in conventions." To avoid verbal bloodshed, the delegates voted to adjourn for a week to let tempers calm. As soon as the rest of the delegates left, the central committee leadership – comprised mostly of the colonels – met and came up with a compromise: A nominating convention would be held August 19 but the townships would hold primaries the week before. "This call ... was made in the interest of harmony," Warren reported, and to ease the differences between the colonels and the kids.[22]

Although the central committee had set August 19 as the date for the nominating convention, the county delegates honored the original adjournment date and met July 30. Once again, the same four townships refused to send delegates. Using this absence as an excuse, Paul Jones, one of the colonels, moved to adjourn, but his motion failed 17-13. Disgusted, all those who had voted for adjournment left the convention. With the floor to themselves, the kids nominated a slate of candidates for the county races. The central committee named its own slate when it met August 19. Its candidates, which included Friedell for county judge and Dixon for sheriff, ran in the general election. Friedell won, but Dixon engaged in a hotly contested race with Judge Thomas Orr, the Republican candidate.[23]

The division in the party ranks was obvious in the sheriff's race, which was literally too close to call. Had Dixon had the full support of the party, he would have won the race by a large margin. However, Dixon had fashioned himself as an upper class gang leader who profited from much of the crime in town. He also came off as a racist and bully, having killed several men in disagreements. Decent people who could put politics aside would have voted for anyone other than Dixon. Although Orr won the election, Dixon had himself declared the winner. Orr contested the election in circuit court, which was presided over by Mitchel, a Republican; the court ruled in Orr's favor. Having already resumed the office of sheriff, Dixon appealed to the state Supreme Court, which upheld the lower court's ruling June 12, 1887. Defeated by the courts, Dixon announced he would have everything ready to turn over to Orr within 15 days – nearly a year after he had illegally usurped the office.[24]

21   Progress and Problems

Despite the dirty politics that obstructed the progress of the town and county, William had reason to anticipate the new year in Texarkana. As he walked to the New Year's Eve program at the Fourth Street Methodist Episcopal Church, he looked forward to a year of personal and civic progress. When the music and program gave way to a time of prayer, he joined the large crowd in praying for the community leaders – himself included – and the future of their city. The prayers ended just as the church bells rang out across town, announcing the new year. The locomotives in the train yards and the manufacturing firms blew their whistles. And men and boys ran into the streets to shoot their guns. The resulting cacophony lasted several minutes. It was official. 1887 had arrived.[1]

William woke up that New Year's morning to a world covered in snow. Undeterred, he dressed in his finest and headed for church to join the faithful few for the Sunday morning worship. Once again "prayers were sent up to heaven, imploring Providence to guide and protect us through the coming year, and rendering Him thanks for His manifold blessings during the year gone by," the local paper reported. After church, William made the customary New Year's calls, which lasted all afternoon and into the evening. His attention was focused on one "fair angel" – Jessie Cook, Joe's little sister.[2]

While romance may have been in William's heart as the new year broke, concern about the future lay heavy on his mind. Just as William was feeling the firm was established enough to ask Jessie to marry him, Joe started getting restless. He wanted out – out of the practice and out of Texarkana. Joe sold his share of the law firm to Professor G.A. Hays, a fellow Mason and a prominent Democrat, that January and headed to Florida to dwell among the orange groves and magnolias. A "real estate dealer" rather than a lawyer, Hays had great ambition and some expendable capital. The new firm of Arnold & Hays purchased the complete set of *Arkansas Reports* from Judge Mitchel and then announced it was open for business January 18 as a collection agency. A few days later, Hays received a commission from Gov. Hughes to serve as a notary public. Like William's old firm, the new one didn't advertise, but Hays took out large ads listing his properties.[3]

The new partnership taught William a thing or two about real estate, but running a collection agency was not his goal in life. He wondered if he and Joe had been too hasty when Joe returned from Florida a few weeks later and announced he would stay in Texarkana after all. William continued to work with Hays a while longer, but by April, Cook & Arnold was in business and Hays had been appointed deputy U.S. district clerk for the future Texarkana branch office of the federal court.[4]

The changes in William's professional life were reflective of the changes taking place in the city. "Texarkana is just now, as it were, in a chrysalis state – arising from a lethargy and assuming city proportions," one of the local papers reported. "Public improvements of every character are being pushed to the front – our enterprising people are wide awake.... Texarkana is no longer a 'one-horse town.' It is assuming city airs, and is in fact a city in wealth, intelligence and population...."[5]

By 1887, the city had a lot to be proud of. Lush vineyards and an oak forest covered the hilly countryside leading up to the city, which now boasted a population of 8,000 equally divided between the Texas and Arkansas sides. The Texas side of the city had water works and electric lights. The Arkansas side was improving its electric system and water works. A street railroad was being discussed, and gas works and incandescent lights were expected in the near future in both sides of the city. The Arkansas town had a large number of stores, two banks, two new hotels that cost more than $35,000 each, one of the most elegant Masonic halls in the Southwest, more than 50 new brick homes, and another 100 residences under construction. While the cotton and timber industries were vital to the city's economy, the railroads were the core. Each day an average of 12 cars of freight came to Texarkana and another 200 passed through the town en route to other cities.[6]

Yes, William and the other townspeople had a lot to be thankful for. But there still was a lot to do to make Texarkana the progressive city of their dreams. The businesses along Broad Street, one of the city's two major thoroughfares, swept their trash onto the street for the scavenger wagons to pick up at night. In the meantime, everyone coming to the business district had to be on the lookout for the garbage littering the street. Having no sewer system, businesses let their sewage run out to either the front or the rear of their buildings; a large pool of foul water had collected in front of Citizens Bank, making it impossible to enter the bank without sloshing through the cesspool. "[T]he unsightly and obnoxious sewer is not made so by their (the bank's) fault alone but from slops and water from Mr. Joe Longinotti's saloon," C.C. Burke, a West Side alderman and chairman of the Sanitation Committee, said in his annual report.[7]

The sanitation committee also took issue with the West Side City Council allowing J.M. Benefield to discharge the sewer from his new hotel into the crossing of the Deutschmann Canal at Broad Street. "The deposit of excrement stopping right in the midst of the populous portion of our city cannot but be fraught with evil that in the near future [may] prostrate our fair city with disease and death," Burke warned.[8]

The city had other problems that created bad impressions for visitors and people passing through on the trains. Although the railroads enriched the city, they were not responsible corporate citizens. In his report, Burke singled out the deplorable conditions at the Texas & Pacific Railroad depot. His committee found the reception room way too small and objected to allowing men to smoke, chew, and drink in the same room where ladies waited for the train. The committee also inspected the public water closets at the depot. "[T]o our horror and disgust, we witnessed one of the most unsightly and disgusting sights it has ever been our misfortune to witness," Burke reported. "They were full to overflowing, and we were informed by the porter that he had to pack the excrement down to make room for more." It looked as if the toilets had not been cleaned since they had been installed. And the committee took issue with the railroad allowing both sexes to use the same facilities. There were no locks on the doors, so there was no privacy for men or women.[9]

Such irresponsibility on the part of the railroads grated on the people trying so hard to clean up their town and make it a city to be proud of. Used to having their hands in the pockets of congressmen and, thus, getting immunity for all their wrongdoings, the railroads often ran roughshod over the rights of local citizens, who, in turn, viewed them as a necessary evil. It didn't take much to get the townspeople in an uproar over the railroads' imperial attitude. One sore spot in Texarkana was how long trains would be parked at the crossing at College Hill, a newer but highly populated part of town. Anyone going to and from town from College Hill had no alternative but to wait for the trains to pass. "The matter is getting to be a nuisance, an outrage upon the citizens that are compelled to go over the crossings," editor Warren commented, "and the railroads don't seem to care a continental.... [W]e fail to see where Texarkana is so peculiarly indebted to the Iron Mt. railroad that her people should continue to tamely submit to all these impositions. If that road is contributing in any matter whatever towards the advancement of this city, we fail to see it, and if its officers and managers have for a long time entertained any friendship for us that friendship has been 'severely' 'hid under a bushel.'"[10]

While city officials were nearly helpless in forcing the railroads to improve their community relations, they had plenty of problems they could fix. A major complaint heard often in town concerned the growing number of vendors and loiterers blocking the streets and sidewalks. The townspeople didn't so much mind the local farmers and food vendors who loudly advertised their produce, which they sold from carts and wagons parked along the road. But the traveling auctioneers who commonly set up shop in the streets were a different matter; some sold their wares, others attracted crowds with lotteries and shell games. The lottery business, in particular, drew such large crowds that pedestrians couldn't get through the streets to conduct legitimate business. "They add nothing whatever to our good name," the *Independent* said, as it raised concerns about swindlers and "fakirism."[11]

Adding to the noise and clutter on the streets were the bootblacks – both black and white – who would set up their boxes on the busiest corners, scattering their brushes all over the sidewalk. But rather than tending to business, they would draw big rings in the ground so they could shoot marbles in a game of "keeps" that was accompanied by foul, blasphemous language. The gambling game often resulted in loud fistfights that sometimes endangered passersby. The daily street scene was not complete without the drunks lying unconscious in the dirt or making loud, obscene remarks to the ladies they stumbled past. Then there were the teenagers of every race and color who spent their idle time throwing rocks and bottles in a reckless manner while intentionally blocking busy sidewalks.[12]

Although city officials could do something about these problems, they rarely did. And when law enforcement officers acted, they had to be forced by public outrage and tended to be heavy handed. The day after the *Independent* complained that no police had been around when three ladies were forced to cross to the other side of Broad Street because the side they had been walking on "was blockaded by drunken noisy men of all colors and nationalities," the police announced they had arrested all the men. Coming upon a drunk sleeping in the street, members of the fire department hosed him to wake him up. When he got angry, they hosed him again. But more often than not, the public cries for law and order went unheard as the police, in full uniform, sat their watch at the gambling tables.[13]

The gambling houses, brothels, and saloons were another issue that did not sit well with Texarkana's growing middle class. If Texarkana were going to succeed as a modern city, its reputation of being a wild frontier town with all the trappings had to be changed. But not everyone in Texarkana – especially those on the West Side – agreed with this middle-class vision. The state of Texas passed a law early in 1887 requiring liquor dealers to execute a $5,000 bond. It also stipulated that there were to be no screens or lewd pictures on the premises where liquor was sold, banned all gaming except billiards, and prohibited anyone younger than 21 from being on the premises. The law mandated a $500 fine for each violation. But like the Sunday blue laws that went unheeded on both sides of the city, West Side officials ignored many of the requirements of the new state law.[14]

This disregard for the law on the part of officials did nothing to curb the violent tendencies even gentlemen showed when it came to settling disputes. In Texarkana, it was second nature to carry a weapon – be it a knife or gun – so arguments frequently became deadly. Using circular reasoning, many respectable citizens carried a gun for "self-defense" in such instances. Elsewhere in Arkansas, travelers were allowed to carry guns while en route even though some cities had passed ordinances otherwise prohibiting guns in city limits. Thus, when Judge Mitchel traveled to Little Rock that January, he holstered his revolver.[15]

On his last day in the city, Mitchel walked into a barbershop across the street from the Capitol Hotel to meet a friend before heading to the train depot. Mitchel was greeted by a Maj. Haines who asked him if he had come to Little Rock to talk to Professor James Mitchell about the eligibility question. (The professor was an editor for the *Little Rock Democrat*, who had written a letter that was highly critical of Mitchel. Once again, some Miller County Democrats were alleging that Mitchel was "loitering and frittering time at the expense of the people," and the allegations were getting publicity throughout the state.) Neither man was aware that Professor Mitchell was sitting within earshot a few chairs away.[16]

"No," the judge replied in an even tone, "I don't have anything to do with these editors."

As the judge turned away, the editor in question got up from a barber chair and tapped Haines on the shoulder. The two spoke briefly before the judge came over to them and started talking to Mitchell about his letter. When the judge accused the editor of lying, the editor said he didn't want any trouble and invited Mitchel to come to his office and discuss the matter there in front of Judge Williams.

As the editor turned toward the door, Mitchel said in a conversational tone, "If you are responsible for the statement you have uttered a damned lie."

The editor took immediate offense and punched the judge with his clenched fist. In the ensuing scuffle, Mitchel drew his revolver and, using it as a bludgeon, struck the editor on the back of his head in an effort to knock him down. Friends of both men tried to separate them as other bystanders called for the police. When officer Sam Speight arrived, he wrested the revolver from the judge, who was holding it at head level. Both men were charged with disturbing the peace, and Mitchel had an additional charge of carrying a pistol. The editor pled guilty to a breach of the peace, and the judge admitted carrying a revolver and using it as a weapon. But he claimed the privilege under the law to carry the gun as a traveler as he had been on his way to the depot. The weapons charge was dismissed, and both men were fined $10.[17]

The incident fed the Texarkana gossip mill for days, but it did little to curb the same kind of violence there. A few months later, Joe Cook got into an argument in front of the City Drug Store with John Kirby, another prominent Democrat who had served with Joe on many committees. In the heat of the argument, Joe drew his pistol and shot John twice – once in the right wrist and once in the right chest area. Before any other shots could be fired, their friends intervened and carried John to a room above the drug store where he was tended to by a doctor. Sheriff Dixon arrested Joe and took him before his old friend Justice Smithers. He was released on $500 bond, which he paid on the spot. As soon as he was well enough, John was carried on a stretcher to the home of his brother Jody Kirby, who lived on College Hill.[18]

That Saturday night, Joe, who was coming home from visiting his fiancé who lived on College Hill, passed near Jody's house. Jody came out, and the two fired at each other – each claiming the other had shot first. Deputies arrested the two men and took them to the Miller County Courthouse where they both swore out a warrant against the other for assault with intent to kill. By this time, a crowd had gathered in the courtroom where

Justice Smithers was to begin investigating the incident. But before the questioning began, Dixon ordered his deputies to search everyone in the courtroom for guns. "This was a wise precaution on the part of the sheriff as it greatly reduced the crowd, many of whom came back down into the city," the *Independent* reported.[19]

Smithers put both men under bond and ordered them to appear before him at 10 a.m. Monday morning for a preliminary trial. William, who had been in Prescott spending the Easter holiday with his parents, returned home just in time to help his partner prepare his defense. The two convinced Smithers to drop the new charges against Joe. Rather than spending time in JP court, Jody waved examination and posted bond for his appearance in circuit court.[20]

By the time the Miller County Circuit Court session opened in June, John Kirby had recovered enough that he and his family were finally able to move from Jody's house to their plantation. Meanwhile, Joe and William were preparing for a unique court session that began with the grand jury indicting both Joe and Jody on a charge of assault with intent to kill. Joe also was charged with carrying a pistol. William missed the regular city council meeting June 14 so he could help Joe prepare for court the next day. The trial began after lunch Wednesday and continued into Friday with Judge Mitchel presiding. While testimony lasted through the morning Thursday, the jury was treated to the lawyers' oratory Thursday afternoon and Friday morning as Joe and William faced off against Prosecutors Webber and W.E. Atkinson, an attorney from Prescott who was serving as Jody's defense lawyer. Late Friday afternoon, the jury returned a verdict of not guilty. The next Monday, Joe and William were back in court for Jody's trial. But when they arrived, they discovered the case had been continued until the next court session in December as Atkinson, Jody's attorney, was too ill to argue the case. Yet the next day, Atkinson was elected by the other attorneys to serve as special judge for the cases in which Mitchel was disqualified.[21]

View of Texarkana, Ark.-Tex. in 1874.

Cotton Market, Texarkana, Texas

Old postcards of Texarkana show it in its earliest days (top) as a frontier town that grew up around the railroad and, a few decades later, as a major trade center (bottom).

BROAD STREET, LOOKING EAST.

Bustling with activity, Texarkana was a thriving city at the turn of the century. The bottom postcard shows the view looking north on State Line Avenue.

The State National Bank (top) hugs the dividing line between Arkansas and Texas. The state names have been written in on the postcard to show where they come together in Texarkana. Where Broad and State Line Avenue meet in Texarkana (bottom) has long been a staging point for parades, political rallies, and street-side crusades. The five-story bank anchors the state line on the right.

Streetcars mingle with pedestrians, horses, and carriages (bottom), making Broad Street the place to be seen and to do business in Texarkana at the turn of the century. W.H. Arnold presented many a case in this federal courthouse and post office building (top), which served both sides of the city.

THE LOBBY—COSMOPOLITAN HOTEL, TEXARKANA, TEXAS

As a railroad hub for both freight and passengers, Texarkana had a thriving hotel industry at the end of the 19th century. Hotels such as the Cosmopolitan (top) offered luxury accommodations for tourists and business travelers. Picnic grounds sprang up around several of the area lakes (bottom). Equipped with boat rentals, concession stands, and pavilions, Spring Lake Park was a favorite for family outings and church and town gatherings.

After years of arguing with the railroads, the people of Texarkana finally convinced railroad officials to build a union depot in town (top). The Miller County Courthouse, bottom, was the scene of many court battles for W.H. Arnold. He was elected by the other lawyers to fill a judicial vacancy and occasionally filled in as a judge when the sitting judge had to recuse himself or was out sick.

W.H. Arnold was admitted to the U.S. Circuit Court for the Eastern District of Arkansas, Texarkana Division, January 10, 1888. G.A. Hays, who briefly served as his business partner, signed his license.

Kate Lewis Arnold with Richard Lewis Arnold

Richard L. Arnold,
the father of Richard S. Arnold and Morris S. Arnold,
as a child

The Arnold family home in Texarkana (top) was built in the 1890s. The Arnold Law Firm had gone through many changes. In 1932 (bottom), it consisted of Richard L. Arnold, left, David C. Arnold, William H. Arnold, Jr., and William H. Arnold, Sr.

W.H. Arnold and Kate Arnold, 1945

The Arnold Law Firm in 1968 included Richard S. Arnold, front left, William H. Arnold, Jr., William H Arnold, III, Thomas S. Arnold, Richard L. Arnold, back left, and Morris S. Arnold.

22 City of the Second Class

The progressives of Texarkana knew they had a lot of work to do to bring the city to respectable maturity. The 1887 spring city elections offered the opportunity to clean house and make some changes. Although the election wouldn't be held until April, the *Independent* began pushing for progress in January, reminding voters that "the most sagacious, far-seeing, practical and competent men are now needed to direct public affairs.... [J]ust now there should be 'no drones in the hive,' but 'queen bees' who will properly direct and lead in those enterprises that are bound to come."[1]

The growing influence of "the kids" in the Miller County Democratic Party gave some progressives reason to hope that it would be possible to clean house. But the party conflict could open the door wider to Republicans – as shown in the recent sheriff's race. And although the Democrats had been taking county and state offices, they had not been as successful on the city level, where voters often ignored party politics. To bolster the Republican chances, Judge Orr, who was still waiting for the courts to declare him sheriff, and a Mr. Battle printed the first issue of the *Texarkana Republican* Sunday, January 30. But undaunted by the obstacles and recent history, the local Democratic Party, now chaired by Joe, was determined to sweep the city election.[2]

The progressives' hopes were renewed February 2 when it was announced that Congressman John H. Reagan, a Palestine, Texas, judge, had defeated U.S. Sen. Samuel Bell Maxey, a Paris, Texas, attorney. Although Maxey, who had been senator since 1875, was a Democrat, the younger party members in Texarkana saw him as part of the old guard and an obstacle to progress. When Congress was considering placement of a new

$50,000 federal courthouse in western Texas, Maxey had ignored the lobbying efforts of his constituents in Texarkana and supported construction of the courthouse in Jefferson, Texas. West Side Mayor Henderson had called a special meeting January 28 to discuss ways to combat Congress' decision. The mayor made the city's views known to President Cleveland, hoping he would veto the appropriation. But with no support from the senator, Texarkanians could do nothing but enviously watch as the courthouse was awarded to the other town. They had other reasons to dislike Maxey – he rarely visited Texarkana, which indicated he didn't recognize the rising status of the border town. Reagan, on the other hand, had come to town several times during his long tenure as a congressman and his campaign to unseat the veteran senator.[3]

Always looking for an excuse to publicize their successes, the Democrats from both sides of the city turned out that Wednesday night to celebrate Reagan's election. Living in a border town gave party members dual allegiance as they viewed both Texas and Arkansas congressmen and senators as their representatives; the same was true with state legislators from that region. Thus, all of Texarkana's leading Democrats hit the streets as the Army of North Virginia came out in full dress parade and bonfires were lit the length of Broad Street. The West Side mayor and other dignitaries made flowery speeches praising Reagan and cheering on the "Democracy."[4]

East Side residents had even more reason to celebrate a few weeks later when the city council adopted a resolution to convert the town into a city of the second class and sent Alderman Sweeney to Little Rock to secure the charter. The council had taken a special census to prove the Arkansas side had sufficient population to warrant the higher status; it was now time to claim the prize. The upgrade in status meant the city could hold elections every two years instead of annually. As the campaigns for the city election intensified, some townspeople questioned whether an election should be held now that Texarkana was becoming a second-class city. Why not let the current administration serve another year? Gov. Hughes said the election wasn't necessary, but William and the other city officials, who questioned the governor's authority to issue a legal opinion, thought it was.[5]

The Democrats and the incumbents, many of whom were not party members, ignored the issue and focused, instead, on winning the election. Joe called the East Side's Democrats to a meeting March 14 to appoint a town central committee. A few days later, the Democrats held ward meetings throughout the East Side to elect delegates for a city nominating convention. Two of the wards elected delegates but gave them no instructions; the Second Ward, however, instructed its delegates to vote for William as city recorder and elected Hays, Joe, and his brother John to serve on the executive committee. The delegates from the wards met Monday, March 22, at Conductors Hall to nominate the Democratic slate for city office. John Cook was elected to preside over the meeting with Hays as secretary. The group also elected a central committee, which included Dixon as chairman. Before the convention closed, a Democratic Club was formed with Dixon as president and Hays as vice president.[6]

The next day, the Democrats published their slate in the *Independent* – as did a nonpartisan group, which called its slate the "Citizens Ticket." The names of William Arnold and H.L. Grigsby, the city attorney, were the only ones to appear on both tickets. The Citizens Ticket, which asked residents to vote for the best man for the office rather than for a party, included several incumbents including Mayor E.A. Schicker. It also included Sam Branch, a respected African American, as an alderman for the Third Ward.[7]

That evening, the Democratic Club held a big rally at the intersection of State Line and Broad Street. More than 100 men marched in the procession, carrying torches and banners promoting the Democratic candidates. The procession, which started at the courthouse, was led by Dixon, who was followed by a brass band. When they reached the downtown intersection, Dixon mounted a platform and addressed the crowd, urging them to make the East Side a Democratic city. The party held an even larger rally Saturday night. More than 200 men, all carrying torches and banners, paraded their horses through the business district, which had been lit up for the occasion at Dixon's request.[8]

As some were still questioning the necessity of the election, Mayor Schicker spoke for all the incumbents on the Citizens Ticket, who believed since they had been elected for only one year, the election should proceed. "This therefore settles the election muddle, and all of the candidates and their friends can now pull off their coats and work for their men," the *Independent* commented. "We congratulate our present officials upon the patriotic view they have taken, for no man should want to serve as an official for a longer term that for which he was elected."[9]

Election Day took on a festive feel that April 5 as court sessions were canceled and the saloons closed. The various candidates had rented every carriage and hack available in the city, decorated them with bright banners, and used them to carry voters to the polls. The Arkansas residents of Texarkana were known for making grand displays. They did not disappoint anyone that Election Day. All was going smoothly until a rabid dog threatened pedestrians on a busy city street. One of the men pulled out his gun and killed the dog. The gunshots caused a ruckus throughout town as residents were sure a political debate had turned violent.[10]

More excitement occurred when the winners were announced. William and Grigsby, who had run without opposition, were re-elected. The surprises came in the other races. Mayor Schicker narrowly defeated his Democratic challenger by 13 votes. Patrick Hardin, the city marshal, beat his Democratic opponent by 120 votes, whereas the city engineer, A.B. Matson, won by only 41 votes. James Mathews, a Democrat, narrowly won the treasurer's seat by 20 votes. The First and Second Wards went solidly for Democrats as aldermen, but the Third Ward elected the Citizens candidates, including Sam Branch. The mixed results showed when it came to city government, Texarkanians still voted for the man – not the party. The vote also could have been a reaction, in part, against Dixon. Even though Dixon did not run for office, he seemed to still be calling the shots for the local Democrats. And he was attracting negative press from other towns for his violent history. A few weeks after the election, a Hot Springs paper condemned both sides of Texarkana for continuing to put up with criminals as law enforcement officers. The article claimed Dixon had killed six men and the West Side marshal had killed one and shot several others.[11]

Putting politics behind it, the city council quickly got back to the business of bringing law and order to the East Side. In the aftermath of Joe's confrontations with the Kirbys, the council passed an ordinance prohibiting people from carrying guns in town. At the same meeting, council members voted to establish a position of chief of police. This move was a slap at Sheriff Dixon, who had volunteered to provide police services to the city for $150 a month.[12]

But the new administration wasn't done yet. As city recorder, William posted a front-page notice from the mayor in the *Independent* to inform citizens that the city's ordinance requiring everyone to keep their property clear of all rubbish and garbage would be strictly enforced. A few weeks later, the city council passed three new ordinances and warned that these ordinances would be strictly enforced. The first one allowed city law officers to shoot all unmuzzled dogs roaming the streets. The second one mandated that all saloons must be closed on Sundays. And the third one prohibited gaming of any kind and called for all gaming houses to be closed. These ordinances did not sit well with Dixon, who owned a saloon and had an interest in several of the gaming houses. But he soon discovered he had nothing to worry about; the ordinances sat on the books virtually unenforced.[13]

Although some of its new ordinances weren't welcomed by a certain group of citizens, the city council continued to legislate – but not enforce – the cleanup of the city. An infestation of huge rats that spring garnered more support for the ordinances about garbage and rubbish. "They destroy chickens so rapidly that it is almost impossible to raise fowls to any size," the newspaper said of the rats. Another problem hurting the city was fire, which continued to be an almost daily occurrence. Armed with ladders, buckets, a few low-pressure hoses, and a horse-drawn wagon, the volunteer hook and ladder company, assisted by every able-bodied man available, had a hard time keeping the flames from spreading to adjacent buildings once a fire got started. It didn't matter that many of these fires were acts of arson; the city council felt compelled to do something more to fight this destructive threat to life and property.[14]

That June, the East Side City Council established a "fire limits," which included the downtown business and residential areas, and then passed an ordinance requiring that all new buildings constructed in the fire limits be built of brick, stone, iron, or concrete and have fireproof roofs of slate, tin, zinc, or slut iron. The ordinance gave the city the right to condemn dilapidated buildings that posed a fire risk and prohibited property owners from rebuilding wooden structures that had suffered at least 50 percent damage. On top of these measures, the council passed an ordinance, based on a recent Arkansas Supreme Court decision, requiring property owners to build and maintain earthen sidewalks in front of all city lots.[15]

While the respectable citizens applauded the ordinances and what they portended, they knew their city still harbored a lot of crime and called for the full weight of the law to be brought against any miscreant – especially if he were a stranger to town. As the city grew, it seemed to attract more and more troublemakers. The townspeople were appalled that spring when law officers, hunting an escaped prisoner awaiting trial on murder charges, dropped in at Wah Lee's Chinese Laundry and discovered a full-blown opium dive. In a room behind the laundry, nine white men, dissipated from their addiction, lay on wooden bunks lining the walls. Some were sleeping while others quietly smoked away, oblivious to the commotion around them. It was evident from the surroundings that the dive had existed for quite some time. The law officers dismantled the place and arrested the proprietor before searching the rest of the town for similar establishments.[16]

Believing strongly in law and order, many of the respectable townspeople of Texarkana – like those elsewhere in the late 1800s – supported public hangings as the just end for the worst criminals. A hanging was as much a spectacle as circuit court; men, women, and children attended the event, seeing it as their civic duty to witness justice carried out. Hangings served as both a morbid entertainment and a moral lesson aimed at keeping the righteous from straying and convincing the unrighteous to repent of their evil ways. Texarkana hadn't witnessed a hanging for a while, so when the day came for Jim Jones, a young black man convicted of killing another black man, to be hanged on the West Side, both sides of the city were in celebration mode. (Although he supported law and order, William abhorred the morbid delight in hangings and made sure he was out of town that week.) Although it was a Thursday, few people were tending to business. They had a hanging to attend.[17]

The Bowie Rifles, a local militia, stood guard at the Bowie County Jail on the West Side as nearly 500 people crowded around the jail entrance so they could be the first to see Jones as he prepared to meet his Maker. At about five minutes before noon, Dixon and his deputies helped their Bowie County counterparts escort Jones from the jail and placed him in an open wagon. Almost in processional form, the crowd followed the wagon to the new pine gallows that had been built for the condemned man near Proctor Springs on the outskirts of town. By this time, nearly 4,000 people had gathered to watch Jones take his final steps up to the 10-foot high platform. Jones appeared calm as the Bowie County sheriff placed the noose around his neck and Rev. H. Booth read from Psalms 51:

> Have mercy upon me, O God,
>   according to thy loving kindness:
>   according unto the multitude of thy tender mercies
>   blot out my transgressions.
>
> Wash me thoroughly from mine iniquity,
>   And cleanse me from my sin.
>
> For I acknowledge my transgressions:
>   and my sin is ever before me.
>
> Against thee, thee only, have I sinned,
>   and done this evil in thy sight:

> that thou mightest be justified when thou speakest,
> and be clear when thou judgest.

As the minister finished his reading, Jones spoke his last words – a proclamation of his innocence; he had killed in self-defense. He smiled as the sheriff placed straps about his feet and arms. And as the black hood was drawn over his face, he remained perfectly cool, the smile still playing about his mouth. At 12:40 p.m., the sheriff sprung the trap; Jones fell six feet. The crowd remained in place, eyes fixated on the death jerks as Jones hung from the rope. Fifteen minutes later, he was pronounced dead from strangulation.[18]

To handle the rise in crime in the region – and perhaps to make amends for snubbing Texarkana when it came to locating the new federal courthouse, both houses of Congress had passed a bill February 28 that made provisions for the federal circuit and district courts for the Eastern District of Arkansas to hold sessions twice a year in Texarkana, Arkansas. To be called the Texarkana Division of the Eastern District, the branch court would hold sessions beginning the second Monday in January and July and would handle cases for Columbia, Howard, Hempstead, Lafayette, Little River, Miller, Nevada, Ouachita, Pike, and Sevier counties. The new court promised to be a boon to both Texarkana's legal profession and its business district – especially if the sessions attracted the crowds the county circuit court brought to town. Dignitaries from the 10-county region came to Texarkana July 11 for the first session of the federal court. Since there was no federal courthouse, the court had to meet in the Miller County Courthouse to hear its one criminal case against a man for running a blind tiger in Prescott. The man was found guilty, sentenced to a year in prison, and fined $100. The session ended after one day.[19]

23   Modernity

Thrust into the midst of the industrialization craze sweeping the country as it prepared for the 20th century, which was little more than a decade away, William and other respectable citizens of Texarkana embraced the concept of modernity and what it had to offer their town. When the opportunity arose, city officials facilitated the connection of the Texarkana telephone exchange to the Hope exchange. The connection expanded the world for that handful of Texarkanians who had telephones by giving them access to not only Hope but Washington, Ozan, Nashville, Centre Point, Antimony City, Prescott, and Emmett. While telephones were still mostly for business and the wealthy, William could visit Judge Mitchel's office and use his phone to contact family, friends, and business associates in other towns. The telephone quickly joined the telegraph and railroads in connecting people, in making what once would have been isolated communities part of a larger world.[1]

While most Texarkanians welcomed the progress such conveniences brought, they often had ambivalent feelings about the way these services were provided – especially when it came to the railroads. In a sense, Texarkana owed its life – or at least a major portion of its prosperity – to the railroads. Yet the townspeople had a sort of love-hate relationship with the industry. Part of the hostility was rooted in Reconstruction days when Gov. Clayton and his cronies had enriched themselves while giving railroad tycoons millions of acres of state land – some of which had been claimed already by settlers. While some of the land was used for the actual railroads, much of it was sold at inflated prices for city lots with the railroads pocketing the money.

Railroad officials ignored the prior claims and, using their political clout, dealt roughly with anyone who stood in their way

– most often by engaging them in lengthy legal battles only the wealthy could afford. The railroads also refused to fence their tracks, which cut across farms throughout Arkansas. When farmers had livestock killed by the trains, their only recourse was the courts. Even though the railroads lost the cases in the end, they appealed as many times as possible in an effort to discourage similar claims and bankrupt or wear down the other party. Such disregard for the rights and property of others increased the public's hostility toward the railroads.[2]

One lawsuit in particular served as a symbol of railroad greed in Texarkana. The origins of Dr. W.H. Cayce v. the St. Louis, Iron Mountain & Southern Railroad Company stretched back to antebellum days. At question was ownership of 120 acres of prime real estate in Texarkana, which had been homesteaded since 1846. But the railroad claimed ownership, saying its predecessor, the Cairo Fulton Railroad, had been granted the land in 1853. The case had dragged through the courts, and the ownership was still in question in 1887. When the commissioner of the General Land Office in Washington, D.C., issued a 30-page ruling in Cayce's favor, Texarkanians rejoiced. The railroad had at last been defeated. Then came word that the commissioner's decision was subject to appeal to the Secretary of the Interior. And, of course, the railroad was appealing. People throughout southern Arkansas reacted. "And thus it seems that our prosperous neighbor on the state line, is to be retarded in its rapid growth and prosperity, by litigation involving the title to a considerable portion ... of its area," the *Camden Beacon* commented.[3]

Since it seemed as if the railroads always won, the people felt powerless to control their own destiny as the economic well-being of their city was so entwined with the railroad. As the railroads were owned by Northern industrialists, such confrontations resurrected the old North-South antagonism – at least in the Southern mind. When the railroads arbitrarily raised freight rates on raw materials heading to Northern factories, Southern newspapers cried, "Foul!" In their eyes, the Southerner was being raped twice – once by the railroad and again by Congress, which continued to heed Northern demands for high tariffs.

Thus, Northern industrialists were conspiring to keep the South impoverished and powerless.

Texarkanians had other reasons to hate the railroads. The trains made it easy for bums and Northern derelicts to head to the warmer climes of the South. Many of these transients chose to make Texarkana a temporary home. While some camped out near the rail yards, others went begging or thieving from door to door. Their presence became even more disconcerting during cholera or yellow fever epidemics. And the respectable citizens who were intent on improving Texarkana society were put off by the vulgar types the railroad often hired for manual labor. Rowdy and uneducated, these men found it amusing to insult women, blaspheme God, and live for pleasure rather than honor. These were the kind who started strikes, who had little care for the lives or property of others. Although most of the townspeople had become somewhat calloused by the behavior of such men, they were calling for blood April 8, 1887. That morning, a brakeman on a Texas Pacific train deliberately threw a 12-year-old black boy from the train as it passed the Bowie Lumber Company in Texarkana. Witnesses watched in horror as the boy fell on the track and the train rolled over his legs. As soon as the train passed, a few of the men carried the boy into a nearby building and summoned a doctor, who could do nothing but numb the pain a bit while the boy waited for death.[4]

On the one hand Texarkanians hated the railroads; with the other, they courted the industry. In 1887, people on the East Side passionately lobbied for two things – a rail line connecting Texarkana to Fort Smith and a new depot. Though it took longer to get the line, the debate on that issue was far less acrimonious as the railroad knew it would make money on the project. People in both Fort Smith and Texarkana had been wishing for the connecting railroad for a number of years, but the talk got serious in 1887. "We have agitated, and intend to continue to agitate because we know what a bonanza that road would be to Texarkana, Fort Smith and to the whole country," Warren reported in the *Independent* that January. "It would do more to advance the prosperity of our city than any other enterprise now spoken of."[5]

A citizens committee, made up mostly of businessmen who would benefit from the extension to Fort Smith, led the charge. The committee contacted railroad officials in St. Louis, trying to interest them in the project. The officials were interested, but they wanted money – $50,000. Committee members responded that they were raising the money. The committee received a letter May 26 from W.L. Whitaker, an official with the St. Louis & Chicago and St. Louis & Colorado railroads in St. Louis, listing more conditions the people would have to meet. He wanted them to give the railroads 30 acres for a yard in Texarkana, get all the required ordinances passed, obtain all the rights of way from Texarkana to the Red River, and agree to transfer all stock from the citizens to the railroads.[6]

Although the additional conditions raised concerns that maybe the railroad wasn't serious about this project, the committee wasted no time in complying. The group met that night to sign contracts pledging the original $50,000 to the Texarkana-Fort Smith line. The group telegraphed Whitaker, telling him the money had been raised but some of his other conditions needed to be clarified. The next day, a larger meeting was held to discuss those conditions. Mr. Roberts, one of the committee members, reported on a conversation he had had with Mr. Hinckley, another railroad official. Roberts said the railroad was serious about building the line – if the conditions were met. However, it would cost $110,000 to meet those conditions. The meeting turned into a pledge drive as members were asked to contribute even more to the project. Before the meeting ended, $32,050 had been pledged with $10,000 of that promised by Whitaker. Some of the residents were hesitant to promise too much; the railroad had broken promises in the past. They wanted a face-to-face meeting with Hinckley and Whitaker.[7]

The railroad gave the committee a June deadline to raise the rest of the money and promised to start laying track as soon as the money was raised. By June 6, the group had raised $102,000. Although they were $8,000 short, the committee members officially accepted the railroad's proposition and promised to raise the remaining $8,000 quickly. But as with so many other railroad promises, this one was derailed. Work on the extension to Fort Smith did not begin in earnest until the 1890s.[8]

While William supported anything that would advance his adopted home, he didn't get involved in pushing for the Texarkana-Fort Smith extension. As city recorder, he was too busy working on the depot issue, which was becoming quite a problem. Of the four railroads coming into Texarkana, only one had a passenger depot in the city by 1887. The passengers from the other lines had to alight from the cars onto a narrow platform. They could then jam into a small dirty waiting room that was often home to a host of filthy transients or walk a considerable distance through the mud or dust (depending on the season) to a hotel.[9]

When Jay Gould came to town January 18 for one of his routine visits of the rail yard, William and several other city officials met with him to request the "speedy construction of a convenient and comfortable depot ... for the accommodation of the large passenger traffic over his roads from this city." The next day, a prominent railroad official sent word that the Gould system had appropriated $170,000 for new buildings in Texarkana. The projects would include a $150,000 two-story, brick depot that would be built from State Line to where the old Marquand Hotel had stood on Vine Street. At first, some Texarkana residents chalked these reports up to rumor – or more empty promises. But when officials with the Iron Mountain and Missouri-Pacific staked the ground for the depot February 10, the residents started to believe the much-needed depot would become a reality. The newspaper reported construction would begin in 10 days.[10]

Texarkanians eagerly watched the site, anxious to see signs of construction. But nothing more happened. Angry rumors circulated that work had stopped because of an ordinance passed by the East Side, requiring the depot to be built at least 200 feet east of the state line. The rumors died down two months later when three train cars loaded with bricks pulled into the yard. Railroad workers spent several days unloading the bricks and taking them to the site of the depot. But once the bricks were unloaded, the workmen left.[11]

Once again, angry rumors flew. This time they were directed at C.C. Dorrian, a former East Side mayor and prominent Democrat, who owned a saloon across from the current waiting room. According to rumor, Dorrian had filed for an injunction against the new depot, which would force the old waiting room to be closed and, thus, hurt his business. When Dorrian heard the allegations, he denied everything, saying he had no problem with the building of a new depot. He gave his own reason for the work stoppage: "The railroad authorities never intended to build a depot ... the sending of three carloads of brick was only another one of their shams and pretenses to quiet the indignation of our citizens at their failure to build a respectable depot."[12]

Three days later, work began once again at the site. But it proved to be another false start. By now, the East Side City Council was getting tired of the game. And it saw some new ways the city could cash in on the railroad business. Sixteen passenger trains rolled in and out of town every day. But some of those trains didn't stop and others stopped only briefly. That meant none of the passengers on those trains had the opportunity to spend a dime in Texarkana stores and restaurants. To remedy this situation, the city council passed an ordinance requiring all passenger trains coming through Texarkana to stop for at least 30 minutes in town.[13]

Instead of praising city officials for looking out for the best interests of the town, the residents turned on them, blaming them for the delay in getting the depot. They started two petitions. One asked the council to repeal the ordinance requiring the depot to be built at least 200 feet from the state line. The other demanded the repeal of the 30-minute ordinance and a pledge from the council that it would not interfere with the building of the depot anywhere between State Line Avenue and Vine Street. At the request of Missouri-Pacific Superintendent Kerrigan of St. Louis, the city council held a special meeting May 21, a Saturday night. Kerrigan submitted plans to build a union depot for all the railroads operating in the city but said it would be built only if the city repealed the 200-foot clearance ordinance. Judge Mitchel then presented the citizens' petition, which supported the railroad's request. Upon looking over the petition, the aldermen recognized only a few names from East Side residents – the others were all from the Texas side of town. When the council refused to repeal the ordinance, Kerrigan returned to St. Louis on his special train.[14]

Rather than yield to the city council and move the depot site a few hundred feet, the railroad ordered the bricks to be moved to another site. When word of this spread, many of the East Side's most prominent residents met June 3 to discuss how to handle the situation. They appointed a committee of five to talk with the city council and encourage it to modify the clearance to 100 feet. But before the committee members met with the city council, they talked to Trainmaster Green and persuaded him to suspend the order to move the brick until after the city council meeting June 7. At its regular meeting that Tuesday night, the city council was confronted by five of the most influential men from the East Side. It had little choice but to agree to amend the clearance ordinance. But it attached a condition – the railroad had to "speedily erect the depot."[15]

Despite all the controversies surrounding the railroads, the people of southern Arkansas enjoyed the ability to travel quickly and easily. As transportation and communication became more convenient, families and friends could keep in touch with loved ones who had moved on, businessmen could extend their opportunities, and people, especially the upper and middle classes, had a lot more time for leisure. With the advent of the cannonball train service, William found it convenient and relatively affordable to slip away for a weekend to visit his family in Prescott. And, just as often, David, Uncle Bill, and his cousin John H. Arnold Jr., a prominent attorney and the mayor of Washington, visited him in Texarkana.[16]

The railroad also made it easier for Texarkanians to participate in festivals and celebrations in other towns by running special trains with discounted rates for the events. Such excursions were a good marketing ploy for the railroads and offered affordable family entertainment to area residents. Special trains were arranged to carry revelers back and forth between Texarkana and Paris, Texas, in June 1887 for a week of festivities that was to conclude Saturday night, June 11, with a magnificent fireworks display. Those who couldn't stay for the whole week piled into the trains headed to Paris for the Saturday extravaganza. Picnickers from all walks of life sat on blankets spread on the grass as they stared expectantly into the night sky, waiting for the first skyrocket to streak across the blackness. As an official ignited the rocket, it sparked. Frightened, the man threw it to the ground, where it continued to dance amid a shower of sparks. At first the crowd laughed at the clownish accident, but laughter turned to panic as the grounded rocket struck Capt. Barry just as he turned to get out of its path. The collision deflected the rocket into the $700 stock of fireworks assembled for the show. A great explosion shook the earth as smoke and fire billowed into the air. The booms of the exploding fireworks could not drown out the groans of the wounded, the terrible shrieks of the women and children, and the snorting of the frightened horses. "The prevailing terror generally created a scene of indescribable horror," an eyewitness reported. In the pandemonium that ensued, at least seven people, including an infant, were killed and more were severely burned or injured when they were run over by buggies in the resulting panic. Three men, who could not swim, had tried to escape the flames by running into a nearby pond, but they found it was deeper than they had expected. Their bodies were found the next morning; they had drowned.[17]

The disaster cast a pall over summer fun for a few days in Texarkana, but it wasn't long before the townspeople were forgetting their troubles at the ball fields. Baseball had hit the town with a passion that year. It had started with the local boys taking on the "Railroad 9" in a challenge match at Beidler Park. But by summer, baseball was big business. The local boys had become the Gate City Club, which was now a part of the South Western League. A new ballpark and grandstands, surrounded by a whitewashed picket fence, had been built near the Miller County Courthouse. The streetcar delivered fans to the gate every Saturday evening there was a home game. Admission for grandstand seating was 50 cents for men and 25 cents for women; ground seating was a quarter. The games were so popular that gate receipts of nearly $130 were realized for the June 13 game against Pine Bluff.[18]

Since the games were played close to the courthouse, William couldn't help but get swept up in the excitement. But he had something more important on his mind that summer than baseball. His wedding suit had arrived by express train May 24, and he was busy preparing for his October 13 wedding to Joe's little sister.[19]

24   Practicing Politics

Jessie and William wasted no time in starting a family. But a month before their first child was due, William left his young bride in the care of her mother and headed to St. Louis to represent Arkansas' Fourth Congressional District at the June 6, 1888, Democratic National Convention. The delegates were in high spirits, sure they would get another four years in the White House with Grover Cleveland. They knew Cleveland had made a lot of enemies during his first term, but he also had introduced much needed reforms. He had taken the railroads to task, halted special interest spending, and threatened the tariffs cherished by Northeastern industrialists. Re-election would be a tough battle, but the delegates meeting at the Exposition Building were confident the party was up for the challenge. Much of the convention focused on selecting a running mate to replace Vice President Thomas Hendricks of Indiana. Cleveland, in an effort to balance his Northeastern roots, chose another Midwesterner, Allen G. Thurman, a former senator from Ohio.[1]

William returned from the convention just in time for the birth of his first child, Jody Claypool Arnold, who was born on the Fourth of July. When it came to childbearing and rearing, not much had changed since the time William himself was born. Infant mortality was still a constant threat. From 1875 to 1900, disease and illness claimed one of every 10 babies before the age of one. "Infant death was such a common occurrence that most extended families – if not the immediate family – were affected by the passing of a little one," historian Ellen M. Plante writes. William was very much aware of the dangers facing his daughter; just the year before, his former partner, G.A. Hays, had mourned as the measles claimed both of his young daughters. Like most new parents, William and Jessie worried over their tiny infant as they got used to the responsibilities of being parents.²

While Jessie tended to their daughter, William went back to practicing politics and law. He took his turn stumping for a second term for Cleveland and attended rallies throughout the county. But Cleveland had initiated one too many reforms. He won the popular vote but lost to Benjamin Harrison in the electoral vote. The country was back in the hands of the Republicans.

With the presidential election over, William resumed his usual routine, which revolved around his law firm, the Democratic Party, the Masonic Lodge, the church, and the family. Nearly three years later, he and Jessie had another daughter, Lucy Arnold – named for William's grandmother Lucinda. Jessie had her hands full taking care of an infant and an inquisitive toddler while William kept up with his busy schedule. Now that he was a father, William became even more concerned about the town where he would raise his children.

Despite all the paper reforms the city council had legislated in 1887, Texarkana in the early 1890s was still a rough town known for gambling, prostitution, and corruption. Businesses routinely ignored the Sunday closure laws as well as the ordinances that prohibited gaming; they knew the most that would happen was a slap on the wrist and a minimal fine. The money they made by breaking the law was more than enough to cover the fine. Wanting something better for his family, William ran for mayor in 1892 on a platform of converting Texarkana into a clean, law-abiding city. Not one to advertise his candidacy with slogans or simple announcements, William appealed to the moral element of the local Democratic Party in a letter that plainly announced his policy and his pledge to rid the East Side of prostitution and gambling and enforce the Sabbath law.³

William found himself in a primary contest against his old mentor and friend, E.A. Warren, editor of the local paper and a progressive. Although Warren had experience, having served as mayor of Camden and Prescott, the Democrats chose the more youthful Arnold. That put him in a general election against incumbent Mayor E.A. Schicker, who was running on the Citizens

Ticket. The owner of a bakery in town and a fellow Mason, Schicker had served as an alderman and mayor. As city recorder, William had worked closely with him, often filling in for him as the judge of the city police court. But this election, William put friendships aside; Texarkana needed change, and he was the man to bring it.[4]

Texarkana was a city swimming in potential when William was elected mayor in April 1892. Once a frontier town in the traditional sense of the word, Texarkana was now conquering what historian Wilbur Cash called the "third frontier" – progress in the form of factories and schools. The population had increased 500 percent, from 3,000 10 years earlier to 15,000 residents equally divided between the East and West sides. That rapid growth accompanied new investment and business enterprises. The city was home to 14 law firms, six grocers, a dry goods store, a liquor store, three newspapers, three first-class hotels with a combined capacity for 400 guests, several smaller hotels and boarding houses, churches of every denomination, a synagogue, two colleges, and four national banks with a total operating capital of $600,000.[5]

It also boasted eight railroads, including a locally owned one that connected to a nearby navigable waterway. Besides the freight trains that rolled in regularly, 28 passenger trains stopped in Texarkana every day. The convenience of the railroad and the area's rich supply of natural resources gave birth to a variety of factories, including several furniture factories, potteries, a mattress factory, a wagon and buggy factory, machinery companies, iron works, sawmills, grist mills, a soap factory, boiler works, cotton seed oil mills, and brick and tile companies. While many of these factories were homegrown, some had moved to Texarkana recently from other cities to take advantage of the resources the border town had to offer. The surrounding area also benefited from Texarkana's growth. In November 1892, George Gould, Jay's son and heir, and a group of Eastern capitalists closed an option on 1,360 acres of land in nearby Brownstown in Sevier County. The group announced plans to build a $300,000 cement plant on the land.[6]

In a few short years, the city's utilities, still privately owned, had seen many improvements. The waterworks had a daily capacity of 3 million gallons; the street railway had four miles of line and another four miles was under construction. Even the electric lights were functioning more smoothly. Other new amenities included a $125,000 federal building, the union depot (scaled back to a $75,000 project), and several large wholesale houses. City leaders often bragged about their town and used its industry and conveniences to recruit more investment and residents.[7]

All this industry served as a magnet to newly arrived immigrants, people tired of the isolation of farm life, and those looking for a way to make a stake. Jobs were plentiful; more than 1,000 railroad workers called Texarkana home. People from all nationalities mingled on the streets where it was common to hear six or seven languages spoken. The city extended an open-door policy to anyone willing to roll up the proverbial shirtsleeves and get to work.[8]

Even in its early days, Texarkana had been home to immigrants, especially a sizable Jewish population, most of which had come from Germany. But by the 1880s, Jews were arriving from Eastern Europe as well. In many parts of the United States, Jews in general were not tolerated, and German Jews did not get along with their eastern cousins, considering them uncouth, low class, and uneducated. But Texarkana had come to embrace all the Jews, appreciating their honesty, work ethic, charity, patriotism, and dependability. The Christians viewed the Jews as authorities on the Old Testament and frequently invited Jewish leaders to teach classes in their Sunday schools and evening training services. In turn, Texarkana's Jewish parents allowed their children to attend Christian Sunday schools (especially at the Methodist churches), where they often had perfect attendance records.[9]

Perhaps because of this acceptance from the Gentile community, there was no friction between the two groups of Jews in Texarkana. When the Episcopalians wanted to build a new church, they sold their old building on Vine Street to the Jewish congregation, which moved it to an empty lot and converted it into Mount Sinai Synagogue. The orthodox Jews (Eastern Europeans) met there early on Saturday for services. Since a minyan was needed to hold the orthodox service, some of the reformed Jews (Germans) attended the service and then stayed for the reformed service that followed.[10]

While this spirit of tolerance and acceptance continued to thrive in Texarkana, by the 1890s, one group had been pushed to the fringes. Although various individuals had demonstrated hatred toward African Americans in previous years, the town had recognized black leaders and offered them a seat at the governing table. But those attitudes gradually changed as the Democrats moved more solidly into power. Seeing the black voter as the tool of the Republican, Democrats refused to let African Americans vote in their primaries. As the Democrats became a one-party system, they effectively shut the black man out of government. He still could vote in the general elections, but those elections were a mere formality. The real decisions were made in the Democratic primary. As the 1890s progressed, the rhetoric against the black man grew ugly, boisterous, and commonplace.[11]

The city also was facing a financial crisis. When the previous administration had come to office in 1890, the city had a surplus of $1,141. But two years later, it was more than $5,000 in debt. Upon taking office, William analyzed the city's books and its bills to find the problem. "The failure of the preceding administration to run the city government within its income, was on account of excessive rates paid to the Water and Light Companies for public service, and keeping the fire team and one employee to wait for fires at the rate of $75 per month," William reported in a message to the people. These three expenses alone exceeded the city's tax revenue by $1,000 a year. The resulting indebtedness forced the city to issue scrip, which doubled the cash price, to pay for labor and materials for any projects. Thus the city was spiraling into more debt. Using his legal skills, William met with officials of the water and light companies to renegotiate the city's contracts. The city ended up with better service for less money – and a $400 reduction in its outstanding bill to the water company.[12]

Besides being mayor, William was serving as chairman of the Miller County Democratic Party. Since it was both a state and presidential election year, William had little time to launch a major crusade to clean up the city in 1892. That summer, he had to be content with routine city business – presiding over the mayor's police court, officiating at weddings, attending city council meetings, getting the budget in order, and representing the city at major events. The rest of his time was devoted to politics and his law practice.[13]

A third party, calling itself the People's Party, had formed that summer throughout Arkansas with a platform calling for government ownership of all railroads, telephones, and telegraph lines. In Miller County, the party put out a full slate of candidates. The Democrats responded by claiming the Republicans would win all the county offices as the new party would drain votes from the Democrats. To keep this from happening, the local Democrats, led by William, planned an aggressive campaign, which included a speaking tour with 16 speakings scheduled throughout the county between August 16 through September 3. The party also called for a grand rally featuring Col. William Fishback, the Democratic candidate for governor.[14]

As county chairman, William traveled to New Lewisville July 11 to represent Miller County at a barbecue where Fishback was speaking. He and two other local Democrats then escorted the gubernatorial candidate to Texarkana. When they arrived at the Cotton Belt Depot at 10:20 that night, they were met by more than 200 members of the Cleveland and Thurman Club, all waving their torches and cheering when Fishback stepped off the train. William and several other prominent Democrats took Fishback to a waiting carriage and rode with him to the Huckins House, where he would be staying. Unmindful of the late hour, a brass band marked the route, followed by the carriage. The faithful Democrats, all mounted on horses, rode behind, lighting up the sky with their torches. Although the colonel was tired after a full day of campaigning, the crowd would not let him retire without a few words. Fishback briefly thanked them for their warm reception and slipped into the hotel as the group gave him three rousing cheers.[15]

Hundreds of Democrats met Fishback at the hotel the next morning. Led once again by the band, the crowd processed with the candidate to Park Byrne for the speaking. William, who had spared no expense in having a nice platform and seats put in the skating rink for the occasion, introduced the "next governor of Arkansas." Most of Fishback's speech focused on the economy – and the damaging effects of the tariff, which hurt the farmer while enriching business. When the country had had a low tariff, Fishback said, the farmers had increased their wealth by 50 percent in a 10-year period. But under the high tariff, farmers had already lost 10 percent of their earnings. Meanwhile, the tariffs had made it possible for the six New England states to accumulate half the total wealth of the country. If the country continued to impose such high tariffs, Fishback predicted a great depression.[16]

It began to rain as Fishback finished his remarks. The crowd waited a few minutes for the rain to stop; then the Republicans introduced Col. Whipple, their gubernatorial candidate. Whipple refuted Fishback's bleak prediction, saying "that the hard time now complained of so much, is not a reality." The People's Party candidate followed Whipple to the platform. But by this time, it was raining so hard, no one could hear his remarks.

William had reason to be proud of the rally he had staged for Fishback. But he didn't have much time to bask in the success. His old friend and mentor, E.A. Warren, was dying. Warren had sold his newspaper a month earlier to J.W. Gardner, editor of the *Picayune* in Nevada County, and announced that he was going to practice law again. On August 23, his 52nd birthday, Warren died of hemorrhaging of the bowels, the same condition that had claimed his father on his 52nd birthday years earlier.[17]

William attended the funeral the next afternoon, but he had no time to grieve for his friend. Following the funeral, Joe got in a heated political discussion with James Crenshaw, the city marshal, at Wright's Saloon. The words turned to blows as the argument intensified. The two were quickly separated, and Joe left the saloon to walk back to his office. But Crenshaw wasn't finished. He caught up to Joe and renewed the fight on the sidewalk in front of the Shepherd Fouke and Company store. After exchanging several blows, Crenshaw screamed out, "He is cutting me."[18]

John Wasden, a city policeman and Crenshaw's brother-in-law, ran up behind Joe and dealt him a "severe blow upon the head which knocked him senseless," the newspaper reported. A doctor was called to examine the two men. Crenshaw had several minor lacerations and a severe cut on his shoulder, but none of them was considered dangerous. Joe, on the other hand, was in critical condition. He was taken to the Cook & Arnold law office above Lightfoot's Drug Store where he remained unconscious for several days. More than a week later, the doctor decided Joe could safely be moved to his home. Wasden was suspended from the police force and arrested the next morning on a charge of assault with intent to kill. The charge was dropped later that year when he pleaded guilty to simple assault; he was fined $75.[19]

In between helping to care for Joe and running their legal practice in what had become a sick room, William attended the speakings throughout the county, introducing all the candidates. The campaign ended September 4 with a large rally at the intersection of Broad Street and State Line Avenue. When the keynote speakers, U.S. Sen. Jake Cranford and Congressman T.C. McRae, were introduced, third party members tried to "capture the stand" for their speaker, but the Democrats ran them off.[20]

The polls opened the next morning with some new challenges for both election officials and voters. The state election marked the first time the secret ballot was being used in Arkansas. Since they couldn't be in the voting booth with their voters, the Republicans printed out a card with instructions on who to vote for. The Democrats, meanwhile, rented carriages to bring in tardy voters or transport those who would not be able to get to the polls otherwise. The new ballot system eliminated the usual disturbances and noise at the polls, but the voting process was much slower. Woodcuts of strutting roosters adorned the *Texarkana Democrat* the next morning as the paper proudly proclaimed a Democratic landslide in Texarkana, Miller County, and throughout the state. Besides electing Fishback governor, the voters had passed a constitutional amendment extending the vote to all males 21 or older who were U.S. citizens or had declared their intention to become one. The amendment set residency requirements of 12 months in the state, six months in the county, and one month in the ward or precinct. Voters also had to have a valid poll-tax receipt. The amendment stipulated that the election judge was to mark the receipt to ensure that each person could vote only once.[21]

25   Fear and Hatred

With the state election over, Texarkana Democrats had nearly two months to campaign for the presidential election. While others enjoyed the county fair and preparations for the World's Fair that would open the next year in Chicago, William found he had little time for leisure. City business and politics were consuming his life. One of his more pressing concerns was the health of the townspeople. A cholera epidemic had started in the Middle East and Europe; 35,000 had died in Persia and 145 in Germany. Numerous cases were being reported in Russia and Belgium. Even though he was across the ocean in Texarkana, William didn't take this epidemic lightly. With increased immigration and travel, epidemics like this spread quickly. Within a few days of the news of the outbreak in Europe, Havana reported cholera.[1]

As a precaution, the United States placed a strict quarantine upon all ships arriving from ports infected with the disease. Passengers were to be quarantined for two to five days before they could leave for the dock, and all baggage was to be fumigated. By mid-September, the epidemic had spread to New York – despite the quarantine. Seven deaths were reported, and Cuba was now placing a quarantine on all ships arriving there from New York and treating ships from other U.S. ports with "suspicion." As the reports affected Wall Street, health officials tried to calm fears of a national epidemic, saying cold weather was setting in and that would end the spread of the disease. Their assurances were ignored when two brothers were hospitalized with the disease in Connecticut.[2]

To prevent a cholera epidemic in Texarkana, city officials had to declare war on all the garbage and filth piling up in the city. They already had passed an unpopular ordinance to prevent hogs from running wild in the city streets. They also had asked local businesses and homeowners to sign a petition approving a local improvement district to fund a city sewer system. In lieu of sewers, private landowners drained their sewage into a large gutter that ran below the depot to the cotton oil mills. The filth of the town had accumulated there for years, becoming a source of pestilence and disease.[3]

William estimated the sewer would cost $18,000 – money the city didn't have. The city was broke. "[O]wing to the large amount required to pay for fire protection and electric lights, no improvements have been made except what were absolutely necessary to make the streets passable," William reported. By law, the city was limited in how much it could assess in taxes. This amount was barely enough to cover ongoing operating expenses – let alone a sewer project. The only way to install sewers was if the landowners paid for them.[4]

"It is remarkable that Texarkana has not been afflicted with a greater amount of fatal sickness during this summer," the mayor said. "There is hardly a street, alley or gutter in the district without pools, of green stagnant and offensive water. Stagnant ponds of water stand under nearly every business house on Broad street several months in the year, and service pipes running from private residences upon the streets, are creating intolerable nuisances daily."[5]

William and the rest of the city officials knew the sewage problems in Texarkana could exacerbate a cholera epidemic. But there was little they could do about that problem until property owners agreed to the improvement district. Instead, they had to focus on what they could do to avoid an epidemic. William posted a notice in the local papers notifying all the residents to clean up their property. Those who refused to do so would be dealt with under the city's nuisance ordinances. As mayor, William had the job of inspecting all the back yards to make sure they were clean. Posting its own notice in the newspaper, the Arkansas Board of Health added its voice to the city's. "Quarantine ... is, not only ineffective in many cases but is exceedingly expensive – the best known preventive, quarantine aside, is to keep the town clean," the board said.[6]

Local concerns about cholera increased with reports of the disease in Gainesville, Texas. C.C. Hamby, acting governor of Arkansas, telegraphed William orders September 20 to establish a strict quarantine against Gainesville at once. The East Side City Council met that day to establish a quarantine camp two miles outside of town – just in case – and appoint a quarantine officer. Dr. W.C. Spearman, the city physician, examined all trains arriving in Texarkana from Texas but found no passengers from Gainesville.[7]

In response to the growing quarantine against Gainesville, Texas Gov. James Hogg issued a quarantine, for both people and goods, against New York and other places with confirmed cases of cholera. His proclamation prohibited people from those areas from entering Texas within a 10-day period of having been in the infected areas. He also ordered that anyone traveling by train into Texas must present to the health inspector an attested health certificate confirming that he had not been in an infected area.[8]

Recognizing how quickly an epidemic could spread through rail travel, Arkansas' Hamby convened the state Board of Health, along with railroad officials, to discuss how to prevent such epidemics. The railroad representatives testified there was nothing they could do about infected passengers until they reached their destination. Adding that the only immigrants coming into Arkansas were Scandinavians and Swedes (European areas not affected by the disease), the railroads tried to alleviate Hamby's fears. In the end, they agreed to notify local governments upon receiving notice of the arrival of immigrant trains or carloads of immigrants.[9]

Once the cholera scare abated, William had to don his political hat again and deal with presidential election issues. Cleveland was running again, this time with Adlai Stevenson of Illinois as his running mate. The Democrats were excited about the possibility of electing the first president to serve two non-consecutive terms, and they were convinced Cleveland's chances were great. William kept busy that fall speaking at rallies throughout the county on behalf of Cleveland and the Democrats. But his big event was the grand rally that would occur on the eve of the presidential election. It was his job to arrange for a spectacular fireworks display and secure prominent speakers.[10]

Just as the local Democrats started to gear up for the election, Republicans once again pushed for a Force Bill as a way to break the Democratic stranglehold in the South and some parts of the North. An article in the *National Republican* said that if the Lodge National Election Law were in effect, there would be a different state of political affairs in the country. It predicted that such a law would allow at least 20 African Americans to be elected to Congress from the South. The article, which was reprinted in the Texarkana paper, went further, stirring up the embers of racism that still lay in the ashes of Reconstruction. The article said the only way to break down the "detestable Bourbonism" of the South was to impose heavy taxes on the property of the white people and repeal state laws against interracial marriage.[11]

Gardner, the new editor of the *Texarkana Democrat*, lashed out against the Republicans and the Force Bill, which, he said, would wrest control of elections from the people. "It is proposed by the Republicans ... to put the negro on top of the white man in the South," Gardner commented. "The first step is to be the abolition of free elections, by turning them over to Federal emissaries, not responsible to the people." Gardner turned his anger on the black community in Texarkana, raging about "those little coons (who) should be made to respect the lads and little girls in the streets." Speaking for many Democrats, Gardner also vented his hatred toward the freedmen who continued to vote for the Republicans. "Sambo is in his glory from all appearances; but he is always that way just before an election," he wrote. "It is disgusting to a gentleman, who is compelled to attend to his daily business, when on every corner some black ape stops him to tell him how much 'fluence' he has."[12]

The more progressive Democrats raised the possibility of co-opting the black vote. "Signs are numerous that the negroes of this country are undergoing a second Emancipation," the *St. Louis Post-Dispatch* reported. The newspaper described this as a slow process in which the black man had begun to think for himself and rely on his own judgment in politics. In so doing, he would find the most conspicuous example of independence "is the wholesale revolt ... against political domination." The *Post-Dispatch* added that African Americans in Alabama, Arkansas, and Georgia were no longer voting Republican and were questioning Republican politics, such as the tariff, which hurt the black farmer as much as it did the white.[13]

Since Congress had not passed the Force Bill, Texarkana Democrats ignored the threats of the Republicans as they focused on the task at hand. The week before the national election was a bustle of activity for the local party leaders. Although they had used the new "Australian ballot" during the state election, this would be the first time they used it in a presidential election. Editor Gardner informed the reading public of what to expect on the new ballot, which would not include the names of the presidential candidates. Instead, it would list the names of electors along with their party affiliations. Each voter would choose eight electors by scratching out or marking off all those he did not want to be an elector.

But President Harrison and the Republicans were not ready to yield on the Force issue. Less than a week before the election, Attorney General William H.H. Miller issued an opinion that, in effect, enforced the tabled Force Bill by ignoring state election laws and making federal authority over the elections paramount. The opinion created such an outcry against the president and his blatant attempts at partisan control of the election that the White House had to respond. With Miller stumping in the West for Harrison, who was mourning the recent death of his wife, Solicitor General Charles H. Aldrich had to handle the issue. But he made matters worse when he ordered U.S. marshals and deputies – namely those in Arkansas, Alabama, and New York – to "invade the polling places and exercise supervisory power." When some states threatened confrontation at the polls, Aldrich retaliated by threatening to bring in federal troops.[14]

For Southern Democrats, the order brought back memories of Reconstruction and federal occupation. They vowed to ignore this dictate from Washington and declared they would maintain and enforce their state laws. Aldrich warned that anyone who tried to interfere with the U.S. marshals would "bring themselves within the scope of the criminal statutes of the United States, regardless of whether or not they act under any State or municipal statute." He promised that any interference would be "rigorously prosecuted."[15]

Stepping back from his inflammatory comments, Aldrich tried to reason with his opponents: "The idea that the United States is not as much the object of the people's love and patriotism as any State is utterly mischievous.... A peace officer of the United States who seeks to prevent illegal voting no more invades the rights of American citizens than does the peace officer of a State. The impression that the Federal Government is a foreign power should be obliterated."[16]

But Democrats throughout the country continued to take issue with both Miller's and Aldrich's stance that U.S. marshals could be sent into any county to serve as an election supervisor. They claimed that marshals could only go into counties with 20,000 or more people. Miller telegraphed U.S. District Attorney General Waters in Little Rock approving his decision to send marshals and deputies into any Arkansas county he thought necessary. Rather than wrapping up a federal grand jury meeting in Little Rock, officials adjourned it until Wednesday, November 9 – the day after the election. This was seen as another intimidation tactic, and rumors quickly spread "that the Grand Jury will indict every Democratic election judge who will not submit to the supervision of Federal officials at the polls."[17]

Arkansas Democrats refused to yield the issue. "The State authorities are fixed in their purpose to allow no interference with their authority," the *New York Times* reported. A notice to Arkansas election officers, published in newspapers throughout the state the Monday before Election Day, demonstrated Arkansas' resolve. The purpose of the notice, issued by state officials, was to make them aware of their duties and the boundaries of federal officials. The notice said the federal court would appoint supervisors for nearly all the voting precincts in the state. These supervisors had the right to "challenge any vote by any person whose legal qualification may be debated." They also had the right to be by the ballot box at all times once the polls opened and until the vote was canvassed. They could scrutinize how the voting was done and how the poll books were kept. They also could scrutinize, count, and canvass each ballot. Despite Arkansas' adoption of the secret ballot, the federal supervisor had the right to see and know everything that transpired between the voter and the judges in the national election.[18]

The notice went on to tell state election officers what these federal supervisors could not do. They could not tell a person how to vote. And they did not have the final say in determining the qualification of a voter – that right belonged to the election judges. While federal supervisors would be in just about every precinct, those supervisors could not be federal marshals, except in Little Rock. The notice quoted federal statutes, which allowed deputy marshals to serve as election supervisors only in cities with at least 20,000 residents. If deputy marshals tried to exercise this authority outside of Little Rock, they were to be arrested by the sheriff.[19]

The controversy intensified the excitement in Texarkana as Election Day approached. Lawyers debated the legal points, and conversations focused on little else. Miller County Democrats reached fever pitch as they put the finishing touches on their rally. The clouds burst open with rain as the cannon opened up at 6:30 Monday night and continued to fire uninterrupted for the next half an hour. No one seemed to mind the rain as hundreds turned out for the processional and 30-minute fireworks display that led up to the main event – the speeches. A platform decked with several American flags and a large Cleveland and Stevenson banner had been erected. William served as emcee, opening the rally and introducing the speakers, the Hon. Minor Wallace of Magnolia, Judge Joe D. Conway of Washington, and W.R. Coats of Kalamazoo, Michigan. But excitement could carry the people only so far. The festive crowd quickly became restless as Wallace droned on for two hours in the cold, wet weather. The other speakers, sensing the mood of the audience, limited their speeches to a few lively comments, which became even livelier when a third-party heckler interrupted them.[20]

Despite the presence of federal supervisors, November 8 passed in Texarkana as a quiet, uneventful election day. Bad weather kept some people away, so voter turnout was light throughout the county. That night, election watchers enjoyed a new treat as several businesses partnered with the Western Union office to sponsor a special telegraphic election display. A stereopticon projected the election results as they came in onto a large illuminated canvas arranged in the window of the local telegraph office. "Thousands can stand in the streets and see and learn the election news from means of this spectacular telegraphic report," the *Democrat* reported. Because of the rain, only hundreds showed up to watch the election results flash across the canvas. But the Democrats didn't mind the rain; they were winning the White House! "Betting was lively in the election last evening, while the bulletins were coming in," the *Democrat* reported the next day. "Jubilant Democrats covered all Republican money, and offered more at odds, which was not taken." The Wednesday issue of the *Democrat*, which proclaimed Cleveland president once again, was covered with woodcuts of roosters crowing. Even though Cleveland had not been able to get rid of the hated tariffs or the threat of a Force Bill in his first term, Democrats were confident he'd get the job done this time.[21]

Several people spent the day after the election toasting the new president at Texarkana's many saloons. First thing that morning, one reveler got a little too drunk and a little too out of control at Con Dorrian's saloon, which was just west of the state line. Marshal Crenshaw, of the East Side, tried to arrest him. But when the man resisted, Crenshaw asked Zach Few, a constable for the East Side, to help him. Possibly having had a little too much celebration himself, J.B. Barkman, a West Side Justice of the Peace, stepped up and threatened to arrest Crenshaw, who was outside his jurisdiction. The marshal, in turn, threatened Barkman with arrest if he continued to interfere. As a result, Few and Crenshaw arrested both the drunken man and Barkman.[22]

While in court, Barkman was joined by his son Joe, who got heated up over the incident and tried to start a fight in the courtroom. Finally, Barkman posted bond and went to drown his complaints at another saloon with his son. Late that afternoon,

Few went into the saloon where the Barkmans happened to be. By this time, the father and son had had quite a bit to drink. They started arguing angrily with Few; in a matter of minutes, bullets were flying. As Few was shooting, he backed out of the saloon. One of his bullets hit Barkman, who crumpled to the floor. The son, firing as he ran, chased after Few. He continued shooting into Few's body even after the policeman fell to the street dead. A stray bullet hit Frank Cassidy, an innocent bystander, killing him almost instantly.[23]

The triple homicide shocked the town and especially William. As mayor, William had been Few's boss. The two had worked closely together in politics as Few had organized the Cleveland and Thurman Club and was one of the up-and-coming young Democrats. Since Few was a Mason, the Masonic Lodge had an emergency meeting to prepare for the funeral. William was appointed to a committee that was to draft a resolution in honor of Few and have it published in the local papers and given to the dead man's family. According to custom, the Masons were asked to wear their usual badges of mourning for 30 days. Since so many of the Masons, like Few, belonged to other secret orders, the group decided not to attend the funeral as a body but to go individually or with the other orders.[24]

It seemed as if the entire town turned out for Few's funeral November 11. William had ordered City Hall to be draped in mourning. And all the businesses on the East Side had closed out of respect for Few's family. "Such an honor was never before paid any deceased citizen of Texarkana," Gardner commented in the *Texarkana Democrat*. Although the Masons didn't attend the funeral as a group, they led off the funeral procession with their black-draped carriages. The hearse slowly followed. Behind it came the carriages of the Knights of Honor. More than 100 carriages lined up for the mournful trek to the cemetery; it was the largest funeral Texarkana had seen.[25]

26   The Crusade

The 1892 election controversy didn't end with Cleveland's victory. The Democrats' fears about the federal grand jury sitting in Little Rock proved real. The grand jury – charged by Judge Williams of the federal court in Little Rock to thoroughly investigate methods used in Arkansas' congressional elections – returned nine indictments against state election officials before adjourning for the session. While no arrests were made immediately, political pundits speculated that the indictments involved violations of the state law that required the appointment of election judges from different political parties.[1]

Another federal court case stemming from the election threatened the future of the Australian ballot just as it looked as if the secret ballot system would be adopted nationwide. A Mr. Dwyer had been indicted in Texas for violating the law when he made out ballots for electors at the table where the presiding election judge sat. Dwyer also used scraps of papers handed him by the electors as ballots and prepared ballots without the assistance of another judge. When Judge Maxey heard the case against Dwyer in the U.S. District Court in San Antonio, he quashed the indictment, saying Dwyer's actions didn't violate the law. "It is considered that the decision seriously affects the supposed safeguards thrown around the ballot by the new Australian law," the *Texarkana Democrat* commented.[2]

Closer to home, Democrats were outraged when "rantankerous Third party cranks" got the federal grand jury sitting in Texarkana in December to indict H.M. Allen, an election judge in Prescott, for interfering with a federal supervisor during the election. Allen and another election judge had made a federal supervisor keep away from the voting booth in compliance with the state's secret ballot law.[3]

Although local Democrats were riled up over the Allen case, the federal case that attracted the most attention that December was one William had to argue. A few years earlier, Mrs. M.A. Tabor, a highly respected society lady and a spiritualist, had tried to hold a séance in Texarkana. Then-Mayor C.C. Dorrian considered a séance the same as a variety show or other stage performance and required Tabor to get a license before holding one. Insisting that she didn't need a license to hold a religious service, the medium ignored the mayor and went ahead with the séance. Dorrian had her arrested and jailed. Tabor, in turn, sued the mayor in federal court, seeking $25,000 in damages. Represented by William and Paul Jones, Dorrian claimed he should not be held personally responsible for performing his duty as mayor.[4]

Because of Tabor's standing in the community, the case became a cause celebre in Texarkana – the "most exciting and sensational civil suit ever tried" in the city. To accommodate all the attorneys involved in the case, the Miller County Circuit Court, which also was in session, adjourned at noon December 1 – just in time for opening arguments in Tabor v. Dorrian. The new courtroom in the Federal Building was packed with the elite of society as William stood to give the opening statement on behalf of the former mayor. Testimony was heard throughout the afternoon and into the evening with Jones giving an eloquent closing argument for Dorrian. The case was handed to the jury at 11 p.m.[5]

William and the other attorneys spent a long night, waiting for the jury to return a verdict. Finally at 5 a.m. Friday, word was sent that the jury was coming in. William returned to the courtroom with Dorrian to hear the jury's award of $1,500 to Tabor. After being up all night, William had only a few hours to freshen up before heading over to the county courthouse where the county circuit court would resume at 9 a.m.[6]

The Tabor case wasn't over. That spring, the district attorney in Washington, D.C., placed séances in the same category with stage shows and required licenses for all mediums. His action had spiritualists worked up throughout the country. They saw this action as an attack on the free practice of their religion.

But officials in Texarkana viewed it as a validation of Dorrian's position. It was with renewed hope that William, now assisted by Joe, appealed to the Federal District Court. This time, the jury returned a sealed verdict – an award of $25 to Tabor. "If not a victory for the defendant, (the verdict) can give but small satisfaction to the plaintiff," the local newspaper reported.[7]

Back in the Miller County Circuit Court, the grand jury was performing one of its annual duties – examining the physical and fiscal condition of the county. The jury's biggest complaints that year had to do with the county jail. The jurors recommended the county build a new courthouse as the current courtroom was too small to seat the court and litigants. And the stench from the jail, which was right under the courtroom, was at times "stifling to the occupants of the entire building." Their other complaint was the cost of boarding and housing idle prisoners. Together, the idle convicts and the residents at the county poorhouse cost Miller County $3,000 a year, "which is one of the highest expense items the county bears."[8]

To reduce the cost, the jury strongly suggested the prisoners should be hired out as provided by law. This suggestion made no concession for the physical and mental health of some of the prisoners. At that time, it was common to jail the mentally ill. In fact, J. Dodson, a young man who had been confined to the jail on a charge of lunacy, died in his cell at about the time the grand jury conducted its investigation. Another prisoner, Tony Stevenson, had been confined in the jail on a pilfering charge for several months before the grand jury convened. After hearing his case, the jury did not indict him. When Stevenson was released, he was "in wretched health and almost entirely helpless."[9]

As part of their solution, the jurors recommended the county sell the poorhouse and buy a farm instead. Then the paupers and convicts could work on the farm for their keep. The county, led by Judge Friedell, put the prisoners to work, but it shelved the farm idea. Instead, it awarded a contract to Thomas Hodge to run the poorhouse. In return for his services, he would receive $7 per inmate per month.[10]

1893 dawned bright and promising for those living in Texarkana. Excited about the idea of a new county courthouse and possibly a real sewage system, they counted their blessings, one of which was the new Federal Building that literally and figuratively straddled the state line. Although parts of the building were already in use, the section housing a new joint post office opened for the first time January 2. An eager crowd lined the sidewalks for a chance to take in the architectural detailing and the native oak woodwork in the courtroom and post office, which would serve both sides of the city. The initial announcement of the merged post office had stirred quite a dispute as both sides, used to having their own post office and the accompanying patronage, fought over whether a Texan or Arkansan should get the coveted post at the new office. When the Postmaster General announced that W.W. Shaw, the East Side's postmaster, would get the new post, those in the Arkansas city were elated. The Democrats didn't care that Shaw was a Republican and had been appointed by a Republican administration. They saw this as a sign that one of their own would succeed Shaw once Cleveland's administration settled into the White House.[11]

Now that they had an actual federal courtroom, the area lawyers looked for ways to more fully utilize it. They called a citizens' meeting January 11 to discuss extending the jurisdiction of the Texarkana Division of the Eastern District into a large portion of Indian Territory. Since crime was rampant in the Indian Territory, the criminal lawyers saw such an extension as a bonanza for their practices. The proposal already had come up in Congress, so their task was to push it through both houses. William was appointed to a committee on finances charged with raising the money necessary to lobby Congress. To garner more local support and help his fund-raising effort, William had the facts and statistics that showed the potential benefits to Texarkana published in the local papers.[12]

With the excitement of the elections, court, and holidays behind him, William turned his attention to city matters. He had campaign promises to keep. One of the first issues that needed tackling was enforcing the Sunday blue laws and closing illegal businesses. Previous administrations had shut their eyes to the Sunday saloon business and issued licenses or fines to shady businesses instead of closing them down. The city then used the license and fine revenue, which amounted to $1,500 a year, to help keep city government afloat. William made it clear from the start that he wasn't going to play that game. "Instead of licensing the dives and other violations of ordinances, our policy has been to surprise them as required by law.... I have yet to believe that it is sound policy to build up the city's finances by encouraging the commission of a crime," he said.[13]

One of his adversaries was Dixon, who was once again sheriff. Profiting from the gambling houses, Dixon didn't want things to change. His gang, which included his deputies, enforced their own brand of law and order, often gunning down anyone who ran afoul of them. He also used civic pressure within the business community and the Democratic Party to get his way. But William refused to bow to Dixon's influence. As part of his cleanup crusade, the mayor ordered raids on the gambling houses and vowed to take on the sheriff's office.[14]

William got his chance to go head-to-head with Dixon when he prosecuted one of the sheriff's deputies in a murder trial. Dixon confronted William outside the courtroom. "[H]e gave me to understand that if I did not relax my efforts he would kill me in the court room," William wrote. The mayor knew this was not an idle threat as he had witnessed Dixon's shooting of the gambler 10 years earlier in that very courtroom. But he didn't flinch under the sheriff's ruthlessness: "I told him that I would not relax and he might kill, as life was not much to me."

William didn't let up – even though he had a wife and three children to worry about. (William Hendrick Arnold, Jr., was born January 30, 1893.) Not only did he continue to prosecute the case, he ordered a raid on the Huey gambling house, which was under Dixon's protection. Once again, the sheriff threatened the mayor. And once again, William ignored him. Many of the residents of the town supported the mayor, sending a clear message to the sheriff and his gang that their kind of law was no longer welcome. Before long, the East Side, at least, was free of brothels, gambling houses, and other illegal businesses.

As another part of his cleanup efforts, William forced the saloons to observe the Sunday blue laws. Enforcing the Sunday law was made more difficult by the state line, which artificially split the town in two. The push for law and order on the Arkansas side was not always mirrored on the Texas side, as the saloons on the West Side did a land-office business when the East Side saloons were forced to close on Sundays. But as 1892 drew to a close, public demands finally resulted in Sunday observance on both sides of the line. "[F]or the first time in the history of our city the Sabbath was universally observed in a business way," the local paper reported, "every business house and saloon being strictly closed with exception of the drug stores and barber shops which were open during the usual Sunday hours.[15]

Following that historic day, there were enough violations of the law that the local paper had to continue its campaign for law and order. "The law which commands men to observe the sanctity of the Sabbath day and prohibits gambling cannot work any real harm or even injustice to any class, as the latter vocation, as a business, is illegal, while there are countless other vocations permitted and approved both by law and society, in which every man may engage," Gardner wrote, "the law exists and it follows necessarily that it should be either repealed or enforced."[16]

William was intent on enforcing it. Violators appeared before him in police court and hotly contested the charges. But they usually walked away with a fine. Often, those charged were represented by Joe, but the fact that Joe was his legal partner didn't seem to sway William. The two had had years of experience opposing each other in their early days of double-barreled law. William's tactics finally won out and earned him the respect of the townspeople in Texarkana as well as other cities. His success forced the West Side to take action against the illegal businesses within its boundaries. In May 1893, the West Side City Council ordered the city marshal to close all "disorderly houses" and gambling houses. The *Texarkana Democrat* noted that this action put the West Side in line with the East Side. The crusade against gambling spread to other cities, and they credited Texarkana with setting the example. "Little Rock is now making it warm for the gamblers as well as Memphis," the local paper quoted from other papers. "Texarkana led the way for maintaining law and order, including the closing of all saloons on Sunday."[17]

While fighting the big battles, William also had to tend to the everyday nuisances of city life. The weather and the deteriorating economy in the winter of 1892-1893 combined to create an ever-growing number of homeless throughout the nation. With the help of the railroads, a proliferation of the homeless and transients found their way to Texarkana, where some of them resorted to "short hand" robbery of the passengers on the trains passing by town. One accosted a woman in her home, causing demands for action. The city marshal made frequent raids to round up "stray tramps" who were then hauled before William in the police court.[18]

Every spring, the city launched a major cleanup campaign, knowing that if the garbage that had accumulated all winter remained on the ground during the heat of the summer, it would be an epidemic in the making. Although they had to be reminded, most people voluntarily participated in the annual spring cleaning; they understood that their lives and the lives of their families depended on it. This year, spring cleaning took on more urgency. City officials remembered too well the cholera epidemic that had swept the world the previous fall.

A more gruesome reminder had occurred at the state penitentiary in Little Rock and a prison work camp in Helena that winter, and health officials were still debating whether the 14 victims of the epidemic had died of arsenic poisoning, cholera, diphtheria, or some other strange, mysterious disease. Following a tour of the facility, the Little Rock chief of police and several inspectors severely condemned the conditions of the prison. They described a dump pile within the walls of the facility as being the size of a city lot and containing "all the manure from the stables, dead calves, offal and kitchen refuse, all in a state of morbid decay. Over this was roaming at will the milch cows of the Penitentiary, and sheep and hogs to be killed for meat." The most recent victim of the epidemic had apparently scavenged some beet pickles from the refuse and eaten them the night before he died.[19]

Soon after the epidemic had broken out in the prison, doctors confirmed three cases of diphtheria in Texarkana. The city marshal had posted yellow flags on the infected houses, and local stores did a good business of selling fumigators. The quick action on the part of city officials had prevented a widespread outbreak. Now that spring was here, they didn't want to take any chances. At a meeting of the East Side Board of Health, Dr. Spearman complained about the filth in the city, warning the board members of what could happen if the garbage wasn't cleaned up. Once again, William had city officials issue notices requiring the townspeople to clean up their property. And once again, he ordered the marshal to rigidly enforce the sanitary ordinances during the "heated term" to prevent sickness. Because of the incident at the Little Rock prison, he also ordered the city scavengers to bury all decaying and vegetable matter at least two feet deep at a safe distance outside city limits.[20]

Soon after getting the city into shape for summer, William was forced to take a sabbatical. The mayor had loaned a horse to Spearman for a few days. The doctor returned the horse, still hitched to his new buggy. When William went out to help Spearman unhitch the animal, the horse spooked and plunged forward just as William was removing Spearman's bridle to replace it with one of his. The mayor was thrown to the ground, and the buggy was smashed to kindling wood. Fortunately, there was a doctor on the premises, who had escaped unscathed. Besides being severely bruised, William fractured the smaller bones in the lower part of his right leg.[21]

The mayor spent the next few weeks at home, having arranged for the city recorder to hold police court in his absence. Convinced he needed the healing waters of Hot Springs, he hobbled into City Hall on crutches May 5 to put everything in order for a prolonged absence. Then he and his family headed to Hot Springs for a month-long rest.[22]

27   The Rule of Violence

Instilling a respect for law and order was not an easy task in what was still seen as the Southern frontier of the 1890s. As a railroad center, Texarkana was easily accessible to people from all walks of life, including the criminal element. And being next door to Indian Territory, it retained a roughness peculiar to frontier towns. Both the railroads and the Indian Territory held a peculiar attraction for gunfighters, robbers, murderers, and just all-around bad guys. Although banks were an easy target for the likes of the Dalton Gang, which did much of its work in this part of the country, trains were an enticing target, especially when they carried large payrolls and wealthy passengers. While robbery was usually the motive, such gangs showed no remorse in ending a few lives along the way. If they were going to hang for a robbery, they might as well hang for a murder. In the meantime, they escaped to Indian Territory to delay the day of reckoning.

The newspapers of Texarkana were filled with the escapades of the Daltons and other gangs. But sometimes it was hard to tell the criminals from the respected community leaders. A gentleman was just as likely as a criminal to reach for his gun or knife when provoked. And many elected officials felt no compunction over stealing from their neighbors. This violence, a perverted outgrowth of the Southern sense of honor, seemed to escalate as the South fell further behind the North in terms of wealth and influence. It had been hard enough to lose the war, to have their property destroyed or stolen, their homes occupied, their governments wrested away from them. But to be constantly reminded of these losses 30 years later, to be punished for the actions of their fathers, to be continually judged and ridiculed by their Northern countrymen was more than some Southerners could take.

The rising leaders of the 1890s had been the children of the Old South. They had been raised "to value honor as much as, if not more than, godly conscience," Southern historian Wyatt-Brown writes. While this code of honor dictated restraint and self-denial when dealing with provocation, it permitted impulsive reactions when necessary to preserve self-esteem and public reputation. This permission had resulted in the antebellum *code duello*. Although duels had been outlawed in the modern world of the late 19th century, Southern society, reared on this concept of honor, did not frown too harshly on men such as Joe Cook who resorted to violence when they couldn't settle their differences with words.[1]

While they didn't always condone such violent behavior from one of their own, respectable citizens could justify it. They understood the frustrations that had led to the outrage. Governed by the honor of the past, Southern society established an unspoken set of rules to help conquer the new frontiers facing the South. A fine line often separated the respected community leader from the hunted and hated criminal, the worthy young debutante from the fallen woman. Society tutted and scolded when one of its own came too close to this line. It offered no forgiveness when the line was crossed – especially by an outsider.

Thus when a dispute between neighbors on College Hill turned ugly in June 1893, no one intervened; they figured the two would settle their differences. After a particularly heated argument with his neighbor Jesse Hale had turned physical, R.E. Lee decided to resolve the dispute over a well for good. He shouldered his shotgun, walked outside, and took aim at the Hales' front porch where both Jesse and his wife were sitting on the hot summer evening. The shots killed Mrs. Hale and wounded her husband.[2]

On the day of his trial in Miller County Circuit Court, Lee was escorted to the courtroom by East Side Constable Joe Vinson and seated at the railing opposite the judge's stand. When Vinson left the courtroom to run an errand in the jail, Hale, leading his two little daughters by the hand, entered the room and walked up to Lee. Ignoring the judge, the prosecutor, and the spectators, Hale dropped his daughters' hand, pulled out a .45 Colt revolver, and began shooting at Lee. As the prisoner dodged behind a large heating stove, a bullet lodged in his thigh. All but the prosecutor and the judge ran pell-mell from the room as Hale continued firing. Hearing the commotion, Marshal Crenshaw rushed upstairs into the courtroom, seized Hale, and disarmed him. Hale was arrested, and Lee's trial was postponed.[3]

Texarkana society recognized a certain kind of justice in Hale's actions; after all, in avenging his wife, he was protecting the honor of his family – something every Southern boy had been taught from the time he was in dresses. But it could not excuse the way he had carried out his vengeance, which jeopardized others. "The action of Hale in thus carrying personal vengeance to the very bar of justice, however just his case, cannot be too severely condemned," the local newspaper commented.[4]

Despite its attitude toward some types of violence, one crime society would not tolerate was official corruption. People could joke about vote stealing and stuffing of ballot boxes (unless their opponents did it); that was part of the game of politics. But they would not stand for anyone getting rich at the public's expense. Thus when former state Treasurer William Woodruff was indicted in December 1892 on charges of embezzling and grand larceny, no one offered him much sympathy. The extent of Woodruff's crime wasn't fully known until 1893. But once the details came out, the newspapers were full of the scandal – and the details of how Woodruff had taken nearly $140,000 of state money during his tenure in office from 1880 to 1890.[5]

More scandal arose – this time closer to home – a few months later. The Bowie County grand jury, meeting in March 1893, indicted several West Side city and Bowie County officials on charges ranging from incompetence to speculating in county scrip. The scandal spread to the East Side that summer when William's and Joe's friend A.S. Blythe, who had replaced

Dixon as Miller County sheriff and tax collector, came up $17,000 short in his tax collections. He admitted using the money to cover personal expenses, saying he had expected to replace it before the revenue was due.[6]

When trustees were appointed for Blythe's bondsmen, who included several of William's Cook in-laws, the court attached all the sheriff's property, which consisted of 35 acres of land adjacent to Texarkana (valued at $5,000-$6,000); three houses and lots in the city ($2,000); his livery stable on the West Side ($4,000); half interest in another livery stable ($2,000); and industrial land in Louisiana ($2,500-$3,500) Ten months later, Blythe still hadn't made good on the shortage. The court ordered him to pay more than $7,000 for the sale of attached stock. When he refused to pay, the debt fell to his bondsmen who had to pay the debt plus 10 percent monthly interest.[7]

The season of scandal didn't end with Blythe. In the spring of 1894, West Side Mayor S.D. Lary was indicted because of his alleged interests in contracts for state improvements. Lary had long been associated with the "tough element" on the West Side, and his administration had been surrounded by numerous rumors and derogatory accusations. Texarkana was not alone in these scandals. Despite the public contempt, reports of corruption in city, county, and state government were common throughout the country.[8]

While society would not tolerate official corruption, it looked the other way – for the most part – when elected officials overstepped the law when it came to settling personal differences or responding to a perceived insult, even when that insult was deserved. In this respect, they were held to no higher standard than the average citizen. When Capt. W.J. Allen of the West Side criticized Bowie County officials in his *Inter-State News* for raising taxes, he was charged with contempt, fined $25 plus interest and court costs. The action gave the county a black eye – at least on the East Side. "We can scarcely credit such action to a nineteenth century court, presided over by enlightened men and held in a civilized country," the *Texarkana Democrat* reported as it accused Bowie County Judge John King of ignoring Allen's inalienable rights.[9]

The Bowie County treasurer met with Allen and offered to give him the $25 to cover the fine. But Allen refused it, saying he would only accept the money from the commissioners themselves. More determined to speak out against the problems in Bowie County, Allen continued to print attacks against the county officials. But now it was personal. Several sharp thrusts aimed at King and the commissioners appeared in the *Inter-State News*. The day after a particularly vicious attack, Allen was walking to G.W. Treher's news store on State Line Avenue when he met King and Howell Runnels, Jr. Before any words could be exchanged, King pulled out a pistol and shot Allen from about six feet away. Allen was carried to a nearby office, and a doctor was summoned. But there was nothing the doctor could do. As he died, Allen gave a statement indicating that King had murdered him in cold blood.[10]

Immediately after the incident, King was arrested and charged with assault to murder. He was released on $5,000 bond only to be arrested a few hours later and charged with murder. Three days later, King appeared before Justice R.J. Haywood of the West Side for a preliminary hearing. When Haywood set bail at $5,000, half a dozen citizens stepped up to provide it. Later that year when the Bowie County grand jury indicted King on the murder charge, Judge John H. Sheppard once again set bail at $5,000, and King was released. The trial was set to begin October 12 before Judge Sheppard. But the prosecutor asked for a change of venue – not to protect King but to ensure justice for the victim. He argued that the people in Bowie County held a great deal of prejudice against Allen and would be biased toward the county judge. Sheppard granted the request, and the trial was moved to Clarksville in Little River County, Texas.[11]

Two months later, a district court jury in Clarksville acquitted King, finding that he had acted in self-defense. In so finding, they ignored Allen's dying words and the testimony of a disinterested eyewitness who verified Allen's version of the incident. Instead, they chose to believe the county officials who came to King's aid by testifying that they had heard Allen threaten to shoot King like a cur. And Runnels, who had been with King at the time of the shooting, said that when Allen had seen the two men approaching him, he had switched his walking stick from his right hand to the left and then moved his right hand toward his hip pocket – a sure sign he was going for a gun.[12]

On the other side of the state line, Miller County Judge Friedell also was involved in an altercation – this one stemming from the problems surrounding the Inter-State College that had opened the previous year on College Hill. Ever since Professor G.L. Bryant had opened the college, he had been besieged with labor disputes with his teachers. Friedell had served as legal counsel in a libel suit brought against Bryant. Convinced that the county judge was trying to ruin him by having a grand jury indict both him and his wife, Bryant went to Friedell's office October 6 and charged him with slander. Friedell denied the professor's accusations and ordered him out of his office.[13]

After that, reports grew muddled as both men claimed the other threw the first punch. The noise of the two men brawling brought Mr. Hallum running out of his office. Trying to stop the fight, he punched Bryant. All three men were taken to the East Side Police Court where they appeared before Recorder Treher on charges of fighting. Ordinarily, William, as mayor, would have been presiding over the police court, but he was out of the office on this day. Treher found Bryant, who looked pretty scratched up, guilty and fined him $2.50 plus court costs. The recorder dropped the charges against Friedell, who was sporting a black eye, and Hallum.[14]

While polite society could countenance violence in a gentleman, it had far less tolerance for those it considered outsiders. A black man, for instance, could not get away with murder – even if it was committed in self-defense. And when a black man's violence was aimed at a white person, mob law usually ruled the day. But even mob law followed an unwritten code. According to that law, the culprit, whether white or black, had to be positively identified and every effort taken to secure a confession. It was easier for a community to justify its actions if it could say the man had confessed. Lynching was the preferred punishment – since that was what the "fiend" would have gotten had an official jury decided his fate. But for outrages against women and children, black offenders often were burned at the stake. In southern Arkansas in the 1890s, certain conditions had to exist for a mob to make itself the law. Either the community was convinced the culprit would not get his just punishment in court or the crime had to be particularly heinous – a grisly murder or the rape of a white woman. The victim or the victim's family usually initiated mob rule and determined the punishment. And the African American community often participated in mob law as spectators and, sometimes, as instigators.[15]

Like their Southern brethren elsewhere, many of the townspeople of Texarkana resorted to mob rule when they felt it was their duty. Such was the case in February 1892 when Mrs. Henry Jewell, a young mother, was raped at her farm a few miles from the East Side. It was a Saturday night, and Henry had left his wife with their five-month-old baby so he could go into town on business. Soon after Henry had left, a man later described as a mulatto came to the door and asked for him, saying he had some hogs to sell him. Mrs. Jewell explained that her husband was gone on business and then conversed with the man for a few minutes. After he left, she decided to visit a neighbor who lived about half a mile down the road. As Mrs. Jewell went to lock the door, the man jumped out from a hiding place and seized her by the throat.

The man dragged the fainting woman out to the barn where he raped her. An hour later, he took off into the woods. When Henry came home a while later, he sounded the alarm; a posse quickly assembled to search for the rapist. Three men who resembled Mrs. Jewell's description of her attacker were arrested. But upon close scrutiny, Mrs. Jewell shook her head. None of them was the man who had defiled her. Meanwhile, Ed Coy, who was later identified as the assailant, was on the run, going back and forth from Texarkana into Little River country in Texas. Thinking the law was after him for a gambling violation, Coy said he talked to some friends about surrendering. But they warned him he would be lynched if he turned himself in.

A week later when he had returned to the Texarkana area, Coy was captured by a farmer and his sons and held hostage overnight. The next morning, East Side Marshal Crenshaw, accompanied by 50 mounted guards, rode out to the home of Calvin Scott and arrested Coy. They took the 32-year-old man to the Jewell farm where Mrs. Jewell identified him. On the way into town, Coy maintained his innocence, but no one was listening. Crenshaw secured Coy in a heavily guarded room and waited for the word to go out to the rest of the posse that the rapist had been captured.

By two that afternoon, everyone had returned. The posse leaders, who most likely included Henry Jewell, were ready to pass sentence on the condemned man. They gathered in the room where he was being kept to discuss the mode of death and the place. They finally agreed – a lynching on Broad Street. As they brought the prisoner out into the street, they were met by a thousand people who had their own idea of a fit punishment. The crowd marched Coy down Broad Street to the Iron Mountain roundhouse, where an even larger crowd had gathered. Someone threw a rope to be used for the lynching, "but the 5,000 throats present set up a shout of 'burn him,'" the *St. Louis Republic* reported. Ignoring the rope, the leaders of the mob secured the frightened prisoner to a large stake supported with guy wires. One of them approached him with a can of coal oil, "and the crowd then knew what fate was in store." The self-appointed leaders doused Coy with the oil.

"Where's Mrs. Jewell?" several people shouted.

"Here," a few people on the edge of the crowd yelled, as they began to push the young woman through the mass of spectators.

"Bring her forward," the man who had taken charge ordered. The code of mob law required the injured party to inflict the punishment.

The crowd parted to let Mrs. Jewell through. Within a minute, she was standing face-to-face with the doomed man. Without uttering a word, the leader placed a torch in her hand. Mrs. Jewell saw the fear in Coy's eyes and then looked from him to the torch to the man in charge, who stood waiting expectantly. She knew what was expected of her, but she didn't want to do it. Let someone else have that on his conscience. Mrs. Jewell stepped back, trying to escape into the crowd. But her neighbors had formed an inescapable wall around her.

"No, no, apply it," the crowd shouted at her.

Averting her eyes from Coy's face, Mrs. Jewell quickly applied the torch to the oil that had pooled about his feet. Without another look at the man, she turned her back and disappeared into the crowd. Coy screamed in agony as the flames licked around his legs and then enveloped his body. Seven minutes later, he was dead. And the respectable people of Texarkana returned to their business.

The gory details of any lynching or a burning spread quickly through the country. While some Northern papers used the Texarkana burning as a way to demonstrate the moral poverty of the South, others were more sympathetic – at first. "The good people of Texarkana deplore the necessity of mob law," the *New York Times* reported, "... but the opinion is general that Coy has been rightly served."[16]

As it was retold, the incident enraged people in the North, who saw it as nothing short of heathen barbarism. A few days after the burning, the *New York Times*, which had somewhat condoned the punishment in its initial report, was compelled to speak against it. "It is simply not possible to describe as a civilized community any community in which a man can be taken by the mob and publicly burned to death without protest on the part of anybody," the *Times* commented. "It does not in the least matter what the crime is of which the victim of such an outrage is accused. It cannot possibly be more brutal and barbarous then the crime which is thus committed upon him."

Equating Texarkanians with "Pi-Utes" and Central Africans, the *Times* continued with racial overtones: "That is a performance that might have occurred in Europe during the Middle Ages, or that might occur in Central Africa at this time, but that could not, we repeat, occur in a civilized community." Pointing to the fact that Mrs. Jewell lit the match, the *Times* said this was how Indians behaved "but civilized men and civilized women can regard it only with disgust."

"The notion that society shall put itself upon the level of the criminal, and, when he has been especially cruel and barbarous, shall be especially cruel and barbarous in its turn, is one that belongs to a low stage of human development, before self-restraint or any other quality that can rights be called moral has begun to operate at all," the *Times* commented. The article conceded that "the offense is one that is especially and with reason dreaded by the South, and one to which the African race is particularly prone." But it concluded that the mob should let the law work and no punishment should be more barbaric than a hanging or shooting.[17]

Texarkanians chafed at the criticism. They saw it as an attack on their way of life, their morals, and their family honor. And they saw it as proof that North and South were still poles apart.

28   North vs. South

A year later, Texarkana mob law was put in motion again, but this time it was over a crime that occurred in Paris, Texas. Henry Smith, an African American, had been arrested in Paris two years earlier for drunken and disorderly behavior. When he resisted, he was clubbed by the arresting officer Henry Vance. Smith swore vengeance. After serving his prison term, Smith returned to Paris and waited his chance to get even with Vance. He took it on a Thursday afternoon in January 1893 when he saw Myrtle, Vance's three-year-old daughter, playing in her front yard. Smith offered the little girl some candy and then picked her up and carried her through the city to a pasture on the edge of town. Whenever he was stopped and questioned, he said he was taking the child to the doctor.[1]

Alone in the pasture with the toddler, Smith vent all his anger toward Vance on the little girl. He started his revenge by raping the child. Then, remembering the clubbing he had received at the hands of the father, he delivered blow for blow on the daughter. When she was senseless, he took a little leg in either hand and literally tore her body apart. As darkness set in, he covered the mutilated, torn body with leaves and brush and then lay down beside the dead child and slept through the night. The next morning, Smith returned home, made his wife cook him a hearty breakfast, and fled.[2]

When Myrtle's body was found, the people of Paris were appalled at the sadistic violence wrought upon the child. How could any human being do such a thing to an innocent little girl? The horror of the murder defied comprehension. Word of the awful deed spread quickly to Texarkana and throughout the surrounding countryside. Since several people had seen Smith with the child, no one doubted the identity of the fiend who had committed such a monstrous crime. Hundreds of men from Paris to Texarkana volunteered to join the manhunt, and the railroads offered free transportation to anyone searching for Smith.[3]

Knowing he would be lynched if apprehended, Smith made his way to Arkansas, skirting Texarkana Sunday night and then hopping a boxcar on a northbound freight train at the coal chute north of town. He left the train at Hope and once again set off on foot for Clow, Arkansas. The manhunt ended Tuesday, January 31, when another black man, wanting to make sure the right man was arrested, led the posse to Smith who was captured in Clow. Smith confessed his crime, in every gruesome detail, to a number of his captors. "The excitement aroused over the news of his capture was intense even in this city, a hundred miles removed from the scene of his devilish crime," the *Democrat* reported. Originally, the posse that had captured Smith planned to bring him by train through Texarkana that night en route to Paris. Thousands of people from both Miller County and Bowie County flocked to the union depot, hoping to catch a glimpse of "this unexampled monster of crime."[4]

At the last minute, the plans were changed, and the posse's departure was postponed till the next morning. When the people waiting for the train Tuesday night were told Smith wasn't on the train, many of them thought is was a ruse "to prevent the citizens here from lynching him, and thus relieving the citizens of Paris of that labor." At the appointed hour Wednesday morning, hundreds of people made their way to the Texarkana depot. "[W]hen the noise of the approaching train was heard, the large platform facing the depot, was a perfect living mass of eager and expectant humanity," the *Democrat* reported. "Over all, however, there brooded an ominous calm, which told more plainly than any overt act could possibly have done, of the deep feeling and deadly passion which lurked in every breast."[5]

Sensing the mood of the people of Texarkana and remembering the burning of Coy, Paris officials took precautions to ensure Smith wasn't lynched in Texarkana. As Smith's train slowed to a stop in front of the depot, 100 armed men lined up alongside the coach that held the prisoner and his guards and escorted them to another train that would take them to Paris. Once

Smith was securely on board, the Paris prosecutor and city marshal appeared on the platform to speak to the waiting townspeople. They thanked the people of Texarkana for their courtesy and help in the manhunt and asked that they not molest Smith but instead let him be delivered to Paris. The townspeople knew what justice awaited Smith in Paris and, according to the code of mob law, that was where he should be "tried." While they had no intention of molesting the prisoner, they demanded to see him.[6]

Surrendering to the crowd, a few guards brought Smith to the car window. "When the head of the grinning wretch appeared at the window for the first time, a deep growl of pent up passion escaped from a hundred lips among the spectators, upon hearing which the frightened brute quickly withdrew his head, and only appeared again at the window at the repeated command of his captors," the *Democrat* reported. A few minutes later when the train pulled away from the depot, several Texarkanians had boarded it, intent on seeing the spectacle they knew awaited them in Paris. On the ride to Paris, the guards told Smith that he was to be tortured and burned for his heinous crime. The prisoner begged the sheriff to shoot him instead. But all had agreed that death by fire was the penalty Smith must pay for committing the most atrocious murder and outrage in Texas history.[7]

When the train arrived in Paris early that afternoon, it was met by an immense crowd. Smith was immediately placed on a carnival wagon and bedecked mockingly as a king upon his throne. The wagon, drawn by six mules, paraded around the square and through town so everyone would get an opportunity to look upon the monster; 5,000 people followed the wagon and another 10,000 lined the streets. They had come from Dallas, Texarkana, Fort Smith, and Hempstead County. They had arrived by train, in wagons, on horseback, and by foot. By order of the mayor, all the saloons in town were closed that day and schools dismissed so the children could witness the justice of the mob. The sheriff stood by, doing nothing to interfere with the mob. He later said it would have been useless "as an army could not stop the vengeance of such a crowd."[8]

The wagon carried Smith to a southern suburb where a scaffold had been built 10 feet above the ground. The doomed man was forced up the steps to the top of the scaffold where a stake had been secured. A can of kerosene had been placed next to a stack of kindling and cottonseed hulls. Vance, his sons, and a few of his brothers greeted the prisoner at the top of the scaffold. Slowly and menacingly, they ripped his shirt from off his body, throwing the scraps of soiled fabric into the crowd, which now numbered 20,000 people, where they were eagerly fought over and grabbed as mementos of the occasion. A photographer from Texarkana set up his camera in a strategic location, knowing there would be a demand for the grisly images he would capture.[9]

After tying Smith securely to the stake, the victim's family began the torture. The men thrust red hot branding irons against Smith's flesh. "Every contortion of his body and every groan that passed his lips brought forth shouts of approval," the correspondent to the *Democrat* reported. "Vainly, he begged for mercy! Vainly, he protested that he did not know it was Vance's child. The red hot irons burned into his flesh deeper and deeper, and he uttered terrific cries – cries that told of untold suffering. Finally the irons were rolled upon and down the stomach, back and arms, the crowd gazing on the terrible scene with a horrible fascination upon the slow process of torture."

The reporter continued, "The climax reached when the irons were thrust into his eyes burning the balls away. Then they were thrust down his throat. Still he lived and writhed and suffered." Their vengeance sated, Vance and his relatives climbed down from the scaffold an hour later. A great mass of kindling and hulls were placed under the scaffold, and oil was poured over Smith, the platform, and the kindling. With a hateful look at his daughter's murderer, Vance set a match to the oil-soaked wood.[10]

"For a time he (Smith) was enveloped in dense volume of smoke," the paper said. "As this passed away and the flames shot upward, Smith was seen amid the fire, swaying back and forth, then became still and all thought him dead. The fire burned him, and he fell upon the burning platform. He then began to toss and roll about as the flames rolled and hissed around him.... His hands burned entirely away, the flesh on his body seemed cooked to a crisp and his feet were burned to a coal.

"... [T]o the surprise of all, with a desperate struggle he pulled himself up by the railing of the burning scaffold, stood up erect, passed his arm over his face and then jumped off the scaffold and rolled out of the fire below." The crowd rushed forward to push him back into the flames. But once again, he rolled out. Finally a rope was tied around his neck, and he was dragged into the fire and held there until his body was cremated. Curiosity seekers waited for the ashes to cool and then carried away everything that was left – including pieces of charcoal – as reminders of the event. A few days later, notices began appearing in the *Democrat* that the local photographer had souvenir photos for sale.[11]

The outrage that had followed the Coy execution in Texarkana was mild compared with what greeted the brutality of the Smith burning, which was reported in great detail throughout the country. Those criticizing the action also mentioned Coy to show that this kind of violence was not isolated to one small Texas town. The protesters called for an end to mob law as, this time, it had gone too far. Once again, the argument took on sectional overtones when Northern newspapers and intellectuals used the two burnings to attack the South.

Northern novelist Julian Hawthorne was among the first to condemn the people of Texas for the torture and death of Smith. The Texarkana papers called Hawthorne's diatribe an unpardonable attack on respectable people, who were forced by the criminal himself to take such horrific actions. These people deserved sympathy – not condemnation, the *Democrat* responded. "A whole community of people are abused, blackened and reviled, without one word of commiseration for their alleged crime nor of condolence for the horrible condition which confronted and forced upon them the necessity of meeting a horrible crime with terrible punishment."[12]

The Northern newspapers ignored the South's claims of self-defense and continued their attacks. "To pile up further evidence of the fact that society in the South is drifting towards barbarism is useless," the *Philadelphia Press* commented. Southern newspapers cried foul when the Northern press raised no similar accusations of barbarism about reports that a white woman had been burned at the stake in Michigan as a sacrificial offering by religious fanatics.[13]

Encouraged by the outrage being expressed by Northern whites, the nation's African American societies spoke out in condemnation of the South. A report from Chicago stated that the "colored protective association, 2500 strong, are [sic] coming to Paris to avenge the burning of Henry Smith." Since such a trip would most likely bring the group through Texarkana, some of the people of Texarkana responded with a letter warning that the protesters had better stay out of their town. The *Democrat* added its voice: "The defamers of the good people of this city and Paris, who so quickly avenged monstous [sic] outrages against a white woman and a little three-year old child, by negro fiends, had better not come to either place soon to add 'insult to injury.' While opposed to mob law in everything else the people of this section propose to mete swift and appropriate punishment upon all such criminals."[14]

Even in the South, some African Americans dared to speak up. The mere mention of the incident produced fighting words as John McQueen, a St. Louis businessman traveling in Indian Territory a few weeks after the burning, discovered. While in a small town on the Frisco line, he alluded to Smith's execution. Overhearing the comment, a black man remarked that when a white man did what Smith had done, it was ignored. Enraged at the "offensive talk," which he perceived as an attack on the honor of Southerners, McQueen seized a wagon spoke and struck the man with it repeatedly. Finally, the black man managed to escape – only to return a little later with several armed friends. To save McQueen's life, a party of white men locked him in his hotel room until they could sneak him onto a train heading to Paris, where the news of his treatment created considerable excitement. The people of Paris vowed that had McQueen "suffered any personal violence at the hands of the mob the same would have been swiftly and surely avenged."[15]

While the people of Texarkana and Paris continued to defend their reputation and actions against the slightest criticism, the South, in general, began to rethink mob law. Perhaps things had gone too far. Judge Sneed, presiding over a criminal court in Knoxville, Tennessee, lectured the grand jury on the evils of mob law and charged them to investigate a recent attempt to lynch a white man who had raped a seven-year-old girl. The judge also appealed to the people of the town to let the law take its course and promised that anyone who suggested mob violence would be indicted.[16]

Texarkanians used the Tennessee case as a retort against the attacks still being leveled at them by Northern papers. "We do most earnestly commend the ... admirable action of a southern judge, presiding over a southern court in a southern state, to the careful consideration of our northern brethren," Gardner wrote in the *Democrat*. Referring to a recent Minnesota lynching, he continued: "Methinks the south will yet be compelled, out of charity and good fellowship, to open an infant's class in the enforcement of law and protection of public peace and personal rights, for the express benefit of our friends of the north and east."[17]

In the article about the Minnesota lynching, Gardner could not restrain from issuing a few more biting digs at the North. "Shades of Abraham Lincoln, Esquire! gaze down on your benighted country and weep. Of course the deed was a damnable one," Gardner said of the Minnesota outrages, "and the crime in every sense diabolical, and yet, and yet, and yet, there is something strong and altogether uncontrollable in the affair after all. By what occult means has this lawless practice, this taking of personal vengeance, without the shadow of legal approval, been transferred from its alleged home in the South to that far off Northern State, where the blood of human passion is converted to icicles ere it reaches the heart." If this lynching had occurred in the South, Gardner said, "the usual cry might now go up from tens of thousands of Republican throats against this people for another of 'those dastardly Southern outrages.'"[18]

As the *Democrat* raged against the hypocrisy of the North, some Southerners embraced the fight to end the violence. Following the lead of a few other Southern governors, Fishback took a firm stand against mob law and offered a $250 reward for the arrest and conviction of each person involved in a recent triple lynching in Beardon, Arkansas. In a letter to Prosecuting Attorney H.P. Smead, the governor said: "It is reported that a mob has murdered three men at Beardon, in Ouachita County. The inference that the courts and officers of the law are utterly insufficient in that county, to which such an outrage leads, is, I feel sure, unjust and false. Yet, however much we may resent such an inference, it will be accepted by the public as true." Not only did mob murder reflect poorly on the county, the entire state was disgraced by such cowardice, the governor added.[19]

"This murdering by mobs is but a species of assassination," Fishback continued. "The assassin hides behind a tree or in the darkness of the night, while the mob takes shelter behind a crowd." The governor concluded his letter to the prosecutor by calling upon him to bring the guilty parties to justice as mob law would only be "broken up by hanging a few of the participants and teaching them that we live in a land of law."[20]

Officials at every level throughout the region soon added their voice to the growing clamor for law and order. In Memphis, a criminal court judge suspended a sheriff who had done nothing to stop a mob from lynching a rapist, who was kidnapped from his jail. The judge placed the coroner in charge of the county and turned the sheriff over to a grand jury. And in Sykeston, Kentucky, with the backing of the National Citizens' Rights Association, the widow of C.J. Miller, who had been lynched for the rape and murder of two sisters, filed for damages against the city marshal and his bondsmen. But Mrs. Miller didn't stop with the sheriff. She also filed suit against members of the posse and citizens of Illinois, Missouri, and Kentucky who had participated in the manhunt and the lynching.[21]

Reading in the local paper of Gov. Fishback's order and the events in other Southern states gave William reason to hope that mob violence, as well as other forms of lawlessness, would soon end its rule in Arkansas – and the South in general. That hope and an accompanying sense of rightness gave him the courage to carry on his crusade in Texarkana.

29   Economic Divide

Mob law was not the only issue separating North and South in 1893. The New England industrialists, who had grown wealthy through their power base in Congress, saw their 30-year stranglehold on the nation's economy eroding with the ascendancy of the Democrats. Looking for someone to blame, they pointed to the South. "Ever since the secession of the Southern Democrats left the Republicans in a majority in the National Senate of 1861 the committees of that body, which shape and to a great extent control the legislation of Congress, have been organized so as to give New England a decided prominence and very great influence," the Manchester, New Hampshire, *Mirror* acknowledged.[1]

Since the war, New England senators had headed the important committees, thus directing the policy of the federal government in most matters. "Through them, New England ideas have prevailed and New England enterprises have been protected," the *Mirror* continued. "Particularly has this been true in dealing with the money and tariff questions." These policies, coupled with the aftermath of the war, had impoverished the South while enriching New England. By 1880, the per capita wealth of the North was $1,186 while that of the South was $376. While the South had made some dollar gains by the 1890s, its per capita wealth remained far below that of the North.[2]

But the New England states weren't concerned about the South. They were worried about continuing their own prosperity – even though it had come at the expense of the rest of the nation. "The ascendancy of Democracy, dominated as it is by the South, changes all that," the *Mirror* said, referring to New England's control of Congress. "For the first time since the war the

Senate has been organized 'against New England' with the openly declared purpose of discrediting her policies and sacrificing her interest, if need be, in order that those of the South and West may prevail."[3]

Recognizing the advantage it finally had now that the Democrats controlled the White House and much of Congress, the South seized every opportunity to pursue that advantage. The Southern governors, at the suggestion of Arkansas' Fishback, held a convention in Richmond to discuss ways to promote the South and push for its development. The governors put together an address, which was sent to the president, reviewing the situation in the region following the war and the abuse it had suffered abroad from the North's misrepresentation. Although the South had much going for it, "the fact stares us in the face that in material advancement these states are far behind their sisters of the north," the governors said in the address. They also called upon the president to provide better representation of the South in other countries in an effort to recruit foreign industrial investment.[4]

Meanwhile, Arkansas was trying to make the most with what it had. Harking back to the values and traditions of the Old South, Fishback presented the governors with a list of statistics demonstrating his state's investment in religion and education. He claimed Arkansas had 3,500 churches within its boundaries – one for every 322 people. More than half of those buildings had been constructed within the past 10 years. This religious activity, though impressive, was surpassed by the state's commitment to education. "Our educational advancement within the past ten years has been at an almost unparalleled pace," the governor said. The increase in school enrollment in Arkansas was two to 50 times that of any state admitted to the Union before or at the same time as Arkansas, which now boasted 3,000 public schools, more than half of which had been built within the past 10 years.[5]

"While within the past thirteen years the South has expended $216,000,000 on the free education of the youths of our section, in Arkansas we have expended during the same period $10,200,000, with an average of 350,000 children," Fishback said. He explained that two-fifths of state tax revenue and half of county taxes went to support the schools, which included 900 black schools. Several schoolhouses for the black children had cost the taxpayer from $10,000 to $20,000 each. The state boasted a university and three normal schools for white students and several colleges and one normal school for black students. It also was home to a number of private colleges and academies, including a free Bible school in Beebe that had an enrollment of 235 students.[6]

The governor used these statistics again a few months later when Congressman Henry Blair of New Hampshire introduced an education bill to force the South to do its duty to educate African American children. In an open letter to New England and Pennsylvania, Fishback retorted: "New England, New York and Pennsylvania not only indignantly deny it (that their conditions are similar to that of the South), but assume the role of missionaries toward this benighted region we call the South, and ... they are so intensely solicitous about the motes in southern eyes, they are permitting a good sized beam to grow in their own eyes." He claimed the white people of Arkansas, who paid about 98 percent of the school tax, were educating not only a larger percentage of white children but also a larger percentage of black children "than New Hampshire, New York, New Jersey, Pennsylvania, Connecticut, Rhode Island and even cultured Massachusetts, are educating their own children, who are bone of their bone and flesh of their flesh."[7]

The economic divide between the North and the rest of the country became painfully obvious that year as the Panic of 1893 set in. Crop failures, low farm prices, high freight rates, high tariffs, and a disastrous monetary policy combined to plunge the nation into a terrible depression, the likes of which had not been experienced previously. As a result, silver miners were starving in the West, White Cappers were wreaking vengeance in the South, banks and businesses were failing throughout the nation, and the Democratic Party, which had celebrated its great victory a few months earlier, was now threatening to split apart.[8]

The bank and business failures had actually started locally in 1892 before Cleveland was elected. When word got out Monday, July 18, 1892, that the bank in Magnolia, Arkansas, had failed over the weekend, people panicked in Texarkana. It was rumored that J.G. Kelso, the sole owner of the Magnolia bank and president of the Gate City Bank in Texarkana, had bankrupted the Magnolia bank by absconding with its funds. Despite the Texarkana bank's assurances that it had "sufficient cash in its vaults to pay every demand against it, and that there is no cause for uneasiness," the rumors created a heavy run on the bank with many depositors withdrawing their funds that Monday.[9]

Even with the withdrawals, the bank was able to cash all checks presented the next day. Assured that the bank was solvent, some of the customers who had withdrawn their funds redeposited them Tuesday afternoon. But the shock created by the Magnolia bank failure continued to reverberate in Texarkana, Little Rock – even in the East. While bank failures had become common in other parts of the nation, this was the first bank failure in Arkansas since 1874. Gate City Bank officials tried to divert blame from Kelso while providing plausible explanations for the failure. They claimed the closure "was due to local jealousies, and not from any inability of Mr. Kelso to meet his indebtedness." Kelso, who had been ill, was out of the state and was probably unaware that his bank had been closed by attachment; but as soon as he was told, he would undoubtedly make everything right, they said. A few days later, Kelso resigned as president of the Gate City Bank.[10]

When railroad freight rates jumped from 22 cents to 76 cents a few months later, the Texarkana Fence Factory was forced to close. It said it could not afford the railroad's "tariff" of $2.28 on a product that only cost $2.75 to make. The closure prompted the *Democrat* to vent against the Northern policies: "These roads are all owned by northern capitalists who wish to keep the South one vast farm, producing raw material for northern manufacturers to convert into products to sell southern consumers – the railroads getting a haul both ways." Coupled with the high tariffs imposed by the North that forced Southerners to buy high-priced products from Northern factories rather than cheaper imports, these practices resembled the colonial mercantile policies England had imposed on 17th- and 18th-century America.[11]

Southern factories weren't the only ones suffering from the high freight rates. Cotton producers, who were getting 8.4 cents a pound for cotton in 1892 despite the fact that the crop was expected to be 35 percent shorter than usual due to early frosts in several states, were rightly concerned about the inflated cost of shipping their crop to market. Still recovering from 1891's unprecedented low of 7.3 cents per pound for cotton, they could not afford the high freight rates. Most of the cotton shippers along the Iron Mountain Railroad signed a petition asking for a reduction in rates on cotton going to St. Louis. The petition recited the disasters brought about by two years of low cotton prices and the difficulties the producers faced because of these prices. The shippers reminded Iron Mountain officials that the railroads reduced shipping rates for grain in the Northwest for similar reasons and asked for the same consideration for cotton. The *Washington Telegraph* called on Fishback to support the shippers' efforts by appointing a committee to go to St. Louis to negotiate with the railroad. "We believe an equitable settlement of rates on cotton would save to the producers of the state not less than a million of dollars," the *Telegraph* said.[12]

Other Texarkana industries limped into 1893. Four days into the new year, the Bowie Lumber Company, one of the oldest lumber companies in the city, was placed in receivership. A week later, the privately held utilities that serviced Texarkana were in trouble. The court ordered a sheriff's sale January 14 of 1,600 shares of capital stock of the gas company and 1,240 shares of the water company to pay a judgment of $6,268 plus interest from January 1892 that had been levied against the utilities. A sheriff's sale also was ordered for 311 shares of the Texarkana Street Railway Company and 100 shares of the Inter-State Land & Building Company. And in the spring, a drug store and a grocery store failed.[13]

Elsewhere, banks continued to fail and the depression deepened. By March, the *Democrat* was saying that the past two years had been "one of the most trying periods in the financial history of the South, since the war." A flurry of bank failures throughout the West later that spring resulted in worries of a "financial panic of fearful proportion." National financial advisers tried to dispel the growing gloom by insisting that the failures were the result of business practices and not an indication of a dying economy. "There has been altogether too much made of the situation," George W. Williams, president of the Chemical National Bank, said. "All that is wanted now is quiet."[14]

Not all the business news was bad in Texarkana as 1892 faded into the new year. While railroads in other parts of the country were starting to show the stress of the souring economy, they were going strong in Texarkana. In mid-November 1892, W.L. Whitaker, now president of the Texarkana & Fort Smith Railroad, proposed building a 50-mile extension to finally complete the connection between the two cities. He promised construction would begin within 60 days and be completed within 18 months. He also offered to make Texarkana the base of operations for the construction – provided Texarkanians raised $40,000 to pay off the railroad's existing encumbrances. The last time the people had raised $110,000 for the extension to Fort Smith, Whitaker had delivered only 30 miles of the proposed line. The businessmen wanted the extension so badly – and the business the construction would bring – that they were willing to meet the railroad's price.[15]

This was a time of railroad mergers and cooperative agreements as companies looked for economical ways to extend their lines in all directions at once. In mid-January, the Kansas City, Nevada and Fort Smith Railroad sent workers in to survey a southern extension and the proposed road from the northern terminus 30 miles north of Texarkana to Fort Smith. From Fort Smith, the track would connect with the Nevada road, giving the cooperating railroads access to Pittsburg and from Kansas City, Missouri, to the Gulf of Mexico. Two weeks later, railroad officials arrived in Texarkana to reorganize the road and begin work on the extension.[16]

Almost before it began, the project hit a hitch. As part of the construction, the railroad wanted to extend the Texarkana & Fort Smith line southward to the Gulf of Mexico. But to do so, the track would have to cross the Texas & Pacific Railroad in

Texas. Bowie County officials gave the company permission to cross the other railroad – provided it pay any damages that might occur. The Texarkana & Fort Smith agreed but the Texas & Pacific stopped construction in February by parking an engine along its track where the crossing was to be built.[17]

When negotiations between the two roads failed, the Texas & Pacific went to court, trying to get a restraining order. Texas Judge John Sheppard refused to issue the order, so the next day the Texas & Pacific took its case to Judge Bryant of the U.S. District Court for the Eastern District of Texas, who issued a temporary restraining order. Two weeks later, Bryant lifted the restraining order when Texarkana & Fort Smith officials filed a $6,000 bond with the clerk of the court as a guarantee of indemnity for any damage that might be done to the other railroad's property.[18]

While construction of the line was delayed, the Texarkana & Fort Smith continued with other projects, converting the ground floor of the Ghio Building into spacious new offices, a depot, and waiting rooms. It also ordered passenger coaches, which were to arrive in mid-March. To help finance the railroad's expansion, Whitaker sold 170 acres of prime development land just beyond Texarkana's western suburbs to the Missouri, Kansas & Texas Trust Company, a wealthy syndicate based in Kansas City, Missouri, for $30,000. The deal was kept secret until it was finalized. Then the syndicate announced plans to build 20 tenement houses on the property. Half of the units would be built for employees of the Texarkana Furniture Manufacturing Company, which employed 109 workers, with the rest being leased to the general public.[19]

As summer settled in, Texarkana society celebrated the successes of their city and tried not to worry about the economic shadows darkening the rest of the country. Many of them took advantage of the railroads' excursion rates to Chicago for the World's Fair, which had opened in May to much criticism and acclaim. Others took advantage of local distractions.[20]

A highlight of the summer season was a performance by Alphonse King. More than 500 people had taken the train that Saturday afternoon to Pleasant Lake where King would amaze them with his aqua acrobatics. It was an extremely hot day and the railroad had forgotten to stock the cars with water, so as soon as the passengers arrived at the lake, they were forced to get lemonade at the concession stand. When the white ladies turned to sit in the shade of the pavilion, they were dismayed to find it occupied by a large number of African Americans. Dixon and Dr. Miller came to the ladies' rescue by ousting the group from the pavilion. In the process, one young black man ran over a white boy. Because of his clumsiness, he and a friend were "dealt with pretty roughly" by several white boys. The whites sitting in the shade laughed as the two unfortunate black men fled into the woods. Then they turned their attention to the amazing King, who walked a wire rope stretched across the lake, walked on the water with the aid of specially designed aquatic shoes, and rode a water bike through the lake.[21]

30   Year of Disaster

Excursions proved only temporary distractions from the worries of the time, which worsened as storms swept through the South, destroying crops and property. Farmers in several counties in southwest Arkansas lost their crops May 30 to a hailstorm that was accompanied by dangerous winds. In many places, fields were so covered with fallen timber that they could not be replanted that year. A day later, what was called a cyclone and hailstorm roared through Hope and nearby Guernsey, killing an entire family, destroying several homes and buildings, and pelting crops with up to eight inches of hail in some fields. "Guernsey ... was swept off the earth," the *Democrat* reported.[1]

There were no federal aid programs to help in times of disaster, and, under Cleveland, there was no hope of any. (In his first administration, the president had refused to assist an area severely damaged by a natural disaster, claiming it would set a bad precedent.) Arkansas Democrats didn't expect government assistance. In Southern tradition, that was not the government's job. Rather, Southern honor obligated neighbor to help neighbor and communities to stand together in times of need. After seeing the extent of the damage, William called a public meeting in Texarkana to raise money for the victims of the storm. Although the depressed economy was taking its toll, Texarkanians, moved by their neighbors' losses, gave what they could. By the time the meeting ended, $130 had been raised and a committee appointed to solicit more donations. Within a week, $305 had been given to the storm relief fund.[2]

Meanwhile, the storm clouds of the economy darkened nationwide. The gloomy forecast had been seeded in 1890 when Democrats, in a compromise, accepted the high Republican-backed tariff in exchange for passage of the Sherman Silver

Purchase Act, which required the federal government to buy 4.5 million ounces of silver a month, much of which was to be coined. The act also allowed notes on the silver to be redeemed in gold. At first, the law was a boon, as it was intended to be, for silver mines in the West as the price of silver escalated overnight. But with the government's monthly purchases nearly matching the output of the mines, the price of silver started to drop. Investors, including foreign governments, exchanged their silver notes for gold, depleting the nation's gold reserves. As silver values dropped, mine operators compensated by cutting the wages of miners. With silver at bargain prices, mines were forced to shut in the summer of 1893, resulting in the layoff of nearly 4,000 miners. By the end of July, 15,000 people in Colorado were in need of immediate aid, and the number of destitute increased daily.[3]

As banks failed and money supplies restricted, businesses ran out of small bills and coins with which to pay their workers. Several textile mills shut down indefinitely in Massachusetts, idling 700,000 spindles and putting 7,000 workers out of a job. "The shortage in currency is the immediate cause of the shut down," the *Democrat* reported. "In many cases the poor state of trade is a greater cause and that will more potentially effect [*sic*] the length of time the mills will be idle."[4]

Convinced the economy could be salvaged simply by repealing the Sherman Act, Cleveland called a special session of Congress to do just that. In his opening address of the session, the president tried to downplay the seriousness of the depression. "Our unfortunate financial plight is not the result of untoward events nor of conditions related to our natural resources, nor is it traceable to any of the afflictions which frequently checked national growth and prosperity...," he said. "Suddenly financial fear and distrust has sprung upon us on every side; numerous moneyed institutions have suspended because abundant assets were not immediately available to meet demands of frightened depositors."[5]

As a result, Cleveland told Congress, banks were wary of loaning money and "loss and failure have invaded every branch of business." He also blamed the crisis on the Sherman Act, saying that because of that legislation, the nation's gold reserve had decreased by more than $132 million since 1890 while its silver reserve had increased by more than $147 million. Although the Sherman Act had been passed to force parity between the two metals, the president said the government could not maintain parity as silver had depreciated too much.[6]

The president had hoped for an early repeal of the troublesome legislation, but many in his own party saw any repeal as a bow to Republicans. They were unconvinced that the Sherman Act was the problem; instead, they pointed fingers across the aisle. The House Democrats called a party caucus as the special session was about to start. Speaker Charles Crisp of Georgia opened the meeting: "The extraordinary condition of affairs throughout the country has necessitated our meeting in extraordinary session." He blamed the economic problems on 30 years of bad laws passed by the Republicans. "We can repeal old laws and can make good ones.... Our financial system should be revised and reformed," Crisp said. "The strictest economy in public expenditures should be observed, and taxation should be equalized and greatly reduced. To these purposes are we thoroughly committed."[7]

But many of Crisp's colleagues were more committed to patronage than to restoring the economy. Disgusted that members of both houses came to him "to talk of nothing but patronage when the fate of the nation was hanging in the balance," Cleveland threatened to make no more appointments until the Sherman Act was repealed. In retaliation, Sen. William Stewart of Nevada, who had switched from the Republican Party to the new Silver Party, introduced a resolution calling for the arraignment of Cleveland before Congress on charges that he was trying to destroy the independence of Congress by seeking to coerce it to repeal the Sherman Act.[8]

The Democrats of Miller County were among those who were more concerned with patronage than economic depression. Labeling the president's policies "mugwumpery," they expressed frustration with what they saw as his insistence on letting Republican officeholders serve out their full terms rather than replacing them with loyal Democrats. The Republicans had had their share of patronage; it was the Democrats' turn.[9]

"It is an outrage that Democrats are not put in charge of the government, from top to bottom," the *Democrat* said. "If the election last November meant anything, it indicated most emphatically that the people were tired of Republican rule, and wanted a change.... There should be some way to effectively rebuke Cleveland." The editor suggested holding indignation meetings to pass resolutions denouncing the president. And he recommended calling for Cleveland's resignation if he didn't clean house and replace the Republicans with loyal Democrats.[10]

The appointments were a concern to both Republicans and Democrats in the South – for different reasons. Using the latest government blue book, which showed the number of political appointments that had been made by state, Congressman John C. Houk, a Republican from Knoxville, Tennessee, compared those numbers with each state's population, based on the 1890 census. His findings showed that most of the states in the South were woefully short of the number of appointments they were "entitled" to, and Arkansas and Texas had the worst showing percentage-wise. According to Houk's reasoning, Arkansas should have had 268 officeholders, but by the end of 1893, only 77 Arkansans held federal positions. Houk called on the Civil Service Commission to make no more appointments from states that already had their share and suggested amending a bill to mandate that federal appointments be proportional to each state's population.[11]

While Miller County Democrats were concerned about the state's overall showing in federal positions, they were most upset about the local postmaster position. Shaw, a Republican, was still serving as postmaster of Texarkana's joint post office. To force an appointment, the central committee decided to nominate a candidate for the position and pass that name along to the postmaster general. Three worthy party members wanted the position. William and several other Democrats pushed for Jeff Sanderson, claiming he was entitled to it "for past active services on behalf of the party, and because he had never heretofore held any office.... The other candidates, it seems to us, have had enough of the 'chicken pie,' and should give others a chance," the *Democrat* reported.[12]

To resolve the issue, Sanderson and William Kelley, the other main contender, signed a request asking the county central committee to hold a primary to select the county's nominee. (With the party pushing for Sanderson, the third candidate had withdrawn his name.) Throughout the county, each township elected delegates to the central committee meeting, during which the party would officially approve a primary and set the date. One of the delegates elected moved out of his township, so T.E. Webber, who had lost the bid to be delegate, assumed he was now the official delegate. Since Webber couldn't attend the central committee meeting, he asked W.F. Kirby, who was a close friend of Kelley, to go as his proxy. When Kirby showed up at the meeting, he was challenged. The voters from the township had sent a signed letter saying they did not recognize Webber as their delegate, thus Kirby couldn't serve as his proxy.[13]

Although he wasn't recognized as a delegate, Kirby stayed through the meeting, in which the committee set the date and the rules for the primary election. The July 18 primary would be open to all who had acted with the party in the past (this wording intentionally shut out any African American voter), and no poll tax would be required. Before the meeting adjourned, Kirby announced that Kelley would not participate in the primary and refused to be bound by its results.[14]

Kelley reiterated his stance before the primary by serving notice to William, as county chairman, that "I will proceed to contest before the State Democratic Central Committee of Arkansas, the action of the Central Committee of Miller county ... and any pretended primary election held ... on account of the many illegal, irregular and undemocratic actions of said committee at their meeting on July twelfth ... which rendered their said actions illegal and void." Despite Kelley's threat to contest the election, the central committee continued with the primary. Sanderson, now with no opposition, won the nomination. His name was given to Congressman Thomas McRae, who had agreed to put forward the name of the primary winner.[15]

Working outside the county system through a network of personal contacts, Kelley took his case directly to the postmaster general. To secure the position for Kelley, his contacts denigrated Sanderson. In October, the postmaster general, ignoring the party's choice, announced Kelley's appointment. His reason stemmed from allegations against Sanderson that went back to 1890 when President Harrison had passed through Texarkana. Sanderson's naysayers claimed he hollered out "Hurrah for Jeff Davis" while shaking his fist at the president and trying to force his way into Harrison's car. Sanderson maintained there was nothing to the charges, but he admitted hollering for Jeff Davis immediately after the band had finished playing "Dixie."[16]

While the local Democrats were waiting for their postmaster to be named, Congress continued debating the Sherman Silver Act and more businesses took last-ditch measures to stay afloat. Many companies, including the Missouri-Pacific Railway, announced plans to cut operating costs and wages. George Gould, president of the road, sent a notice to the heads of departments throughout his system, detailing the wage cuts. Monthly salaries of $100 or more would be reduced by 10 percent. Workers making less than $100 a month would not be affected. The railroad also reduced the workweek in some places. In North Little Rock, for instance, workers would be restricted to a 40-hour week – five eight-hour days with Saturday off.[17]

The argument over silver ended in the House August 28 when the Wilson Bill, which repealed the Sherman Act, was passed by a two-thirds majority and sent to the Senate. Trying to make the bill more palatable to the silver interests, several congressmen attached amendments, which all failed. "All of the Arkansas members, except [C.R.] Breckinridge, voted for silver coinage every time, and against the Wilson bill," the *Democrat* bragged.[18]

Perhaps coincidentally, the economic forecast immediately brightened. The same day the House approved the Wilson Bill, 6,000 men went back to work at two iron mills in Pittsburgh, 4,800 people returned to work at four paper mills in Ohio. Bank failures had about stopped, and money was easier to get. Several idled factories had started up or announced plans to reopen in

September. "The commercial condition of the country is improving every hour," the Texarkana paper reported, while pointing out that Texarkana had been almost immune to the economic upheaval.[19]

"Texarkana is about the only city we know of that the panic has not stopped building," Gardner commented in his paper. "We have some twenty or more handsome new residences now going up. This speaks volumes for the permanent and solid growth and development of our city." A few days later, Gardner announced that construction of the Texarkana & Fort Smith railway, which had been temporarily suspended because of the general financial depression, had resumed.[20]

But the upturn in business proved a mirage. Texas officials announced September 30 that the state treasury was nearly – if not completely – depleted. The state had $65,000 in cash on hand, and no more revenue was expected until December. But the monthly bills, which were due that day, totaled $150,000. As a result, the state would not pay the teachers or clerks until December 1. In Texarkana, businesspeople were dismayed to learn the Kansas City, Pittsburgh & Gulf Railroad (formerly the Kansas City, Nevada & Fort Smith Railroad) was going to halt its expansion projects in the Texarkana area. This was bad news. The fact that expansion of the track to Fort Smith and south to the Gulf had continued off and on for most of the year while almost every other railroad project in the country had been stopped had given Texarkanians a false sense of security in the economic crisis. Yes, a few businesses had closed, and farmers were hurting. But as long as the railroad was building, there was work to be found and business to conduct. The people lost this security when the depression forced the railroad to stop construction.[21]

Disastrous farm prices that fall also hurt the town's economy as well as that of the nation. The price for cotton, the area's primary cash crop, had dropped to 7 cents a pound. Wheat, at a record low of 52.1 cents a bushel, was 10.3 cents lower than ever before. Barley was at a record low of 40.6 cents; and corn and oats had continued a three-year drop in price. Hay producers were the only ones making money as hay was selling at a near record high of $9.18 a ton.[22]

Trying to stave off total ruin by forcing an increase in the price of cotton, a loose organization of cotton producers, called "White Caps," formed in Louisiana and Mississippi and quickly spread into Arkansas, Texas, and almost every other cotton-producing state. To achieve their goals, the White Caps dedicated themselves to preventing the ginning and marketing of the 1893 cotton crop until the price reached 10 cents a pound. They posted cease-and-desist warnings on gin houses in the Texarkana area and threatened to burn down the houses if they persisted in ginning cotton.[23]

The movement grew more violent as the economy darkened. In Mississippi, the White Caps became a "terror to the country" as they beat and murdered those farmers who sold their cotton. In Texas, they threatened a farmer who had sold his cotton, giving him a few hours to leave the state. He chose to buy a Winchester instead. The violence spread from farmers to laborers as the financial situation worsened. Unemployed white workers aimed their frustration at black men who still had jobs. Wooden signs were posted along the Gate City Railroad line, giving all African Americans working and living along the line a few hours to vacate the country. It proved an empty threat, but it added to the tension created by the depression.[24]

The Senate, which had spent 61 days arguing about the Sherman Act, could no longer ignore the condition of the country. Following a marathon 14-day session of deliberations, the Senate passed the Wilson Bill to repeal the Sherman Act October 30. The president signed the bill three days later. But the damage already had been done. The economy continued its tailspin. R.G. Dun's weekly business report for the last week in October 1893 showed 358 businesses had failed that week in the United States. Two weeks later, another 361 businesses failed – for a 172 percent increase in business failures over the same week in 1892.[25]

The depression deepened as the federal reserves seemed to melt away. With just under $89 million in the treasury by the end of the year, the government was reporting its lowest currency balance in years. The customs receipts for December of less than $9 million were the lowest of any month since 1865 when the country's population had been half what it was in the 1890s. Meanwhile, government expenditures for December exceeded the monthly revenue receipts by nearly $5.3 million. If receipts continued to drop off, the gold reserve would be exhausted. To avoid such a disaster, the government considered issuing bonds to cover the shortfall. Preferring taxes to deficits, Democrats pushed a bill that would initiate an income tax – two percent on all income over $4,000. The income tax bill also would add a two percent tax on decks of playing cards and a $1 tax on every gallon of distilled spirits.[26]

In Texarkana, consumer confidence remained strong throughout the 1893 Christmas season, and holiday sales were good. But they were not enough to salvage many of the town's businesses. The Saturday before Christmas, the Texarkana Furniture Company, the largest of 29 furniture factories in the city, went into receivership. Just a year earlier, the company had been heralded as the most prosperous business in town, manufacturing more than $10,000 worth of furniture a month and shipping out three carloads of furniture a week. The day after Christmas, the stock of Julius Scherer was attached by creditors and Sam Falk's holdings, J.C. Whitner's hardware store, and Mrs. Levy's second-hand store were all assigned to the bank. That same day, the Santa Fe Railroad went into receivership.[27]

31   A Change of Times

For many people ravaged by the Panic of 1893, their only hope was a fresh start. Thus, when the Cherokee Strip opened in Indian Territory to homesteaders early that year, thousands of desperate people flocked to the Strip. They had sold their few possessions, borrowed money, lied, and cheated to gamble that they would be among the hundreds to emerge with a parcel of land. Many of those who lost in the Great Land Race found themselves stuck, and penniless, in the Territory with no means of returning home. And many of the winners lacked the capital, the skills, and the time to put up proper shelter or plant a crop before winter set in. Boom towns, resembling Texarkana in its younger days, sprang up, offering a new frontier to those seeking to escape settled civilization. The rampant crime made these towns a bonanza for criminal lawyers like Joe Cook, who had been looking for a new place to settle for several years. It came as no surprise when Joe announced in September 1893 that he was relocating to Perry, one of the leading towns in the newly opened Cherokee Strip.[1]

So it was that Cook & Arnold became just Arnold. The years had been good to William – despite the depression. He made plans to build a handsome new residence in the Fouke neighborhood in Texarkana and divided his time between his lucrative law firm and his duties as mayor. With Joe gone, William devoted his practice to civil cases, of which he had plenty. When the Miller County Circuit Court convened in December 1893, it had to change its schedule when William got sick. He was counsel on nearly every civil case on the docket.[2]

As mayor, William continued to spend considerable energy delivering on his campaign promises and preparing Texarkana for the next century. Both efforts were hampered, at times, by the state line, which artificially divided the town. This boundary became "an insurmountable obstacle in the path of every important project for internal improvement," the *Democrat* reported. Besides creating the expense of supporting two city governments, this dual existence resulted in Texarkana being viewed as two towns rather than one city. Together, the two sides of the city had the population to classify as a city of the first class, a designation that would provide more benefits to the residents and help with the development of infrastructure.[3]

One benefit the residents wanted was free postal delivery. Federal law allowed any city of 8,000 people or more to have free postal delivery in residential areas and gave the postmaster general the discretion to offer free delivery to cities of 5,000. By 1893, Texarkana had a combined population of 15,000 to 20,000. "Now, that the Postoffice of the city is consolidated the two corporations may be considered as one city," the editor of the *Democrat* argued, "at least as far as Uncle Sam is concerned."[4]

Although free delivery had been on everyone's wish list for at least a year, no one pursued the issue until 1894 when William, as mayor, began corresponding with the postmaster general's office through Congressman McRae about the issue. He was told to get free postal delivery, both towns would have to name and sign all their streets, number the houses, and create permanent sidewalks throughout the residential and business areas. Promised a visit by a postal inspector within a few days, city officials put up signs and house numbers. Property owners were asked to help create raised earthen sidewalks, and city prisoners were used to improve some of the existing sidewalks. Without notifying anyone that he was in town, the inspector quietly assessed conditions on both sides of the city. After his visit, the inspector informed city officials that his report would not be very favorable because the houses on the West Side weren't all numbered and the streets weren't all signed. He also noted large puddles of water standing on sidewalks in several locations on the West Side.[5]

William received a letter from McRae a month later that detailed the adverse report the inspector had submitted. In addition to the other problems, the inspector had cited poor sidewalks and insufficient lighting in residential areas throughout the city. In the letter, which was read at an East Side City Council meeting, McRae said if the defects were corrected by July 1, Texarkana would get free postal delivery. Arrangements were made for the inspector to visit the city again; but this time, he would meet with city officials.[6]

Another issue that would have been easier to address had Texarkana been one city was sewage disposal. The East Side's efforts to finance a sewer system through a local improvement district had failed because not enough residents in the district had agreed to form the district. Recognizing that it could not afford the heavy expense of building a sewer system, the East Side negotiated with the West Side to build a joint system. Rather than using public funds, both sides passed similar ordinances clearing the way for the project, which would be privatized through a joint bid process. The contracts set sewer rates from $8 to $15 a year for residences with proportionate rates for businesses. Although the contract was for a 20-year franchise, each side reserved the right to purchase the system in 10 years.[7]

Other improvements in town were slowed by the depression. Work on a new courthouse, which was to cost no more than $35,000, had begun in April 1893. Since Miller County had only $12,000 on hand for the project, County Judge Friedell made an oral agreement to borrow the rest of the money. That fall, the contractors were ready to lay the cornerstone. The local Masons planned elaborate ceremonies for the installation of the stone and prepared a time capsule, which included Masonic documents, an 1836 silver half dollar to recognize the year of Arkansas' statehood, an 1893 silver quarter, copies of local newspapers, and statements from prominent residents. The ceremony began Monday morning, October 23, with a Masonic procession from the lodge to the site of the new courthouse. As the selected orator for the Masons, William gave a "timely address," in which he reviewed the history of the Masons. The event concluded with a few remarks from Friedell and the placing of the cornerstone.[8]

The excitement aroused by the ceremony may have been premature. Because of the financial panic, Friedell's funding agreement fell through in January 1894. With no written contract, the county could not force the other party to make good the promised loan. The contractor refused to do any more work until he was paid, so construction stopped with the courthouse two-thirds completed. To finish the project, the county had to issue scrip, which more than doubled the cost of the building.[9]

William had his own problems to deal with. Knowing his time as mayor was running out, he addressed some of the infrastructure issues that had troubled the city for years. One of these was the College Hill crossing of the St. Louis, Iron Mountain & Southern Railway Company, which posed a life-threatening hazard to anyone traveling to and from that neighborhood. In September 1893, the East Side City Council passed an ordinance forcing the railroad to make the crossing safe and convenient for passage of people, animals, and vehicles of all kinds. The ordinance gave the railroad two months to install gates with arms or build a bridge or tunnel at the crossing. If it chose to install gates, it had to assure that people passing through the crossing had no more than a three-minute delay. The railroad chose the cheaper option and installed gates. It hired a gatekeeper to operate the gates from 7 a.m. to 6 p.m.[10]

Two months later, Martin Leverett was crossing the railroad at College Hill in his dairy wagon when a fast-moving switch engine raced through the crossing without sounding a warning whistle or ringing its bell. The engine plowed into Leverett's wagon, smashing it to pieces and throwing him onto the tracks where he was horribly mutilated when the engine rolled over his body. The broken man was carried to his home to die. A coroner's jury found the railroad negligent in the accident, and the *Democrat* suggested it was time for it to build a bridge over the crossing.[11]

Another safety problem the city faced on an almost daily basis was fire. When William had taken over as mayor, the city had a volunteer fire department. Its firefighting equipment included a one-horse team, which was stabled at City Hall; 1,000 feet of hose; a hose-truck; an engine house; an alarm system;

and 30 hydrants with four miles of water mains. Whenever the fire alarms sounded – night or day – all able-bodied men in the city were expected to help fight the fire. Soon after taking office, William had recommended the city privatize the fire department to keep the city from sliding further in debt. In February 1893, the city sold its horses and contracted with two men to maintain the fire equipment and convey it to the scene of every fire for use by the volunteers. The contract saved the city $1,500 a year, but it raised concerns among residents over the response time to fires. To ease these concerns, the city agreed to pay half the expense of installing a telephone in the office of Mr. Reid, one of the men contracted to provide firefighting services. As there were only 56 telephones in the city at this time and few of them were in homes, the installation of a phone was more symbolic than practical.[12]

The privatization was questioned whenever a rash of serious fires broke out. A large portion of the East Side's business district was lost in August 1893 when a fire started at night in former-Mayor Schicker's bakery. The flames quickly spread to a meat market located in the same two-story frame building. Soon the entire building was engulfed in the fire, which then spread to the two adjoining brick buildings. Before the flames were extinguished, they had destroyed a second meat market; a harness shop; a saloon; the Texarkana Hardware Company; the law offices of A.M. Garrison; the office of H.M. Abbey, the auditor for the Southern Pine Lumber Company; and the office of J.C. Edwards, justice of peace. As the business owners watched their property being destroyed, they started arguing over the cause of the fire and reached for their guns; fortunately, no one was injured in the hail of bullets. Their differences settled, they wasted no time in finding new quarters. The next morning, it was business as usual – only in a new location – for several of the businesses.[13]

While Texarkanians complained about their lack of protection from fire, they were reminded that they had it much better than others when a fire all but destroyed the business district of nearby Fulton. Set by arsonists in the middle of the night, the fire, within three hours, destroyed every business but one. Having no fire company, the residents had to form a bucket brigade as their sole defense against the flames. While many risked their lives to try to save the city, others were looting the stores before they burned and helping themselves to whiskey. The next morning, the East Side jail was filled with Fulton's hung-over looters.[14]

A few months later, Texarkanians were once again questioning William and his cost-cutting efforts when several fires – many of them set in an attempt to conceal robberies – damaged businesses throughout the city. "Protection from fires is a matter of first importance," the *Democrat* stated. "Five large insurance companies had withdrawn from Texarkana leaving only twelve others and they talk of doing the same thing, because of the inefficiency of the fire department." In response, the East Side City Council held a special meeting a few days later to order 500 feet of a superior quality fire hose and issue a notice that the owners of frame buildings on Broad Street had until April 1, 1894, to remove them.[15]

Another disastrous fire hit Texarkana a month later, but this one was on Walnut Street on the West Side. It started in a storehouse and spread to three homes and the Jewish synagogue, which had recently been moved to the area and renovated. As there was no fire hydrant in the neighborhood, the fire departments from both sides had to connect their hoses to get water to the site.[16]

William learned that cost-cutting efforts often carried a high price. While his decision regarding the fire department opened him to public complaint, another decision his administration made cost him a friendship. William's friend Dr. Spearman voluntarily served on the East Side's Board of Health along with the mayor, the city attorney, and three aldermen. As a member of the board, which was charged with protecting the city against "contagious, malignant and infectious diseases," the doctor was asked to investigate an alleged case of diphtheria, which had caused the schools to close. After doing so, Spearman presented the city with a bill of $50 for his services. City officials denied the bill, saying they had understood Spearman was acting as a member of the Board of Health – not as a private physician.[17]

A few months later, Spearman filed a suit against the city in the JP court, which ruled in the city's favor. He then appealed to the Miller County Circuit Court. After hearing the case, the jury was instructed that if it concluded Spearman had performed the services as a member of the Health Board and at the request of the board, it should find against him. The jury ruled in the city's favor. Objecting to the instruction given the jury, the doctor appealed to the Arkansas Supreme Court, which agreed in January 1894 that the jury instruction was in error and sent the case back to the lower court. The case had created such a stir throughout the state that the Little Rock newspapers printed the complete text of the Supreme Court's ruling.[18]

Texarkanians had more cause for excitement a month later when East Side officials broke up yet another gambling den on State Line Avenue. *The Daily Texarkanian* (the new name of the *Daily Texarkana Democrat*) praised their efforts. "The law is plain and explicit on this subject and its enforcement will meet with the unqualified approval and support of the law-abiding people of our city," the paper said as it called on the West Side to follow suit and establish law and order throughout Texarkana.[19]

Meanwhile, law officers had other crime to avert. Several gangs of bank robbers, each with its own signature style, were working their way through the country, hitting any banks that hadn't yet failed. One gang made a habit of posting warnings on the doors of a bank a few days before the intended robbery. Such a notice appeared on the door of the Gate City Bank in February. The notice informed bank officials that it would be visited February 22 and "all its ready cash appropriated and carried away." Bank officials prepared for the robbery, but two days after the appointed date, nothing had happened yet. Marshal Crenshaw continued to keep an eye out for the would-be robbers. About a week after the date set for the robbery, Crenshaw's suspicions were aroused when a gang of heavily armed men came into town, passing themselves off as cattlemen. When the men learned the marshal and his deputies were onto them, they left town.[20]

Excitement of a different kind embroiled the mayor in a controversy involving his church. In a Sunday paper, the new editor of the Inter-State News ran an article titled "Sambo at the Front" that attacked the Fourth Street Methodist Church and its pastor for worshipping with African Americans on an equal basis. Implying that it was common for blacks to worship alongside whites at the church, the article chided Brother Littleton, the pastor, for addressing two black men in the rear of the church as "brother" and inviting them to take seats in the front. As they came forward, the paper claimed, the minister met them at the rail, saying he was there to save souls regardless of color.[21]

The article caused such a commotion that the board members of the church felt compelled to respond. They started by setting the record straight. It was not Brother Littleton but Dr. M.S. Hard, one of the secretaries of the Methodist Episcopal Extension Society, who had extended the invitation to the two black men, who were the pastor and presiding elder of the Colored Methodist Church on the West Side. Dr. Hard, who worked with both white and black churches throughout the country, did not meet them at the rail or shake hands with them; he offered them a hymnbook.[22]

The board members saw no impropriety in the visiting brother's actions. Instead, they commended him. "[A]ll the churches (in the denomination) are now reaching out a helping hand to help their 'Brother in Black,'" the board members said. They informed the new editor that previous pastors of the Texarkana church – as well as evangelists – had preached to black and white alike.[23]

Gardner, the editor of the *Texarkanian*, printed the card submitted by the church board. But his reaction, coupled with the comments of the other editor, showed the Methodists had become a minority in their relationship with their black brothers and sisters. Referring to the card, Gardner responded, "[W]e believe that to exclude a human being from the House of God or deny him the privilege of hearing his holy word, is a sin against high Heaven, while for a white man to controvert God's expressed will, by attempting to place an inferior race in equality with their superiors, is a crime against humanity. The highest and lowest of the human races were no more intended for the same plane of social life than the natural growth of the Occident and Orient are intended for the same climate. There is then only one way to reconcile these conflicting conditions and that is for the higher and more powerful race to concede every just and righteous claim of their inferiors, at the same time scrupulously guarding their own rights."[24]

Looking back on his childhood, William recalled all the Methodist camp meetings he had attended with his parents in which former slave worshipped alongside former master. He remembered white and black alike calling out for a sermon by Uncle Sam, whom his grandfather had trained in the ministry. No one then had protested the right of a black man to stand before a white congregation, espousing the truths of God. Times had definitely changed.

32 Elections and Epidemics

With a little more than a month left in his term as mayor, William could look back with pride on his administration and the officials who had helped him bring law and order to what had been known as a frontier town. Many residents encouraged William to run for a second term, but he declined. He had fulfilled all of his promises. Texarkana was well on its way to becoming a progressive city. It was time for him to step down and let someone else hold the city reins. Besides, he had a full plate what with his solo law practice, a growing family, and his party obligations. And politics had just become a lot more exciting. A Republican and three Populists had joined with Senate Democrats to repeal the odious election law that had allowed federal supervision of elections. The 39-28 vote marked the end of "an important era in the country's history," the *Texarkanian* commented. "As the laws to be repealed were the outgrowth mainly of the war of the rebellion and have their origin during reconstruction days," they were the last vestige of the South's defeat. The Democrats could truly look forward to a new century.[1]

But before William could step down, nature gave him one more mess to clean up. Texarkana reported its heaviest rain in several years March 18, 1894. As creeks turned into impassable waterways and railroads washed out, the city was cut off. In Swampoodle, the swollen streams swept away years of accumulated filth. Nineteen inches of water flooded the city water works, where pipes were popping like heavy artillery and the furnaces glowed red hot as they struggled to keep the pumps working.[2]

As soon as the water dried up, the Democrats got serious about the upcoming city election. The local newspapers called for candidates who would maintain the progress William had started. "On the East side, under Mayor Arnold's excellent administration, the city has advanced in every way, and its affairs have prospered continually," editor Gardner commented. Since the West Side was still ruled by a "rough element," respectable citizens on the East Side rightfully feared the unruly characters would cross the state line unless another strong law-and-order candidate were elected. Although several candidates stepped forward, none committed himself to preserving law and order.[3]

On the eve of the Democratic primary, a voter wrote a letter commending William and calling upon the candidates to follow in his steps. "He (William) came out squarely before the election and announced his policy plainly," the voter said in his letter to the editor. "He was elected and he fulfilled every pledge. Prostitution has been banished, gambling driven out, and the saloon keeper has not been allowed to profit by violating the law. Is our city ready to turn back to the old way? Has the moral administration of Mayor Arnold done harm to our city?"[4]

Pointing out that neither mayoral candidate had taken a public stand, the letter writer asked them: "Gentlemen, are you afraid to come out like men and let the people know your sentiments? The moral element of the Democratic party desire to know this, and they are a power in the land if once aroused. If you do not stand for good moral government in Texarkana, Arkansas, hundreds of Democrats will scratch your name from the ticket."[5]

The next day, the Democrats nominated J.C. Edwards, who had served as justice of the peace, as their candidate for mayor. Once again, a Citizens Ticket was promoted with former Mayor Schicker leading the slate as the mayoral candidate. Since no Democrats appeared on the Citizens Ticket, Gardner claimed it really was a Republican ticket, which he said did an injustice to the two-thirds of the party that was black in that it included no African American candidates.[6]

Respectable people on both sides of the state line were just as concerned about the West Side election and the need to retire the "tough," corrupt element that had run the city for years. Commenting on an article from the *Inter-State News*, Gardner said, "[I]t correctly states that the way Texarkana, Arkansas, got rid of such damnable domination was by her mayor and officers having had sufficient back-bone to enforce law and order. It closes the article with the hope that the West side 'can meet our East side neighbors on an equal law and order plane.'"[7]

The Democrats won easily on the East Side, but the reformers had a close fight on the West Side. Judge P.A. Turner defeated incumbent Mayor S.D. Lary, who had been indicted on corruption charges, by 10 votes. Turner's first act as mayor of the West Side was to order the police to run the toughs out of town, close all the gambling houses, and notify the saloon keepers that no whiskey was to be sold on Sundays. Although he had not taken a stand on law and order, Edwards, the East Side's new mayor, gave a forceful speech when he was sworn in April 9 warning that "the tough element of the West side shall not find on the East side a haven of refuge, when driven from their present habitation."[8]

William returned to the life of a private citizen, assured that his advancements in city government would be continued. The only change the new administration made was to repeal the ordinance that banned hogs from running loose on the city streets. The local paper had spoken against the repeal: "[T]here should be no step backward in relegating the hog to the rear, as he is a nuisance if allowed to run free in the streets." But the administration bowed to public pressure, expressed in a petition, and gave the hogs free run of the streets.[9]

The new city officials soon found themselves too preoccupied with a smallpox epidemic to do much else that spring. The first hint of the epidemic occurred two days after the new administration was sworn in. Two African Americans had reportedly died of chicken pox. But rumors quickly spread that smallpox actually was to blame as chicken pox was rarely fatal and generally infected children – not adults. Following the deaths, four new cases of the disease were reported on College Hill and two cases in the northern suburbs – all in black communities. A day later, an infant and an elderly man died of the disease and several new cases were reported in town. Dr. Simmons, the city's health officer, confirmed the cases were chicken pox – not the dreaded smallpox. When another case was reported April 20, two other doctors were brought in. They diagnosed the disease as smallpox, but Simmons continued to insist it was chicken pox.[10]

To fight the growing epidemic, the city ordered that yellow quarantine flags be placed on all the houses where the disease had been reported. Schools were closed, and a pest house established a mile outside the city along the Iron Mountain Railroad. Finally, the Board of Health, over Simmons' objections, made it official – the East Side was in the midst of a smallpox epidemic. Twenty-seven cases were confirmed in the black community April 25.[11]

Hoping to keep the epidemic under control, the board ordered that anyone who had been exposed must be kept under strict quarantine. Those who couldn't care for themselves were to be taken to the pest house. Anyone who violated these rules would be arrested and forcibly placed in quarantine. City officials promised to provide food for those who needed it. All East Side residents were ordered to "thoroughly clean, cleanse and disinfect" their premises immediately with lime. If they couldn't afford it, the city would provide it. The Sanitary Board would inspect everyone's home and business and report any nuisances or unsanitary conditions; violators would be prosecuted.[12]

As more deaths were reported, some doctors began offering vaccinations. Dr. Simmons, who continued to insist that the city was dealing with chicken pox, resigned, and the city appointed a new health officer, who reported another death and one new case for a total of 22 cases April 26. Nineteen other people who had been exposed were being quarantined in a separate building some distance from the pest house.[13]

Although local townspeople were concerned about the disease, the epidemic was causing three times as much alarm outside the city as it was in Texarkana. The start of the epidemic had been linked to members of Fry's Army, which had come through town en route to join Coxey's Army in Washington for a protest against the nation's monetary policies. Two of the "soldiers," too sick to continue, were left behind in Texarkana.[14]

When smallpox was first rumored, several people in Texarkana fled the city in panic, spreading wild rumors about how bad the situation was. The white townspeople who stayed weren't overly concerned since the epidemic was confined to the black population and officials had taken all necessary precautions. But the reaction outside Texarkana, whipped up by false and exaggerated reports, threatened to devastate the city's economy. To protect themselves from the disease, surrounding towns in both Arkansas and Texas declared a quarantine against Texarkana. Little Rock, Prescott, Hope, Fulton, New Lewisville, Camden, Paris, Dekalb, Bonham, and Mount Pleasant cut off all trade and travel to the border town.[15]

While the epidemic was not a cause of concern for white Texarkanians, the quarantine, and its impact on business, was. Texarkana's businessmen appointed a committee to write a report condemning the false rumors spreading in the other towns and asking the other cities to lift their quarantine. Panicked by the crisis, the new mayor sent a telegram to Gov. Fishback, saying: "We have small pox. What assistance can we expect from the State." The businessmen condemned the mayor's telegram, contending that it would make the situation worse as it would send the message that the epidemic was out of control. Besides, cities were supposed to handle their own problems; the state didn't have the resources to help.[16]

By the end of April, many Texarkanians began to panic as the word on the street was worse than the truth, and it was getting difficult to tell truth from rumor. To calm the fears, the city Health Board called a citizens meeting to give the townspeople a first-hand official report of the situation. About 200 people attended. City officials confirmed that 400 people – black and white – had been exposed but only 30 to 35 cases had developed, and all those were in the African American community. "[A]nd most of them were in the lower class ... whose filthy and exposed condition, aggravated the disease," the reporter covering the meeting said. The townspeople were told that health officials from other cities in Arkansas and Texas had inspected the situation and reported that everything was under control and that there was no need for a quarantine against Texarkana. They also were told that several doctors were offering free vaccinations to those who couldn't pay for them. A plea went out for used clothes for the people in quarantine as all their old clothes would have to be burned.[17]

The meeting may have reassured people in Texarkana, but it did nothing to ease the anxiety in the surrounding area. T.L.L. Temple, a prominent Texarkana lumberman who had been on a business trip in St. Louis ever since the epidemic had broken out, was traveling home when his train stopped in New Lewisville. When Temple tried to get off the train, he was forced to reboard at muzzle point. The same thing happened when he tried to get off the train at a mill station a mile east of New Lewisville. Texarkana's Board of Health was in large part to blame for the panicked reaction. While the board was instructed to keep U.S. health authorities apprised of the situation, it was reluctant to give official reports to anyone else. Thus, railroad operators who were being forced to give daily reports in St. Louis and Little Rock had to rely on the exaggerated reports being heard in the streets. Those reports were then picked up by newspapers throughout the region and publicized as fact.[18]

The official reports were bad enough. New cases continued to break out, and they were spreading from the East Side out into the county and across the state line. There was more cause for concern among the white population when two cases were reported in white families living in Miller County May 1. Ten family members had been exposed to the disease. Since the county didn't have a pest house or the money to establish one, the county Health Board asked East Side officials to take care of the infected and exposed people in the county. But city officials refused; they were spending $100 a day just to take care of their own people.[19]

The next day, a white woman who had refused medical attention died, and several more cases were reported in the county. As the epidemic spread through the county, surrounding towns maintained their quarantine against Texarkana. Some set armed guards at their train depots to ensure no one from Texarkana or Miller County disembarked. Sam Jones, a prominent Georgia evangelist, canceled his much advertised lecture in Texarkana, citing the smallpox scare. Editor Gardner and his wife were not allowed to attend the Arkansas Press Association meeting in Little Rock because of that city's quarantine against Texarkana.²⁰

To keep the disease from reaching epidemic proportions on the West Side, city officials there imposed compulsory vaccinations on the black community. In Miller County, Judge Friedell agreed to use county funds to feed the infected but he would do nothing to provide medical treatment.

To add insult to injury, heavy rains and storms aggravated the situation by causing considerable damage throughout town. Several coffins, together with their "ghastly contents," had been washed up and were lying along the embankment road between the Iron Mountain and Cotton Belt crossings leading to College Hill. In the early days of Texarkana, there had been a paupers' cemetery on the site, but all the coffins supposedly had been dug up and interred in another cemetery. Elsewhere in the county, the Red River was flooding, and people in Fulton were forced to leave their homes. About 200 feet of Iron Mountain track was under six to eight feet of water. Railroad workers guarded trestles as the flood waters threatened embankments.²¹

After an exhausting few weeks, the people of Texarkana finally could relax and recoup their losses. The flood waters receded, the coffins had been reburied, and the smallpox epidemic had run its course. Schools reopened May 8. Three days later, the other towns started lifting their quarantines against Texarkana.²²

33 Reconstructing the Ideal

As the new administration handled the smallpox epidemic, William devoted his newfound free time to his law practice and family. At about that time, Robert Brady Williams, a prominent lawyer from Washington, moved to Texarkana and went into practice with William as Williams & Arnold. Ten years older than William, Robert brought a lot of prestige and connections to the law firm. The son of Judge Abner B. Williams, Robert had studied the classics at Washington and Lee University and then studied law with his father. After being admitted to the bar in 1876, he had gone into practice with his father in Hempstead County.[1]

Robert and William had much in common. Both of their mothers were devout Methodists. Their fathers were Whigs-turned-Democrats. Both lawyers were Masons. Both were interested in politics. Both were involved in the Democratic State Central Committee. Where there were differences, Robert represented the ideal the younger man longed to achieve. Robert's parents, who had already made it into the ranks of the elite when the Civil War broke out, emerged from the war and Reconstruction with their social and economic status fairly intact. But David and Tempie, William's parents, were younger. Given five to 10 more years, they would have become the elite. But the war ended their progression, and they struggled to hold onto their position in the upper middle class. Thus, William was denied the education and advantages Robert had received from his family.[2]

Starting with that solid foundation handed down from his father, Robert was able to build financial security for himself. While practicing law in Washington, Robert had acquired or inherited large real estate holdings, including 6,000 acres in farm land and some property in town. Robert also was considered a businessman and financier; he served as vice president of the Hempstead County Bank and had stock and interests in numerous other successful enterprises in southwest Arkansas.[3]

The partnership with Robert changed the way William practiced law. With Robert's contacts and business interests, the firm focused on business law rather than criminal. In 1896, William wrote the charter for the State Bank and served as its attorney for several years. Eventually he was providing legal counsel to such companies and utilities as the State Savings & Trust Company, Texarkana Water Corporation, Texarkana Gas & Electric Company, insurance companies, and many others.

In working with Robert, William fully understood, perhaps for the first time, the birthright he had lost to the war and Reconstruction. It was a loss his parents' generation had recognized years earlier. "The wound has never healed, and when touched the abrasion shows acute inflammation.... [M]y life was potent with golden dreams, which that cruel war turned into hydra form. The scenes we forgot are not erased," Elmira Snodgrass, who was a young woman during the war years, wrote several decades later. Despite her own wounds and painful memories, Elmira, like David and Tempie, sensed that the biggest impact was to the children. "The Federal army robbed my children of their rights before they were born! The Old South was theirs by inheritance," she wrote. "[B]ut in lieu of its (the Old South's) advantages, they have been made a part of the brick and mortar worked into the building of the New South," she added.[4]

While his partnership with Robert may have made William more aware of his loss, it also girded and focused his ambitions. Robert had grown up with the educational and business advantages that should have been William's. Although the war had ended such dreams for his father, William was not about to give up his personal aspirations that encompassed all the teachings of Southern honor, the values of the Old South, the dedication to family, the virtue of a gentleman.

William clung to the belief that Arkansas offered those who were willing to work an opportunity for upward social mobility.

While the war had dampened the optimism and the degree of certainty that had surrounded such mobility, it had not erased the hope or the possibility. That sense of Southern honor refused to let these hopes die. Honor itself had pointed a way out of the chaos the war had rained on the South. From birth, William had accepted the Southern code of honor and lived by it. He knew no other way. The resulting worldview, handed down from his parents, had molded him; it shaped how he acted and reacted; it determined his judgments and opinions; it created the filters through which he looked upon the world. He, in turn, would hand this worldview, this vital code, down to his children, instilling in them a respect of education, an obligation to their country, and the pride and responsibility of being an Arnold.

Through Robert, William also understood the advantages his partner had gained by following his father into the law. All of the prestige and influence Abner had gained reflected upon Robert, making his course a bit easier. William expanded his dream – not only would all his children receive a good education but his sons would follow in his steps and become lawyers. For his male descendents, the responsibility of being an Arnold would mean pursuing a legal career.

As William approached the turn of the century, he had every reason to be optimistic. He was a partner in a prominent law firm. He was respected in his community. He held influential positions in the legal profession and the Democratic Party. He had the wherewithal to educate his children and live the life he desired.

But 1900 proved a difficult year. Robert died in April, leaving William to practice alone once again. Jessie died August 27, making William a single father with five children, ranging in age from four to 12 years old. (His third daughter, Ruth Arnold, was born in 1894 a few months after he retired from city office, and a second son, David Christopher Arnold, was born in 1896.) As William adjusted to these tragedies, he decided to practice alone. "My purpose was to keep the place open for the admission of my sons, whom I hoped would all be lawyers," William wrote years later.[5]

In mourning, William immersed himself in work, church obligations, and civic duty. With his children in school, he took great interest in their education, serving as a member and president of the school board. Through his involvement on the school board, he met a young teacher, Kate Lewis, a graduate of Peabody College in Nashville. Two and a half years of struggling as a single parent were enough for William. In 1903, at the age of 42, he married the 21-year-old Kate. Richard Lewis Arnold, another lawyer for the Arnold firm, was born three years later.[6]

For a while, life settled into a routine for the Arnold family. In the summers when it was too hot to work, the family traveled. Sometimes they went to Canada or took a cruise; other times, they took short trips to Baker Springs, where they would spend leisurely days along the Cossatot River. William, though still involved in the local party, seemed to forget about politics, devoting most of his time to his family, his career, and the legal profession in general.[7]

As vice president of the Arkansas Bar Association in 1906, William lobbied tirelessly to have the bar's annual meeting be a joint convention with the Texas Bar Association. What better place to have it than Texarkana, which straddled both states? Recognizing the advantage to them, the businessmen of the city joined William in his efforts to bring the joint convention to town. When the joint meeting convened in the Miller County Courthouse July 10, 1906, about 500 lawyers were in attendance. In his opening speech, William "praised Texas in the grand style of the day and to an extreme seldom lavished on the Lone Star State by people from Arkansas." Because of the success of the convention, others followed, demonstrating the need for a convention center and auditorium in Texarkana. For his efforts, William was recognized as being "largely responsible for Texarkana's fame as a convention city."[8]

Soon William's ambition and his commitment to public service could no longer be satisfied by making a name for himself with the bar association or serving on the school board. He needed a new challenge. As a lawyer, one of his biggest frustrations was the increasing complexity of the law brought about by the volumes of new laws being passed every legislative session.

Many of these laws were unclear or contradictory, which made it difficult for both lawyers and judges to do their job effectively. His solution? He announced he would be running in the Democratic primary for a state Senate seat. William approached the Senate campaign much as he had the mayoral race. Instead of running a small card announcing himself as a candidate, he wrote a lengthy article for the newspaper, detailing and explaining his platform. In the letter, he advocated several changes in the state Constitution, including a 60-day limit on legislative sessions and four-year terms for all legislators and state officers.[9]

"[M]y object in making the race was to expose the outrage upon the public of the long, windy, unnecessary and expensive legislative sessions and the absurdity of the continual agitation in the election of State officers every two years," he wrote. Out of those sessions came a voluminous amount of enactments, many of which were unnecessary. He pointed out that the acts of the 1889 General Assembly filled a volume of 186 pages. In comparison, the 1905 Assembly had produced 845 pages. Two years later, the acts of the General Assembly filled 1,255 pages. (The 1911 Assembly – the one for which William ran – met for an unprecedented 141 days and passed enough acts to fill nearly 2,000 pages.)

William's opponents – Judge Friedell and W.B. Owen, a former state representative – announced no platform. When the three candidates addressed voters, William discussed issues; the other two ran on their name. William attended as many speakings in the county as he had time for. When stumping on the campaign trail, he would stack up all the law books of the state to illustrate his point about the numerous laws being passed. Then he would vow that if he were elected, he would not vote for any new laws. Most of William's campaigning was confined to Texarkana, whereas the other candidates toured the county. Taking advantage of William's absence in the outlying areas, Friedell adopted the former mayor's platform and circulated it as his own. When the results of the primary were announced, William was the clear winner in Texarkana, having received more votes than the other two combined. But his failure to campaign throughout the county cost him the Senate seat. Friedell, receiving enough votes in the county to offset William's lead in Texarkana, beat him by 39 votes.[10]

After the election, several of William's friends told him they hadn't voted for him because they thought Friedell, whom they called an old Confederate soldier, needed the job more than William, whose law practice had become quite lucrative. "It was also alleged that he [Friedell] was a strong prohibitionist, and the tendency of the times now is that a man's qualifications to represent the people depends upon some minor collateral issue like that," William wrote later. "Prohibition was not involved at all in this race, but it was brought in as though it were a vital proposition." As a Methodist, William would have been for temperance himself. But he refused to make an election about a single issue; he wanted to tackle the bigger problems facing the state.[11]

In conceding the election, William announced that he would never sit as a member of the state Legislature in either house. But he wasn't through with politics – or with trying to improve the law. When John H. Rogers, the federal judge for the Western District of Arkansas, died in April 1911, the lawyers of Texarkana unanimously endorsed William for the position. They were joined by lawyers in Hope, Camden, and several other Arkansas towns. "We thought that as Judge Rogers was a Democrat and the party rules somewhat relaxed in judicial matters that a Democrat might possibly be elected to succeed," William wrote.

William was one of 12 applicants for the position; most of the others lived in Fort Smith where the Western District Court was seated. The lawyers pushing for William weren't discouraged by the populated field. They lobbied long and hard to get their man appointed judge. But the Republicans were pushing for one of their own. H.L. Remmel, chairman of the Arkansas Republican Party, sent a telegram to President Taft April 18: "Our state organization in due time will present for your consideration for appointment the name of a republican lawyer in every way qualified for the position." And other candidates, such as W.H.H. Clayton of McAlister, Oklahoma, used personal contacts to try to arrange interviews with the president.[12]

William had his own contact – Texas Congressman Morris Sheppard, who met with President Taft on William's behalf May 4. Following that meeting, Morris met with Sen. James P. Clarke of Arkansas to request his endorsement for William's application. The congressman reported on this meeting in a follow-up letter to the president: "Senator Clark (*sic*) stated that he knew Mr. Arnold to be entirely qualified, and that he came up to the requirements of a federal judge, and that if you asked him for his opinion he would give Mr. Arnold his unqualified endorsement." But Clarke told Morris he would give several other applicants the same approval if their names were submitted to him.[13]

Neither Morris nor William was discouraged. Morris commented to local newspapers on his meeting with the president. He said he interpreted "Taft's diplomatic remarks to mean that Mr. Arnold stood a very good chance of receiving the appointment and stood higher than any other Democrat." Although Remmel was lobbying for Fort Smith District Attorney John T. Worthington, Frank Youmans, a Republican attorney in Fort Smith, seemed to be the leading candidate. "[A] well-known national figure at Washington stated 'the cards were stacked for Youmans' and that no other candidate would have a chance," the newspaper reported. "Mr. Arnold laconically replied: 'Well if the cards have been stacked, the hand hasn't been played.'"[14]

Ignoring the rumors, William did everything he could to ensure he was dealt the winning hand; he was playing for his life's dream. He spent considerable time assembling his application, which included a carefully written biographical sketch and resolutions adopted by the Texarkana, Hope, and Camden bar associations supporting his candidacy. It also included a large number of endorsements from prominent attorneys in Arkansas, Texas, and Louisiana. Among the endorsements were letters from Morris, which reminded the president of their meeting, and Charles G. Dawes of Chicago, who said William had been his attorney for years. But apparently, the cards were stacked. When the hand was played, Youmans was named judge.[15]

Although discouraged, William wasn't ready to give up on politics. On March 10, 1915, he announced he would allow his name to go before the next Arkansas Democratic primaries, which would be held the following year, as a candidate for governor. "In offering himself for the position ... Judge Arnold does so solely from a patriotic impulse," the *Texarkanian* reported. "The emoluments of the office from a financial standpoint are certainly not sufficient to attract a lawyer of Judge Arnold's position and earning capacity." (William had earned the title *judge* by filling in when other judges had to recuse themselves from specific cases and in filling a six-month vacancy.)[16]

In announcing his candidacy, William said the governor's office should be conducted like a successful business. His platform included improving public schools and universities, changing state terms from two years to four, and setting term limits. His announcement surprised all but a few of his closest friends. Although the election was a year away, the possible field of candidates was getting crowded. And most of the names bandied about belonged to prominent politicians – such as Gov. G.W. Hays, Little Rock Mayor Charles Taylor, Congressman C.J. Floyd of Yellville, Secretary of State Earle W. Hodges, and Attorney General W.L. Moose. Having held no office higher than mayor of Texarkana, William was an unlikely candidate.[17]

After mulling over his prospects and examining the amount of money previous candidates had spent on a gubernatorial race, William made another announcement that June. This time, he said he would not run for governor. In explaining his decision, William said he had considered running only after being approached by lawyers from all over the state and several people in Fort Smith. But the cost of running was an obstacle. "The item of expense seems to be a barrier to a man of ordinary means who would aspire to the honors of such a office," William said in the announcement, "judging from the expense account of other candidates, and I am not in position to spend anything like the amount of money it has cost other candidates to make the race."[18]

He pointed out that in the 1912 gubernatorial race, George W. Donaghey had spent nearly $18,000 in the campaign and Joe

T. Robinson, the winner of the election, had spent nearly $12,000 – for a two-year term that paid only $4,000 a year. "If the recent past is to be a guide for success in the aspirations for such an office, the eligible are limited to a very narrow circle, and I do not feel I am eligible to make the race under those circumstances," William said. Although he cited finances, family may have been a bigger consideration. Kate was quite content with a behind-the-scenes role in politics, but she did not want her husband running for office. He had been disappointed enough by politics.[19]

34   A Civic Duty

Discouraged by politics and disappointed in his quest for a judicial post, William turned his concern about the law to another matter – the 1874 Arkansas Constitution. Written as a response to Reconstruction and its ministers, the Constitution did not reflect Southern values in that it legislated a distrust of public officials and their actions. To get around its stringent limitations, lawmakers had worked overtime creating massive volumes of legislation that allowed the government to function. The true Southern way, at least in theory, had been to elect honorable, enlightened leaders who could be trusted to do what was right for the people. They did not need legislative limits. Their code of honor would hold them in check. William, like other Arkansans, was ready to let Southern honor – and its accompanying values – guide the state. Working with the law on a daily basis, he also understood the need for a more progressive document. A better constitution would alleviate the need for the volumes of legislation coming out of the General Assembly every two years.

His only hope was a constitutional convention to correct the underlying problem. After losing the Senate race, "I ... stated that we should have a new constitution in this state, and if a constitutional convention should ever be called that I would like to be a delegate to that convention," he recalled. He immediately acted upon these sentiments. As an influential member of the Arkansas Bar Association, he lobbied hard for a constitutional convention to replace the document adopted as vengeance on Reconstruction.[1]

His efforts paid off when the Arkansas Bar began its lobbying efforts in earnest in 1914. At its annual meeting in 1916, it devoted one of the five main addresses to the need for a new constitution. In a 40-page address, W.H. Rector pointed out many – but not all – instances "wherein the present constitutional system fails adequately to provide for the efficient expressions of the various functions of governmental power." The following year, the bar's entire annual meeting focused on a new constitution. By this time, it had created a Special Committee on the New Constitution, which remained active through 1920.[2]

The inflexibility of the 1874 Constitution was felt more by lawyers and government officials perhaps than by any other group. The document contained no provision for local bond issues, tax reforms, or other progressive acts of government. The desire for a new constitution, however, was not limited to lawyers. The Democratic Party endorsed calling for a constitutional convention at its state conventions in 1914, 1916, and 1918. The *Arkansas Gazette*, the *Arkansas Democrat*, and Gov. Charles Brough, inaugurated in 1917, all added their voices to the plea for a convention. Brough tackled the issue in his inaugural address: "The ghost of the past no longer walks. The people are secure in their enjoyment of the rights vouchsafed by a real democracy; the day of the 'carpetbagegr' [*sic*] and 'scalawag' has gone, never to return.... The keynote of the present is expansion rather than contraction, progress, rather than limitations, confidence in our lawmakers and public servants, rather than suspicion of them."[3]

The General Assembly yielded to the demands for a convention and called for one to be held in the fall of 1917. Each county was to elect the same number of delegates as it had House members along with 14 delegates at large – two from each of the state's seven congressional districts. In setting up the convention, the General Assembly approved a minimal per diem of $4 for each delegate and restricted the total appropriation for the convention to $25,000. The per diem resulted in much criticism as it limited who could afford to be a delegate. In defending the minimal pay, state Sen. J.A.O. Bush of Prescott said the "object was to get a select body of men who could afford to serve practically without pay." Other proponents insisted "patriotism, duty, and civic satisfaction should more than compensate for the inadequate amount."[4]

William announced his candidacy as a delegate from the Fourth District by running an article in the local paper, detailing his platform. He wanted to do away with local bills having to go through the General Assembly; expand the Supreme Court by adding two more justices; increase the salaries for state officials; increase the governor's term to four years; enact a workers' compensation law; provide for educational reforms; and remove the constitutional ban on women voting. As a nod to those who revered the old Constitution, William acknowledged that it was "framed by great and patriotic men and in its day was a remarkable model for protection against oppression, tyranny, waste and extravagance." But as one of the oldest state constitutions still in existence, he added, it needed to be "brought abreast of the times."[5]

Also running for the Fourth District delegate positions were Mr. Hardin of Fort Smith and James Head, who was admittedly partial to the existing Constitution. He called it a "paragon of excellence" that needed only slight modification. Recognizing how important this convention was and that it would stand and fall on the strength of the delegates elected, William campaigned more for this position than he had for any other office and paid for newspaper advertising. Although the campaign season was brief, he visited the county seat of each of the 11 counties in the Fourth District. "I did not undertake to make a campaign in the accepted sense, but gave my views upon the subjects to be considered by the Constitutional Convention through news-papers without making a personal appeal for votes," he said.[6]

Whenever he addressed voters, William reminded them how much the state had changed since 1874. "Our present Constitution was framed ... at the most trying period of the State's history, when its population was less than half a million; bowed down to suffering and sorrow, and depleted by war and reconstruction," he said, adding that Arkansas' population in 1917 was nearly 2 million. William's strategy worked. The *Times-Record* of Fort Smith endorsed him, saying his progressive platform had the "right ring." The paper continued: "The new constitution means our emancipation from the narrowness of an outworn document.... This is a new age and we imperatively need a new constitution.... This is no time for mere politicians, this is a time for statesmanship."[7]

When the Democrats held their primaries – restricted to white men – April 14, 1917, most of the candidates were lawyers. They were among the few who could afford the financial sacrifice. The winners of the Democratic primary were assured of winning the seats at the general election in June as the Republicans could not offer much opposition. Although the Arkansas General Assembly had passed a bill that spring giving women the vote, women could not serve as convention delegates or vote in the April primary for the convention delegates. John Arbuckle, the state attorney general, had ruled that the Riggs Law would not go into effect until June 8, 1917. (This suffrage law, the first of its kind in the South, was quickly declared unconstitutional as the 1874 Arkansas Constitution expressly prohibited women from voting.)[8]

The primary votes were counted April 22; William was in the top two for his district. Since there was no Republican opposition, he was assured one of the two delegate seats from the Fourth District. But the intense devotion Arkansans had to the old Constitution showed in the vote. Head, running on a platform of little change, received the most votes – 3,092. William received 2,330, and Hardin had 2,208. Voter turnout was light for the general election as many considered it a "simon pure" democratic affair. "The Democratic primary settled the affair, insofar as more than seventy counties were concerned," the *Arkansas Democrat* reported. As a result, some townships didn't bother to hold a general election as the "farmers were too busy to 'fool with the election.'"[9]

Several states were considering holding constitutional conventions in 1917. The *New York Times* warned them not to expect too much from the conventions. "We New York folks, who have seen a mighty good revised Constitution rejected by a colossal majority, look with a certain humorous pity upon the efforts of other States to patch the fundamental laws," the paper said.[10]

A Civic Duty

The efforts of William and the other progressives were doomed from the beginning. Months before Arkansas' convention was to open, the nation entered the World War. As the United States sent troops to Europe, protesters denounced efforts in Congress to initiate a draft – some of them going as far as suicide to demonstrate their disapproval. To counter such unpatriotic activity, a flag-raising ceremony was held April 27 at the Miller County Courthouse. As a new American flag was raised over the courthouse, William, whose two oldest sons enlisted, spoke of the needs of the Army and Navy and heartily endorsed the selective draft bill before Congress. Other community leaders spoke of the need to demonstrate patriotism through increasing food production and making munitions. All that summer and throughout the war, William served as a Four-Minute Speaker, making brief speeches in Miller and surrounding counties to rally support for the troops and raise money for the war effort as part of the Liberty Loan drives. He also was appointed by Provost Marshal General E.H. Crowder to organize advisory boards in each county in the state to provide legal advice to the young men registering for the draft.[11]

While William and many others worked behind the scenes to muster support for the war effort, protesters stole the headlines as they continued to clamor for peace. To curb the dissent, lawyers were disbarred for making "disloyal" statements, and judges and politicians (including a Supreme Court justice and the mayor of Chicago) were accused of disloyalty. The protests became so strident that the state Council for Defense strongly suggested that all circuit judges open their court sessions with a patriotic address.[12]

With the war overshadowing the necessity of changing the state Constitution, several delegates suggested adjourning the convention before it began. Gov. Brough, in a speech to Arkansas mayors and city officials on the eve of the constitutional convention, attacked such suggestions as the "rankest cowardice." "He also pledged to speak out daily for the adoption of a new constitution even if it meant his political suicide," the *Arkansas Democrat* reported.[13]

William and the other delegates began arriving in Little Rock Saturday, November 17. When the 110 delegates met in the House chamber that Monday to be sworn in, 10 found themselves without chairs. One of those who remained standing proposed holding a lottery for the seats – even though lotteries were illegal in the state – but the 100 with seats voted down the suggestion. Those without seats took to the floor or leaned against the wall. After the delegates had elected a president, one of the first proposals was adoption of a resolution pledging support to President Woodrow Wilson and his war policies. Delegate Mitchell of Boone County opposed the resolution, saying the convention couldn't be sincere in its sentiments if it stayed in session to "draw a constitution the people don't want and won't adopt." If the delegates sincerely supported the war effort, Mitchell said, they should adjourn so they could devote their efforts to winning the war. When the resolution supporting Wilson came to a vote, the delegates sprang to their feet in a show of patriotism; Mitchell remained seated.[14]

On the third day of the convention, the delegates yielded to public pressure and voted almost unanimously to recess until the first Monday of July 1918. In the meantime, committees were to draft specific sections that would then be reviewed when the convention resumed. William, one of the more vocal delegates of the convention, was appointed chairman of the committee on the legislative department and as a member of the committee on the judiciary and the committee on submitting the document to the people.[15]

The committee members spent most of the winter and spring debating and drafting their sections. Since the committees had been working independently, the final reports conflicted greatly with one another. Rather than resolve the conflicts, the codification committee printed the reports as they were so the convention as a whole could settle the problems when it reconvened in July. As soon as the delegates gathered that July at the new Statehouse, a motion was made to adjourn because of the war. When that motion was defeated, some delegates tried to recess until October 1919. But the majority of the delegates were committed to presenting the people of Arkansas with a new, workable constitution as soon as possible.[16]

The war continued to cast its shadow over the proceedings as the delegates labored eight hours a day, six days a week in the heat and humidity of the Little Rock summer. The new Statehouse had no cooling system, and drinking water was in short supply. As temperatures soared into the 100s and the days went by with no noticeable progress, tempers flared. The state's funding had run out, and delegates were not assured of being paid even the minimal $4 a day. After 10 weeks and several threats, the delegates finally managed to agree on a new document that allowed for female suffrage, prohibition, restrictions on local legislation, four-year terms, and salary increases for state officers, liberalized initiative and referendum procedures, expansion of the Supreme Court, creation of kindergartens and juvenile courts, authorization of a workers' compensation law, and creation of the office of lieutenant governor.[17]

The people of Arkansas were asked to vote on the proposed constitution in a special election December 14, 1918. All of the elements worked against the election. The World War continued to steal the headlines and interest of the people; a deadly flu epidemic swept through the state; and the weather refused to cooperate. Freezing temperatures in the north and flooded rivers in the south, coupled with the flu epidemic, forced polls to open late or not at all. About 63,000 people voted – slightly more than a third of the average voter turnout. Of those, 61 percent voted against the proposed constitution.[18]

Disappointed once again by the voters of Arkansas, William returned to his law practice. But he did not let disappointment keep him or his children from public service. He supported his son David when he ran for the state legislature in 1920. At 24, David was the youngest representative elected. Embracing his father's views on oppressive legislation, David devoted his efforts to remedial legislation and the repeal of laws that had grown out of the abuse of legislative power. Particularly odious was a law that allowed speculators and contractors to get local improvement districts passed without the consent of the landowners who had to pay the taxes. "Many farm localities in the

State had become practically bankrupt by reason of the creation of improvement districts by legislative acts fixing the entire tax upon lands in the building of highways.... The farmers of Miller County were in revolt against this type of ruthless legislation." David introduced a bill to repeal the 1920 act that had created the South Miller County Highway District and got it through the House. But the legislation, opposed by a powerful combination of companies and individuals who would profit from the road building and the opening of swamplands, was blocked in the Senate.[19]

David took his fight to the Senate by running against the incumbent, Judge Friedell, two years later. Much to William's satisfaction, David defeated his father's old rival by a majority of almost two to one. "He was very popular," Richard Arnold said of his uncle, "the only Arnold who ever was, really. People liked David." Although it was his first term as a senator, David was named president of the Senate, serving as acting governor when necessary. And he went to work on his legislation again. This time he got it passed by both houses. When the governor vetoed the bill, David successfully led the charge to get the legislators to override the veto. David's work in the General Assembly was seen as constructive in that it paved the way for road construction to be paid with gasoline taxes instead of through state-imposed local improvement districts. Like his father, David believed in citizen legislators rather than career politicians. When his term was finished and his work accomplished, he left the Legislature, giving up a promising political career to return to Arnold & Arnold.[20]

While David was busy in the General Assembly, William was trying to reform the legal system on the national level. As a prominent member of the American Bar Association, he joined with a group of leading judges, lawyers, and teachers to form the Committee on the Establishment of a Permanent Organization for the Improvement of the Law. This committee conducted a study that identified two chief defects – uncertainty and complexity – in the law, which had produced a "general dissatisfaction with the administration of justice." The study claimed the uncertainty stemmed from a lack of agreement among the law profession on the fundamental principles of common law, a "lack of precision in legal terms," "conflicting and badly drawn statutory provisions," the "great volume of recorded decisions," and the "number and nature of novel legal questions." The complexity was due to the "lack of systematic development" of the law and the numerous variations within the different jurisdictions in the country.[21]

As a result of this study, the American Law Institute was created. William was one of the founding members – along with U.S. Chief Justice William Howard Taft, who had denied William a judicial post when he was president. As part of his involvement in the Institute, William attended several annual meetings at the Mayflower Hotel in Washington and worked with his colleagues on restating basic legal subjects so judges and lawyers would be clear on what the law actually said. William also joined the National Conference of Commissioners on Uniform State Laws, which worked closely with the American Law Institute to develop and monitor a Uniform Commercial Code.[22]

35 In Search of Public Honor

The 1920s brought a new face to politics in Arkansas and the entire nation. The Ku Klux Klan had gained credibility with both the Republican and Democratic parties by taking a strong stance against bootleggers, prostitution, and gambling. What had begun as "mainly an instrument of masked terrorism, a movement for violent moral and social reform, had become essentially a political organization, dedicated to influencing nominations and elections everywhere and placing its favorites in office." To build its influence, the Klan took the credit when its endorsed candidates were elected to city, county, and state office. It had helped get governors elected in Oregon, Colorado, Maine, Georgia, Ohio, and Louisiana. The Klan, which had almost complete control of Indiana, also took credit for electing U.S. senators from Texas and Oklahoma as well as congressmen from several states. In many cases, these candidates were not Klansmen and they had not sought the endorsement. The Klan's power also was felt in Arkansas, where it had influenced municipal elections in Little Rock and found a sympathetic ear for its prohibition and law-and-order reforms.[1]

In its zenith in 1924 with more than 5 million members nationwide, the Klan aimed its influence at the national conventions of both parties. But the organization – with its white, Protestant supremacist doctrine – had become an issue in and of itself as a groundswell of opposition began to surface. Going into the primaries, some candidates criticized the Klan even though they knew it could be political suicide. And within both parties, elements were at work to adopt a plank denouncing the Klan by name. The Klan threatened to replace the Teapot Dome scandal, which had implicated leading Republican officials and tainted a Democratic contender, as the overriding issue of the Democratic convention. To protect its interests, the Klan sent its leaders to lobby behind the scenes at both the Republican and Democratic conventions.[2]

When the Democratic State Central Committee met in Little Rock in April 1924, it selected 18 delegates, including William, to attend the National Democratic Convention. With one of its leaders, Virgil C. Pettie, a member of the Arkansas delegation, the Klan figured it could count on Arkansas to vote against any plank repudiating it. Although the central committee requested the delegation to vote for Arkansas' favorite son Sen. Joseph Robinson, who was endorsed by the Klan, it gave the delegates no instructions regarding the party platform. So William and the other Arkansas delegates packed their bags and headed for Madison Square Garden. It was William's fourth national convention. When the Democrats arrived in New York for the June convention, they were confident that whomever they chose would be elected president since the Republican chances had been hurt by Teapot Dome.[3]

The floor fight began when the delegates met Saturday, June 28, to approve the party platform. It was standing room only in the Garden as immigrants, both men and women, packed into the upper galleries. Signs prohibiting smoking and spitting on the floor were printed in both English and Italian. The crowd kept quiet as most of the platform was read. When a meaningless plank referring to religious liberty was read, Andrew Erwin of Georgia, defying the rest of his state's delegation, tried to amend it to repudiate the Klan by name. A spontaneous demonstration erupted in which anti-Klan delegates marched toward the Georgia delegation as a band played "While We Go Marching Through Georgia." Enraged, Klan supporters booed and hissed.[4]

Pandemonium seized the galleries as the spectators jeered. In an effort to restore order so the next speaker could take the floor, police rushed into the space reserved for the delegates. The police stood in continuous lines in every aisle except the center one, which had delegates sitting in it. By now it was early morning, and the platform had yet to be approved. William Jennings Bryan rose as the final speaker against the anti-Klan amendment. As he stood to speak, he was booed and hissed by the masses in the gallery. Hundreds of police reserves were called as reinforcements to those already in the Garden. As Bryan tried to speak, the crowd continually interrupted him. In response, some of the delegates demanded that the galleries be cleared of the hoodlums, and Bryan made disparaging remarks about "Northern rudeness." Finally, it was time to vote on the amendment. The Arkansas delegation solidly supported the majority report of the platform committee, which did not include the controversial amendment. The anti-Klan plank lost by one vote. The convention recessed at 2 a.m. Sunday.[5]

Another floor fight began with the first ballot to select the Democrats' presidential candidate. Several names were in the running, but the two with the biggest following were Alfred E. Smith, governor of New York, and William Gibbs McAdoo, President Wilson's son-in-law and his secretary of the Treasury. The Klan was not thrilled with either man. Smith, a "wet" Catholic, stood for everything the Klan opposed. McAdoo, a staunch prohibitionist, had irritated the Klan by refusing to take a stand on the organization. As the balloting progressed, Smith and McAdoo clearly emerged as the frontrunners, but neither could get the two-thirds majority required to secure the nomination. Throughout the first day of balloting, the Arkansas delegation stood faithfully behind its candidate, Sen. Robinson. During a recess following the ninth ballot, McAdoo's supporters tried to persuade the Arkansas delegates to leave their favorite son, who didn't have a chance of winning the nomination, in favor of their candidate. But when the convention reconvened that night, the Arkansas delegates gave all their votes to Robinson.[6]

The balloting continued for days with no one willing to yield. After an especially long, heated day of voting July 2, one of McAdoo's supporters took Robinson to McAdoo's suite in the Madison Square Hotel where McAdoo tried to persuade him to withdraw. But Robinson refused. When the balloting began the next day, the Oklahoma delegates switched their votes from McAdoo to Robinson. Finally, after eight days and nights of balloting, McAdoo and Smith, realizing they could not get the required votes, released their delegates. A hundred ballots had been taken with no nominee. The convention recessed at 4 a.m. July 9.[7]

That afternoon, the delegates reconvened. After three more ballots, John W. Davis, a constitutional lawyer from West Virginia, was chosen as the Democratic candidate for president. Recognized as one of the most outstanding, brilliant members of the party, Davis had served in Congress and as ambassador to Britain. Davis won the nomination with no support from Arkansas, as all the Arkansas delegates followed their instructions to the end, voting for Robinson on every ballot.[8]

When he hit the campaign trail as the Democrats' anointed, Davis came out against the Klan, condemning the organization by name for raising "the standard of religious and racial prejudice" and doing "violence to the spirit of American institutions." The Republican nominee, Vice President Calvin Coolidge, kept his thoughts about the Klan to himself. That fall, when Coolidge won the election, the Klan claimed victory. But that victory did not extend to Arkansas where Davis, despite his anti-Klan stance, received more than two votes to every one cast for Coolidge. With their vote, Arkansas Democrats proved that party allegiance was paramount.[9]

After the 1924 convention, William stepped back from politics temporarily but not from public service. The next year, he served as a special associate justice on the Arkansas Supreme Court to decide whether Amendment 13, known as the Initiative and Referendum Amendment, had been legally adopted by a majority of voters. The court decision had far-reaching effects as it changed the former construction of the law. In the past, constitutional amendments had been adopted by a majority based on all votes cast in the election. Under the new ruling, amendments were adopted by a majority of the votes cast upon that particular amendment. William, viewed as the dean of the local bar, had other opportunities to impact the law of Arkansas as he frequently was elected by the other lawyers to serve as a special judge in circuit court when the presiding judge was disqualified or was ill.[10]

William did not let age slow him down or deter him from duty. When Jesse C. Hart, chief justice of the Arkansas Supreme

Court, died in 1933, William, then 72, said he would be a candidate whenever Gov. Junius Futrell called a special election to choose a new chief justice. But William refused to be a candidate for the interim position. When that honor went to 45-year-old Texarkana Chancellor C.E. Johnson, there was speculation that Johnson would be the leading candidate in the special election. The state Democrat Central Committee held a convention in July to choose its candidate for the special election. William refused to oppose the younger man on the convention floor, opening the door for Miller County party officials and attorneys, including William's son David and several of the Cooks, to endorse Johnson's candidacy.[11]

Johnson was opposed in the general election by an independent, Judge Woods, who had served as an associate justice of the court from 1893 until January 1929. When he had stepped down, Woods gave ill health and "advanced age" as his reasons. But now at 75, Woods wanted back on the bench. A longtime Democrat, Woods ran as an independent when he lost the Democratic nomination to Johnson. The younger man easily defeated Woods in the general election.[12]

William took one more stab at politics. Since his wife had been on the committee representing Arkansas at the Roosevelt-Garner inauguration, William thought he might have enough political clout to get a diplomatic appointment. Using every connection he and Kate had, William lobbied President Franklin D. Roosevelt for an appointment as ambassador to Tonga. Once again, his efforts failed. "I think it disappointed him greatly," his grandson Buzz Arnold says.

William had lived a life devoted to public service, working tirelessly to clean up his town and put Democrats in office. In all his dealings, he had followed the Southern code of honor. Looking back on his life with all of its accomplishments and disappointments, he perhaps felt cheated of the public recognition demanded by that code. Yes, his friends and neighbors admired and respected him. The townspeople of Texarkana were in his debt. He had made his mark on Arkansas through his law practice and political loyalties. He had accomplished more than most people. But despite all his efforts, he had never been granted the opportunity to demonstrate that he could be great in the annals of mankind. What perhaps frustrated him most was knowing he would have made a damn good judge – or senator or governor or ambassador.

To prove to himself and others that his life had been lived honorably and to the benefit of his family and community, William had to proclaim his honor to others. Thus, his biographical sketch, which detailed his political, legal, and societal activities, appeared in law and history journals, books that recognized community leaders in Arkansas – and European restaurants and hotels, where he gained a celebrity status he was denied at home. At the age of 74, William prepared for an autumn tour of Europe. But before setting sail from San Francisco August 9, 1935, he dictated a personal historical sketch to a public stenographer at the hotel where he was staying. The sketch was the story of his judicial and private life set down in the cold, precise language of a lawyer. It included a bibliography of seven reference books in which he was mentioned. In a day before copy machines, William had the stenographer type out dozens of copies of the sketch for him to take to Europe.[13]

William's first act upon arriving at the Savoy Hotel in London was to deposit a copy of his sketch with the hotel manager. As he traveled through Europe that fall, William left copies at every hotel and restaurant he visited. The unusual practice became a topic of conversation at the top hotels and restaurants on the continent and in London. It soon attracted media attention. Gwyn Lewis, a reporter with the *London Sunday Express*, dubbed William "The Man Who Cannot Lose Himself" in an article he wrote. The label spread over Europe as hotel and restaurant officials anticipated a visit from this American man. Lowell Thomas, a national news commentator in the United States, picked up on the story, spreading William's newfound fame to his home country.[14]

"I do not want to lose myself this far from home," William replied when asked why he was leaving a trail of personal history. "Anything might happen to me during this trip. I might be knocked down and killed by an omnibus in London or a taxicab in Paris. I might lose my memory, and then where would my six children be? Now, as a result of the traces I leave behind, the hotels will know how to act."[15]

While a bow to the old Southern code that demanded William put himself forward for public recognition, the "traces" also demonstrated William's rigid sense of duty to his family. When it came right down to it, his whole life was lived for his family – past and future. He had done right by his children in providing them with a solid, classical education and in assuring his sons a respected career as leaders in the legal community. He had given them a legacy of citizenship, of duty to God and country. But there was one thing more that the Southern code demanded he leave his descendants – a tribute to family honor. As time permitted, William corresponded with war officials and distant relatives to piece together a rough history of his Arnold ancestors. His wife and daughters joined the Daughters of the American Revolution, and he was a member and state president of the Arkansas Society Sons of the American Revolution. Toward the end of his life, he gathered all of his research and correspondence together and convinced West Publishing, a major publisher of law books, to print his manuscript as *The Arnold Family*. Throughout his book, William presented the Arnolds as "men of education, large property interests, extensive influence, and high character, patriotic, and [who] stood for the traditions of the land in which they lived."

Reflecting on the sketches and stories he had shared, he concluded: "It affords me gratification to say that members of the Arnold family ... have performed great service in the upbuilding of the country and the sustaining of the rights and liberties of the people. They have responded nobly when called upon to defend our constitutional rights in times of war, and in peace have occupied the high and responsible position of peoples of high ideals, aspirations and force of character." He then challenged future generations of Arnolds to live up to their lineage.

Whether consciously or subconsciously, William made a concerted effort to live the life of a learned Southern gentleman. His life demonstrated a personal interpretation of this ideal, one that was reconstructed for his time. But in his mind, William was not necessarily reconstructing the Southern ideal; he merely was living the life expected by his parents, his uncles, the entire Arnold lineage. This then was the legacy William left his children and grandchildren. It was a legacy of family pride, of high ideals, of aspirations, of service to community, of duty to God. It was the legacy his parents had given him. It was the legacy of Southern honor.

36   The Arnolds in the 20th Century

Although the past was important to him for the lessons it taught, William lived for the future. As a result, he invested in his children's education. Believing that a good education was the gateway to their personal El Dorado – and perhaps feeling somewhat limited because of his own lack of a college degree – William spent considerable sums on his family's schooling. "The girls were sent to college just like the boys.... They weren't expected to have careers ... but they were well educated," William's grandson Buzz says. "He thought that whether they were going to be the breadwinner or not, it was important to have a college education.... To my knowledge, he never accumulated a substantial amount of money or property. What he had, he spent on his children." His wealth was his family and law firm.[1]

William's oldest daughter, Jody, went from the Texarkana public schools to Belmont College in Nashville, Tennessee. She also attended Randolph Macon Woman's College in Lynchburg, Virginia, and the Drexel Institute in Philadelphia. Lucy, the second daughter, received her bachelor's degree from Randolph Macon in 1911. Ruth received her high school education at the Girton School in Winetka, Illinois, and attended Vassar and the University of Chicago.

Having made a name for himself, William had high expectations for his sons. They, in turn, fulfilled his ambitions for them. William Hendrick, Jr., graduated as salutatorian from the Western Military Academy in Alton, Illinois, before graduating from Phillips-Exeter Academy in Exeter, New Hampshire, in 1911. He received a bachelor of arts from Harvard and then attended Oxford on a Rhodes Scholarship. His Oxford years were interrupted by service in World War I. Following his schooling, he joined his father's law firm. William's second son, David Christopher, attended public and private schools in Texarkana before going on to Phillips-Exeter in 1913. From there, he went to the University of the South in Sewanee, Tennessee. He entered his father's law office as a student in 1915 and then volunteered for action as soon as World War I broke out. Following the war, he returned to what became Arnold & Arnold. The youngest son, Richard, also attended Phillips-Exeter, graduating with a classical diploma in 1925. He received his bachelor's from Yale and his law degree from Harvard. He, too, returned to Texarkana to practice law with his father.[2]

William's legacy lives on. In time, several of his grandsons joined the Arnold & Arnold law firm, which still exists in Texarkana. His children and grandchildren continued to demonstrate a commitment to education, the desire to serve the community, the need to reach the top of their profession. And they adhered to that sense of family pride – of being an Arnold.

In his book, William wrote proudly of his oldest son's accomplishments. He said William Jr. "has established a high reputation in his professional work and has been called to offices of distinction because of his abilities. Aside from his legal activities, he has had a splendid military record, is a public-spirited citizen and the possessor of a most attractive personality, all of which have given him a great popularity and brought a professional clientele of much value." In William's judgment, his son lived the Southern ideal.

William was no less proud of his second son. "I may say that David made a very fine record in the Senate, as he had done in the Lower House ... the previous term," William wrote. While in the General Assembly, David served on the Judiciary Committee in the House and chaired the same committee in the Senate. David used his influence to pass the Arnold Bill (No. 136, Acts 1925), "which provided for construction of a bridge across the Red River at Fulton ... over the opposition of a powerful combination in control of the ferry and bridge franchises granted to them by County Courts of Hempstead and Miller counties," William said. The validity of the act was questioned all the way to the state Supreme Court, where Arnold & Arnold served as special counsel to assist the attorney general, who represented the state Highway Commission in the case. The court upheld the act, making it possible to build bridges in other parts of the state where ferry companies had maintained a monopoly. David also was successful in court, taking one case to the U.S. Supreme Court (267 U.S. 572-574, 45 S. Ct. 228). One of the hardest days of William's life occurred in 1936 when David, at the age of 40, died of a massive heart attack while arguing a case in Miller County Circuit Court.

His youngest son had just started out in life when William published his book. But the father found many things to praise about Richard. Besides his educational achievements, William was proud of his son's marriage to Janet Sheppard, the oldest daughter of U.S. Sen. Morris Sheppard of Texarkana, Texas.

William, who died December 8, 1946, is a vague memory to his grandsons. Ten years old at the time, Richard S. Arnold remembered that his "Pappy," though disappointed by life time and again, insisted on looking to the future. "The night he died, he was talking about going to Mexico," Richard said. "There was always something new to do."[3]

William died before his grandsons established themselves in the legal profession. But if he were to come back, he would be proud of – but not surprised at – their achievements. They have lived the lives he expected; they have realized the dreams he helped make possible. They have carried on the Arnold legacy.

William Hendrick "Bill" Arnold III, who was 23 when his grandfather died, attended Rice University and the University of Texas. He was admitted to the Texas Bar in 1950 and the Arkansas Bar in 1953. His legal career included serving as circuit judge for the Eighth Judicial District of Arkansas. Bill's younger brother, Thomas Saxon Arnold, also went to Rice and the University of Texas. He was admitted to the Texas Bar in 1952, the Arkansas Bar in 1953, and the Colorado Bar in 1977.

Richard's two sons accomplished their grandfather's ultimate dream – they became federal judges. Richard S. Arnold, born March 26, 1936, followed his father and uncle in receiving a classical diploma from Phillips-Exeter. He graduated first in his class at Yale and then earned his law degree from Harvard, again graduating at the top of his class. After serving as a law clerk to Supreme Court Justice William J. Brennan, Jr., he returned home to practice law at the family firm. Like his grandfather, he tried his hand at politics – unsuccessfully. But he set his sights a little higher; he ran for Congress against fellow Democrat David Pryor. He also followed his grandfather's lead in serving as a delegate to the Arkansas Constitutional Convention. Although held half a century later, this convention still was aimed at getting rid of the much-patched relic of 1874. The document that came out of the convention met the same fate as the one William had worked on in 1918.[4]

Richard also followed his grandfather in being nominated for a federal district judgeship. But by the 1970s, the tides of politics had changed, and a Democrat could be appointed to such a position. Richard became the federal district judge for the Eastern and Western District Court of Arkansas in 1978. Two years later, he was named to the U.S. Court of Appeals for the Eighth Circuit. In 1992, he became the chief judge of the circuit court and subsequently was a finalist for a U.S. Supreme Court appointment. When Richard died in 2004, he was lauded as one of the brightest legal minds of the time.

Richard's brother, Morris S. "Buzz" Arnold, took another route to the court. By his own admission, Buzz chafed at the family practice and wanted to choose his own path. After receiving a classical diploma at Exeter and studying at Yale for two years, Buzz transferred to the University of Arkansas, where he earned a bachelor's degree in engineering. He quickly realized he was not cut out for the life of an engineer and stopped fighting his genes. He got his law degree from the University of Arkansas, graduating at the top of the class. After a short stint with the family firm in Texarkana, he attended Harvard Law School, where he received an LL.M. in 1969 and an S.J.D. in 1971, and was a Knox Fellow at the University of London.[5]

Instead of pursuing politics or private practice, Buzz chose an academic career. He taught law at Indiana University and became associate dean of the University of Pennsylvania Law School. While at Penn, he served as vice president of the university and was a visiting professor at Stanford Law School and taught in summer sessions at Michigan and Texas. His career took him to Cambridge University as a visiting fellow at Trinity College. He eventually returned to Arkansas as the Ben J. Altheimer Distinguished Professor of Law at the University of Arkansas at Little Rock. Just as he could not turn his back on the law, Buzz found he could not completely reject politics. While in Little Rock, he became state chairman of the Republican Party – a fact that might have given way to a grandfatherly lecture had William been alive.[6]

In 1985, Buzz was appointed a federal district judge for the Western District of Arkansas – 75 years to the day his grandfather had been denied the position. After more than seven years on the bench, Buzz was appointed to the U.S. Court of Appeals for the Eighth Circuit. It was the first time in the history of the American federal judiciary that brothers served together on a federal court of appeals. Despite the political differences, William would have been beaming. But what would make him even prouder is the distinction and praise his grandsons earned from the recognized lights of the legal profession.[7]

The *Minnesota Law Review* published a symposium about Richard in November 1993. In that symposium, Justice Brennan praised Richard as a "courageous and stalwart supporter of individual rights" and a consistent protector of "the First Amendment guarantees of freedom of the press and freedom of speech, even in cases in which the protected expression was controversial, distasteful, or hateful." Brennan also cited Richard's "heroic efforts" as the chairman of the Budget Committee of the Judicial Conference. He concluded: "A tribute to Judge Arnold cannot confine itself to his jurisprudential achievements.... The unfortunate fact is that the wheels of justice too often turn slowly and always at great expense. Judge Arnold has played a prominent role in ensuring that the Third Branch is provided with the resources necessary to enable us to fulfill our vital mission of efficiently resolving legal disputes, fairly enforcing the laws, and vigorously safeguarding our most cherished rights and freedoms."[8]

Meanwhile, Buzz has continued to garner acclaim both as a judge and a scholar. His books and articles on English legal history and Arkansas legal and governmental history are source books for many other works. "Suffice it to say that although his job is as a judge, he was a scholar before that and will probably always remain a scholar first and foremost. However, that is a good thing particularly in an appellate judge," writes Robert R. Wright, the Donaghey Distinguished Professor of Law Emeritus at the University of Arkansas at Little Rock.[9]

While his grandsons have lived up to William's expectations, they admit it has not always been easy. Richard and Buzz were raised with the idea that, as Arnolds, more was expected of them. They were viewed as "bluebloods" in Texarkana, Buzz says. There were times he wished he were not an Arnold, that he could live a life of fewer expectations. To some extent, Exeter offered the boys an escape. "The atmosphere there was very free," Richard said of the New England preparatory school. "Nobody cared who you were or where you came from. What they looked to was solely your intellectual ability. Either you had it or you didn't.... It was very democratic in the sense that they didn't care ... what your name had been before you got there; they cared what you could do after you arrived."[10]

Richard and Buzz not only showed what they could do after they arrived, they lived up to their name, which to their grandfather was as important as their deeds. In writing his book, William dedicated it to "the young members of the Arnold family with the hope that the reputations and lives of members of the family will inspire them to strive to live honorable and useful lives, and to be of some account in the world's affairs."

With their upbringing so steeped in the best of Southern tradition, William's grandsons had little choice. The Southern ideal that their grandfather had so carefully crafted shaped their dreams and ambitions. Its accompanying concept of honor as something inviolable and precious imposed definite standards of conduct. The result was the culmination of William's legacy.

A larger-than-life painting of William dominates the lobby of Buzz's office. Costumed in the long coat symbolic of his profession, William stiffly gazes from the canvas, invoking Wilbur Cash's description of the classic Southern lawyer at the turn of the century: "And as of old, there was the inevitable great lawyer, towering, leonine, long of coat and mane, the breathing epitome of the Confederacy, to drop a familiar hand upon his shoulder and warm his heart with confidential chat." Although he died more than half a century ago, William and those of his generation symbolize a presence that cannot be ignored. Their antebellum values, Southern honor, and strength of character live on. And through them – through their grandchildren – pass the hopes and dreams of all those who conquered one frontier or another without sacrificing that underlying commitment to family, that responsibility to community, and that duty to God that embody the Southern ideal.[11]

Appendix A: Selected Arnold Genealogy

The following is a selected genealogy for the descendants of Benjamin and Anne Hendrick Arnold:

1 Benjamin Arnold, farmer[1]
Born ca. 1712 in Presque Isle, King William County, Va.
Married ca. 1736 Anne Hendrick (ca. 1719-1806)
Died ca. 1796 in Greenville County, S. C.

  2 iii Hendrick Arnold, farmer
  Born ca. 1752 in Virginia.
  Married ca. 1773 Ruth Howard Cash
  Died 1795[2] in Laurens County, S. C.

    3 i William Arnold[3], called "Squire"
    Born ca. 1775[4] in Virginia
    Married Elizabeth Neighbors (had seven children)
    Married Mary Tierce
    Died in Cobb County, Ga.

    3 ii Ira Arnold, farmer; justice of peace; land speculator
    Born Dec. 25, 1791[5], in Laurens County, S.C.
    Married 1813 Mary "Polly" Saxon (Oct. 23, 1796- April 1878)
    Died 1858 in Laurens County, S.C.

      4 iv Hendrick Howard Arnold, doctor; farmer; legislator
      Born Jan. 2, 1822, in Laurens County, S.C.
      Moved 1843 to Clark County, Ark.

Married July 19, 1849, Ann Hendrick T. Ross (see below) in Clark County, Ark.
Died April 30, 1898, in Arkadelphia, Ark.

5 i Edgar Ross Arnold,
Born July 31, 1852, in Arkadelphia, Ark.
Married Nov. 18, 1873, Josephine Ross (see below) in Clark County, Ark.
Died July 28, 1930, in Arkadelphia, Ark.

6 ii Charles H. Arnold, farmer
Born Oct. 14, 1875, in Arkadelphia, Ark.
Married 1900 Lizzie Outlaw

7 v Howard Arnold
Born 1910

8 W.H. "Dub" Arnold, Arkansas Supreme Court Justice

5 ii William Brown Arnold, farmer
Born April 2, 1871, in Arkadelphia, Ark.
Married Oct. 1, 1892, Ollie Wells

4 v Clarissa Arnold
Born April 10, 1824, in South Carolina
Married 1848 Dr. John T. Pressly (a dentist) in South Carolina (they had six children)

4 vii David Saxon Arnold, schoolteacher; businessman; farmer, Prescott, Ark., mayor
Born Nov. 11, 1828,[6] in Laurens County, S.C.
Moved 1849 to Clark County, Ark.
Married Dec. 31, 1856, Temperance L. Arnold (see below) in Union County
Died 1903 in Sweetwater, Texas

Appendix A

5 i David Saxon "Sax" Arnold, Jr.
Born 1857 near Lisbon, Ark.
Married Oct. 15, 1885, Rebecca Lee
Died April 15, 1935, in Marshall, Texas

5 ii Mary Lucy Arnold
Born 1859 near Lisbon, Ark.
Married ca. 1878 James S. Regan
Died Oct. 13, 1930, in Prescott, Ark.

5 iii William Hendrick Arnold, schoolteacher;
Texarkana mayor; lawyer
Born Feb. 15, 1861, near Lisbon, Ark.
Married Oct. 13, 1887, Jessie Cook (Jan. 27, 1870-Aug. 27, 1900) in Lewisville, Ark.
Married Feb. 17, 1903, Kate Lewis (born Dec. 9, 1881)
Died Dec. 8, 1946, in Texarkana, Ark.

  6 i Jody Claypool Arnold, home economics teacher
  Born July 4, 1888, Texarkana, Texas
  Married Nov. 23, 1917, Carl L. Smith

  6 ii Lucy Arnold, high school math teacher
  Born April 13, 1891, Texarkana, Texas
  Married 1922 Booker Ellis, Sr.

  7 Booker Ellis, Jr.

  6 iii William Hendrick Arnold, Jr., lawyer
  Born Jan. 30, 1893, in Texarkana, Texas
  Married Dec. 26, 1921, Grace Hendricks
  Died Nov. 6, 1977

    7 i William Hendrick Arnold III, lawyer; circuit judge
    Born Nov. 2, 1923

7 ii Thomas Saxon Arnold, lawyer
Born Aug. 3, 1928

8 i Clark Arnold, lawyer

8 ii Steve Arnold, lawyer

6 iv Ruth Arnold
Born Oct. 24, 1894, in Texarkana, Texas
Married May 9, 1917, Allen Anderson McCurdy

7 i William Arnold McCurdy
Born ca. 1921
Died 1930

7 ii Allen McCurdy

7 iii Donald McCurdy

7 iv Elizabeth Katherine McCurdy

6 iv David Christopher Arnold, lawyer; state legislator; state senator
Born July 6, 1896, in Texarkana, Texas
Married Oct. 4, 1919, Hilda Manley
Died 1936 in Texarkana, Ark.

7 i David C. Arnold, Jr.
Born July 19, 1920

7 ii Hilda Arnold
Born Nov. 5, 1922

7 iii Jessie Katherine Arnold
Born Aug. 11, 1926

6 v Richard Lewis Arnold, lawyer
Born Dec. 30, 1906, in Texarkana, Texas

Married June 9, 1934, Janet Sheppard (born 1911 in Texarkana, Texas; died 1955 in Texarkana, Ark.)
Died 1988 in Texarkana, Ark.

7 i Richard Sheppard Arnold, lawyer; federal judge
Born March 26, 1936, in Texarkana, Texas
Married June 14, 1958, Gale Ann Palmer Hussman (born July 17, 1935, in Texarkana, Ark.) in Camden, Ark.
Divorced May 1, 1975
Married Oct. 27, 1979, Karen "Kay" Sue Kelley (born Dec. 2, 1953, in Heber Springs, Ark.; lawyer; corporate vice president) in Little Rock, Ark.
Died Sept. 23, 2004, in Minneapolis, Minn.

8 i Janet Sheppard Arnold, lawyer
Born July 4, 1963, in Washington, D.C.
Married Richard John Hart (born May 29, 1964, in Naples, Italy; lawyer; investment broker)

9 i Evan Antonio Hart
Born April 24, 1997, in Palo Alto, Calif.

9 ii Saxon McGrath Hart
Born July 10, 2000, in Palo Alto, Calif.

8 ii Lydia Palmer Arnold, lawyer
Born Aug. 28, 1969, in Texarkana, Texas
Married Sept. 14, 1996, Terry Lynn Turnipseed (born Dec. 18, 1964, in Jackson, Miss.; lawyer) in Washington, D.C.

9 i Lucile Mae Turnipseed
Born Sept. 9, 2000, in Washington, D.C.

9 ii Grace Arnold Turnipseed
Born Aug. 27, 2002, in Washington, D.C.

7 ii Morris Sheppard "Buzz" Arnold, law school professor/dean; author; federal judge
Born Oct. 8, 1941, in Texarkana, Texas
Married Oct. 16, 1992, Gail Marie Kwaak
(born Jan. 13, 1944, in Bayshore, Long Island) in Sheridan, Ark.

5 iv Sally Temperance Arnold, schoolteacher
Born March 24, 1863, most likely near Garland City, Ark.
Married Aug. 29, 1878, Dr. Alphonso Harris
Died in Dallas, Texas

5 v Carrie Ella Arnold, schoolteacher
Born Sept. 4, 1865, most likely near Garland City, Ark.
Married Oct. 14, 1883, W.E. "Bud" Barrow
Died May 16, 1909, in Sweetwater, Texas

5 vi Robert Esterbrook Arnold, civil engineer
Born Feb 13, 1870, near Lisbon, Ark.
Died March 31, 1907, in Colina, Mexico

5 vii Martha "Mattie" Hill Arnold
Born Dec. 19, 1871, in Union County, Ark.
Married Sept. 13, 1892, Israel Shell Focht
Died in Sweetwater, Texas

5 viii Clara Pressley "Violet" Arnold
Born Jan. 20, 1875, near Prescott, Ark.
Married June 5, 1895, Seaborn Cole (born Aug. 14, 1865)
Died in Sweetwater, Texas

5 ix John Thomas "Samp" Arnold
Born April 1, 1878, in Prescott, Ark.
Died in Dallas, Texas

Appendix A

> **5 x Emma "Dot" Arnold**, schoolteacher
> Born July 18, 1880, in Prescott, Ark.
> Married April 27, 1908, George M. Pavey
> Died in Dallas, Texas
>
> **5 xi Henry Lee Arnold**
> Born Oct. 25, 1887, in Prescott, Ark.
> Died in 1928 in Dallas, Texas

2 vi Thomas Arnold, Revolutionary soldier; farmer
Born Oct. 5, 1763[7], in Buckingham County, Va.
Married Oct. 26, 1786, Mary Bidestone[8] (May 13, 1766-Dec. 9, 1857)
Died March 23, 1844, in Autauga County, Ala.

> **3 i Temperance Arnold**
> Born Nov. 25, 1789, probably in Rutherford County, N.C.
> Married Aug. 13, 1804, Peter Ross (1770-Feb. 5, 1850) in Logan County, Ky.
> Moved 1842 to Clark County, Ark.
> Died Sept. 23, 1870, in Clark County, Ark.
>
>> **4 i Mary A. Ross**
>> Born Sept. 6, 1807, Logan County, Ky.
>> Married Feb. 18, 1830, Lovin Ross
>> Moved 1842 to Clark County, Ark.
>> Died Oct. 9, 1870
>>
>> **4 vi David Carroll Ross**, doctor; farmer
>> Born June 26, 1818[9], in Logan County, Ky.
>> Moved 1842 to Clark County, Ark.
>> Married Aug. 11, 1842, Caroline M. Arnold (see below) in Hempstead County, Ark.
>>
>>> **5 i David Ross**
>>> Born ca. 1852 in Union County, Ark.

5 ii William Ross
Born ca. 1856 in Union County, Ark.
Married March 31, 1874, Clara Hillams (born ca. 1840) in Union County, Ark.
Died Dec. 10, 1874, in Lavaca County, Texas

4 vii William Brown Ross, farmer
Born April 4, 1821, in Dallas County, Ala.
Moved 1842 to Clark County, Ark.
Married Oct. 17, 1845,[10] Nancy Peeples Bozeman (died ca. 1848) in Clark County, Ark.
Married July 31, 1867, Martha Arnold (see below) in Union County, Ark.
Died Sept. 6, 1871

5 i William Peeples Ross, businessman; farmer; publisher
Born Feb. 1, 1847, in Clark County, Ark.
Married Sept. 25, 1873, Alice B. Sloan (born ca. 1854) in Clark County, Ark.
Married Feb. 8, 1849, Eliza Sloan (Oct. 23, 1832-1866) in Clark County, Ark.

5 vii Josephine Ross
Born July 28, 1852
Married Edgar Arnold (see above)
Died in Clark County, Ark.

4 ix Ann Hendrick T. Ross
Born Aug. 5, 1834, in Burnsville, Ala.
Moved 1842 to Clark County, Ark.
Married Hendrick Howard Arnold (see above)
Died March 28, 1920

3 ii William Bideston Arnold (1), sheriff; Methodist preacher; farmer
Born July 1, 1791, in Logan County, Ky.

Appendix A

Married 1823 Lucinda Powell Hardin (born April 12, 1800, in Newton County, Ga.; died July 9, 1879) in Montevallo, Ala.
Moved ca. 1839 to Hempstead County, Ark.
Died 1847 in Hempstead County, Ark.

4 i Sarah Elizabeth Arnold
Born 1823 in Alabama
Moved ca. 1839 to Hempstead County, Ark.
Married Lawson Smith
Died 1856 in El Dorado, Ark.

4 ii Mary Blanton Arnold
Born in 1825[11] in Alabama
Moved ca. 1839 to Hempstead County, Ark.
Married William H. Baird
Died 1873 in Hempstead County, Ark.

4 iii Caroline M. Arnold
Born 1826 in Alabama
Moved ca. 1839 to Hempstead County, Ark.
Married Dr. David Carroll Ross (see above)
Died ca. 1869 in Gonzales, Texas

4 iv Louiza Jane Arnold
Born 1827 in Alabama
Moved ca. 1839 to Hempstead County, Ark.
Died 1846 in Hempstead County, Ark.

4 v John Hardin Arnold, Sr., farmer
Born Oct. 25, 1828, in Alabama
Moved ca. 1839 to Hempstead County, Ark.
Married 1857 Luvisa A. Baird (Sept. 5, 1829-April 14, 1883)
Married March 5, 1885, Mary Sherman Burk
Died Aug. 25, 1903, in Hope, Ark.

5 i Carrie Jane Arnold
Born Nov. 27, 1861, in Hempstead County, Ark.
Married Jan. 15, 1885 John Jackson Moore (Aug. 19, 1857-1910)

5 ii John Hardin Arnold, Jr., lawyer; mayor of Preston and Washington
Born Feb. 27, 1864, in Daingerfield, Texas
Moved to Arkansas after the Civil War
Married Nov. 7, 1894, Jimmie Meriwether Duncan (born Nov. 5, 1873)
Died July 19, 1925, in Hope, Ark.

5 iii William Bideston Arnold (2)
Born June 13, 1867
Died Nov. 26, 1912

4 vi Martha H. Arnold
Born ca. 1832[12] in Alabama
Moved ca. 1839 to Hempstead County, Ark.
Married William Brown Ross (see above)
Married 1878 Col. W.T. Steel
Died 1898 in Oklahoma

4 vii Thomas A. Arnold
Born ca. 1835 in Alabama

4 viii William Edward Arnold, doctor
Born ca. 1834[13] in Alabama
Moved ca. 1839 to Hempstead County, Ark.
Married Dec. 27, 1868, Mary McCollum (March 13, 1847-died Jan. 3, 1885) in Hempstead County, Ark.
Died Feb. 23, 1923, in Prescott, Ark.

5 Ella Arnold
Born Oct. 13, 1869, in Hempstead County, Ark.
Married Jan. 16, 1901, Joe Lee Davis (they had four children)

4 ix Temperance "Tempie" Lucinda Arnold
Born March 2, 1839, in Autauga County, Ala.
Moved ca. 1839 to Hempstead County, Ark.[14]
Married David Saxon Arnold (see above)
Died Sept. 16, 1928, in Sweetwater, Texas

4 x Robert Esterbrook Arnold (1), doctor, member of first Arkansas Board of Health
Born ca. 1841 in Hempstead County, Ark.
Died 1887 in Tilden, Texas

3 iv Thomas Hendrick Arnold, farmer; miller
Born March 7, 1797, in Logan County, Ky.
Married Dec. 1, 1819, Mary "Polly" Wilson (1802-1843)
Moved ca. 1837 to Hempstead County, Ark.
Married Jan. 4, 1846, Sarah W. Pridgeon

3 vi Ann Hendrick "Nancy" Arnold
Born June 22, 1802
Married March 11, 1824, Hance H. Dunklin

Other relatives of note:
Mary "Polly" Saxon Arnold, wife of Ira Arnold, was the daughter of Lewis Saxon (Dec. 10, 1765-Oct. 31, 1813) and Sally Allen Saxon McNees.[15] The children of Ira and Mary grew up in Laurens County, S. C., surrounded by their Arnold, Allen, and Saxon relatives. One of these cousins, David P. Saxon, seems to have been like a brother to David Saxon Arnold. Just a few years apart in age, they apparently moved to Arkansas together, lived as neighbors in Union County, and enlisted together in Company F of the 19th Arkansas in El Dorado.

David Park Saxon,[16] lawyer, farmer, merchandiser, state legislator
Born May 10, 1830, in Laurens County, S.C.
Moved to Union County, Ark., in the late 1840s

Married Feb. 9, 1858, Mary Medora Reeves (born April 7, 1840; died May 20, 1912) in Union County, Ark.
Died Oct. 20, 1912

Robert L. Saxon, gynecologist, surgeon in Little Rock, Ark.
Born April 7, 1874, in Lisbon, Ark.
Graduated from the University of Arkansas and the University of Nashville; did post-graduate work in New York, Vienna and London
Died Aug. 9, 1959

Appendix B: Selected Arnold Military Record

Revolutionary War:

Thomas Arnold –
When he was about 16, Thomas enlisted in the 96th District of South Carolina in 1779, serving 18 months as a private under Capt. John Ridgeway. After marching to Rutherford County, North Carolina, his unit joined Morgan's Army. Thomas was at the battles of Long Cane, Hammond's Store, and Cowpens. Although he was at Cowpens, he was unable to fight because of a wound he had received at Hammond's Store. After recovering from the wound in North Carolina, Thomas returned to South Carolina where he was in several skirmishes.

Thomas enlisted again in March 1783, this time for a 12-month stint with Capt. George Martin's company in the South Carolina Troops serving under Col. Levi Casey. He received a pension of $30 a year beginning January 3, 1834.[1]

Lewis Saxon –
While living in the 96th District of South Carolina, Lewis enlisted in 1778 under Lt. Col. Robert McCrary and Col. James Williams. He was at the Battle of Stono. In December 1780, he served under Capt. William Harris. Promoted to captain in 1781, he saw action at Cowpens, the siege of the 96th District, and Eutaw Springs. He was taken prisoner at Haye's Station.[2]

Hendrick Arnold –
Hendrick served as acting district commissioner for supplying the troops in Amherst County, Virginia. Besides supplying beef to the army, he paid his nephew Benjamin Arnold to serve in the army in his place.[3]

Benjamin Arnold –

While living with his grandfather Benjamin Arnold in Laurens County, South Carolina, the younger Benjamin enlisted at the age of 17 (about 1779). He served as a private in the companies of Capt. John Ford and Capt. David McDowell, both part of Col. Benjamin Cleveland's regiment. Benjamin then moved with his grandfather back to their property in Henry County, Virginia, where he enlisted and served as a private under Capt. George Harston and Capt. David Woodruff under Col. Peter Perkins and Col. Merriwether.

During his last six-week tour of service, Benjamin served as a substitute for his Uncle Hendrick Arnold. Altogether, Benjamin served 10 months in the war and saw action at Cowpens.[4]

Civil War:

David Saxon Arnold –

David first enlisted March 1, 1862, for 12 months as a third lieutenant with Capt. William Langford's Company F, an infantry unit that served in the Arkansas 19th Regiment as a part of Brig. Gen. Albert Rust's Brigade. David first saw battle at Fort Pillow, a Confederate-built earthen fort with batteries of cannons overlooking the Mississippi River from the Chicksaw Bluffs in Tennessee. The Arkansas soldiers joined Company B (the Claiborne Rangers) of the 12th Louisiana Volunteers that March in defending the Tennessee fort against a Union bombardment that lasted 60 days.

As April gave way to May, the 19th Arkansas and parts of the 12th Louisiana evacuated Fort Pillow and headed to Corinth, Mississippi, where the Army of the Mississippi was under the command of Gen. P.G.T. Beauregard. The first order of business after the 19th arrived at Corinth was a reorganization and election of regimental officers. Col. Thomas P. Dockery was elected as the new commander of the regiment May 12. A few weeks later, the Confederate troops packed up and slipped out of town, leaving Corinth to the Union forces. David, on the point

Appendix B

of physical collapse, was relieved of duty June 3 as his unit was setting up camp in Tupelo, Mississippi.

After recovering from his illness, David enlisted March 12, 1863, as a private in Company A of the 13th Louisiana Battalion, a partisan rangers unit under Lt. Col. Samuel Chambliss. The unit was in several skirmishes in northern Louisiana but did not participate in a regular battle or general engagement. David's first few months with the 13th were spent riding picket at Lake Providence and trying to foil Gen. Ulysses Grant's advances on Vicksburg, Mississippi. When Chambliss resigned April 30, Maj. Richard Capers was promoted to lieutenant colonel and James H. Capers, the commanding officer of Company A, was promoted to major of the battalion. David was elected captain and commanding officer of Company G, a unit of about 100 men from Union County, Arkansas, and Claiborne Parish, Louisiana.

The fall of Vicksburg July 4, 1863, forced the 13th to move west to Delhi, Louisiana, where it became part of Col. Isaac Harrison's Cavalry Brigade. Besides annoying the enemy, Harrison's Brigade built bridges, foraged for food, and loaded wagons. Badly outnumbered and weakened by disease, the brigade retreated toward Monroe, Louisiana, late in July. There the soldiers continued harassing Yankee forces, destroying crops, skirmishing with Union gunboats, and doing their part to keep Gen. Nathaniel P. Banks from advancing any farther up the Red River.

Early in 1864, David's battalion was reorganized as the Fifth Louisiana Calvary Regiment, and Harrison's Brigade became part of the Sub-District of North Louisiana. David retained his command of Company G. The brigade followed the progress of Adm. David Porter's Union gunboats and transports upriver from Alexandria to Shreveport, Louisiana, in an effort to slow the progress of the Navy, take out as many ships as possible, hinder the enemy's foraging efforts, and stall its proposed rendezvous with Banks' land troops. The Fifth Regiment raided Pineville, Louisiana, where Union forces were camped April 24. Then it defeated a sizable Union force in a skirmish at nearby Hadnot's Plantation. Camp Hadnot was David's last stop with

Harrison's Brigade as his health once again gave out and he was forced to go home.

Dr. Hendrick Howard Arnold –

Between March 20 and April 1, 1864, there were four skirmishes in Arkadelphia, Ark., where Hendrick lived. The semi-retired doctor had been 39 when the war started and, thus, exempt from the Conscription Act. But when the war came to him, Hendrick enlisted under Capt. R.E. Reeds as an army surgeon.

Hendrick was with the Confederate army that attacked Gen. Frederick Steele's troops April 18 near Poison Spring. His unit, under the command of Gen. James F. Fagan, also attacked a Union supply train April 25 near Marks' Mill. Following the fighting, Hendrick was responsible for moving the wounded into makeshift hospitals set up in the homes of Wat Smith, Bill Davis, and Warren Crane, who all lived in the vicinity of the Marks plantation and the gristmill that lent the skirmish its name.

Dr. William E. Arnold –

Just out of medical school, Bill enlisted in the early stages of the war in 1861 as a private under Col. P.H. Cleburne in Company A of the First Arkansas Regiment, which served under Col. James F. Fagan with the Army of Virginia. Stationed in Evansport on the mosquito-infested Potomac River for the remainder of 1861, Bill contracted malaria.

Still suffering from malaria, Bill fought at Shiloh, Tennessee, in April 1862. Although he survived the battle, his health broke due to exhaustion, stress, and the endless rain. As soon as the Confederate forces retreated to Corinth, Mississippi, Bill traveled to Murfreesboro, Tennessee, where he went before the Confederate Medical Board and was subsequently made an assistant surgeon with the rank of captain.

At the Battle of Atlanta, Bill was in the center rear of the fighting troops, tending to the wounded. As he was bandaging a fallen soldier, he was struck in the arm by shrapnel. After being treated in a hospital for a month, the wounded doctor was sent home to Arkansas to recuperate.

Before he had completely recovered, Bill was called back to his regiment, which was serving under Gen. John B. Hood in Franklin, Tennessee. As the war ended, Bill was serving under Gen. Joseph E. Johnston, who surrendered his army April 26, 1865, near Greensboro, North Carolina. After the surrender, Bill and the other Arkansas soldiers in his regiment boarded a train for the long ride home. They got as far as Knoxville, Tennessee, when the train ran off a bridge and plunged into the French Broad River, killing eight soldiers and wounding 50 others. After assisting the wounded, Bill hopped a boxcar from Knoxville to Memphis where he switched to river transportation. He was forced to walk the final leg of the journey to Little Rock and then walked 18 hours from Little Rock to visit his family in Arkadelphia for a few days. Late that May or early June, he made it home.

Dr. Robert E. Arnold –

Robert was seriously injured at the Battle of Spotsylvania Courthouse in Virginia in the spring of 1864 when a bullet or shrapnel hit his windpipe. He was confined to an army hospital until he was well enough to go home.

World War I:

William H. Arnold, Sr. –

From 1917-1919, William made speeches throughout Miller County, Arkansas, and surrounding counties in support of the war. He also served as a Four-Minute Speaker in Texarkana to raise war funds in the Liberty Loan drives. As vice president for Arkansas of the American Bar Association, he was appointed by Maj. Gen. E.H. Crowder, Provost Marshal General in Washington, as a member of the Central Committee charged with organizing advisory boards in each county to provide legal advice to registrants under the Selective Service Law. In 1918, he served on the Arkansas committee that set up legal boards to advise drafted men and their families.

William Hendrick Arnold, Jr. –

William interrupted his law studies at Oxford to enlist June 23, 1917, in Motor Truck Company No. 8 of the Arkansas Guard in Texarkana, Arkansas. He transferred to Reserve Officers' Training Camp at Camp Pike in Little Rock, Arkansas, and then to Leon Springs, Texas. While in Texas, he qualified in the Coast Artillery Corps and was assigned to The Presidio in San Francisco. He was discharged November 26, 1917, so he could accept a commission as second lieutenant in C.A.R.C. Company 8 at Fort Winfield Scott in California. He was then stationed at Fort Barry, California, where he was trained in the use of heavy artillery. After organizing 130 men into the 14th Company of Coast Defense, he was transferred to Company A, 62nd Artillery, 33rd Artillery Brigade.

William's company sailed from New York in May 1918, landing at Le Havre, France. The company was stationed at St. Emilion, Gironde. William returned to the United States on the *Powhatan* in February 1919, landing at Norfolk, Virginia. He was honorably discharged May 26, 1919, at Camp Zachary Taylor in Louisville, Kentucky. He returned home with a gold chevron for service with the American Expeditionary Forces and the Victory Medal.

David Christopher Arnold –

Soon after being admitted to practice law in the Chancery Court of Miller County, David volunteered in May 1917 at the outbreak of U.S. involvement in the war. He entered the officers' training camp at Little Rock, but the medical staff rejected him. David returned to his father's law firm and was admitted to practice in the Supreme Court of Arkansas January 28, 1918.

As the war heated up, David enlisted again in July 1918, entering Camp Pike as a soldier in training in Company 34, Ninth Training Battalion, 162 Depot Brigade. He was transferred September 12, 1918, to Infantry Central Officers' Training School as a member of Company 6, Battalion 3. He was honorably discharged December 8, 1918, at Camp Pike.

Appendix C: Selected Slave Records of the Arnold Family

Greenville County, S.C., Slave Records:

July 12, 1810 – Benjamin Arnold freed Prince, "a Negro lad slave," when 12-year-old Prince and his father, Roger, a freedman, paid him $400. Because he was under age, Prince remained legally under the full authority of Benjamin's family until he turned 21. During this time, Prince earned wages and saved up his money. In March 1817, the teenager paid William Wright $381 for land that bordered Benjamin's property along the South Fork of Horse Creek.[1]

January 20, 1817 – Benjamin freed Daniel Arnold when Daniel and Rodger[2], who is described as Benjamin's "secretary and a man of color," paid him $700. The record describes Daniel as a mulatto, about 36 years old, six feet tall with two scars on his left cheek.[3]

February 10, 1817 – William Arnold, Ira's brother, freed Amy when Samuel Taylor paid him $400. Amy, who may have been Samuel's wife, was 38 or 39, about five feet tall with a "yellow" complexion. Samuel had been freed by Arthur Taylor, who lived in Laurens County, in 1800. After being freed, Samuel bought at least two parcels of land and deeded two acres, including the meetinghouse spring and burying ground, to the Baptist Society for use of the Society of Columbia Meeting House.[4]

January 17, 1818 – Ira Arnold freed Moses after Samuel Taylor paid him $900. The emancipation was recorded Feb. 19, 1818, and Benjamin Arnold presided over the legal proceedings as the justice of the quarter section. Moses was about 17 years old and four feet nine inches tall.[5]

March 1, 1819 – Ira freed Cupid when Samuel Taylor paid him $1,200. Again, Benjamin presided over the proceedings, which were recorded March 30. William Arnold was listed as one of the witnesses. Cupid was about 20 years old and nearly six feet tall with a blemish in his left eye.[6]

U.S. Census Slave Schedules:

1830 Laurens County, S.C.
William Arnold – 11 slaves
1 male 0-10, 1 male 10-24, 3 males 36-55, 1 female 0-10, 3 females 10-24, 3 females 36-55

1830 Dallas County, Ala.
Thomas Arnold – 9 slaves
1 male 0-10, 3 males 36-55, 3 females 10-24, 1 female 24-36, 1 female 55-100

William Bideston Arnold – 10 slaves
2 males 0-10, 1 male 10-24, 1 male 36-55, 3 females 0-10, 3 females 10-24

1840 Laurens County, S.C.
Ira Arnold – 19 slaves
7 males 0-10, 3 males 10-24, 1 male 24-36, 4 females 10-24, 1 female 24-36, 2 females 36-55, 1 female 100+

1850 Laurens County, S.C.
Ira Arnold – 7 slaves
1 male 13, 1 male 37, 1 female 3, 1 female 16, 1 female 19, 1 female 25, 1 female 60

1850 Hempstead County, Ark.
Lucinda Arnold – 6 slaves
1 male 18, 1 male 22, 1 male 23, 1 male 50, 1 male 52, 1 female 34

Appendix C

1850 Clark County, Ark.
Hendrick H. Arnold – 4 slaves
1 male 13, 1 male 14, 1 female 15, 1 female 16

Temperance Ross – 6 slaves
1 male 22, 1 male 35, 1 female 8, 1 female 18, 1 female 50, 1 female 60

1860 Clark County, Ark.
Hendrick H. Arnold – 16 slaves
7 males 0-9, 2 adult males, 4 females 0-5, 3 adult females

Temperance Ross – 5 slaves

1860 Union County, Ark.
David S. Arnold – 16 slaves
2 males 5; 1 male 7, 1 male 9. 1 male 13, 1 male 22,
1 male 34, 1 female 2, 2 females 7, 3 females 17,
2 females 19, 1 female 22

David Carroll Ross – 29 slaves
9 males 19-50, 9 females 11-48, 11 children

Notes

Introduction

1. Carl N. Degler, *Place Over Time: The Continuity of Southern Distinctiveness* (Baton Rouge: Louisiana State University Press, 1977), xi; F.N. Boney, *Southerners All* (Macon, Ga.: Mercer University Press, 1984), 3, 14, 22; Wilbur J. Cash, *The Mind of the South* (Garden City, N.Y.: Doubleday Anchor Books, 1941), 225.
2. Cash, 44, 45; Eugene D. Genovese, *The Southern Tradition* (Cambridge, Mass.: Harvard University Press, 1994), 14; C. Vann Woodward, *The Burden of Southern History* (Baton Rouge: Louisiana State University Press, 1960), 24, 35.
3. Bertram Wyatt-Brown, *Honor and Violence in the Old South* (New York: Oxford University Press, 1986), 14, 22, 30, 41, 42, 51.
4. *Ibid.*, 17, 39, 62.
5. *Ibid.*, 16, 75, 63-69.
6. *Ibid.*, 63-69.
7. Jean E. Friedman, *The Enclosed Garden: Women and Community in the Evangelical South, 1830-1900* (Chapel Hill, N.C.: The University of North Carolina Press, 1985), 10; Genovese, 8.
8. Emory M. Thomas, *Robert E. Lee: A Biography* (New York: W.W. Norton & Co., 1995), 19; Wyatt-Brown, 44, 45.
9. Thomas, 33, 41.
10. Aristotle, *Politics*, Book 1, Chapter 5.
11. Cash, 80, 86.
12. Wyatt-Brown, 40; Cash, 81, 82.
13. Carl H. Moneyhon, *The Impact of the Civil War and Reconstruction on Arkansas* (Baton Rouge: Louisiana State University Press, 1994), 56; Cash, 88; Boney, 2, 14, 15, 26, 28.
14. Frank Lawrence Owsley, "Plain Folk and Their Role in Southern History," *The South: Old and New Frontiers,* ed. Harriet Chappell Owsley (Athens, Ga.: The University of Georgia Press, 1969), 36, 43; Boney, 14, 15.
15. IMA.
16. Cash, 81, 82, 86; Woodward, 285; Wyatt-Brown, 32, 50.
17. Genovese, 51.
18. Friedman, 7.
19. *Letters of Richard D. Arnold, M.D. 1808-1896*, ed. Richard H. Shryock, 1929, in Eric Foner, *Reconstruction: America's Unfinished Revolution 1863-1877* (New York: Harper & Row Publishers, 1988), 128.
20. Foner, 235, 273.
21. *Ibid.*, xxii, xxiii; Cash 14.
22. Charles Orson Cook, "'The Glory of the Old South and the Greatness of the New:' Reform and the Divided Mind of Charles Hillman Brough," *AHQ* 34 (autumn 1975), 227-228, 240.

1 Arkansas: A New Frontier

1. Hazel Arnold MacIvor, *Some Ancestors and Descendants of Benjamin Arnold: King William County, Virginia and Greenville, South Carolina* (Lake Orion, Mich.: The Arnold Family Association of the South, 1974). William's father, Thomas Arnold (1763-1857), had started life in Buckingham County, Virginia, but later moved to Laurens County, South Carolina. From there he, along with several extended family members, moved to Caldwell County on the mouth of the Cumberland River in Kentucky. A few years after the exodus to Kentucky, the family scattered further, with Thomas and his immediate family moving on to Alabama. William's grandfather, Benjamin Arnold (ca. 1712-1790), was most likely born in King William County, Virginia. Land records show that he farmed in various places throughout Virginia before moving to South Carolina late in life.
2. MacIvor.
3. Marian Elias Lazenby, *History of Methodism in Alabama and West Florida* (1960), 113. There is no record of William's conversion or of his attendance at this meeting. However, he was one of the few settlers in the area at the time. The records of the meeting, included in Lazenby, indicate that most of the area settlers participated. There also is a brief family record that William's older sister, Temperance, converted to Methodism in this time period. It is probable that William converted when Methodism was first introduced to this part of Alabama.
4. *1830 U.S. Census for Dallas County, Alabama.* According to this census, William had the following slaves: two boys under 10, one young man between 10-24, a man between 36-55, three girls under 10, and three girls between 10-24.
5. Lazenby, 254; Horace Jewell, *History of Methodism in Arkansas* (Little Rock, Ark.: Press Printing Company, 1892), 381.
6. Lazenby, 258.
7. *Ibid.*, 149; *ACA*.
8. MacIvor; *Hempstead County, Arkansas, Federal Land Records,* comp. Joy Fisher (ARGenWeb); Mary Medearis, ed., *Sam Williams: Printer's Devil* (Hope, Ark.: Etter Printing Company, 1979), 304. The part of Hempstead County that included Terra Rouge became Nevada County in 1871 (*BHM*, 550).
9. Arnold family tradition holds that William's family moved in 1840; and the 1840 Census places him in Arkansas. The federal land records give the year of filing as 1839. William may have filed on the land in 1839 and moved his family the next year, but the family may have moved in 1839 when he filed on the land. Medearis has Thomas and William moving together to Hempstead County about 1834. While Thomas may have relocated in 1834, William did not. He officiated at the Autauga County, Alabama, weddings of Edward Gilbert and Elizabeth Simmons, March 3, 1837; William P. King and Sarah P. Taylor, May 17, 1837; and William P. Shackleford and Martha E. Taylor, February 28, 1838 (ACA). The 1850 U.S. Census for Hempstead County, Arkansas, gives Temperance's birthplace as Alabama, but the 1860 Census gives it as Arkansas. Temperance, William's youngest daughter, was born March 2, 1839, in Alabama. (MacIvor).

10. Jewell, 121; *BHM*, 377; Carolyn Gray LeMaster, *A Corner of the Tapestry: A History of the Jewish Experience in Arkansas 1820s-1990s* (Fayetteville, Ark.: The University of Arkansas Press, 1994), 6.
11. S. Charles Bolton, *Arkansas 1800-1860: Remote and Restless* (Fayetteville, Ark.: The University of Arkansas Press, 1998), 19.
12. *BHM*, 377-387; LeMaster, 5-7; James M. Woods, *Rebellion and Realignment: Arkansas' Road to Secession* (Fayetteville, Ark.: The University of Arkansas Press, 1987), 36-37.
13. *BHM* does not indicate where the other four post offices were located in Hempstead County. However, the two earliest towns in the county besides Washington were Fulton and Columbus. Fulton, the first settlement in the county, was an important shipping point on the north side of the Red River. Columbus, which had a post office by 1834, was located five miles west of Washington (Montgomery, Donald Ray, "Simon T. Sanders: Public Servant," *AHQ* 39 [summer 1980], 160-161).
14. John Gould Fletcher, *Arkansas* (Chapel Hill, N.C.: University of North Carolina Press, 1947), 108-110.
15. Bolton, 16; LeMaster, 7-8.
16. *1840 U.S. Census for Hempstead County*; Bolton, 51-52, 116-117.
17. Jewell, 32-36, 138. Lucy's tombstone in the Artesian Cemetery in Nevada County identifies her as the "wife of Rev. W.B. Arnold" (Hempstead County, Arkansas, Cemeteries Book 4 [Hope, Ark.: Hempstead County Genealogical Society, 1990], 115).
18. Friedman, xii.
19. Bolton, 118-119; Ellen M. Plante, *Women at Home in Victorian America* (New York: Facts on File, Inc., 1997), 15-16.
20. Jesse Ross moved from Alabama to Clark County, Arkansas, in the early years of the state's history. His daughter, Susan Ross Barton, who was born in Dallas County, Alabama, moved with her family to Clark County in 1844 – at about the same time Peter and Temperance moved. Another Ross family, Drury and Mary Ross, also moved from Dallas County to Clark County in 1846. Drury, Susan, and Peter were most likely cousins – if not siblings (*BHM*, 124-125, 161-162, 377-387).
21. *Hempstead County, Arkansas, 1820-1881: Computer Indexed Marriage Records* (North Salt Lake: Hunting for Bears, Inc., n.d.); Friedman, 10. David Ross' younger brother William Brown Ross, after being widowed twice, married Caroline's younger sister Martha Arnold in 1867.

2 Shadows

1. Jewell, 126-127.
2. *Ibid.*
3. *DCA*, 9.
4. Bolton, 113, 117. Formed in 1810 in Kentucky, the Cumberland Presbyterians were a breakaway group that disagreed with the fatalistic predestination held by the Westminster Presbyterians and believed that the preaching ability of a minister was more important than his academic credentials (*BHM*, 100).

5. Bolton, 128.
6. Jewell, 130.
7. Lazenby, 255.
8. Jewell, 128-129.
9. *Ibid.*, 129, 135, 138, 140; *Clark County, Arkansas, Marriage Records, 1821-1879*, comp. Bobbie Jones McLane (1974), 180.
10. Jewell; Montgomery, 164. The seminaries, which operated until the end of the Civil War, educated many of the area's future leaders. The first college in Alabama, LaGrange opened a year before Alabama State University was founded. John Ross served on the first board of trustees of the Alabama school and B.B. Ross was on the first faculty (Jewell; Lazenby, 1030-1032).
11. Bolton, 149, 168; Fletcher, 119, 120. There is no record of William's political leanings, but it is known that other Arnolds of the time were diehard Whigs. Most Whigs opposed the war, which would explain why none of the Arkansas Arnolds, who came from a line of patriot soldiers (see Appendix B), participated in the Mexican War.
12. Michael Emery and Edwin Emery, *The Press and America: An Interpretive History of the Mass Media*, 7th ed. (Englewood Cliffs, N.J.: Prentice Hall, 1992), 112-114.
13. Bolton, 149, 150. Much of this dispute may have been political in nature. As a Whig newspaper editor, Pike was not a fan of Yell. Even though he was a Whig, Pike's involvement in the war can be explained by his ambition. Wool, a career military man, served where his country sent him – regardless of his political philosophy.
14. Bolton, 150, 151.
15. *Ibid.*
16. *Ibid.*, 153-155.
17. Emery, 113-114.
18. Friedman, xii; *1850 U.S. Census for Hempstead County, Arkansas*; *1850 Slave Schedule for Hempstead, Arkansas*.
19. Bolton, 121; MacIvor, 68-70; Mary Davis Woodward, "Dr. W.E. Arnold – A Personality Sketch," *AHQ* 8 (winter 1949), 331; *BHM*, 824, 829.
20. Jewell, 363; Joanna Miller Lewis, "Equality Deferred, Opportunity Pursued: The Sisters of Wachovia," *Women of the American South*, ed. Christie Anne Farnham (New York: New York University Press, 1997), 84; Friedman, 36, 100; Plante, 7.

3 In Search of El Dorado

1. *Marriage Bonds and Ministries Returns of Union County, Arkansas: 1829-1870*, comp. Annie Laurie Spencer (El Dorado, Ark.: El Dorado Printing Co., 1962), viii.
2. There were several Benjamin Arnolds in the family. The slave records do not provide enough information to reveal if this Benjamin was the uncle or the cousin.

3. *Abstracts of Some Greenville County, South Carolina, Records Concerning Black People Free and Slave, 1791-1865* vol. 1, comp. Anne K. McCuen (Spartanburg, S.C.: The Reprint Company Publishers, 1991), v, 33-47; *Head of Families: First Census of the United States – 1790, South Carolina* (Washington: Government Printing Office), 70. See Appendix C for details of the Arnolds' interaction with slaves.

4. Joan E. Cashin, "According to His Wish and Desire: Female Kin and Female Slaves in Planter Wills," *Women of the American South*, 106; MacIvor, 52-53; *Laurens County, South Carolina, Will Book A- 2, 1840-1853*, comp. Frances Terry Ingmire (St. Louis: Ingmire Publications, 1982), 123-124.

5. Cash, 35; *Abstracts of Early Records of Laurens County, South Carolina, 1785-1820*, comp. Sara M. Nash (1982); *Laurens County, South Carolina, Wills, 1784-1840*, comp. Colleen Elliott (Easley, S.C.: Southern Historical Press, 1988); *Laurens County, South Carolina, Will Book D-E, 1810-1825*, comp. Frances Terry Ingmire (St. Louis: Ingmire Publications, 1982), 123.

6. Family tradition holds that David's maternal grandfather, Lewis Saxon, was related to George Washington through his mother.

7. *BHM*, 124-125.

8. *Abstracts of Early Records of Laurens County, South Carolina, 1785-1820*; *Laurens County, South Carolina, Wills, 1784-1840*.

9. *1840 Census for Laurens County, South Carolina*; *1850 Census for Laurens County, South Carolina*; *1850 Slave Schedule for Laurens County, South Carolina*; Cashin, 104. Sally (Sarah) McNees, Polly Arnold's mother, states in her will, dated June 17, 1846, that she had given Polly (along with other heirs) an advancement on her inheritance. She instructs the executor to distribute proceeds from the sale of her estate, which included several slaves, equally among her heirs. Then on November 25, 1847, Sally added a codicil: "It is my will that the distributive share of my estate, to which my daughter, Polly Arnold, may be entitled, be secured in trust, and I hereby give the same to Samuel Barksdale (Polly's son-in-law) and my son, Joshua Saxon, in trust for her sole and separate use and benefit during her natural life and at her death, it is my will that the said share or what may be remaining in their (the trustees above named) hands be equally divided between her children." Polly's brother, Hugh Saxon, left similar instructions in his will of November 11, 1851. In the will itself, Hugh instructs that $1,000 is to be given to Capt. Samuel Barksdale in trust for the sole use and benefit of Polly. At her death, whatever is left is to be divided equally among her children. Later in the will, Hugh leaves the remainder of his estate, which has not been specifically given to someone, to be divided equally among his heirs, including Polly. The next day, he added a codicil to clarify that anything left to Polly was to be conveyed to Samuel in trust for her sole benefit (Wills in W.H. Arnold, The Arnold Family [St. Paul, Minn.: West Publishing Co., 1935]).

10. *BHM*, 182; Cash, 26; Bolton, 19; *Clark County, Arkansas: A Genealogical Source Book*, comp. Pauline Williams Wright and Barbara McDow Caffee (Baltimore: Gateway Press, Inc., 1982), 4. Arnold family tradition sets the year for David's arrival in Arkansas as 1849, but it does not provide a month.

11. Bolton, 17, 19; Fletcher, 111.

Notes (pp. 25-30)

12. Woods, 44-47.
13. Ibid.
14. Ibid., 23, 44-47.
15. Bureau of Land Management Records, including Homestead and Cash Entry Patents; *1850 Census for Clark County, Arkansas*; *Centennial History of Arkansas*, vol. 3 (Chicago: The S.J. Clarke Publishing Co., 1922), 821. Hendrick filed on two other 40-acre government parcels – one in 1855 and another in 1860. By the 1880s, he had 700 acres of farm and timberland – far more than the average farmer in Clark County (*BHM*, 125).
16. *BHM*, 383-388; Davis Woodward, 331-334; Wyatt-Brown, 32. According to Union County federal land records, David Carroll Ross acquired his first tract of government land, 40 acres, April 1, 1850. The records show 10 other land transactions for David Ross in Union County from 1856-1859, involving a total of 640 acres.

4   Settling In

1. Degler, 56.
2. D.W. Harris and B.M. Hulse, *The History of Claiborne Parish, Louisiana* (New Orleans, 1886), 73; Owsley, 36; Degler, 56; *BHM*, 829; Bolton, 55.
3. Moneyhon, 37-45.
4. Ibid., 38, 43, 51; *BHM*, 817-820.
5. *BHM*, 829; *1860 Census for Union County, Arkansas*, 285-286; Pattie Wright Hedges, "How Women Supported the Family," *CWA*, 62; Foner, 11; David Y. Thomas, *Arkansas and Its People* (New York: The American Historical Society, Inc., 1930), 7, 95; MacIvor, 67, 70. Union County land records show that Frederich Hawthorne filed on two parcels of land in 1855. The "old Hawthorne place" most likely was the land he had farmed prior to this filing. Much of the land first settled in the early 1840s played out quickly. "But in a few years the lands washed badly and began to fail, when they should have been in their prime" (Harris, 73).
6. *1860 Census for Union County, Arkansas*. By 1860, a skilled slave was selling for $2,000, and a field hand was valued at $1,000 (Moneyhon, 29, 34).
7. IMA; *Marriage Bonds and Ministries Returns of Union County, Arkansas 1829-1879*, 4, 152, 158; Friedman, 34; Fletcher, 131. The courtesy titles of *Mr.* and *Miss* were generally reserved for those with high social rank. Very few entries in the Union County records contain these titles. The marriage record lists David's and Temperance's ages as 30 and 18, respectively. However, the birth dates listed in MacIvor would make them 28 and 17 at the time of their marriage, and U.S. Census records show them as being 30 and 18 in 1860. An infare feast traditionally was held at the home of the bridegroom's oldest living relative. Because of the distances involved, David and Tempie may have broken with this tradition and celebrated at her sister's house instead.
8. *1860 Census for Union County, Arkansas*; H.K. Thatcher, *Camden and the Ouachita River* (Ouachita County, Ark.: Ouachita River Valley Association, 1952), 8, 9; Owsley, "Pattern of Migration and Settlement on the Southern Frontier," *The South: Old and New Frontiers*, 15; Woods, 27, 31; Foner, 127.

The *1860 Slave Schedule for Union County, Arkansas*, shows that David had two male slaves, aged 34 and 22; five male slaves ranging in age from 5 to 13; six female slaves ranging in age from 17 to 22; two 7-year-old female slaves; and a 2-year-old female.

9. Fletcher, 131; Medearis, 305-306.
10. Clyde W. Cathey, "Slavery in Arkansas," *AHQ* 3 (spring 1944), 80; Suzanne Lebsock, *Virginia Women, 1600-1945: A Share of Honour* (Richmond: Virginia State Library, 1987), 76-77.
11. Eugene Genovese and Elizabeth Fox Genovese, "The Religious Ideals of Southern Slave Society," *The Evolution of Southern* Culture, ed. Numan V. Bartley (Athens, Ga.: The University of Georgia Press, 1988), 24-25; *BHM*, 56,125, 557, 825.
12. Ray V. Denslow, *Civil War and Masonry in Missouri* (Missouri: Grand Lodge, Ancient Free and Accepted Masons and the State of Missouri, 1930); "Secret Brotherhood of Freemasonry," *History's Mysteries*, History Channel (2003). While there is no extant family record of David being a Mason, the circumstantial evidence is great. His father, brother, brothers-in-law, friends, and son were all high-ranking Masons. And when he enlisted, he joined a unit formed by a Masonic leader.
13. Fletcher, 140, 141; Woods, 29; Cathey, 73-74. The General Assembly postponed this expulsion date in early 1861, pushing it back to January 1, 1863 – ironically, the date the Emancipation Proclamation would go into effect.
14. Woodward, 63, 64.
15. *Ibid.*, 65; Cathey, 76.
16. Woods, 92.
17. Moneyhon, 82-83. David's son, William, expressed these ideas in his book and ascribed their basis to conversations he had with the men who had fought for the Confederacy. These men included his father, uncles, and schoolteacher.
18. Six of the eight Arkansas delegates at the convention walked out even though they had been instructed not to for any reason. Most of the newspapers in the state criticized the two delegates who remained. The blame for the walkout was placed on the leading presidential candidate, Stephen Douglas, rather than on those who left (Woods, 99-103).
19. *Ibid.*, 105. The Whigs, as a political party, had died out in the 1850s, but those like David who had been strong supporters of Whig principles had difficulty finding a new political home, especially during the strife of the late 1850s. Although Whigs tended to support a strong central government, they opposed extensive executive power, which they viewed as political abuse. Influenced by evangelical religion, Whigs spoke up for morality and humanitarianism and were more tolerant of African Americans and Native Americans (Bolton, 168). Whigs also tended to be wealthy and better educated than their neighbors. The larger slaveholders were generally Whigs. Before the Whig Party faded, The *Washington Telegraph* and the *Arkansas Gazette* espoused the party's views (Woods, 36-37). David likely subscribed to both newspapers.
20. Fletcher, 140, 141; Woods, 109.
21. *Diary of Judge John Brown*, 6 November 1860, in Woods, 109.
22. Woods, 116-118; Jewell, 165.

23. Woods, 116-118.
24. *Ibid.*

5 Road to Secession

1. Fletcher, 138; Bolton, 17, 19.
2. Woods, 25, 27; Moneyhon, 60; Bolton, 98, 128-133. Slave mortality in Arkansas for the year ending June 30, 1850, was 18:1,000; the white mortality for the same period was 13:1,000. The slave birth rate was 25:1,000; the white birth rate was 34:1,000. Thus the natural increase for slaves was 7:1,000, while the natural increase for whites was 21:1,000 (Bolton, 133).
3. Woods, 122, 129, 130.
4. Woods, 127-129; Bolton, 185. Sources disagree on the number of troops sent to reinforce the Little Rock arsenal. Jack B. Scroggs claims there were 60 troops of artillery transferred from Kansas to Little Rock (Scroggs, "Arkansas in the Secession Crisis," *Arkansas and the Civil War*, ed. John L. Ferguson [Little Rock: Pioneer Press, 1965], 21).
5. Lebsock, 67; Plante, 74-75.
6. Plante, 74-75; Lebsock, 67; M. Jane Johansson, ed., *WBT*.
7. Bolton, 185; Woods, 130-132, 142. As a youngster, William Hendrick was called "Willie" (1870 Census for Union County, Arkansas). His nickname changed to "Dick" in his teen years.
8. Woods, 132-135, 143, 146; Bolton, 185.
9. Woods, 154.
10. *Ibid.*, 148, 153-159, 249; Fletcher, 146; Bolton, 185-186; Owsley, *op cit.*, 20.
11. Woods, 157; Scroggs, 38-39.
12. Francis Irby Gwaltney, "A Survey of Historic Washington, Arkansas," *AHQ* 17 (winter 1955), 360-361.
13. Woods, 157.
14. Jesse N. Cypert, "Secession Convention," Publication of the Arkansas Historical Association, in Scroggs, 41; A.W. Bishop, *Loyalty on the Frontier* (St. Louis, 1863), 9, in Scroggs, 141-142; Woods, 157-161; *BHM*, 53-54, 73; Bolton, 185-186.
15. Fletcher, 148; Woods, 134, 160-161; *BHM*, 75; Stewart Sifakis, *Compendium of the Confederate Armies: Florida and Arkansas*, vol. 4 (New York: Facts on File, 1992), 29.
16. Cathey, 76.

6 Call to Arms

1. *BHM*, 557; Fletcher, 142; Hedges, 62-63.
2. Laura Govan, "The Daughter of the First Arkansas Regiment," *CWA*, 144; Davis Woodward, p. 331. Atlanta Medical College became part of Emory University. Col. Fagan was promoted to general before the war ended.

3. Kate Beasley, ed., "Three Civil War Letters," *AHQ* 3 (Summer 1944), 184; David Y. Thomas, "Getting out of the Union," *Arkansas and the Civil War*, 44. Many of these soldiers later joined the war effort again.
4. Thomas, 44. Several references mention Bushy Creek in passing but give no detail as to where it was located in Arkansas. However, the only action on the western front at this time was in Missouri. Thus, it is reasonable to assume that what was called Bushy Creek was on Arkansas' northern border.
5. Davis Woodward, 331; John L. Ferguson, ed., "A Chronology of the Civil War in Arkansas," *Arkansas and the Civil War*, 285. Ferguson defines a *skirmish* as "a small encounter usually incidental to a larger military movement" and *action* as "active, frequently sharp, offensive and defensive movements."
6. Denslow, 8, 31; *BHM*, 819.
7. *BHM*, 819; Arthur R. Buckalew and Robert B. Buckalew, "Hillsboro's Soldier-Citizen: Horatio Gates Perry Williams," *AHQ* 31 (spring 1972), 37. Gus Scott, captain of Company E of the First Louisiana Cavalry, wrote this letter shortly before he was killed while retreating toward Knoxville, Tennessee, June 22, 1863 (Howell Carter, *A Cavalryman's Reminiscences of the Civil War* [New Orleans: The American Printing Co., n.d.], 78-79).
8. 19th-F; *BHM*, 819, 825; Leo E. Huff, "The Memphis and Little Rock Railroad During the Civil War," *AHQ* 23 (autumn 1964), 264.
9. Huff, 266; Buckalew, 37-39.
10. Buckalew, 37-39; Report of Maj. Gen. Henry W. Halleck, U.S. Army, St. Louis, Missouri, 10 March 1862, in "Pea Ridge," *Arkansas and the Civil War*, 81.
11. Instead of taking the boat/coach/train passage from DeValls Bluff to Hopefield, some travelers chose to take a steamer down the White River to the Mississippi and then up to Memphis. However, this route usually took about 24 hours longer. Since time was a luxury, the Confederacy used the Memphis and Little Rock Railroad extensively to transfer troops east of the Mississippi. After Memphis fell to the Union in June 1862, the Confederacy could use only the western portion of the railroad, the part that stretched from Little Rock to DeValls Bluff (Huff, 264-267).
12. *Ibid.*
13. *BHM*, 85; Buckalew, 39-40; Harris, 192-193.
14. *Fort Pillow State Historic Park*, Tennessee State Parks, www.state.tn.us/environment/parks/pillow/history/htm.
15. Harris, 206.
16. 19th-SD; 19th-F; Harris, 195-199.
17. Kenneth C. Barnes, "The Williams Clan: Mountain Farmers and Union Fighters in North Central Arkansas," *Civil War Arkansas: Beyond Battles and Leaders*, ed. Anne J. Bailey and Daniel E. Sutherland (Fayetteville, Ark.: University of Arkansas Press, 2000), 159; Ken Durham, "'Dear Rebecca': The Civil War Letters of William Edwards Paxton, 1861-1863," *LH* 20 (spring 1979), 185; 19th-F. Sgt. Gilson Harbin was discharged from Company F at Fort Pillow April 15, 1862, and Pvt. T.J. Bustin was discharged four days later. No reason is given for the discharges. Both men enlisted March 1 at El Dorado with David Arnold.

18. 19th-F; John Q. Anderson, "Joseph Carson, Louisiana Confederate Soldier," *LH* 1 (winter 1960), 48-49; Theophilus Perry to Harriet Perry, Pine Bluff, Ark., 11 April 1863, *WBT*, 123.
19. Ludwell H. Johnson, *Red River Campaign: Politics and Cotton in the Civil War* (Baltimore: Johns Hopkins Press, 1958); Jewell, 167; *Fort Pillow State Historic Park*.

7 On the Homefront

1. Hedges, 63.
2. *Ibid.*, 64-65; Carl H. Moneyhon, ed., VDG, *AHQ* 42 (spring 1983), 53; Clara B. Eno, "Activities of the Women in Arkansas During the War Between the States," *AHQ* 3 (spring 1944), 6.
3. Eno, 6, 24.
4. *Ibid.*, 8; Moneyhon, 56-57; Hedges, 64. The illnesses that claimed the lives of so many soldiers also hit the towns and villages, where people were dying of the measles, dysentery, and influenza. With so many doctors engaged in the war and the limited supplies of medicine and bandages reserved for the battlefront, people at home were dying for lack of medical resources.
5. Hedges, 63; Theophilus Perry to Thomas A. Person, 6 May 1862, *WBT*, 3.
6. Ulysses S. Grant, *Memoirs and Selected Letters* vol. 1 (New York: Literary Classics of the United States, 1990), 226-227; William C. Davis, *Rebels & Yankees: The Battlefields of the Civil War* (San Diego: Thunder Bay Press, 1999), 43-46.
7. Grant, 226-227; Davis, 43-46.
8. Johnson, 158-160; Davis, 43-46; Carter.
9. Davis Woodward, 331-332; Grant, 239.
10. Davis, 38-49; Davis Woodward, 331-332.
11. Grant, 238, 246.
12. Harris, 192-193, 206; *Fort Pillow State Historic Park*; Davis, 43. When Confederate Gen. Albert E. Johnston was killed at Shiloh, command fell to Beauregard, who has been largely blamed for the defeat.
13. Buckalew, 39-40; 19th-SD; Durham, 188; Theophilus Perry to Harriet Perry, 23 July 1862, *WBT*, 7; 19th-F.
14. Margaret Greene Rogers, "Corinth 1861-1865," Publication No. A-0002 (Corinth, Miss.: Northeast Mississippi Museum Association, 1990); Grant, 222; Durham, 186-190; Theophilus Perry to Harriet Perry, 21 September 1862, *WBT*, 35.
15. Theophilus Perry to Harriet Perry, Confederate camp near Lewisville, Ark., 5 August 1862, *WBT*, 17.
16. Theophilus Perry to Harriet Perry, Camp Holmes, 21 September 1862, and Theophilus Perry to Levin Perry, 17 August 1862, both in *WBT*, 17-18, 35.
17. Durham, 188.
18. Grant, 250-255.
19. Buckalew, 40; Rogers.
20. 19th-F; Rogers.

21. Grant, 255.
22. *Ibid.*
23. 19th-F; *BHM*, 819. No description is given of David's illness other than that it was quite serious. It had a lasting impact on his health.

8 A Discharge of Duty

1. Michael B. Dougan, "Life in Confederate Arkansas," *AHQ* 31 (spring 1972), 15-17; David Y. Thomas, "Under the Confederate Flag," *Arkansas and the Civil War*, 74; Theophilus Perry to Harriet Perry, Camp Bayou Meto in Little Rock, 10 December 1862 and Harriet Perry to Theophilus Perry, Spring Hill, Texas, 23 December 1862, both in *WBT*, 69, 75; Fletcher, 155.
2. Wyatt-Brown, *Southern Honor: Ethics and Behavior in the Old South* (New York: Oxford University Press, 1982), 220; James J. Hudson, ed., "From Paraclifta to Marks' Mill: The Civil War Correspondence of Lt. Robert C. Gilliam," *AHQ* 17 (autumn 1958), 283.
3. *BHM*, 77-78; Anderson, 48.
4. 19th-F.
5. MacIvor, 64; Hudson, 291. When David hid the cotton is unknown, but this chronology is both logical and possible. This practice of hiding cotton was common. For instance, one family hid two bales in a wheat house and another bale under the gin house (Hudson, 291).
6. Johnson, 10, 13, 19-24.
7. *Ibid.*, 101-103.
8. Dougan, 16; Theophilus Perry to Harriet Perry, Lewisville, Ark., 5 August 1862, *WBT*, 17. There is no record of when the family moved to Garland City, which was about 20 miles southeast of what was to become Texarkana. However, it is unlikely that they would have moved before David enlisted at El Dorado or while he was away. They also could not have moved close to Tempie's due date.
9. Farrar Newberry, "Harris Flanagin," *Arkansas and the Civil War*, 65.
10. *Records of Louisiana Confederate Soldiers and Louisiana Confederate Commands*, vol. 1, comp. Andrew J. Booth (Spartanburg, S.C.: The Reprint Co., 1984), 78; Harris, 231-232; Theophilus Perry to Harriet Perry, Pine Bluff, Ark., 23 April 1863, and Theophilus Perry to Harriet Perry, Delhi, La., 20 June 1863, both in *WBT*, 127, 143.
11. Van D. Odom, "The Political Career of Thomas Overton Moore, Secession Governor of Louisiana," *LHQ* 26 (October 1943), 1022-1023; Carter, 11; *Confederate Partisan Rangers*, U.S. Civil War Center, www.civilwarhome.com/partisanrangers.htm; Daniel E. Sutherland, "Guerillas: The Real War in Arkansas," *Civil War Arkansas: Beyond Battles and Leaders*, 135-153.
12. Harris, 232.
13. Anderson, 60; Odom, 1022-1023; Theophilus Perry to Harriet Perry, 18 July 1862, *WBT*, 6.
14. Arthur W. Bergeron, Jr., *Guide to Louisiana Confederate Military Units 1861-1865* (Baton Rouge: Louisiana State University Press, 1989), 61; Davis, 144.

15. Theophilus Perry to Harriet Perry, Alexandria, La., 27 May 1863, *WBT*, 135. Theophilus Perry was an officer in a Texas cavalry unit charged with similar objectives as the 13th Louisiana and in the same region of the state. Following the fall of Vicksburg, the two units rode together in the same brigade. The situation in the Alexandria area was not as devastating as in other parts of Louisiana. This has been credited to the fact that Col. William T. Sherman had, before the war, served as the first superintendent of the Louisiana State Seminary of Learning & Military Academy, which opened in 1860 in Pineville, La., (near Alexandria) and later evolved into Louisiana State University. When the war started, Sherman left his post to serve in the Union army. But because of his friendships and ties to this part of Louisiana, Sherman ordered the Union forces not to burn the houses in the area.
16. Theophilus Perry to Harriet Perry, Delhi, La., 20 June 1863, *WBT*, 143.
17. Theophilus Perry to Harriet Perry, Lacroix Landing, La., 29 May 1863, and Theophilus Perry to Harriet Perry, near Mt. Lebanon, La., 18 May 1863, both in *WBT*, 132.

9 Fall of Vicksburg

1. Bergeron, 61; Grant, 256, 283; Theophilus Perry to Harriet Perry, Alexandria, La., 27 May 1863, *WBT*, 135.
2. Bergeron, 61; Michael Sharpe, *Historical Maps of Civil War Battlefields* (London: PRC Publishing, Ltd., 2000), 15; Grant, 295. While the 13th spent most of the spring of 1863 opposing Grant's march through northern Louisiana, several of its companies joined skirmishes at Caledonia and Pin Hook in May. There is no record of whether David's company was one of those assigned to these skirmishes.
3. Bergeron, 61; Sharpe, 15; Davis, 139-153.
4. Booth, 78; Bergeron, 60-61; Theophilus Perry to Harriet Perry, Campti, La., 23 May 1863, *WBT*, 133.
5. "Troops under Fire," *DTD*, 17 November 1893, 1.
6. Theophilus Perry to Harriet Perry, Lacroix Landing, La., *WBT*.
7. Theophilus Perry to Harriet Perry, west side of Bayou Tensas, La., 1 June 1863, *WBT*, 138.
8. *Ibid.*
9. *Ibid.*; Theophilus Perry to Harriet Perry, Delhi, La., 20 June 1863, *WBT*, 142-143.
10. Theophilus Perry to Harriet Perry, Delhi, La., 11 June 1863, *WBT*, 140-141.
11. Theophilus Perry to Harriet Perry, Camp Holmes, 21 September 1862, and Delhi, La., 20 June 1863, both in *WBT*, 142-143.
12. Powell A. Casey, *Encyclopedia of Forts, Posts, Named Camps, and Other Military Installations in Louisiana, 1700-1981* (Baton Rouge: Claitor's Publishing Division, 1983), 69, 103; Bergeron, 47, 61; "Goodrich's Landing," *CWSAC Battle Summaries*, The American Battlefield Protection Program, www2.cr.nps.gov/abpp/battles/la014. htm; Allen W. Jones, "Military Events in Louisiana During the Civil War, 1861-1865," *LH* 2 (summer 1961), 301-321; Anderson, 55.

13. Powell A. Casey, *Encyclopedia of Forts, Posts, Named Camps, and Other Military Installations in Louisiana, 1700-1981* (Baton Rouge: Claitor's Publishing Division, 1983), 69, 103; Bergeron, 47, 61; "Goodrich's Landing," *CWSAC Battle Summaries*, The American Battlefield Protection Program; Allen W. Jones, "Military Events in Louisiana During the Civil War, 1861-1865," *LH* 2 (summer 1961), 301-321; Anderson, 55.
14. Theophilus Perry to Harriet Perry, Delhi, La., 12 July 1863, *WBT*, 147-148.
15. *Ibid.;* Theophilus Perry to Harriet Perry, Delhi, La., 9 July 1863, *WBT*, 145.
16. Theophilus Perry to Harriet Perry, Delhi, La., 9 July 1863 and 12 July 1863, both in *WBT*, 144-145; 149.
17. Theophilus Perry to Harriet Perry, Delhi, La., 12 July 1863, *WBT*, 149.
18. Durham, 191-195; Grant, 389.
19. Durham, 191-195; Theophilus Perry to Harriet Perry, Delhi, La., 12 July 1863, and Trenton, La., 17 July 1863, both in *WBT*, 149-150; Odom, 1021.
20. Levin Perry to Theophilus Perry, Spring Hill, Texas, 20 July 1863, and Theophilus Perry to Harriet Perry, Trenton, La., 17 July 1863, both in *WBT*, 150, 153-154.
21. Theophilus Perry to Harriet Perry, Delhi, La., 12 July 1863, both in *WBT*, 147-148.
22. Harriet Perry to her mother, Mrs. Person, Harrison County, Texas, 13 December 1863; Theophilus Perry to Harriet Perry, Fourdoche, La., 8 December 1863; and Theophilus Perry to Harriet Perry, Marksville, La., 8 January 1864, all in *WBT*, 174, 179-180, 191; Hudson, 281.
23. Harriet Perry to Theophilus Perry, Spring Hill, Texas, 18 January 1864, and Theophilus Perry to Harriet Perry, Marksville, La., 18 January 1864, both in *WBT*, 196-197.
24. Bergeron, 48, 61; Theophilus Perry to Harriet Perry, Marksville, La., 29 January 1864, and Pearl Lake, La., 9 March 1864, both in *WBT*, 205, 224-225. Since men in the cavalry had to provide their own mounts, they received a higher rate of pay than the infantry. When these units were dismounted, the Confederate Army paid them at the infantry rate – even though they had enlisted as cavalry. A private in the cavalry was paid $110-$120 Confederate a month (Theophilus Perry to Harriet Perry, Camp Holmes, 21 September 1862, *WBT*, 34).
25. Johnson, 209, 211.
26. *Ibid.*, 213-214; Bergeron, 47-49.
27. Johnson, 223.
28. *Ibid.*, 223-225.
29. Casey, 73.

10 The War at Home

1. Harriet Perry to Theophilus Perry, Texas, 30 October 1862, 3 December 1862, and 23 December 1862, all in *WBT*, 51, 67, 74. (Harriet Perry, who lived on the Texas side of the Red River area, had a lot in common with Tempie, as both were educated women from respected families. The women were close in age and both were devout in their faith.

It is reasonable to suggest that Tempie's thoughts toward childbirth while her husband was off to war would have been similar to the fears Harriet shared in letters with her husband, who also was fighting west of the Mississippi.)
2. Eno, 25. By 1864, writing paper, which was still made from rag, had become scarce and expensive, as was anything made from cotton. For $30, a person could buy 72 sheets of foolscap and 96 sheets of rough notepaper – when it was available. Such prices forced frugality (Harriet Perry to Theophilus Perry, Spring Hill, Texas, 29 January 1864, *WBT*, 202).
3. Harriet Perry to Theophilus Perry, Spring Hill, Texas, 20 July 1863, *WBT*, 155;VDG, September 1863, 52.
4. Plante, 90; Lebsock, 88.
5. MacIvor, 64.
6. Eno, 19.
7. Wyatt-Brown, *Honor and Violence in the Old South*, 71, 80; MacIvor, 61.
8. Dougan, 24; Hedges, 64; Eno, 20.
9. The date of this visit is not clear. It may have occurred during the late fall or winter of 1863 as part of a recruiting trip.
10. Dougan, 20, 363.
11. VDG, 18 September 1863, 60.
12. Theophilus Perry to Harriet Perry, Delhi, La., 12 July 1863, and Levin Perry to Theophilus Perry, Spring Hill, Texas, 20 July 1863, both in *WBT*, 147-148, 153-154; Moneyhon, *The Impact of the Civil War*, 120.
13. Moneyhon, *op. cit.*, 17, 23; Bergeron, 48-49, 61; Dougan, 16-17, 25, 28; Hudson, 280; Gwaltney, 362; Carl H. Moneyhon, "Disloyalty and Class Consciousness in Southwestern Arkansas, 1862-1865," *Civil War Arkansas: Beyond Battles and Leaders*, 117-132; Jeffrey Alan Owens, "The Burning of Lake St. Joseph," *LH* 32 (fall 1991), 411.
14. Sallie E. Jordan, "Sketch of Mrs. Lutetia M. Howells, of Clarksville," *CWA*, 31-32.
15. *Ibid.*
16. *Ibid.* Fourteen other houses were burned in the area that day.
17. VDG, 26 September 1863, 61.
18. Gwaltney, 355; W.H. Arnold, "Rondo, Miller County, Arkansas: Brief Historical Sketch," 31 October 1930.
19. Dougan, 22; Fletcher, 174-175.

11 A State Divided

1. Gwaltney, 369-370; Hudson, 282.
2. Arnold.
3. Gwaltney, 370.
4. Fletcher, 184-187.
5. Hudson, 288.
6. In his family history, William H. Arnold specifically names four male slaves. More generic references imply that the family at this time included several other slaves – both male and female. There is no record of whether any of the slaves were impressed or if any of them ran away.

During the war, many women hired their slaves out for economic reasons and their own inability to force the slaves to work (*WBT*, 82). Again, there is no record of whether Tempie hired out any of her slaves.

7. Mrs. A.A. Tufts, "Reminiscences of Mrs. E. S. Scott," *CWA*, 48.
8. *WBT*, 39, 235-236; VDG, 160-161; *CWA*, 18.
9. Gwaltney, 369, 375; *BHM*, 382; Harriet Perry to Mary Temperance Person, Marshall, Texas, 22 October 1862, *WBT*, 45.
10. *WBT*, 166. In the Perry family, for example, there were five deaths – all children – in the summer of 1863. Before the war ended, Harriet had mourned both of her children, her husband, two brothers, her father-in-law, and several young brothers- and sisters-in-law.
11. An *affair* is defined as a fight, an *expedition* as "a journey for a specific purpose," and an *operation* as "a complete military action or mission of some kind" (Ferguson, 292-294).
12. Ira Don Richards, "The Battle of Poison Spring," *AHQ* 28 (winter 1959), 338-349; Joseph P. Blessington, *Walker's Texas Division*, 201, in *WBT*, 241.
13. Edward Atkinson, "The Battle of Marks Mill," *AHQ* 14 (winter 1955), 381-384; Ira Don Richards, "The Engagement at Marks' Mills," *AHQ* 19 (spring 1960), 51-60; Johnson, 191. Accounts differ on the size of the supply train. Atkinson, a private engaged in the battle, claims in his account, which was written 55 years later, that the supply train consisted of 400 wagons.
14. Atkinson, 381-384; Richards, "Mark's Mill," 51-60.
15. Bergeron, 48.
16. Davis Woodward, 332.

12 The End

1. Moneyhon, *The Impact of the Civil War*, 119.
2. Dougan, 17.
3. VDG, 141, 158.
4. *Ibid.*, 159-160.
5. Beasley, 187.
6. *BHM*, 382; Gwaltney, 381; Johnson, 49-78.
7. Fletcher, 200-202.
8. Gwaltney, 390; Jack B. Scroggs, "Arkansas in the Secession Crisis," *Arkansas and the Civil War*, 7, 15.
9. David Y. Thomas, "Under the Confederate Flag," 76-77.
10. *Ibid.*
11. Gwaltney, 380.
12. *Ibid.*, 381, 383; VDG, 165.
13. Davis Woodward.
14. Fletcher, 197; Gwaltney, 386.
15. It is not clear from family records when the Arnolds returned to Union County. But given Bill's return to the family farm near Garland after his surrender and the impending birth of another child late that summer, it is probable that the move was made after the fall harvest and the birth of the baby.

16. Gwaltney, 385, 388, 391.
17. *Ibid.*, 359; Fletcher, 197-198; Foner, 130.
18. Temperance Arnold to William H. Arnold, 22 May 1911, in *The Arnold Family*.
19. "The Loss of the Civil War," *TDT*, 13 April 1894, 4. This article quotes from a June 1893 report that appeared in the *New York Sun*.
20. Woods, 9-10. According to William Arnold's memoirs, his parents had at least 20 cattle when they returned to Union County.
21. *BHM*, 557, 819; Gwaltney, 382; Foner, 130; Friedman, 92; Cash, 113.
22. Moneyhon, *The Impact of the Civil War*, 45.

13 The Aftermath of War

1. Foner, 129. In the Alabama plantation country, per capita wealth by 1870 was one-sixth of what it had been before the Civil War started.
2. Friedman, 101.
3. Johnson, Boyd W., "Cullen Montgomery Baker: The Arkansas-Texas Desperado," *AHQ* 26 (autumn 1961), 232-237; Eugene Genovese and Elizabeth Fox-Genovese, "The Religious Ideals of Southern Slave Society," *The Evolution of Southern Culture*, ed. Numan V. Bartley (Athens, Ga.: The University of Georgia Press, 1988), 24-25.
4. Cash, 121.
5. *BHM*, 827.
6. Gwaltney, 392; Mary Brunson, "Federal Raiders of Mississippi," *CWA*, 141-142; Cash, 172.
7. *BHM*, 826; Foner, 140-141.
8. *BHM*, 826.
9. Woods, 25; Foner, 125; Spencer, viii; Moneyhon, *The Impact of the Civil War*, 58, 178.
10. Cash, 156, 171.
11. Moneyhon, *The Impact of the Civil War*, 230; Foner, 140-141.
12. Foner, 140-141; Moneyhon, *The Impact of the Civil War*, 230-232.
13. Fletcher, 200-202.
14. *Ibid.*; Moneyhon, *The Impact of the Civil War*, 200.
15. Foner, 273; Fletcher, 203; Moneyhon, *The Impact of the Civil War*, 242.
16. Moneyhon, *The Impact of the Civil War*, 242; Fletcher, 211-212; Richard Owings, "The Brooks Baxter War," *Arkansas Encyclopedia*, B (2000-2003); Woods, 211-212. The final vote counts in Pulaski and Jefferson counties exceeded the number of registered voters by 1,925 (Owings).
17. "Arkansas. What Led to the Recent Contest," *NYT*, 25 May 1874, 1; Owings.
18. Moneyhon, *The Impact of the Civil War*, 234; Foner, 140-141.
19. Moneyhon, *The Impact of the Civil War*, 235-237. Seven cents a pound was the break-even price for cotton. While 17 cents produced some profit in a normal year, it was not enough to clear accumulated debt at a time when other prices were terribly inflated (Woodward, 186).

20. Moneyhon, *The Impact of the Civil War,* 184; 1860 Census for Van Buren Township in Union County; 1870 Census for Garland Township in Union County; 1860 Census for Caddo Township in Clark County; 1870 Census for Caddo Township in Clark County. David moved from Lisbon to Pleasant Grove near Mount Holly shortly before the 1870 Census. This move may have affected his property values.
21. Moneyhon, *The Impact of the Civil War,* 119. Men in their 40s were considered old (*WBT*).

14 Hard Lessons

1. Cash, 93, 140; *BHM*, 121-122; Frank Lawrence Owsley, "Plain Folk and Their Role in Southern History," 45-46; C. Vann Woodward, *Origins of the New South 1877-1913* (Baton Rouge: Louisiana State University Press, Littlefield Fund for Southern History, and University of Texas, 1951), 63.
2. Owsley, 43.
3. *Ibid.*, 46; Woodward, *Origins of the New South*, 61-63; Woods, 93; Cash, 140.
4. Wyatt-Brown, *Honor and Violence*, 45-47. Thomas Jefferson encouraged his nephew to study the classics. Harry "Lighthorse" Lee gave this same advice to his sons, who in turn ensured that their sons also had a classical education.
5. *BHM*, 96; Wyatt-Brown, *Honor and Violence*, 46-50.
6. Theophilus Perry to Harriet Perry, Uncle Godwin's place, 17 September 1863, *WBT*, 165.
7. Cash, 140; Owsley, 46; *BHM*, 187-188; Plante, 92.
8. *Hempstead County, Arkansas 1820-1881: Computer Indexed Marriage Records* (North Salt Lake: Hunting for Bears Inc., n.d.), 3. The Artesian Church was located about two or three miles from the present town of Prescott. William Arnold gives 1873 as the year for Bill and Mollie's wedding. MacIvor used Arnold as her source for this, so she also gives 1873 as the wedding year. Several online genealogical sites give 1868 as the marriage year. This makes more sense as their first child, Ella Arnold, was born Oct. 13, 1869.
9. In "Origin of Confederate Memorial Association," *CWA*, 119.

15 The Shadow of Reconstruction

1. *BHM*, 821.
2. Moneyhon, *Impact of the Civil War,* 239, 257. Floods or drought impacted the Arkansas cotton crop in 1868, 1869, and 1874. An army of cutworms attacked the crop in 1869.
3. Owings; "Governor Elisha Baxter of Arkansas," *National Governors Association Online*, 16 November 2003, www.nga.org/governors.
4. Owings; "Governor Elisha Baxter of Arkansas;" "Arkansas. What Led to the Recent Contest." A report submitted to Congress in February 1875 following a congressional investigation found that Brooks probably had won the popular vote.

But Baxter polled more votes as his people controlled more voting places (Owings). The amount of fraud by all parties makes it difficult to determine the true winner.

5. "What Led to the Recent Contest;" "Governor Elisha Baxter of Arkansas." Baxter denied Brooks' claims about the officer in the courtroom.
6. Owings; "Governor Elisha Baxter of Arkansas."
7. Owings; Woodward, 185; Moneyhon, *Impact of the Civil War,* 260-261; Edgar Ross Arnold to William Arnold, 13 February 1913, and Ann H. Arnold to William Arnold, 1913, both in *The Arnold Family*; *Centennial History of Arkansas* vol. 3 (Chicago: The S.J. Clarke Publishing Co., 1922), 821.
8. Owings; "What Led to the Recent Contest." Leading the charge against the governor were Sens. Clayton and Dorsey, who Baxter claimed had tried to bribe him to assure themselves re-election through vote fraud. His refusal to issue railroad bonds that would have benefited them also turned the senators against him.
9. "Arkansas. Governor Baxter Ousted by the Contestant, Brooks," *NYT,* 16 April 1874, 5; Owings; "Governor Elisha Baxter of Arkansas."
10. "Governor Baxter Ousted by the Contestant, Brooks;" Owings.
11. Owings; "Governor Elisha Baxter of Arkansas;" "Governor Baxter Ousted by the Contestant, Brooks."
12. "The Two Governors of Arkansas," *NYT,* 13 May 1874, 4; Owings.
13. Owings. The cannon had been brought in by Gen. Hindman to defend Arkansas during the Civil War (Powell Clayton, *The Aftermath of the Civil War in Arkansas* [New York: Negro Universities Press, 1969]). The cannon is on display at the Old State Capitol in Little Rock.
14. Owings.
15. *Ibid.*
16. *Ibid.;* "The Two Governors of Arkansas."
17. Owings; "Playing with Fire," *NYT,* 12 May 1874, 4.
18. "Playing with Fire."
19. *Ibid.*
20. Owings; "The Two Governors of Arkansas."
21. Owings; "Effect of the President's Decision – Probable Breaking Up of a Corrupt Ring," *NYT,* 16 May 1874, 1.
22. "The State of Arkansas," *NYT,* 19 May 1874, 1.
23. *Ibid.*
24. *Ibid.* The General Assembly had formed Clayton County March 24, 1873, from pieces of existing counties in northeast Arkansas. Although the House voted May 19, 1874, to change the name of the county, the final name change was not approved by both chambers until December 6, 1875, when it was officially made Clay County in honor of Henry Clay. Dorsey County was formed April 17, 1873, from parts of Bradley, Jefferson, and Lincoln counties. It was finally renamed Cleveland County March 5, 1885, to commemorate Grover Cleveland's election as the first Democratic president since the war.
25. "Arkansas. Baxter Again in the State-House," *NYT,* 20 May 1874, 1.
26. *Ibid.* Clayton served in the Senate until 1877 when he returned to Arkansas where he went into the railroad business. He served as the U.S. ambassador to Mexico from 1897-1905 (Owings).

27. "Arkansas. A Review of the Situation," *NYT*, 30 May 1874, 2. Owings estimates that 200 people died in the month-long conflict.
28. "Two Governors of Arkansas;" "Playing with Fire;" "What Led to the Recent Contest."
29. Owings.

16 Coming of Age

1. Woodward, *Origins of the New South*, 108, 111; LeMaster, 98; Cash, 164.
2. Woodward, *Origins of the New South*, 108; LeMaster, 52, 98; *BHM*, 829. In his book on the Arnolds, William Arnold said his family moved to Marysville in 1872. However, the 1870 Census for Union County places the family in the Marysville area at least two years earlier.
3. Davis Woodward, 331.
4. *BHM*, 550-554; Davis Woodward, 331.
5. *BHM*, 557. Ansley was elected to the General Assembly in the fall of 1873 to fill the term of C. Thrower (*BHM*). Uncle John is John Hardin Arnold, Tempie's brother.
6. Owsley, "Plain Folk and Their Role in Southern History," 46.
7. Cash, 131. Ansley, Dick's teacher, had enlisted in the Seventh South Carolina Volunteer Infantry June 6, 1861. He served with the Seventh until April 1862 when he was forced to return to Arkansas because of the climate. That June, he joined the 33rd Arkansas, Company F, and was elected first lieutenant and then later promoted to captain. He served with the regiment until the surrender in 1865 (*BHM*, 557).
8. Cash, 118.
9. Owsley, "Plain Folk and Their Role in Southern History," 43; Cash, 185.
10. Robert Ross Wright, *Old Seeds in the New Land: History and Reminiscences of the Bar of Arkansas* (Fayetteville, Ark.: M and M Press, 2001), 204, 207; Cash, 30.
11. *BHM*, 66.
12. *Ibid.*
13. Cash, 30; Owsley, "Plain Folk and Their Role in Southern History," 42.

17 In Pursuit of the Law

1. This examiner may have been A.W. Wilson, who finished his education at St. John's College in Little Rock in 1874. He taught public school himself four years before getting a county position. He eventually became county clerk (*BHM*, 180).
2. *BHM*, 121. "Cousin Lewis" Saxon was related to Mary "Polly" Saxon Arnold, William's paternal grandmother. "Cousin Lewis" may have been Polly's cousin. He is not to be confused with the Lewis Saxon who was her father.

3. By the late 1880s, the average salary in Nevada County for a man with a first-grade teaching certificate was $45 a month and $37.50 for a second-grade certificate; a woman with either a first- or second-grade certificate averaged $30 (*BHM*, 551).
4. *BHM*, 67, 551, 553.
5. *Ibid.* "Bluff City" was a misnomer as this hamlet was simply a post office at a crossroad.
6. *Ibid.*, 550-554.
7. *Ibid.* Mitchel served as state senator from 1879-1881 and did not win his bid for Congress. His father, Charles Mitchel, had represented Arkansas in Congress several terms before the Civil War, so the son grew up in politics.
8. Morris S. "Buzz" Arnold, "The Arnolds of Southwest Arkansas," *The Arkansas Lawyer* 18 (July 1984), 137.
9. *BHM*, 551. There is disagreement between William Arnold and *BHM* on the spelling of Smoote's name. Arnold spells it as *Smoot*. Smoote had a classical education and studied under a noted Tennessee poet, David Reeve Arnold. By 1890, Smoote was in a firm with John H. Arnold, Jr., William's cousin. A New York publisher released Smoote's small volume of poetry, *The Mississippi and Other Songs* (*BHM*, 551).
10. *BHM*, 552.
11. *Ibid.*, 191. Colonel Cook was the brother-in-law of George Christopher, the clerk of the court at Prescott who had hired William briefly before he was admitted to the bar. The colonel's wife, Cornelia Christopher Cook, was George's sister. Arnold states that Cook died in 1883; *BHM* (191*)* gives two conflicting years for his death – 1882 and 1884.
12. *BHM*, 184, 186; W.H. Arnold, Sr., "Historical Statement of Texarkana Arkansas to Feb. 7, 1917," *AHQ*, 5 (spring 1946), 345-346; Cash, 18.
13. *BHM*, 183, 186; Arnold, "Historical Statement," 344, 347; LeMaster, 71, 72. Goldberg had been trained as a rabbi in Germany. When he first came to the United States, he worked as a peddler. He became seriously ill and was taken in by a Christian family. After converting to Christianity, he became a minister. Despite his conversion, he served as a rabbi to the Texarkana Jewish community for nearly 10 years and prepared many of the boys for their bar mitzvah (LeMaster).
14. Arnold, "Historical Statement," 346; Cash, 186.
15. Woodward, *Origins of the New South*, 120; MacIvor, 61. Stonewall Jackson Roland, William's cousin who was born in 1862, moved from South Carolina to Arkadelphia in the 1880s (MacIvor).
16. Arnold, 341-344.
17. Untitled, *DTI*, 17 May 1886, 1; "The East Side City Council," *DTI*, 12 January 1887, 3; untitled, *DTI*, 20 May 1886, 4; untitled, *DTI*, 4 June 1886, 1. The city council later passed an ordinance to prohibit the Monarch band from parading in the street.
18. *BHM*, 183, 185; Woodward, *Origins of the New South*, 160.
19. "Local News," *DTI*, 2 May 1887, 4. While W.H. Arnold placed the courtroom shooting in 1883, *BHM* places it in 1885. The incident occurred while Dixon was sheriff, a post he held from 1882-1884. He wasn't re-elected until 1886.

18 Planting Roots

1. Arnold gives no other information about this case that stirred up so much public sentiment. Although *BHM* briefly mentions a few infamous cases in each county, it does not include any case that would fit this vague description.
2. *BHM*, 191-192. The Little Rock Law Class, founded in 1868, brought in prominent local attorneys to lecture students. This was the only formal law training available in Arkansas until 1890 when a Department of Law was established at the university in Fayetteville. The Fayetteville program failed after one year, and its dean, Frank Goar, moved to Little Rock and reorganized the Little Rock Law Class into the Law Department of the Arkansas Industrial University (Wright, 207).
3. Arnold does not identify this sheriff, nor does he give a date for this comment. W.T. Hamilton succeeded Dixon as sheriff in 1884, but Dixon was re-elected in 1886. A.S. Blythe won the position two years later (*BHM*, 184).
4. "A Bold Burglar!" *DTI*, 2 June 1886, 4; "Local News," *DTI*, 3 June 1886, 4.
5. IRA.
6. "Local News," *DTI*, 26 May 1886, 4; "Local News," *DTI*, 14 May 1886, 4. Even though William used his given name professionally, friends continued to call him "Dick" the rest of his life.
7. In the 1880s, individual Texarkana candidates did not run display ads. Instead, they paid to place a small "card" or a line announcing their candidacy in the local newspaper. These ads, which ran in the upper left column on Page 2 in the *DTI*, blended in with the rest of the news and editorial comments on the page. The parties occasionally ran display ads, which listed all of the party's candidates. Throughout most of his career, William refused to pay for an individual ad.
8. W.H. Arnold, "When Texarkana Celebrated Grover Cleveland's Election," January 1934 newspaper clipping in Scrapbook 10, *Judge Morris Arnold Manuscript Collection*, Torreyson Library Archives, University of Central Arkansas.
9. Arnold remembers being paid $50 a month as city recorder. But articles on the city council meetings in *DTI* show that sometimes he received as little as $20 ("The East Side City Council," *DTI*, 12 January 1887, 3).
10. "Society Letter," *DTI*, 27 December 1886, 3.
11. "Society Letter," *DTI*, 10 April 1886, 3; untitled, *DTI*, 14 April 1886, 1; untitled, *DTI*, 16 April 1886, 1; untitled, *DTI*, 17 April 1886, 4.

19 Upheaval

1. "That Interview," *DTI*, 30 April 1886, 1, reprinted from the *Globe Democrat*, 27 April 1886.
2. *Ibid.*
3. *Ibid.*; "Local News," *DTI*, 10 May 1887, 4.
4. "The Strike. East St. Louis in Flames," *DTI*, 10 April 1886, 4.
5. *Ibid.*

6. *Ibid.*; "The Strike," *DTI*, 10 April 1886, 4. *DTI* first reported that Deputy Williams had been killed in the shootout. Three days later, it reported that he was recovering (*DTI*, 13 April 1886).
7. "The Strike," *DTI*, 12 April 1886, 1; "Farmers Beware!" *DTI*, 19 April 1886, 1.
8. "The Strike," *DTI*, 13 April 1886, 1; "Timely and Appropriate," *DTI*, 14 April 1886, 4.
9. "The Strike," *DTI*, 13 April 1886, 1; "Lumber Business Review," *DTI*, 13 April 1886, 1; "The Strikes," *DTI*, 23 April 1886, 4.
10. "The Strike," *DTI*, 20 April 1886, 4; "The Outrage Last Night," *DTI*, 22 April 1886, 1.
11. "The Strikes," *DTI*, 23 April 1886, 4; "The Congressional Committee," *DTI*, 11 May 1886, 4.
12. "The Strike," *DTI*, 20 April 1886, 4; "The Strike," *DTI*, 10 April 1886, 4; "The Strikes Everywhere," *DTI*, 22 April 1886, 1; untitled, *DTI*, 27 April 1886, 1.
13. "That Interview," *DTI*, 30 April 1886, 1.
14. Local News," *DTI*, 3 May 1886, 4; "The Congressional Committee," *DTI*, 11 May 1886, 4.
15. "Local News," *DTI*, 10 May 1887, 4; "The Gate City Guards," *DTI*, 13 May 1887, 1; "untitled," *DTI*, 26 May 1887, 2.
16. "Untitled," *DTI*, 20 May 1886, 4; "untitled," *DTI*, 27 May 1886, 4; "Can't It Be Stopped!" *DTI*, 7 May 1886, 4.
17. George Edwards, "A Card," *DTI*, 14 May 1886, 4; "Outrageous Conduct," *DTI*, 12 May 1886, 1. Edwards claimed he slapped the evangelist, but the other newspaper accounts say he knocked Wolfe down.
18. "That Mass Meeting," *DTI*, 13 May 1886, 4.
19. Edwards.
20. "Yes! That 'Do Settle It!'" *DTI*, 25 May 1886, 1; "The Edwards Case," *DTI*, 26 May 1886, 4.

20 Politics, Texarkana Style

1. *Little Rock Arkansas Gazette*, 3 February 1889, in Woodward, *Origins of the New South*, 56.
2. "A Card," *DTI*, 21 May 1886, 1. According to Arnold, Mitchel's sensitivity to the things said about him because of his joining the Republicans impaired his effectiveness on the bench. He also was extravagant and always in debt. As a result, he later moved to Oklahoma for a clean start, got in debt there, and failed. He returned to Arkansas where he died a disappointed and broken-hearted man.
3. "The Miller County Democratic Convention," *DTI*, 31 July 1886, 1.
4. Untitled, *DTI*, 22 May 1886, 4.
5. Untitled, *DTI*, 26 May 1886, 4.
6. Untitled, *DTI*, 1 July 1886, 4.
7. "A Jolly Time," *DTI*, 15 May 1886, 4; "Society Letter," *DTI*, 26 May 1886, 3. While the picnic article mentions that "local dignitaries" Dick Arnold and Joe Cook were at the picnic, it doesn't mention whether they had dates. Subsequent articles reveal that Joe was getting quite serious about a young lady and hint at a love interest in Dick's life.

8. "The Pic Nic at Old River," *DTI*, 16 June 1886, 4. The newspaper article does not indicate that this was a political event, but given the timing and the speeches, it most likely was a Democratic rally. This would explain why court was recessed for the event as virtually all of the lawyers attending court would have been Democrats.
9. Untitled, *DTI*, 17 June 1886, 1.
10. Untitled, *DTI*, 19 June 1886, 4; "Emancipation Day," *DTI*, 21 June 1886, 4.
11. Untitled, *DTI*, 18 June 1886, 4.
12. "Society," *DTI*, 12 June 1886, 3. This suit may have been the one William had bought for his friend's wedding.
13. Untitled, *DTI*, 9 July 1886, 1.
14. Untitled, *DTI*, 1 July 1886, 4; untitled, *DTI*, 8 July 1886, 1. Only a few businesses had telephones by 1886, so service was quite limited.
15. Untitled, *DTI*, 9 July 1886, 1.
16. Untitled, *DTI*, 7 July 1886, 4; "To Electric Light Consumers," *DTI*, 15 July 1886, 4.
17. Untitled, *DTI*, 6 July 1886, 4; untitled, *DTI*, 8 July 1886, 4; William H. Arnold, "Senatorial Convention," *DTI*, 9 July 1886, 1. It is unclear from the *DTI* coverage of the convention whether William went as an alternate delegate or as an observer. William is not listed as an alternate in accounts of the Miller County Central Committee's selection of delegates, but later newspaper accounts imply he was an alternate.
18. "The Senatorial Convention," *DTI*, 10 July 1886, 4; "The Senatorial Convention," *DTI*, 14 July 1886, 4.
19. "Announcement," *DTI*, 26 June 1886, 2; "Announcement," *DTI*, 29 June 1886, 2; Woodward, *Origins of the New South*, 52.
20. Woodward, *Origins of the New South*, 52.
21. "Democratic Township Convention," *DTI*, 17 July 1886, 1; "Texarkana (Garland) Township Convention," *DTI*, 19 July 1886, 1; "The Democratic Miller County Convention," *DTI*, 26 July 1886, 1.
22. "The Democratic Miller County Convention," *DTI*, 26 July 1886, 1; untitled, *DTI*, 26 July 1886, 4. The *Independent* frequently left the "e" off Joe's name.
23. "The Miller County Democratic Convention," *DTI*, 31 July 1886, 1.
24. "Additional Locals," *DTI*, 13 June 1887, 1.

21 Progress and Problems

1. Untitled, *DTI*, 3 January 1887, 3; "Happy New Year!" *DTI*, 1 January 1887, 4.
2. "Additional Local," *DTI*, 3 January 1887, 1.
3. "Local News," *DTI*, 18 January 1887, 4; "Local News," *DTI*, 22 January 1887, 4; advertisement, *DTI*, 22 January 1887, 4. In the ad he ran January 22, Hays listed 43 properties. The title "professor" seemed to be applied to college-educated teachers. Once the person had the title, he kept it even though his profession changed.

4. "Local News," *DTI*, 3 February 1887, 4; "Local News," *DTI*, 28 May 1887, 4; "Local News," *DTI*, 12 April 1887, 4. Hays earned his law license June 21, 1887 ("Local News," *DTI*, 21 June 1887, 4). He later had a law partnership with William's other brother-in-law, John Cook.
5. "The City Elections," *DTI*, 14 January 1887, 4. Throughout its early history, Texarkana was home to several newspapers. At this time, the *Independent*, though not an organ of the Democratic Party, generally espoused Democratic principles. Republican papers came and went as did other independent papers. By 1887, the *Independent* reported that *The Dallas News*, Little Rock papers, and Hot Springs papers also had sizable circulations in the area, arriving the day of publication by regular train or cannonball express (untitled, *DTI*, 28 May 1887, 2).
6. "Texarkana," *DTI*, 1 January 1887, 4; "Local News," *DTI*, 26 January 1887, 4.
7. C.C. Burke, "Letter to the Editor," *DTI*, 19 January 1887, 4.
8. *Ibid*. Deutschmann Canal was named for Joseph Deutschmann, a German Jew who settled in the Texarkana area in the early 1870s. "He bought some undesirable land called the 'sand flat' in the area, drained it, and developed it into a black residential site (which later became known as Swampoodle). When a spring flood hit in 1874, the land was flooded along with other low areas of the town. Deutschmann's tenants were marooned, and one drowned. Having had some engineering training, he built a canal that not only drained his property but others as well. Known as 'Deutschmann's Canal,' it became an annual reminder of his contribution to the town" (LeMaster, 201).
9. *Ibid.*
10. Untitled, *DTI*, 17 January 1887, 4.
11. Untitled, *DTI*, 17 January 1887, 4; "Local News," *DTI*, 19 February 1887, 4.
12. "Local News," *DTI*, 28 February 1887, 4; J.F.S., "The St. Gamin, or Arab," *DTI*, 17 January 1887, 1; untitled, *DTI*, 2 April 1887, 1; untitled, *DTI*, 18 January 1887, 4; "Local News," *DTI*, 19 February 1887, 4.
13. Untitled, *DTI*, 18 January 1887, 4; untitled, *DTI*, 19 January 1887, 4; untitled, *DTI*, 2 April 1887, 1; "Additional Local," *DTI*, 18 January 1887, 1.
14. "Texas Liquor Laws," *DTI*, 25 April 1887, 4; untitled, *DTI*, 6 May 1887, 4. Even Sheriff Dixon's Telephone Saloon remained open on Sundays.
15. "The Mitchel-Mitchell Altercation," *DTI*, 17 January 1887, 1.
16. *Ibid.*; "An Unprecedented Record," *DTI*, 10 January 1887, 2; "Additional Local," *DTI*, 15 January 1887, 1. Warren defended his former law partner by publishing an abstract prepared by court clerk George W. Terry that showed that Mitchel had handled more than 100 cases, issued 73 decrees, and incurred only $2,200 in expenses during a 15-day court session in Nevada County.
17. "The Mitchel-Mitchell Altercation," *DTI*, 17 January 1887, 1.
18. "An Unfortunate Difficulty," *DTI*, 8 April 1887, 4. Jody also was known as "Jo" Kirby.
19. "More Shootings," *DTI*, 11 April 1887, 4; "Local News," *DTI*, 11 April 1887, 4.
20. "More Shootings," *DTI*, 11 April 1887, 4; "Local News," *DTI*, 11 April 1887, 4; "Local News," *DTI*, 16 June 1887, "Local News," *DTI*, 13 April 1887, 4.

21. Untitled, *DTI*, 29 May 1887, 1; "Miller County Circuit Court," *DTI*, 12 June 1887, 4; "Local News," 16 June 1887, 4; "Local News," *DTI*, 17 June 1887, 4; "Local News," *DTI*, 18 June 1887, 4; "Additional Local," *DTI*, 20 June 1887, 1; "Local News," *DTI*, 21 June 1887, 4.

22 City of the Second Class

1. "The City Elections," *DTI*, 14 January 1887, 4.
2. "Local News," *DTI*, 31 January 1887, 4; "Attention Democrats," 14 March 1887, 4. The *Texarkanian Republican* folded a few months later for lack of funding. Joe and William represented the St. Louis Type Foundry in its repossession of the paper's presses, type, and other material ("Local News," *DTI*, 28 May 1887, 4).
3. "The Cannons Boom," *DTI*, 2 February 1887, 4; "Federal Court," *DTI*, 29 January 1887, 4; "Maxey, Samuel Bell, 1825-1895," *Biographical Directory of the United States Congress*, 5 December 2003, bioguide.congress.gov/scripts/bio display.pl?index=M000265; "Reagan, John Henninger, 1818-1905," *Biographical Directory of the United States Congress*, 5 December 2003, bioguide.congress. gov/scripts/biodisplay.pl?index= R000098.
4. "The Cannons Boom," *DTI*, 2 February 1887, 4.
5. "East Side City Council," *DTI*, 14 February 1887, 1; "Additional Local," *DTI*, 31 March 1887, 1.
6. "Attention Democrats," 14 March 1887, 4; "The Ward Meetings," *DTI*, 18 March 1887, 4; "The Democratic City Convention," *DTI*, 23 March 1887, 4.
7. "The Democratic City Convention," *DTI*, 23 March 1887, 4.
8. *Ibid.*; "Additional Local," *DTI*, 23 March 1887, 1; "Local News," *DTI*, 24 March 1887, 4; "Additional Local," *DTI*, 25 March 1887, 1; "The Parade," *DTI*, 28 March 1887, 4.
9. "Additional Local," *DTI*, 1 April 1887, 1.
10. "Local News," *DTI*, 5 April 1887, 4; "Local News," *DTI*, 6 April 1887, 4.
11. "The City Elections," *DTI*, 6 April 1887, 4; "The Democratic City Convention," *DTI*, 23 March 1887, 4; "Local News," *DTI*, 2 May 1887, 4. Although Reconstruction had ended more than 10 years earlier, respected African Americans continued to play leadership roles in Texarkana through the 1880s. The East Side had a black policeman in 1887, and Judge Mitchel appointed H.M. Watkins, a black man, to serve on a committee along with two doctors to select the jurors for the December 1887 term of the Miller County Circuit Court (untitled, *DTI*, 18 June 1887, 4).
12. "East Side Council," *DTI*, 14 May 1887, 4.
13. "Notice," *DTI*, 14 May 1887, 1; "The Ordinances will be Enforced," *DTI*, 30 May 1887, 1.
14. Untitled, *DTI*, 19 May 1887, 1.
15. "Fire Limits," *DTI*, 29 June 1887, 1; "Local News," *DTI*, 16 June 1887, 4.
16. "An Opium Dive," *DTI*, 9 May 1887, 4.
17. "Gone to Eternity," *DTI*, 13 May 1887, 1.
18. *Ibid.*
19. "Official Bill," *DTI*, 28 March 1887, 1; "Federal Court," *DTI*, 11 July 1887, 4; "The Federal Court," *DTI*, 12 July 1887, 4.

23 Modernity

1. "Telephone Extension," *DTI*, 3 June 1887, 4.
2. Untitled, *DTI*, 22 January 1887, 2.
3. "Settled at Last," *Globe Democrat*, 29 March 1887, reprinted in *DTI*, 30 March 1887, 4; "Important Land Decision," *Camden Beacon*, reprinted in *DTI*, 6 April 1887, 3. Similar cases stemmed from railroad claims in Hot Springs, Arkansas.
4. "Additional Local," *DTI*, 8 April, 1887, 1. The brakeman's only justification was that the boy had hopped the train at the junction; freeloaders were not welcome.
5. Untitled, *DTI*, 10 January 1887, 4.
6. "The Fort Smith R.R.," *DTI*, 26 May 1887, 4.
7. "The Rail Road Meeting," *DTI*, 27 May 1887, 4; "Another Meeting," *DTI*, 28 May 1887, 4.
8. "All Aboard for Fort Smith," *DTI*, 6 June 1887, 4.
9. "Have no Depot," *DTI*, 27 May 1887, 4.
10. "Jay Gould," *DTI*, 18 January 1887, 1; "Local News," *DTI*, 19 January 1887, 4; "Local News," *DTI*, 22 January 1887, 4; "It Now Looks Like It," *DTI*, 10 February 1887, 4. The Marquand Hotel had been destroyed in a fire in 1886.
11. "That Depot," *DTI*, 12 April 1887, 1.
12. *Ibid.*
13. Untitled, *DTI*, 15 April 1887, 4; untitled, *DTI*, 16 May 1887, 4. In addition to the passenger trains, 54 freight trains arrived in Texarkana every day by May 1887.
14. "The Depot Muddle," *DTI*, 23 May 1887, 4; "Local News," *DTI*, 25 May 1887, 4.
15. "The Depot Meeting Last Night," *DTI*, 4 June 1887, 4; "East Side City Council," *DTI*, 8 June 1887, 4.
16. The cannonball trains made fewer stops and kept more reliable schedules than the regular trains (Untitled, *DTI*, 16 May 1887, 4). John H. Arnold, Jr., served as mayor of Washington from 1886-1887 and mayor of Prescott in 1890 (*Marriages Hempstead County, Arkansas, 1875-1900.* Hope, Arkansas: The Hempstead County Genealogical Society, n.d., i; *BHM*, 554).
17. "Terrible Disaster at Paris," *DTI*, 6 June 1887, 1.
18. "Local News," *DTI*, 24 February 1887, 4; "Texarkana Wallops Camden," *DTI*, 2 May 1887, 4; "Base Ball Park," *DTI*, 6 June 1887, 1; "Texarkana Again Victorious!" *DTI*, 13 June 1887, 1. Admission prices went up in June for league games. Men had paid 25 cents while women were admitted free.
19. "Personal," *DTI*, 24 May 1887, 4.

24 Practicing Politics

1. W.H. Arnold, "When Texarkana Celebrated Grover Cleveland's Election;" "Grover Cleveland," *The White House*, 7 December 2003, Washington: U.S. Government, www.whitehouse.gov/history/presidents. Vice President Hendricks died in office. There is some confusion in Arnold's book whether William attended the 1888 or the 1892 convention as he uses both dates.

2. Plante, 75; "Additional Local," *DTI*, 8 April 1887, 1.
3. "How About It!" *TDT*, 13 March 1894, 1.
4. *BHM*, 187, 204-205, 207. The *Independent had* changed its name to the *Daily Texarkana Democrat* by 1892. Soon after J. Gardner bought the paper from E.A. Warren, he bought another paper in town and merged it with the *Democrat*. In 1894, he changed the paper's name to *The Daily Texarkanian*.
5. Cash, 209; *BHM*, 185-187; ad, *DTD*, 19 November 1892, 3. "Colleges" offered a high school education. Texarkana's public school system offered a free elementary education to all students. But a "college" education was available only through the private schools.
6. *BHM*, 186-187; ad, *DTD*, 19 November 1892, 3; "Texarkana's Factories," *DTD*, 7 April 1893, 1; "Big Enterprise," *DTD*, 23 November 1892, 1.
7. *BHM*, 187; ad, *DTD*, 19 November 1892, 3. In 1893, Miller County's total taxable value was $3,120,720 ("Our Taxable Values," *DTD*, 14 January 1893, 1).
8. Ad, *DTD*, 19 November 1892, 3; *BHM*, 186-187.
9. LeMaster, 89-90, 92.
10. Untitled, *DTD*, 18 September 1893, 4; LeMaster, 92.
11. Even a superficial reading of the *Independent* of the 1880s and the *Texarkanian* and *Democrat* of the 1890s will reveal a drastic change in the editorial and societal treatment of African Americans. This change becomes more obvious in the late 1892, 1893, and 1894 issues, which reflect the opinions of a new editor. However, the change cannot be solely attributed to the new editor as African Americans began disappearing from most government positions at this time.
12. W.H. Arnold, "Message of Mayor Arnold," *DTD*, 20 April 1893, 1. The new light contract, which went into effect in July 1892, gave the city 22 streetlights for $2,500 a year. This was an annual savings of $1,020 over the old contract. The new water contract, which went into effect in February 1893, gave the city 40 fire hydrants for $2,200 a year. Under the old contract, the city paid $2,815 a year for 31 hydrants.
13. Untitled, *DTD*, 21 September 1893, 4; *Marriages Hempstead County, Arkansas, 1875-1900*. Using his credentials as mayor, William performed two weddings in Hempstead County in 1892.
14. "Borrowed Ideas," *DTD*, 30 July 1892, 2; untitled, *DTD*, 21 July 1892, 4; "Public Speaking," *DTD*, 12 August 1892, 1; "Lo, He Cometh!" *DTD*, 11 August 1892, 1.
15. "Lo, He Cometh!" *DTD*, 11 August 1892, 1; "The Torch Light Parade," *DTD*, 12 August 1892, 1.
16. "The Candidates," *DTD*, 12 August 1892, 1.
17. "Good-bye," *DTD*, 18 July 1892, 4; "Col. E.A. Warren Dying," *DTD*, 23 August 1892, 4; "Col. E.A. Warren Dead," *DTD*, 12 August 1892, 4.
18. "A Bloody Affray," *DTD*, 24 August 1892, 4.
19. *Ibid.*; "Lawyer Joe Cook No Better," *DTD*, 25 August 1892, 4; "Local News," *DTD*, 25 August 1892, 4; "Attorney Joe Cook Much Better," *DTD*, 3 September 1892, 4; "Circuit Court Proceedings," *DTD*, 20 December 1892, 1.
20. "The Rally – Torch Light Processional Saturday Night," *DTD*, 5 September 1892, 4.

21. "The Battle On! Democrats Use Every Effort to Win To-day," *DTD*, 5 November 1892, 1; "The Battle Won!" *DTD*, 6 September 1892, 1; "Proposed Amendment to the Constitution of the State of Arkansas," *DTD*, 19 July 1892, 3. Revenue from the poll tax benefited the public school system ("A Law," *DTD*, 24 February 1893, 1).

25 Fear and Hatred

1. "Cholera Spreading," *DTD*, 27 August 1892, 1.
2. "The Threatened Scourge," *DTD*, 27 August 1892, 1; "Cholera in the United States," *DTD*, 16 September 1892, 1.
3. W.H. Arnold, "Sewerage," *DTD*, 20 July 1892, 1.
4. *Ibid*. With bonds issued at six percent interest, William figured the sewer project would cost $4.80 per $1,000 valuation per year for 10 years.
5. *Ibid.*
6. "Official," *DTD*, 18 July 1892, 4; "Local News," *DTD*, 14 September 1892, 4; "Council Proceedings," *DTD*, 14 September 1892, 4; Arkansas Board of Health, "Notice to Citizens," *DTD*, 22 September 1892, 1. As part of the hog ordinance, the city set up a pound for loose hogs. The marshal, who was paid 25 cents for each hog impounded and 10 cents a day to care for each hog, was to post a bulletin outside the mayor's office with a description of the impounded hogs. Any animal not claimed within five days was to be sold to the public.
7. "Quarantine Against Gainesville, Texas." *DTD*, 20 September 1892, 4.
8. "Quarantine Proclamation," *DTD*, 22 September 1892, 1.
9. "State Board of Health," *DTD*, 21 September 1892, 1.
10. "Local News," *DTD*, 3 November 1892, 4; "Fireworks and Speaking," *DTD*, 5 November 1892, 1.
11. "Is the Force Bill Dead?" *DTD*, 8 October 1892, 2.
12. *Ibid.*; untitled, *DTD*, 3 November 1892, 4.
13. "A Second Emancipation," *St. Louis Post-Dispatch*, in *DTD*, 26 October 1892, 1.
14. "Mr. Harrison's Blunder," *NYT*, 6 November 1892, 2; "Clubs Will Be Trumps," *NYT*, 6 November 1892, 2; "A Resort to Force," *DTD*, 5 November 1892, 1.
15. "A Resort to Force," *DTD*, 5 November 1892, 1; "Clubs Will Be Trumps."
16. "Clubs Will Be Trumps."
17. "Marshals in Arkansas," *NYT*, 4 November 1892, 2.
18. *Ibid.*; "Here is the Law," *DTD*, 7 November 1892, 1.
19. "Here is the Law," *DTD*, 7 November 1892, 1.
20. "Fireworks and Oratory."
21. "Election Bulletins," *DTD*, 7 November 1892, 4; "Local News," *DTD*, 8 November 1892, 4; "Glorious News. Cleveland Elected Beyond a Doubt," *DTD*, 9 November 1892, 1.
22. "Triple Killing," *DTD*, 10 November 1892, 1.
23. *Ibid.*
24. "Resolution and Respect to the Memory of Z.T. Few," *DTD*, 11 November 1892, 1.
25. "Local News," *DTD*, 11 November 1892, 4; "Last Tribute," *DTD*, 14 November 1892, 1.

26 The Crusade

1. "Nine Indictments," *DTD*, 22 November 1892, 1.
2. "The Australian Ballot," *DTD*, 6 May 1893, 1.
3. "An Imposition and Outrage," *DTD*, 17 May 1893, 1.
4. "A New Decision," *Arkansas* Democrat, reprinted in *DTD*, 14 April 1893, 1; "Fifteen Hundred Dollars," *DTD*, 2 December 1892, 1.
5. "Fifteen Hundred Dollars."
6. *Ibid.*
7. "A New Decision;" "Federal Court Notes," *DTD*, 22 November 1893, 1. Under federal procedure, the minimum amount upon which suit could be brought in federal court was $500. Since the jury awarded Tabor only $25, Dorrian did not have to pay court costs ("Federal Court Notes," *DTD*, 23 November 1893, 1).
8. "Grand Jury Report," *DTD*, 16 December 1892, 1.
9. *Ibid.*; "One More Unfortunate," *DTD*, 9 December 1892, 1; "Local News," *DTD*, 1 December 1892, 4.
10. "Grand Jury Report;" "County Court Proceedings," *DTD*, 29 December 1892, 1.
11. "The New Postoffice," *DTD*, 3 January 1893, 1; W.H. Arnold, Sr., "Historical Statement of Texarkana," 348; "W.W. Shaw Secures the Plum," *DTD*, 16 December 1892, 1.
12. "Proceedings of the Citizens' Meeting," *DTD*, 12 January 1893, 1.
13. W.H. Arnold, "Message of Mayor Arnold."
14. An indication of Dixon's influence in the town and the local Democratic Party can be found in the fact that neither the *Independent* nor the *Texarkana Democrat* ever criticized the sheriff or reported on the city's raids of his establishments. In the 1880s, editor Warren promoted Dixon's Telephone Exchange Saloon at every opportunity. And when the saloon closed, the paper attributed it to a problem Dixon had with his manager. In the 1890s, Gardner continued Warren's habit of always speaking kindly and respectfully of the sheriff.
15. "Local News," *DTD*, 30 November 1892, 4; "A Real Sunday," *DTD*, 5 December 1892, 1.
16. "Brave and Manly, *DTD*, 7 January 1893, 1.
17. Untitled, *DTD*, 18 May 1893, 4; "East Side City Court," *DTD*, 1 June 1893, 1; "Good for the West Side," *DTD*, 5 May 1893, 1; untitled, *DTD*, 15 February 1893, 1.
18. "Petty Thieving," *DTD*, 15 December 1892, 1; untitled, *DTD*, 16 February 1893, 4. A "short hand" robber would today be called a "pickpocket." Towns in the warmer areas of the country, especially those along the railroad, traditionally attracted the homeless during the winter months. In 1893, northern Louisiana had suffered a major crop failure due to weather. As a result, many people were starving in that region, and some of them may have swelled the ranks of the homeless. Also, the homeless who might otherwise have gone to northern Louisiana had to find alternative winter quarters.
19. "In the Dead House," *DTD*, 3 January 1893, 1; "The Dying Convicts," *DTD*, 31 December 1892, 1; "Poisoned Convicts," *DTD*, 20 December 1892, 1. About 110 convicts, most of them African Americans, were working in ankle-deep mud along the railroad bed near Helena when 18 came down with symptoms resembling arsenic poisoning. Several eventually died from the illness.

Given the living conditions – they were crammed into four or five boxcars at night and took their meals outside in the mud – the deaths may have been the result of the bad weather and unsanitary conditions. However, poison was not ruled out as unemployed laborers in the area had protested when convicts were brought in to do the jobs that they thought rightfully belonged to them. Rumors spread that some of these protesters had poisoned the convicts' food, which was left outside and unattended all day.

20. "Report of Board of Health," *DTD*, 23 December 1892, 4; "East Side Board of Health," *DTD*, 6 April 1893, 1.
21. "A Painful Accident," *DTD*, 25 April 1893, 1.
22. Untitled, *DTD*, 29 April 1893, 4; "Local News," *DTD*, 5 May 1893, 4; "Local News," *DTD*, 26 May 1893, 4; untitled, *DTD*, 5 June 1893, 4.

27 The Rule of Violence

1. Wyatt-Brown, *Honor and Violence in the Old South*, 74.
2. "Sensational Shooting," *DTD*, 3 July 1893, 1.
3. *Ibid.*
4. *Ibid.*
5. "Woodruff Indicted," *DTD*, 14 December 1892, 1; "Another Steal Discovered," *DTD*, 26 January 1893, 1; Woodward, *Origins of the New South*, 69.
6. "Sheriff Blythe Short!" *DTD*, 23 August 1893, 1.
7. *Ibid.* "Demand of Bondsmen," *TDT*, 2 May 1894, 1.
8. "Mayor Lary Indicted," *TDT*, 21 March 1894, 4.
9. Untitled, *DTD*, 30 June 1893, 4; untitled, *DTD*, 1 July 1893, 4. Allen had revived the *Inter-State News*, which was published in Texarkana, Texas, in February 1887. The paper was Democrat in its politics.
10. "A Deplorable Tragedy," *DTD*, 5 August 1893, 1.
11. *Ibid.*; "Released on Bail," *DTD*, 8 August 1893, 1; untitled, *DTD*, 30 September 1893, 1; "Change of Venue Granted," *DTD*, 13 October 1893, 4.
12. "Judge King Acquitted," *DTD*, 14 December 1893, 1; "Released on Bail."
13. "The Inter-State College," *DTD*, 20 August 1892, 4; "Fistic Encounter," *DTD*, 6 October 1893, 1.
14. "Fistic Encounter," *DTD*, 6 October 1893, 1; untitled, *DTD*, 7 October 1893, 4.
15. The Texarkana newspapers for 1892-1894 chronicle numerous lynchings and "roastings" in Arkansas and throughout the country – even in the North ("A Minnesota Outrage," *DTD*, 10 May 1893, 1; "An Illinois Lynching," *DTD*, 5 June 1893, 1). White men as well as black men were lynched, but the only accounts of an offender being burned at the stake involved African Americans. Though mob law generally was used in heinous crimes, there were a few cases in which black men were lynched for petty theft ("Work of a mob," *DTD*, 21 November 1893, 1). No one resorted to mob law when a widowed, childless white woman was raped by a black man. Instead, the culprit was arrested and tried and sentenced in court ("To What End," *DTD*, 29 July 1893, 1). A black mob reportedly burned D.T. Nelson, a black man accused of hacking another black man to death ("Terrible Punishment," *DTD*, 15 November 1893, 1).

The African American community helped with the burning of a black transient in Fort Gaines, Georgia, who had robbed and murdered a businessman ("Death at the Stake," *DTD*, 18 April 1893, 1). More than 1,000 African Americans in Ohio threatened to lynch six white men who had raped a respected black woman ("Justice Demanded," *DTD*, 29 September 1892, 1). Mob law is not to be confused with random lynchings used by hate groups such as the Ku Klux Klan to intimidate African Americans.

16. "A Negro Burned Alive," *NYT*, 21 February 1892, 6. This article features a report from the *NYT* special correspondent in Arkansas and an article from the *St. Louis Republic*.
17. "Mob Law in Arkansas," *NYT*, 21 February 1892, 4.

28 North vs. South

1. "Another Negro Burned," *NYT*, 2 February 1893, 1; "The Fiend Caught," *DTD*, 1 February 1893, 1. Henry Smith was an alias for Bob Dowery, but the newspaper accounts refer to him as Smith.
2. "Another Negro Burned," *NYT*, 2 February 1893, 1; "The Fiend Caught," *DTD*, 1 February 1893, 1.
3. "Another Negro Burned," *NYT*, 2 February 1893, 1.
4. "The Fiend Caught," *DTD*, 1 February 1893, 1.
5. "Local News," *DTD*, 1 February 1893, 1; "The Fiend Caught," *DTD*, 1 February 1893, 1. *NYT* reported that 5,000 people were waiting at the Texarkana depot.
6. "Another Negro Burned," *NYT*, 2 February 1893, 1; "The Fiend Caught," *DTD*, 1 February 1893, 1.
7. "The Fiend Caught," *DTD*, 1 February 1893, 1; "Another Negro Burned," *NYT*, 2 February 1893, 1.
8. "The Fiend Caught," *DTD*, 1 February 1893, 1; "Another Negro Burned," *NYT*, 2 February 1893, 1.
9. "The Fiend Tortured," *DTD*, 2 February 1893, 1; "Another Negro Burned," *NYT*, 2 February 1893, 1.
10. "The Fiend Tortured," *DTD*, 2 February 1893, 1. *NYT* gave a similar account that was just as detailed of the torture.
11. *Ibid.*; "Another Negro Burned," *NYT*, 2 February 1893, 1.
12. "Julian Hawthorne," *DTD*, 7 February 1893, 1.
13. "Drifting Toward Barbarism," *DTD*, 7 February 1893, 1.
14. "Coming, 2500 Strong," *DTD*, 15 February 1893, 1.
15. "Attacked by Negroes," *DTD*, 18 February 1893, 1.
16. "A Plucky Judge," *DTD*, 10 May 1893, 1.
17. *Ibid.* A white man had enticed two little girls into the woods at Iron Mountain, Minnesota, and raped them. One of the girls was expected to die. When he was found hiding behind a pile of rubbish in the rear of a saloon, he was half dragged, half carried to an opening in the woods where he was hanged. Just as his body made the final death twitch, the miners who had captured him fired a score of bullets into his body ("A Minnesota Outrage," *DTD*, 10 May 1893, 1).
18. "A Minnesota Outrage."

19. "Governor Fishback Speaks," *DTD*, 13 May 1893, 1. Three black men were hanged from telegraph poles along the line of the Cotton Belt Railroad near Beardon May 9, 1893. The three were accused of robbing and murdering Jesse Norman, a prosperous white businessman. Norman's skull was crushed with an ax before he was left for dead in a flooded ditch ("The Beardon Lynching," *DTD*, 10 May 1893, 1).
20. "Governor Fishback Speaks."
21. "Lynching Aftermath," *DTD*, 26 May 1893, 1; "Suit for Damages," *DTD*, 15 July 1893, 1.

29 The Economic Divide

1. In "A New Era for the South," *DTD*, 14 April 1893, 2.
2. *Ibid.*; Woodward, *The Burden of Southern History*, 17; Moneyhon, *The Impact of the Civil War*, 69. Per capita wealth in the South in 1880 was equivalent to that of Germany and Russia (Woodward). Before the Civil War, the average per capita income of Southerners (including slaves) was $1,086 – about two-thirds that of Northerners (Moneyhon). In 1860, the South possessed 30 percent of the national wealth; 10 years later, it had only 12 percent.
3. In "A New Era for the South."
4. "The Governors' Convention," *DTD*, 14 April 1893, 1.
5. "Arkansas' Advancement," *DTD*, 14 April 1893, 1. The governor's statistics included a breakdown of churches and membership, by denomination, in the 1890s. The Baptists were the largest denomination in the state with 1,772 churches and nearly 100,000 members. The colored Baptists had 558 churches and nearly 37,500 members. The Methodist Episcopal Church had 1,033 churches and 195 parsonages worth $1 million plus education buildings (used for academies and colleges) valued at $200,000. Ten years earlier, the denomination had 525 churches worth $45,000. In 1893, the colored Methodists had 173 churches, nearly $233,500 in property, and almost 28,000 members.
6. *Ibid.*
7. William Meade Fishback, "New England Illiteracy," *DTD*, 9 June 1893, 1. In this letter, the governor refers to Henry Blair as "senator." Blair served as senator from New Hampshire from 1889-1891. But in 1893, he was once again representing his state in the lower house.
8. Woodward, *Origins of the New South*, 264-265, 272-273; "Tillman Explodes," *TDT*, 10 April 1894, 1.
9. Untitled, *DTD*, 18 July 1892, 1; untitled, *DTD*, 19 July 1892, "Kelso's Bank," *DTD*, 21 July 1892, 1; "Official Statement of the Gate City National Bank," *DTD*, 28 July 1892, 1.
10. Untitled, *DTD*, 19 July 1892, 4; "Official Statement of the Gate City National Bank;" "Kelso's Bank;" untitled, *DTD*, 19 July 1892, 1; untitled, *DTD*, 25 July 1892, 1. In one untitled article, *DTD* claims this was the first bank failure since 1874. But in "Kelso's Bank," it says it is the second. The closure was not cleared up, and Kelso was implicated in the bank's failure.
11. "To Suspend," *DTD*, 22 September 1892, 4.

12. "Six Million Bales," *DTD*, 22 November 1892, 1; "Reduced Freight Rates," *Washington Telegraph*, reprinted in *DTD*, 2 November 1892, 1.
13. "Before the Courts," *DTD*, 5 January 1893, 1; "Business Complications," *DTD*, 14 January 1893, 1; untitled, *DTD*, 10 April 1893, 4; untitled, *DTD*, 11 April 1893, 4.
14. "Arkansas and Texas," *DTD*, 31 March 1893, 1; "The Hopeful View," *DTD*, 15 May 1893, 1.
15. "Railroad Extension," *DTD*, 16 November 1892, 1; "Pushing Its Line," *DTD*, 16 January 1893, 1.
16. "Pushing Its Line;" "To Commence Work," *DTD*, 27 January 1893, 1.
17. "Unseemly Obstruction," *DTD*, 6 February 1893, 1.
18. Untitled, *DTD*, 7 February 1893, 1; "Restraining Order Granted," *DTD*, 8 February 1893, 1; "The Bond Filed," *DTD*, 21 February 1893, 1.
19. "New Offices," *DTD*, 13 March 1893, 1; "An Important Deal," *DTD*, 21 March 1893, 1; "Contracts Let," *DTD*, 29 March 1893, 1; "Texarkana's Pride, The Texarkana Furniture Manufacturing Company," *DTD*, 22 September 1892, 1.
20. The *DTD* was filled with articles about the preparations for the World's Fair in 1892 and articles on the opening, exhibits, accidents, and reaction from April through September 1893.
21. "Alphonse King's Exhibition," *DTD*, 26 June 1893, 1. Editor Gardner was appalled at the audacity of the African Americans to sit in the pavilion and was greatly amused at the beating the two young black men received. The language he used to describe this incident is quite racist.

30 Year of Disaster

1. "Glorious News," *DTD*, 15 June 1893, 1; "Cyclone at Hope," *DTD*, 1 June 1893, 1. Guernsey was about five miles west of Hope.
2. "Public Meeting," *DTD*, 7 June 1893, 1; untitled, *DTD*, 13 June 1893, 4.
3. "Congress Convened," *DTD*, 9 August 1893, 1; "Colorado's Needy Thousands," *DTD*, 28 July 1893, 1.
4. "Currency Still Scarce," *DTD*, 7 August 1893, 1; "700,000 Spindles Idle," *DTD*, 7 August 1893, 1.
5. "Congress Convened."
6. *Ibid.*
7. "Party Caucus Held," *DTD*, 7 August 1893, 1.
8. "Sad But True," *DTD*, 17 August 1893, 4; "A Stab at Cleveland," *DTD*, 25 September 1893, 1. Sen. Stewart switched back to the Republican Party in 1901.
9. "More Mugwumpery," *DTD*, 21 April 1893, 1. Republicans favoring reform helped put Cleveland in office in 1884. These Republicans were known as "mugwumps."
10. *Ibid.*

11. "The Southern States," *DTD*, 17 January 1893, 1. By Houk's reasoning, Arkansas and Texas had only 29 percent of the officeholders they should have had – the lowest in the South. (Texas had 156 people in office but was "entitled" to 531.) Nationwide, three states had lower percentages: Oklahoma, 13 percent (2/15); Utah, 14 percent (7/49); and Washington, 28 percent (24/83). In real numbers, 17 states – all with smaller populations – had fewer appointments than did Arkansas, but 25 states had smaller populations. That meant eight states that were smaller than Arkansas had greater representation. Houk's numbers showed that Maryland, Virginia, and the District of Columbia were well in excess of their share of appointments. But he did not take into consideration that many of the officeholders living in these three areas came from other states.
12. "The Contest for Postmaster," *DTD*, 11 July 1893, 4.
13. "Miller Central Committee," *DTD*, 14 July 1893, 1; "Col. Kelley to Contest," *DTD*, 19 July 1893, 4.
14. "Miller Central Committee," *DTD*, 14 July 1893, 1; "The Primary Election," *DTD*, 19 July 1893, 1.
15. Col. Kelley to Contest"; "The Primary Election."
16. "Col. W.R. Kelley Appointed Postmaster," *DTD*, 23 October 1893, 1.
17. "Cutting Down Expenses," *DTD*, 12 August 1893, 1.
18. "The Wilson Bill Passed," *DTD*, 29 August 1893, 1.
19. "Outlook Brightening," *DTD*, 29 August 1893, 4.
20. Untitled, *DTD*, 29 August 1893, 4; "Railway News," *DTD*, 2 September 1893, 4.
21. "Texas Sensation," *DTD*, 30 September 1893, 1; "Railroad News," *DTD*, 10 February 1893, 1; "Local Application," *DTD*, 21 October 1893, 1.
22. "The Farmer Suffered," *DTD*, 12 January 1894, 1. This article was a reprint of a U.S. Department of Agriculture year-end report of average farm prices.
23. "Let the Law Prevail," *DTD*, 17 October 1893, 1.
24. "Mississippi White Caps," *DTD*, 9 August 1893, 1; untitled, *DTD*, 18 October 1893, 1; untitled, *DTD*, 21 August 1893, 4. Similar warnings had been posted along the Gate City Railroad two years earlier, but nothing had come of them.
25. "Silver Defeated," *DTD*, 31 October 1893, 1; "The Fight is Over," *DTD*, 2 November 1893, 1; "R.G. Dun's Report," *DTD*, 11 November 1893, 1. The Senate's debate on the issue filled five volumes of the Congressional Record with 20 million words. Dun's report for the second week of November 1892 showed 210 businesses had failed. This most likely was up from previous years as the depression was already setting in by November 1892.
26. "Cash in the Treasury," *DTD*, 12 January 1894, 1; "Income Tax Bill," *DTD*, 24 January 1894, 1. Of the $88,914,096 in the treasury December 31, 1893, $6,889,300 was in currency. The rest was in gold. The December customs receipts were half what they had been the previous year.
27. "Several Big Failures," *DTD*, 26 December 1893, 1; "Texarkana's Pride, The Texarkana Furniture Manufacturing Co.," *DTD*, 22 September 1892, 1; "Gone Under," *DTD*, 26 December 1893, 4.

31 A Change of Times

1. "The Cherokee Strip," *DTD*, 15 March 1893, 1; "Boomers Starving," *DTD*, 27 October 1893, 1; untitled, *DTD*, 23 September 1893, 4. The Cherokee Bill, passed by Congress in March 1893, paid the Cherokee Nation more than $8.3 million for the Strip, which was opened to homesteaders in the Great Land Race later that year. Those who secured a 160-acre parcel had to pay $2.50 an acre in the eastern part of the Strip and $1.50 an acre in the western portion. About 75,000 were unsuccessful in their bid for land. The Cherokee Bill was part of the government's strategy to bring statehood to the area occupied by the Five Civilized Tribes by inducing them to become U.S. citizens, forsake their tribal relations, and take up their land in severalty ("The Cherokee Strip").
2. Untitled, *TDT*, 12 March 1894, 4; untitled, *DTD*, 6 December 1893, 4.
3. "Question Revived," *DTD*, 22 September 1893, 1.
4. "Free Delivery," *DTD*, 4 January 1893, 1; "The Texarkana Postoffice," *DTD*, 13 February 1893, 1.
5. "Free Delivery Yet Possible," *TDT*, 1 May 1894, 1; "Demands Prompt Attention," *TDT*, 5 February 1894, 1; untitled, *TDT*, 7 March 1894, 4.
6. "Council Meeting," *TDT*, 25 April 1894, 1; "Free Delivery Yet Possible." Although he was no longer mayor in April 1894, William continued to work on securing free postal delivery on behalf of the city.
7. "Sewerage in Sight," *DTD*, 15 November 1893, 1; "Sewerage Secured!" *DTD*, 10 January 1894, 1.
8. "The New Court House," *DTD*, 13 April 1893, 1; "New Courthouse," *DTD*, 24 January 1894, 4; "Corner Stone Ceremonies," *DTD*, 20 October 1893, 1; "Corner Stone Ceremonies," *DTD*, 24 October 1893, 1.
9. "New Courthouse," *DTD*, 24 January 1894, 4. The finished courthouse cost the county $75,000 (W.H. Arnold, Sr., "Historical Statement of Texarkana," 347).
10. "An Ordinance," *DTD*, 14 September 1893, 1; "Martin Leverett Killed," *DTD*, 11 December 1893, 1.
11. "Martin Leverett Killed;" "Iron Mountain Crossing," *DTD*, 12 December 1893, .1.
12. *BHM*, 186; "Council Meeting," *DTD*, 6 February 1893, 1; "Message of Mayor Arnold," *DTD*, 20 April 1893, 1; "East Side City Council Proceedings," *DTD*, 1 July 1893, 1; "Telephones in Use," *DTD*, 24 July 1893, 1. Most of the telephones were located in businesses; only a few professionals had installed one in their home. Neither City Hall nor William had a phone at this time. Telephone numbers were one or two digits, based on the order in which they were installed – the number for the first telephone installed was 1, the second was 2, etc.
13. "A Destructive Fire," *DTD*, 17 August 1893, 1.
14. "Fulton in Ashes," *DTD*, 5 October 1893, 1.
15. Untitled, *DTD*, 5 December 1893, 4; untitled, *DTD*, 9 December 1893, 4.
16. "Last Night's Fire," Untitled, *DTD*, 3 January 1894, 4.
17. "Cause Celebre," *DTD*, 15 January 1893, 1.
18. *Ibid.*

19. Untitled, *TDT*, 12 February 1894, 4.
20. Untitled, *TDT*, 24 February 1894, 4; "Tried to Make It Good," *TDT*, 2 March 1894, 4.
21. Board members of the Fourth Street Methodist Church, "A Card," *TDT*, 12 February 1894, 4.
22. *Ibid.*
23. *Ibid.* Bishop Hargood of the Methodist Episcopal Church South had recently published a book titled *Brothers in Black*.
24. Untitled, *TDT*, 12 February 1894, 4.

32 Elections and Epidemics

1. "To Be Wiped Out," *TDT*, 7 February 1894, 1; "The Federal Election Law," *TDT*, 8 February 1894, 1. The House had already repealed the law.
2. "The Heavy Rains," *TDT*, 19 March 1894, 4; untitled, *TDT*, 19 March 1894, 4; "Local News," *TDT*, 20 March 1894, 4.
3. "City Elections," *DTD*, 23 January 1894, 1.
4. Democratic Voter, "How About It!" *TDT*, 13 March 1894, 1.
5. *Ibid.*
6. "Result of Primary," *TDT*, 15 March 1894, 4; "Citizens Ticket ad, *TDT*, 17 March 1894, 4; untitled, *TDT*, 17 March 1894, 4; untitled, *TDT*, 19 March 1894, 4.
7. Untitled, *TDT*, 28 March 1894, 4.
8. "Good Government!" *TDT*, 4 April 1894, 1; untitled, *TDT*, 10 April 1894, 4; "Our New Officers," *TDT*, 10 April 1894, 4.
9. "Local News," *TDT*, 10 April 1894, 4; "Council Meeting," *TDT*, 25 April 1894, 1.
10. "Alarming Symptoms," *TDT*, 12 April 1894, 4; "Scarry [sic] Rumors," *TDT*, 13 April 1894, 1; untitled, *TDT*, 21 April 1894, 4.
11. Untitled, *TDT*, 23 April 1894, 4; untitled, *TDT*, 25 April 1894, 4.
12. "Board of Health Resolutions," untitled, *TDT*, 25 April 1894, 1; "Sanitary Notice," *TDT*, 25 April 1894, 1.
13. Untitled, *TDT*, 26 April 1894, 4; "Small Pox News, *TDT*, 26 April 1894, 4; "Small Pox Situation," *TDT*, 27 April 1894, 1.
14. "Small Pox Situation;" "Citizens Mass Meeting," *TDT*, 30 April 1894, 1; "Quarantine Against Us," *TDT*, 26 April 1894, 4. Groups of people from all over the country, especially from the West, commandeered railcars, rode their horses, marched – whatever they had to do – to join Coxey's Army for a "peace protest" in Washington. Destitute, most of them were reduced to begging for food when they passed through towns. Jacob Coxey, a greenbacker and populist, organized the march to protest the high interest on bonds and seek relief "for the suffering people, burdened by unjust class legislation for thirty years past." As the various "divisions" of the army traveled through towns on their way to the nation's capital, they were sometimes blocked by police. By the time the army paraded in Washington May 1, 1894, only 400 soldiers had made it the entire distance ("Coxey's Little Army," *TDT*, 1 May 1894, 1; "Coxey at Washington," *TDT*, 2 May 1894, 1).
15. "Quarantine Against Us."

16. "Small Pox Scare," *TDT*, 28 April 1894, 1; untitled, *TDT*, 26 April 1894, 4; "State Board of Health," *DTD*, 21 September 1892, 1. During the cholera scare in 1892, the state Board of Health was helpless to do any thing as it had no funding.
17. "Citizens Mass Meeting;" untitled, *TDT*, 30 April 1894, 4. Neither Dr. Simmons nor Dr. Spearman offered free vaccinations. Simmons still refused to believe this was a smallpox epidemic. And Spearman, one of the first doctors to advertise the vaccinations, charged for them.
18. Untitled, *TDT*, 1 May 1894, 4; "Small Pox Situation;" untitled, *TDT*, 1 May 1894, 4.
19. "Small Pox Situation;" untitled, *TDT*, 4 May 1894, 1.
20. Untitled, *TDT*, 5 May 1894, 4; untitled, *TDT*, 8 May 1894, 4.
21. Untitled, *TDT*, 5 May 1894, 4; untitled, *TDT*, 10 May 1894, 4; untitled, *TDT*, 3 May 1894, 4; "Red River Booming," *TDT*, 4 May 1894, 1.
22. "Small-pox Situation," *TDT*, 8 May 1894, 4; untitled, *TDT*, 11 May 1894, 4.

33 Reconstructing the Ideal

1. *BHM*, 448.
2. *Ibid.*, 448-449.
3. Robert most likely moved to Texarkana following his father's death (*Ibid.*).
4. Elmira F. Snodgrass, "Reminiscences of the Old South," *CWA*, 129-130.
5. Ruth Arnold was named for William's Aunt Ruth (his father's sister), who had been crippled from childhood. David Christopher Arnold was named for William's father and Jessie's mother's (Cornelia Christopher Cook) family.
6. IRA.
7. IMA.
8. Wright, 98; "He Made City Convention Conscious," newspaper clipping, Scrapbook 10. In 1926, the bar associations for Arkansas, Texas, and Louisiana held a joint convention in Texarkana with 600 lawyers in attendance.
9. Newspaper clippings, Scrapbook 2, *Judge Morris Arnold Manuscript Collection.*
10. IRA.
11. In his book, William questions Friedell's claim of being a Confederate soldier.
12. Frances Ross, handwritten notes taken on the federal application file of William H. Arnold.
13. *Ibid.*
14. *Ibid.*; "Arnold not Discouraged," undated newspaper clipping in Scrapbook 2. Remmel had set up an appointment May 5 with the attorney general to "present our candidate for judge of the Western District of Arkansas." He was accompanied by Worthington (Ross).
15. Ross; "Arnold not Discouraged."
16. "Judge Arnold to Make Race for Governor," *TDT*, 10 March 1915, in Scrapbook 2.
17. *Ibid.*; "Judge W.H. Arnold Will Offer Himself for Governor," *Four States Press*, 11 March 1915, in Scrapbook 2; "Gubernatorial Race in Arkansas to Have Many in the Running," *TDT*, 18 March 1915, in Scrapbook 2.

18. "Judge Arnold Has Not Made Announcement," *The Texarkanian*, 5 June 1915, in Scrapbook 2.
19. *Ibid.*; IMA.

34 A Civic Duty

1. Calvin R. Ledbetter, Jr., "The Constitutional Convention of 1917-1918," *AHQ* 34 (Spring 1975), 5.
2. "The Constitutional Convention of 1917-1918;" Wright, 104.
3. Ledbetter, 5-6.
4. *Ibid.*, 9-11.
5. "Judge Arnold Decides to Offer as Delegate to Important Session," *The Texarkanian*, 21 February 1917, in Scrapbook 3, *Judge Morris Arnold Manuscript Collection*.
6. "Hon. James D. Head for Delegate at Large," undated newspaper clipping, Scrapbook 3; W.H. Arnold, paid political ad, *The Texarkanian*, 23 April 1917, in Scrapbook 3.
7. "William H. Arnold," *Arkansas Gazette*, 8 April 1917, in Scrapbook 3.
8. *Ibid.*, 11, 14, 20; "Light Vote Is Cast in County Primary," *Arkansas Democrat*, 14 April 1917, 6.
9. "No Republican Vote Expected Tuesday," *Arkansas Democrat*, 25 June 1917, 4; "Little Interest Shown," *Arkansas Democrat*, 14 April 1917, 3.
10. "Constitution Repairing," *NYT*, 1 June 1917, 7.
11. *Arkansas Democrat*, April 1917 - November 1917; "Flag Raising Yesterday at Miller County Court House," *Four States Press*, 28 April 1917, in Scrapbook 3.
12. *Arkansas Democrat*, April 1917 - November 1917; "Ask Judges to Awaken People," *Arkansas Democrat*, 3 November 1917, 4.
13. "Brough Declares for Compulsory Arbitration Law," *Arkansas Democrat*, 15 November 1917, 1.
14. "Many Convention Delegates Arrive," *Arkansas Democrat*, 17 November 1917, 8; "State Convention Is Scene of Many Unusual Features," *Arkansas Democrat*, 21 November 1917, 14; Ledbetter, 14-15.
15. "Convention Takes Recess Until July," *Arkansas Democrat*, 21 November 1917, 1; *Proposals of the Committees of the Constitutional Convention of Arkansas, to be Presented to the Convention at its Meeting on the First Monday in July, Nineteen-eighteen*, Little Rock: Arkansas State Government, n.d.
16. *Proposals*, 1-2; Ledbetter, 19.
17. Ledbetter, 10, 15, 19-20, 29.
18. *Ibid.*, 33.
19. *History of Arkansas and Its People*, Vol. 3 (American Historical Society, 1930), 253-256, in W.H. Arnold, *The Arnold Family* (Minneapolis: West Publishing Co., 1935), 14, 15.
20. *Ibid.*, 15, 16; IRA.
21. "About the American Law Institute" (American Law Institute), www.ali.org, 6 February 2005.
22. *Ibid.*

35 In Search of Public Honor

1. Leah M. Taylor, *The Democratic Convention of 1924*, unpublished master's thesis in history, Louisiana State University, 1966, 206-208.
2. *Ibid.* Charles C. Alexander, "White Robes in Politics: The Ku Klux Klan in Arkansas, 1922-24," *AHQ* 22 (autumn 1963), 72-73. The Teapot Dome scandal broke in January 1924 when it was learned that the Republican secretary of the Interior had arranged illegal oil leases for his friends. William McAdoo, seen by many as the Democratic frontrunner, was not involved in the scandal, but, as a lawyer, he had represented one of the defendants.
3. Alexander, 72-73.
4. Taylor, 157-203. The religious liberty plank was a mild comment aimed against the Klan, but it did not mention the organization by name. Opponents to the plank wanted implicit repudiation of the Klan.
5. *Ibid.*; Alexander, 210.
6. Taylor, 13, 17, 87, 208-210, 211, 355.
7. *Ibid.*, 236-237; 309.
8. *Ibid.*, 18.
9. Alexander, 211, 213.
10. George B. Rose, "William H. Arnold," *Arkansas Law Review and Bar Association Journal* 1 (summer 1947), 72; "Elected Special Judge," *Arkansas Democrat*, 23 June 1917, 7; "Sketches of Seven Texarkana Men Appearing in Latest Issue of 'Who's Who in America'," *Texarkana Gazette*, in Scrapbook 9, *Judge Morris Arnold Manuscript Collection*; "Judge W.H. Arnold Will Offer Himself for Governorship;" "Remarks of W.H. Arnold Special Judge in Opening Circuit Court November 26, '29," *Twin City News*, undated, in Scrapbook 7, *Judge Morris Arnold Manuscript Collection*.
11. "Judge Arnold Will Seek Chief Justice Place at Election," *Texarkana Press*, undated, in Scrapbook 9; "W.H. Arnold to Seek Post of Chief Justice," newspaper clipping, Scrapbook 9; "Supported by Home Folks," *Texarkana Press*, 14 July 1933, in Scrapbook 9.
12. "Democratic Nominee," *Arkansas Gazette*, 15 July 1933, in Scrapbook 9.
13. Gwyn Lewis, "A Man Who Cannot Lose Himself," *London Sunday Express*, 6 October 1935, in Scrapbook 10.
14. *Ibid.*; "Prominent Texarkana Attorney Becomes Subject of Broadcast During His Travels in Europe," *Texarkana Daily News*, 8 October 1835, in Scrapbook 10.
15. "Prominent Texarkana Attorney Becomes Subject of Broadcast During His Travels in Europe;" "A Man Who Cannot Lose Himself."

36 The Arnolds in the 20th Century

1. IMA.
2. Ironically, some of the men from David Arnold's company were taken as prisoners to Alton, Illinois, during the Civil War (19th [Dockery's] Arkansas).
3. IRA.

4. Transcript of Richard Sheppard Arnold interview, June 17 and July 10, 1969, State College of Arkansas Oral History Research Office, 1, 4; Wright, 372.
5. IMA; Wright, 375.
6. Wright, 376.
7. *Ibid.*, 374, 376.
8. In Wright, 373-374.
9. *Ibid.*, 376
10. IMA; transcript of Richard Sheppard Arnold interview.
11. Cash, 218.

Appendix A

1. Benjamin's parents are listed as Benjamin and Anne Arnold. The first Benjamin was born ca. 1660 in New Kent County, Virginia. He was married to Anne, who was born in 1672, by September 1690. A planter and land speculator, this Benjamin served his community as a surveyor and sub-sheriff of King William County. He died ca. 1720.
2. Hendrick's will – mentioned in "Laurens County Estate Book A-1," *The South Carolina Magazine of Ancestral Research* 8:3 (Summer 1980), 144 – was dated July 15, 1795.
3. William raised his younger brother Ira after their father's death.
4. The 1790 census shows Hendrick with one son under the age of 16; however, William was named the executor of his father's will in July 1795, a task that required him to be of age at the time.
5. The 1850 U.S. Census for Laurens County, S.C., lists Ira Arnold's age as 57, which would make his birth year 1792.
6. David S. Arnold is listed as 30 in the 1860 U.S. Census for Van Buren Township in Union County, Ark. The census also lists his wife, Temperance, as 18 and gives her birthplace as Arkansas instead of Alabama.
7. The Revolutionary War Pension Records, compiled by Kathleen Paul Jones and Pauline Jones Gandrud in *Alabama Records, Vol. 75: Autauga County*, 1980, give two possible birth years for Thomas Arnold – 1763 and 1766. The earlier date, also listed in family records, is more plausible given the fact that Thomas enlisted in 1779 in the 96th District of South Carolina and served 18 months as a private in the South Carolina Troops under Capt. John Ridgeway. Had Thomas been born in 1766, he would have been only 13 when he enlisted.
8. This name originally may have been *Boydston* or *Boidstone* (MacIvor, 66). It also is spelled *Bedeston* in the *Roster of South Carolina Patriots in the American Revolution*.
9. Census records agree with the 1818 birth year, but according to David Ross' 1874 marriage record to Clara Hillams, he was 53 at the time, which would make his birth year about 1821.

10. William B. Arnold officiated at this wedding, which was held at the home of Michael Bozeman. *Clark County, Arkansas Marriage Records 1821-1879*, comp. by Bobbie Jones McLane, 1974.
11. The 1850 U.S. Census for Hempstead County, Ark., lists Mary's age as 23, which would give her a birth year of 1826 or 1827.
12. While family records show Martha was born about 1836, the 1850 U.S. Census for Hempstead County, Ark., shows she was 17 at the time, which would make her birth year 1832 or 1833. Marriage records give her age as 35 when she married her cousin William B. Ross in 1867; this coincides with the census record.
13. The 1850 U.S. Census for Hempstead County, Ark., gives William E. Arnold's age as 13, which would make his birth year 1836 or 1837.
14. The 1860 U.S. Census gives Tempie's birthplace as Arkansas, but family tradition holds that she was born in Alabama.
15. Lewis Saxon and Sally Allen were married Feb. 1, 1787.
16. Marriage records indicate that David Saxon was 25 when he was married in 1858, which means he would have been about five years younger than his cousin David Arnold. But according to Arkansas census records, there was only a year difference between the two men. There also is a discrepancy about when David Saxon moved to Arkansas. One entry in *The Centennial History of Arkansas Vol. 3* has him moving in 1841 and immediately starting a farm. A subsequent entry in the same volume says he moved to Arkansas in the late 1840s. It is more likely that he moved with his cousin in 1849 or 1850 as neither man shows up in the 1850 Arkansas census. The 1860 Census shows David Saxon, listed as 29, living with Frederick Reeves, a relative of his future wife, in Union County. He had no personal estate in 1860.

Appendix B

1. "Autauga County," *Alabama Records, Vol. 75*, compiled by Kathleen Paul Jones and Pauline Jones Gandrud (Betty Wood Thomas, 1980), 45-46; *Roster of South Carolina Patriots in the American Revolution*, compiled by Bobby Gilmer Moss (Baltimore: Genealogical Publishing Company, Inc., 1983), 27.
2. *Roster of South Carolina Patriots in the American Revolution*, 847.
3. MacIvor, 60.
4. Moss, 27.

Appendix C

1. *Abstracts of Some Greenville County, South Carolina, Records Concerning Black People Free and Slave, 1791-1865*, 33, 43.
2. Since name spellings vary widely in the slave records, it is probable that this Rodger is the father of Prince.
3. *Abstracts*, 44.
4. *Ibid.*, 35-46.

5. *Ibid.*, 45.
6. *Ibid.*, 47.

Bibliography

Books:

Abstracts of Early Records of Laurens County, South Carolina, 1785-1820. Sara M. Nash, comp. 1982.
Abstracts of Some Greenville County, South Carolina, Records Concerning Black People Free and Slave 1791-1865 vol. 1. Anne K. McCuen, comp. Spartanburg, S.C.: The Reprint Company Publishers, 1991.
Alabama Records vol. 106. Kathleen Paul Jones and Pauline Jones Gandrud, comps. Betty Wood Thomas, 1980.
Arkansas Confederate Veterans and Widows Pension Applications. Frances T. Ingmire, comp. St. Louis: Ingmire Publications, 1985.
Arnold, William Hendrick. *The Arnold Family*. St. Paul, Minn.: West Publishing Co., 1935.
Autauga County, Alabama Records vol. 75. Kathleen Paul Jones and Pauline Jones Gandrud, comps. Betty Wood Thomas, 1980.
Autauga County, Alabama Records vol. 224. Kathleen Paul Jones and Pauline Jones Gandrud, comps. Betty Wood Thomas, 1980.
Bailey, Anne J. and Daniel E. Sutherland, eds. *Civil War Arkansas: Beyond Battles and Leaders*. Fayetteville, Ark.: University of Arkansas Press, 2000.
Bartley, Numan V., ed. *The Evolution of Southern Culture*. Athens, Ga.: The University of Georgia Press, 1988.
Bergeron, Arthur W. *Guide to Louisiana Confederate Military Units, 1861-1865*. Baton Rouge: Louisiana State University Press, 1989.
Biographical and Historical Memoirs of Southern Arkansas. Chicago: Goodspeed Publishing Co., 1890.
Bolton, S. Charles. *Arkansas, 1800-1860: Remote and Restless*. Fayetteville, Ark.: The University of Arkansas Press, 1998.
Boney, F.N. *Southerners All*. Macon, Ga.: Mercer University Press, 1984.
Carter, Howell. *A Cavalryman's Reminiscences of the Civil War*. New Orleans: The American Printing Co., n.d.
Casey, Powell A. *Encyclopedia of Forts, Posts, Named Camps, and Other Military Installations in Louisiana, 1700-1981*. Baton Rouge: Claitor's Publishing Division, 1983.
Cash, Wilbur J. *The Mind of the South*. Garden City, N.Y.: Doubleday Anchor Books, 1941.
Centennial History of Arkansas vols. 2, 3. Chicago: The S.J. Clarke Publishing Co., 1922.
Clark County, Arkansas: A Genealogical Source Book. Pauline Williams Wright and Barbara McDow Caffee, comps. Baltimore: Gateway Press, Inc., 1982.
Clark County, Arkansas, Marriage Records, 1821-1879. Bobbie Jones McLane, comp. 1974.
Clark County, Arkansas, Obituaries and Death Notices, 1869-1900 vol. 1. Allen B. Syler, comp. Hot Springs, Ark.: Arkansas Ancestors, 1991.

Clayton, Powell. *The Aftermath of the Civil War in Arkansas*. New York: Negro Universities Press, 1969. Reprint of 1915 edition.

Confederate Women of Arkansas in the Civil War, 1861-'65: Memorial Reminiscences. Little Rock: The United Confederate Veterans of Arkansas, 1907.

Dallas County, Alabama Records vol. 90. Kathleen Paul Jones and Pauline Jones Gandrud, comps. Betty Wood Thomas, 1980.

Davis, William C. *Rebels and Yankees: The Battlefields of the Civil War*. San Diego: Thunder Bay Press, 1999.

Degler, Carl N. *Place Over Time: The Continuity of Southern Distinctiveness*. Baton Rouge: Louisiana State University Press, 1977.

Denslow, Ray V. *Civil War and Masonry in Missouri*. Missouri: Grand Lodge, Ancient Free and Accepted Masons and the State of Missouri, 1930.

Emery, Michael and Edwin Emery. *The Press and America: An Interpretive History of the Mass Media*, seventh ed. Englewood Cliffs, N.J.: Prentice Hall, 1992.

Farnham, Christie Anne, ed. *Women of the American South*. New York: New York University Press, 1997.

Ferguson, John L. *Arkansas and the Civil War*. Little Rock: Pioneer Press, 1965.

Fletcher, John Gould. *Arkansas*. Chapel Hill: University of North Carolina Press, 1947.

Foner, Eric. *Reconstruction: America's Unfinished Revolution 1863-1877*. New York: Harper & Row Publishers, 1988.

Friedman, Jean E. *The Enclosed Garden: Women and Community in the Evangelical South, 1830-1900*. Chapel Hill, N.C.: The University of North Carolina Press, 1985.

Genovese, Eugene D. *The Southern Tradition*. Cambridge, Mass.: Harvard University Press, 1994.

Grant, Ulysses S. *Memoirs and Selected Letters* vols. 1, 2. New York: Literary Classics of the United States, 1990.

Harris, D.W. and B.M. Hulse, eds. *The History of Claiborne Parish, Louisiana*. New Orleans: Press of W.B. Stansbury & Co., 1886.

Head of Families: First Census of the United States – 1790, South Carolina. South Carolina Heritage Series 6. Washington: Government Printing Office, 1908.

Hempstead County, Arkansas, Cemeteries Book 4. Hope, Ark.: Hempstead County Genealogical Society, 1990.

Hempstead County, Arkansas, 1820-1881: Computer Indexed Marriage Records. North Salt Lake: Hunting for Bears Inc., n.d.

Hendrick, Burton J. *The Lees of Virginia: Biography of a Family*. Boston: Little, Brown, and Co., 1935.

Hewett, Janet B., ed. *The Roster of Confederate Soldiers, 1861-1865* vol. 1. Wilmington, N.C.: Broadfoot Publishing Co., 1995.

Jewell, Horace. *History of Methodism in Arkansas*. Little Rock, Ark.: Press Printing Co., 1892.

Johansson, M. Jane, ed. *Widows by the Thousand: The Civil War Letters of Theophilus and Harriet Perry, 1862-1864*. Fayetteville, Ark.: The University of Arkansas Press, 2000.

Johnson, Ludwell. *Red River Campaign: Politics and Cotton in the Civil War*. Baltimore: Johns Hopkins Press, 1958.

Judicial Staff Directory. Winter 1999. Alexandria, Va.: Congressional Quarterly, 1999.

Laurens County, South Carolina, Will Book A, 1840-1853 vol. 2. Frances Terry Ingmire, comp. St. Louis: Ingmire Publications, 1982.

Laurens County, South Carolina, Will Book D-E, 1810-1825. Frances Terry Ingmire, comp. St. Louis: Ingmire Publications, 1982.

Laurens County, South Carolina, Wills, 1784-1840. Colleen Elliott, comp. Easley, S.C.: Southern Historical Press, 1988.

Lazenby, Marion Elias. *History of Methodism in Alabama and West Florida.* North Alabama Conference and Alabama-West Florida Conference of the Methodist Church, 1960.

Lebsock, Suzanne. *Virginia Women, 1600-1945: A Share of Honour.* Richmond: Virginia State Library, 1987.

LeMaster, Carolyn Gray. *A Corner of the Tapestry: A History of the Jewish Experience in Arkansas, 1820s-1990s.* Fayetteville, Ark.: University of Arkansas Press, 1994.

MacIvor, Hazel Arnold. *Some Ancestors and Descendants of Benjamin Arnold, King William County, Virginia, and Greenville, South Carolina.* Lake Orion, Mich.: The Arnold Family Association of the South, 1974.

Marriage Bonds & Ministries Returns of Union County, Arkansas, 1829-1870. Annie Laurie Spencer, comp. El Dorado, Ark.: El Dorado Printing Co., 1962.

Marriages Hempstead County, Arkansas, 1875-1900. Hope, Ark.: The Hempstead County Genealogical Society, n.d.

Medearis, Mary, ed. *Sam Williams: Printer's Devil.* Hope, Ark.: Etter Printing Co., 1979.

Moneyhon, Carl H. *The Impact of the Civil War and Reconstruction on Arkansas.* Baton Rouge: Louisiana State University Press, 1994.

Nagel, Paul C. *The Lees of Virginia: Seven Generations of an American Family.* New York: Oxford University Press, 1990.

Owsley, Frank Lawrence. *The South: Old and New Frontiers: Selected Essays of Frank Lawrence Owsley.* Harriet Chappell Owsley, ed. Athens, Ga.: The University of Georgia Press, 1969.

Plante, Ellen M. *Women at Home in Victorian America.* New York: Facts on File, Inc., 1997.

Proposals of the Committees of the Constitutional Convention of Arkansas, to be Presented to the Convention at Its Meeting on the First Monday in July, Nineteen-eighteen. Little Rock: Arkansas State Government, 1918.

Records of Louisiana Confederate Soldiers and Louisiana Confederate Commands vol. 1. Andrew B. Booth, comp. Spartanburg, S.C.: The Reprint Co., 1984.

Richardson, James M. *History of Greenville County, South Carolina.* Spartanburg, S.C.: The Reprint Company Publishers, 1980.

Roster of South Carolina Patriots in the American Revolution. Bobby Gilmer Moss, comp. Baltimore: Genealogical Publishing Co., Inc., 1983.

Sharpe, Michael. *Historical Maps of Civil War Battlefields.* London: PRC Publishing, Ltd., 2000.

Sifakis, Stewart, ed. *Compendium of the Confederate Armies: Florida and Arkansas* vol. 4. New York: Facts on File, 1992.

_____. *Compendium of the Confederate Armies: Louisiana.* New York: Facts on File. 1995.
Sloan, William David, ed. *Media and Religion in American History.* Northport, Ala.: Vision Press, 2000.
Thatcher, H. K. *Camden and the Ouachita River.* Ouachita County, Ark.: Ouachita River Valley Association, 1952.
Thomas, David Y. *Arkansas and Its People.* New York: The American Historical Society, Inc., 1930.
Thomas, Emory M. *Robert E. Lee: A Biography.* New York: W.W. Norton & Co., 1995.
Union County, Arkansas Marriage Records, 1829-1902. John Calvin Head, comp. Shreveport, La.: J&W Enterprises, 2000.
Who's Who in the South and Southwest, 24th ed. New Providence, N.J.: Marquis Who's Who, 1995.
Woods, James M. *Rebellion & Realignment: Arkansas' Road to Secession.* Fayetteville, Ark.: The University of Arkansas Press, 1987.
Woodward, C. Vann. *The Burden of Southern History.* Baton Rouge: Louisiana State University Press, 1960.
_____. *Origins of the New South, 1877-1913.* Baton Rouge: Louisiana State University Press, Littlefield Fund for Southern History, and University of Texas, 1951.
Wooley, James E., ed. *A Collection of Upper South Carolina Genealogical and Family Records.* Easley, S.C.: Southern History, 1979.
Wright, Robert Ross. *Old Seeds in the New Land: History and Reminiscences of the Bar of Arkansas.* Fayetteville, Ark.: M and M Press, 2001.
Wyatt-Brown, Bertram. *Honor and Violence in the Old South.* New York: Oxford University Press, 1986.
_____. *Southern Honor: Ethics and Behavior in the Old South.* New York: Oxford University Press, 1982.

Journals & Essays:

Alexander, Charles C. "White Robes in Politics: The Ku Klux Klan in Arkansas, 1922-1924." *Arkansas Historical Quarterly* 22. Autumn 1963.
Anderson, John Q., ed. "Joseph Carson, Louisiana Confederate Soldier." *Louisiana History* 1. Winter 1960.
Arnold, Morris Sheppard "Buzz." "The Arnolds of Southwest Arkansas." *The Arkansas Lawyer* 18. July 1984.
Arnold, William H., Sr., "Historical Statement of Texarkana, Arkansas, to Feb. 7, 1917." *Arkansas Historical Quarterly* 5. Spring 1946.
_____. "Rondo, Miller County, Arkansas. Brief Historical Sketch." Mss. Oct. 31, 1930.
Atkinson, Edward. "The Battle of Marks Mill." J.H. Atkinson, ed. *Arkansas Historical Quarterly* 14. Winter 1955.
Atkinson, J.H. "Personal Notes." *Arkansas Historical Quarterly* 6. Spring 1947.
"The Bar of Early Arkansas: Excerpts from George B. Rose's Address on May 6, 1903, to the Sixth Annual Meeting in Little Rock, Arkansas." *The Arkansas Lawyer Special Centennial Issue.* 1998.
Beasley, Kate, ed. "Three Civil War Letters." *Arkansas Historical Quarterly* 3. Summer 1944.

Buckalew, Arthur R. and Robert B. Buckalew. "Hillsboro's Soldier-Citizen: Horatio Gates Perry Williams." *Arkansas Historical Quarterly* 31. Spring 1972.

Cathey, Clyde W. "Slavery in Arkansas." *Arkansas Historical Quarterly* 3. Spring 1944.

Cook, Charles Orson. "'The Glory of the Old South and the Greatness of the New:' Reform and the Divided Mind of Charles Hillman Brough." *Arkansas Historical Quarterly* 34. Autumn 1975.

Dougan, Michael B. "Life in Confederate Arkansas." *Arkansas Historical Quarterly* 31. Spring 1972.

Durham, Ken, ed. "'Dear Rebecca': The Civil War Letters of William Edwards Paxton, 1861-1863." *Louisiana History* 20. Spring 1979.

"1829 Census of Laurens District." *The South Carolina Magazine of Ancestral Research* 4. Spring 1976.

Eno, Clara B. "Activities of the Women of Arkansas During the War Between the States." *Arkansas Historical Quarterly* 3. Spring 1944.

Gwaltney, Francis Irby. "A Survey of Historic Washington, Arkansas." *Arkansas Historical Quarterly* 17. Winter 1955.

Hollandsworth, James G. "The Execution of White Officers from Black Units by Confederate Forces During the Civil War." *Louisiana History* 35. Fall 1994.

Hudson, James J., ed. "From Paraclifta to Marks' Mill: The Civil War Correspondence of Lt. Robert C. Gilliam." *Arkansas Historical Quarterly* 17. Autumn 1958.

Huff, Leo E. "The Memphis and Little Rock Railroad During the Civil War." *Arkansas Historical Quarterly* 23. Autumn 1964.

Johnson, Boyd W. "Cullen Montgomery Baker: The Arkansas-Texas Desperado." *Arkansas Historical Quarterly* 26. Autumn 1961.

Jones, Allen W. "Military Events in Louisiana During the Civil War, 1861-65." *Louisiana History* 2. Summer 1961.

"Laurens County Estate Book A-1." *The South Carolina Magazine of Ancestral Research* 8. Summer 1980.

Ledbetter, Calvin R., Jr. "The Constitutional Convention of 1917-1918." *Arkansas Historical Quarterly* 34. Spring 1975.

Moneyhon, Carl H., ed. "Life in Confederate Arkansas: The Diary of Virginia Davis Gray, 1863-1865, Part 1." *Arkansas Historical Quarterly* 42. Spring 1983.

Montgomery, Donald Ray. "Simon T. Sanders: Public Servant." *Arkansas Historical Quarterly* 39. Summer 1980.

Nelson, Grace Benton. "Early Lumber Industry in Clark County." *The Clark County Historical Journal* 1. Spring 1974.

_____. "Federal Invasion of Clark County." *The Clark County Historical Journal* 2. Winter 1975.

Odom, Van D. "The Political Career of Thomas Overton Moore, Secession Governor of Louisiana." *The Louisiana Historical Quarterly* 26. October 1943.

Owens, Jeffrey Alan. "The Burning of Lake St. Joseph." *Louisiana History* 32. Fall 1991.

Richards, Ira Don. "The Battle of Poison Spring." *Arkansas Historical Quarterly* 28. Winter 1959.

_____. "The Engagement at Marks' Mill." *Arkansas Historical Quarterly* 19. Spring 1960.

Rose, George B. "William Hendrick Arnold." *Arkansas Law Review and Bar Association Journal* 1. Summer 1947.
Woodward, Mary Davis. "Dr. W.E. Arnold: A Personality Sketch." *Arkansas Historical Quarterly* 8. Winter 1949.

Newspapers:

Arkansas Democrat. 1917-1918. Microfilm.
Daily Texarkana Democrat. 1893. Microfilm.
Daily Texarkana Independent. April 1886-June 1887, 1892. Microfilm.
The Daily Texarkanian. 1894. Microfilm.
New York Times. April - May 1874; February 1892; November 1892; February 1893. Microfilm.
The Texarkanian. 1917-1918. Microfilm.

Misc.

"About the American Law Institute." American Law Institute. www.ali.org.
"Arkansas Rivers List." *The Ozark Whitewater Page*. Bill Herring, comp. 19 November 2003. www.ozarkpages.com/whitewater/AR.html#Cossatot.
Biographical Directory of the United States Congress, 5 December 2003, bioguide.congress.gov.
Confederate Partisan Rangers. U.S. Civil War Center. www.civilwarhome.com/partisanrangers.htm.
Correspondence with Morris Sheppard "Buzz" Arnold., 1998-2003.
Correspondence with Richard Sheppard Arnold., 2002-2003.
"Fort Pillow State Historic Park." *Tennessee State Parks Website*. www.state.tn.us/environment/parks/pillow/history.htm.
"Goodrich's Landing." *CWSAC Battle Summaries*. The American Battlefield Protection Program. www2.cr.nps.gov/abpp/battles/la014.htm.
"Governor Elisha Baxter of Arkansas." 5 December 2003. National Governors Association Online. www.nga.org/governors.
"Grover Cleveland." *The White House*. 7 December 2003. Washington: U.S. Government, www.whitehouse.gov/history/presidents.
Hempstead County, Arkansas, Federal Land Records, Joy Fisher, comp. AR GenWeb.
Interviews with Morris Sheppard "Buzz" Arnold. 10 December 1998 and 25 June 2003, Little Rock, Ark. Audio tape.
Interview with Richard Sheppard Arnold. 3 April 1999, Fayetteville, Ark. Audio tape.
Judge Morris Arnold Manuscript Collection. Torreyson Library Archives, University of Central Arkansas.
19th (Dockery's) Arkansas Infantry Regiment Confederate States of America: Co. F." Edward G. Gerdes, comp. www.couchgenweb.com/civilwar/dockeryf.html.
"19th (Smead's-Dockery's) Arkansas Infantry Regiment." *Arkansas Confederate Infantry Regiments*. www.aristotle.net/~tomezell/AR_infy.htm.
Owings, Richard. "The Brooks Baxter War." *Arkansas Encyclopedia*, B. 16 November 2003. www.geocitien.com/arkencyclo/brkbax.html.

Rogers, Margaret Greene. *Corinth, 1861-1865.* Publication #A-0002. Corinth, Miss.: Northeast Mississippi Museum Association, 1990. www2.tsixroads.com/corinth_MLSANDY/corcwh.html

Ross, Frances. Unpublished notes from the federal file on the 1911 application of William H. Arnold for the position of U.S. District judge.

"Secret Brotherhood of Free Masonry." *History's Mysteries.* HistoryChannel.com, 2003.

Taylor, Leah M. *The Democratic Convention of 1924.* Unpublished master's thesis in history at Louisiana State University, 1966.

Transcript of Richard Sheppard Arnold interview. Conway, Ark.: State College of Arkansas Oral History Research Office, 1969.

U.S. Census for Autauga County, Alabama, 1830, 1840.

U.S. Census for Clark County, Arkansas, 1850, 1860, 1870.

U.S. Census for Dallas County, Alabama, 1830, 1840.

U.S. Census for Hempstead County, Arkansas, 1840, 1850, 1860.

U.S. Census for Laurens County, South Carolina, 1820, 1830, 1840, 1850.

U.S. Census for Union County, Arkansas, 1850, 1860, 1870.

U.S. Slave Schedules for Clark County, Arkansas, 1850, 1860.

U.S. Slave Schedules for Hempstead County, Arkansas, 1840, 1850, 1860.

U.S. Slave Schedules for Union County, Arkansas, 1860.

Index of Place Names

Africa 13
   Central 267
Alabama 1, 3, 4, 8, 9, 11, 18, 22, 39, 46, 153, 246
   Autauga County 1
   Burnsville 9
   Canebrake region 3
   Chambers County 1
   Dallas County 9
   LaGrange 14
   Mulberry Creek 9
   Pickens County 9
Arkansas xxviii, xxix, xxx, 4-10, 12, 14-18, 24, 25, 26, 27, 28, 30, 32, 33, 34, 35, 36-37, 39-47, 49-55, 58, 67-68, 70, 71, 77, 88, 90, 94-95, 96, 98-99, 100-101, 103-106, 109-115, 117, 125-126, 127, 128-129, 133-134, 135, 140-150, 152, 154, 159, 162, 165, 166, 170, 171, 178, 197, 201, 206, 217, 219, 225, 230, 233, 238, 239, 240, 244, 246, 247-248, 251, 254, 256, 265, 270, 276, 277-279, 289, 290, 292, 296, 300, 307, 311, 313, 315, 316, 317, 319, 321-323, 325, 328, 329, 330, 331, 332, 333, 339, 340
   "Anthony County" 148
   Antimony City 224
   Argenta 179
   Arkadelphia 10, 23, 95, 101, 104-105, 113, 141, 162
   Arkansas River 41, 52, 71, 109
   Artesian 155
   Ashley County 124
   Baker Springs 313
   Bayou Meto 24
   Bear Creek 126
   Beardon 276
   Beebe 279
   Benton County 50
   Bentonville 51
   Bluff City 163
   Boone County 324
   Brownstown 235
   Bushy Creek 51
   Caddo 131
   Camden 26, 36, 104-106, 110, 234, 307, 315, 316
   Centre Point 224
   Clarendon 53
   Clark County 9, 26, 101, 161
   Clarksville 96, 98
   Clayton County 148
   Clear Lake 188
   Clow 270
   Columbia County 192-193, 223
   Cossatot River 313
   Dekalb 307
   DeValls Bluff 33, 53
   Dorsey County 148
   El Dorado 28, 52, 56, 66, 69, 121, 124
   Elkhorn 53
   Emmett 163, 224
   Fayetteville 15, 33, 44, 143, 145, 171
   Fort Smith 36, 46, 145, 147, 226-228, 271, 282, 291, 315, 316, 317, 321
   Fulton 298-299, 307, 309, 337
   Garland City 70, 104, 108, 113, 114, 116
   Guernsey 285
   Helena 41, 45, 47, 257
   Hempstead County 4, 5, 6, 7, 8, 10, 11, 12, 15, 18, 71, 137, 154, 163, 223, 271, 310, 337
      Military Road 15
      Missouri Township 8
   Hollywood 161-162

Hope 224, 270, 285, 307, 315, 316
Hopefield 33, 54
Hot Springs 176, 182, 220, 258
Howard County 223
Huntsville 52
Lafayette County 69, 192-193, 223
Lewisville 55, 192
Lisbon 10, 18, 26-29, 31, 114, 121, 152, 153
Little River County 223
Little Rock 5, 7, 15, 24, 33, 41-42, 43, 44, 52-53, 71, 84, 95, 98-99, 101, 104, 105, 111, 113, 143, 145, 147-150, 154, 171, 182, 201, 217, 247, 248, 251, 256, 257, 258, 280, 300, 307, 308, 309, 317, 324, 325, 328, 329, 340, 341
   Camp Pike
   Main Street 98, 143-144, 145, 149
Madison 33, 54
Madison County 47
Magnolia 248, 280
Marks' Mill 106
Marysville 152-154
Miller County 69, 165, 178, 182, 186-187, 189, 190, 192-193, 201, 202, 203, 209, 216, 223, 238, 241, 248, 252-253, 260, 262, 264, 270, 287, 288, 294, 296-297, 300, 308, 309, 313, 323, 326, 332, 337, 338
   Garland Township 194
Monroe County 47
Mount Holly 18, 152-154
Mount Pleasant 307
Mount Prairie 8
Nashville 224
Nevada County 8, 137, 154, 163, 164, 182, 223, 239
New Gascony 145
New Lewisville 238, 307, 308
North Little Rock 290
Old River 189
Ouachita County 29, 223, 276
Ouachita River 27
Ozan 224

Palarm 145
Pea Ridge 53
Pike County 223
Pine Bluff 41, 105, 106, 144-145, 149, 190, 232
Pleasant Grove 368
Pleasant Lake 283
Poison Spring 105-106
Pope County 147
Prescott 116, 154, 155, 157, 162, 163-165, 166, 172, 173, 182, 203, 223, 224, 230, 234, 251, 307, 320
Preston 340
Pulaski County 140, 143, 186
Red River xxx, 7, 11, 69-70, 89, 90, 104, 106, 116, 227, 309, 337
St. Francis River 33, 53
Sevier County 223, 235
Sugar Creek 51
Terra Rouge 4
Texarkana 165-168, 169-170, 172-173, 174-176, 177-184, 186-187, 188-193, 196, 197-201, 202, 204-209, 216-217, 219, 221-223, 224-231, 234-238, 241, 242-246, 248-250, 251-258, 259, 260, 261, 262, 265, 267, 268, 269-272, 273, 274, 275, 276, 280, 281-282, 283, 285, 288, 290-292, 293, 294-301, 303-304, 306-309, 310, 313, 314-315, 316, 317, 332, 336, 337, 339, 341
   Broad Street 165, 169, 198, 200, 205-206, 207, 217, 218, 240, 243, 266, 299
   College Hill 188, 199, 202, 260, 264, 297, 305, 309
   Deutschmann Canal
   "East Side" 165-166, 184, 190, 217-218, 220, 226, 228-230, 234, 235, 249-250, 254, 255-256, 260, 261, 262, 265, 296-300, 304-306, 308
   First Ward 219
   Fouke neighborhood 294
   Second Ward 218, 219

Index of Place Names

Spring Lake Park 208
State Line Avenue 165, 192, 205, 206, 218, 228, 229, 240, 300
Swampoodle 303
Third Ward 218, 219
Vine Street 228, 229, 236
Union County 10, 18, 24, 26-30, 33, 34, 49, 51-52, 58, 62, 65, 66, 67, 69, 71, 77, 114, 116, 117, 121, 123, 124-126, 130-131, 139, 141
Van Buren Township
Van Buren 33, 36
Washington 5-6, 14-15, 98, 100, 101, 103, 112, 121, 224, 230, 248, 310
White River 53
Yellville 317
Belgium 242
California 24
San Francisco 333
Canada 313
Cannae xxii
Colorado 286, 328
Connecticut 242, 279
Cuba 242
Havana 242
England, Britain 20, 110, 281, 331
Gloucester 42
London 333
Europe 110, 242, 267, 323, 333
Eastern 165-166, 236
Florida 39, 44, 196-197
Fort Pickens 43
Pensacola 43
France 110
Paris 333
Georgia 12, 39, 44, 46, 246, 287, 308, 328, 329
Atlanta 107
Cass County 162
Savannah xxvi
Germany 236, 242
Gulf of Mexico 38, 282, 291
Illinois 36, 66, 179, 244, 276
Alton 336
Chicago 180, 242, 274, 283, 316, 323
Lake Shore 180
East St. Louis 179-180
Winetka 336
Indiana 233, 328
Indian Territory 5, 15, 25, 46, 254, 259, 274, 294
Cherokee Strip 294
Fort Towson 5
Perry 294
Kentucky 4, 17, 22, 35, 69, 276
Frankfort 43
Lexington 9
Logan County 1
Louisville 13
Mill Springs 51
Sykeston 276
Louisiana 7, 18, 33, 37, 39, 40, 52, 64, 65, 68, 69, 71-74, 76, 79, 80, 83, 84, 85, 88, 94, 120, 262, 292, 316, 328
Alexandria 74, 86, 87
Baton Rouge 76
Bayou Des Cedars 87
Black River 84
Camp Ford 81
Campti 87
Claiborne Parish 77
Dallas Station 73
Delhi 73, 83
East Carroll Parish 73
Goodrich's Landing 81
Grand Ecore 87
Homer 55
Lake Providence 73-74, 80-81
Loggy Bayou 87
Mansfield 88
Monroe 73, 83
New Orleans 6, 7, 16, 27, 29, 38, 40, 121
Ouachita River 84
Pineville 88
Port Hudson 76-77
Red River 84, 86-87, 104, 106
Sabine Crossroads 87
St. Maurice 87
Shreveport 16, 86, 106
Sniders Bluff 79
Yazoo Delta 76
Yazoo Pass 79
Yazoo River 68
Young's Point 80

Maine 328
Maryland
  Baltimore 35
Massachusetts 13, 279, 286
Mexico 15-16, 338
  Agua Nueva 17
  Buena Vista 17
  Cantana 17
  Encanscion 16
  Saltillo 16, 17
Michigan 274, 339
  Kalamazoo 248
Middle East 242
Minnesota 275
Mississippi 34, 37, 39, 40, 62, 128, 168, 292
  Corinth 59, 61-65, 69
  Iuka 69
  Tupelo 65-66
  Vicksburg 62, 68, 73-75, 76-83, 94-95
Mississippi River 33, 45, 53-54, 59, 61-62, 68, 70, 73, 76-77, 79, 80, 81, 84, 88, 100, 113, 121
Missouri 40, 46, 69, 129, 276
  Kansas City 282, 283
  Oak Hills 50
  St. Louis 33, 42, 143, 227, 229, 230, 233, 274, 281, 308
  Wilson's Creek 50
Nevada 287
New England 13, 239, 277-278, 279, 341
New Hampshire 279
  Exeter 336
  Manchester 277
New Jersey 279
New World 20
New York 242, 244, 246, 279, 322, 330
  New York City 6, 13, 16, 329
    Wall Street 242
  Poughkeepsie 171
North Carolina xxiv, 44, 46, 113
  Greensboro 113
Ohio 233, 290, 328
Oklahoma 328, 330
  McAlister 316
Oregon 328
Pennsylvania 128, 279

  Gettysburg 84, 111
  Philadelphia 336
  Pittsburg 282, 290
Persia 242
Rhode Island 279
Russia 242
Sea of Galilee 2
South Carolina xxiv, 9, 20, 23, 24, 27, 28, 39, 44, 46, 154, 166
  Brewerton 20, 23
  Charleston 35
  Charleston Harbor 43
  Cherokee Boundary 22
  Fort Sumter 43-44, 46, 102
  Greenville County 20, 21
  Horse Creek 22
  Laurens County 20, 24
  Newberry County 24
Tennessee 36, 40, 41, 44, 53-54, 59, 61, 62, 84, 275
  Chickamauga 84
  Chicksaw Bluffs 54
  Fort Donelson 51
  Fort Henry 51
  Fort Pillow 54-56, 61-62, 71
  Franklin 108
  French Broad River 113
  Island No. 10 54
  Knoxville 113, 275, 288
  Memphis 41, 51, 54, 76, 113, 256, 276
    Poplar Street 54
  Murfreesboro 61
  Nashville 62, 313, 336
  Plum Point Bend 55
  Sewanee 337
  Shiloh 59-62, 64, 65
  Tennessee River 53, 62
Texas 15, 16, 24, 36, 39, 40, 70, 71, 80, 96, 101, 117, 120, 125, 126, 143, 152, 165, 167, 170, 183-185, 197, 200, 206, 217, 230, 244, 251, 254, 256, 265, 271, 273, 283, 288, 291, 292, 307, 313, 316, 328, 339
  Bonham 307
  Bowie County 184, 222, 261, 262-263, 270, 283
  Buchanan 33
  Clarksville 263
  Dallas 36, 271

Index of Place Names

Deniston 180
Gainesville 244
Jefferson 217
Little River County 263, 265
Palestine 216
Paris   216, 230-231, 269-271, 274, 275, 307
Rio Grande 16
San Antonio 16, 251
Sweetwater 166
Texarkana 184-185, 197, 200-201, 217, 223, 226, 262, 300, 338
  Broad Street 183, 198, 217
  Proctor Springs 190, 222
  State Line Avenue 263
  Walnut Street 299
  "West Side" 183, 184-185, 198, 200-201, 217, 220, 222, 235, 249, 256, 261, 262-263, 295-296, 299, 300, 301, 304-305, 309

Tonga 332
Union 4, 25, 34, 37
United States, America 13, 15, 17, 36, 110-111, 122, 127, 174, 236, 242, 247, 281, 292, 323, 333
Virginia xxiv, 20, 33, 41, 44, 49, 107
  Appomattox 112
  Bull Run Creek 50
  Evansport 49
  Fredericksburg 188
  Harper's Ferry 32-33
  Lynchburg 336
  Manassas 50
  Old Dominion 49
  Potomac River 49
  Richmond 35, 49, 278
  Spotsylvania 106
Washington, D.C. 41, 43, 49, 111, 128, 144, 147, 148, 181, 225, 246, 252, 306, 316, 327
West Virginia 331

Index of People

A

Abbey, H.M. 298
Abrams, Col. 98
Aldrich, Charles H. 246-247
Allen, Henry 88
Allen, H.M. 251-252
Allen, W.J. 262-264
Altheimer, Ben J. 340
Anderson, ____ (farmer) 11
Anderson, Robert 44
Andrew, James O. 12-13
Ansley, John 154-155
Arbuckle, John 322
Aristotle xxii
Arnold, Ann H.T. Ross 24, 162
Arnold (Barrow), Carrie Ella 116
Arnold, Benjamin 20, 21
Arnold, Benjamin 21
Arnold, Clark (slave) 119-120
Arnold, David Christopher 213, 312, 323, 325-326, 332, 336-338
Arnold, David "Sax" Saxon, Jr. 32, 58, 91, 120, 126, 127, 132-133, 153, 155, 166
Arnold, David Saxon, Sr. 20-38, 39, 42, 44-45, 48, 49-57, 59, 61-66, 67-75, 77-88, 89-90, 94-96, 98-99, 101-104, 106, 108, 109-118, 119-126, 127, 128, 129, 130-131, 133-137, 139, 141, 146-147, 149, 152-157, 161, 163, 172, 173, 230, 310-312
Arnold (Dunklin), Ann Hendrick "Nancy" 9
Arnold (Ellis), Lucy 234, 336
Arnold (Harris), Sally Temperance 89
Arnold, Hendrick 20, 21, 22, 42
Arnold, Hendrick Howard 9-10, 22, 23, 24, 26, 31, 42, 95, 101, 104-106, 115, 131, 141, 145, 146, 148, 152, 154, 162
Arnold, Ira 9, 20, 21-23
Arnold, Jessie Cook 196, 233-234, 312
Arnold, John Hardin, Jr. 155, 230
Arnold, John Hardin, Sr. 155, 166
Arnold, Kate Lewis 211, 213, 313, 318, 332
Arnold, Louiza Jane 14
Arnold, Lucinda "Lucy" Powell Hardin 4-9, 14, 18, 70-71, 89-90, 107-108, 114, 116-117, 234
Arnold, Mary "Molly" McCollum 137
Arnold, Mary "Polly" Saxon 23
Arnold (McCurdy), Ruth 312, 336
Arnold (Moore), Carrie Jane 155
Arnold, Morris Sheppard "Buzz" 164, 212, 215, 332, 336, 339-341
Arnold (Regan), Mary "Lucy" 34, 58, 91, 126, 127, 132-133, 155
Arnold, Richard D. xxvi
Arnold, Richard Lewis 211-213, 215, 313, 337, 338
Arnold, Richard Sheppard 172, 212. 215, 326, 338, 339, 340-341
Arnold, Robert Esterbrook 8, 18, 106-107, 115, 155, 157
Arnold (Ross), Caroline M. 10, 18, 26, 27, 31
Arnold (Ross), Temperance 9, 24, 26
Arnold (Smith), Jody Claypool 233-234, 336
Arnold, Temperance "Tempie" Lucinda Arnold 5, 18-19, 26, 29-34, 38, 39, 42, 44, 45, 48, 49-52, 58-59, 67, 69-71, 78, 86, 88, 89-90, 92-94, 99, 102-104, 106-108, 109-118, 120-121, 123-124, 126,

Index of People

127, 132-133, 137, 139, 149, 154, 155, 157, 163, 310-312
Arnold, Thomas (1) 11-12
Arnold, Thomas (2) 23
Arnold, Thomas Hendrick 4, 7
Arnold, Thomas Saxon 215, 338
(Arnold), "Uncle" Sam (slave) 3, 30, 302
Arnold, William 21, 22-23
Arnold, William Bideston 1-10, 11-12, 14-15, 18, 42, 302
Arnold, William Edward "Bill" 18, 26, 42, 49, 51, 59-61, 107-108, 113, 114, 115, 116, 137, 154, 155-156, 170, 230
Arnold, William Hendrick, Jr. 213, 215, 255, 323, 336, 337
Arnold, William Hendrick, Sr., "Willie," "Dick" xxix-xxx, 42, 51, 58, 90-94, 99, 107-108, 115, 116-117, 120, 121, 123, 126-127, 132-137, 153-158, 160, 161-168, 169-173, 174-176, 177, 182, 186, 187-189, 191, 192, 193, 194, 196-197, 198, 203, 207, 209-210, 213, 214, 217, 218-219, 220, 222, 224, 228, 230, 232, 233-235, 237-240, 242-245, 248, 250, 252-258, 261-262, 264, 276, 285, 288, 289, 294-299, 301, 302, 303-305, 310-318, 319-327, 329, 331-335, 336-342
Arnold, William Hendrick "Bill", III 215, 338
Atkins, Jerry 123-124
Atkinson, W.E. 203
Aurelius, Marcus xxii

B

Bacon, Roger xxii
Banks, Nathaniel P. 70, 74, 84, 86-87, 104, 106
Barkman, J.B. 249-250
Barkman, Joe 249-250
Barksdale, Samuel 23
Barrow, Carrie Ella Arnold 1116
Barry, ____ Capt. 231
Bartlett, Frank 80
Battle, ____ Mr. 216
Baxter, Elisha 111, 139-150
Beauregard, P.G.T. 61, 64

Bell, John 36
Benefield, J.M. 198
Betts, Samuel D. 69
Blair, Henry 279
Block, Abraham 6
Blythe, A.S. 261-262
Boney, F.N. xix, xxiv
Booth, H. 222
Borland, Solon 15-16, 46
Bozeman (Ross), Nancy Peeples 14
Branch, Sam 218-219
Breckinridge, C.R. 290
Breckinridge, John C. 35-36
Brennan, William J., Jr. 339, 340
Brooks, Joseph 129, 140-150
Brough, Charles xxiii-xxix, 320, 323
Brown, John (abolitionist) 32-33
Brown, John (judge) 36
Bryan, William Jennings 329-330
Bryant, ____ Judge 283
Bryant, G.L. 264
Burgess, John W. xxvii
Burke, C.C. 198-199
Burt, Cicero 65
Bush, J.A.O. 320
Butler, Benjamin 70
Byrne, Lawrence 190, 193

C

Caesar xxii
Capers, James H. 77
Capers, Richard 77
Carrigan, A.H. 170
Cash, Wilbur J. xix, xxiii, xxv, xxvii, 135, 151, 152, 156, 157, 166, 235, 341
Cassidy, Frank 250
Catterson, R.F. 142
Cayce, W.H. 225
Chambliss, Samuel 73, 77
Christ (Jesus) 2, 3, 29, 100
Christopher, George 164
Clampitt, George N. 29
Clarke, James P. 316
Clay, Henry 32, 34
Clayton, Powell 129-130, 139-141, 143-144, 147, 148, 149, 224
Clayton, W.H.H. 316

Cleveland, Grover 174, 217, 233-234, 244, 248, 249, 251, 254, 279, 285, 286-288, 292
Coats, W.R. 248
Collins, Charlie 81
Conway, Elias 32
Conway, Joe D. 248
Cook (Arnold), Jessie 196, 233-234, 312
Cook, Charles Orson xxix
Cook, Joe 171-172, 174, 175, 184, 187-189, 190, 191, 194, 196-197, 202-203, 216, 218, 220, 232, 239-240, 253, 256, 260-261, 294
Cook, John, Jr. 188, 218
Cook, John, Sr. 165, 171
Coolidge, Calvin 331
Coulter, ____ Col. 126, 153
Cowser, J.B. 69
Coy, Ed 265-267, 2770, 273
Crane, Warren 106
Cranford, Jake 240
Crenshaw, James 239-240, 249, 261, 265-266, 300
Crisp, Charles 287
Crowder, E.H. 323
Curtis, Samuel 98

D

Dalton Gang 259
Davis, Bill 106
Davis, Jefferson 41, 42, 44, 290
Davis, John W. 331
Dawes, Charles G. 316
Dearing, Harrison L. 28
Degler, Carl N. xix, 27
Deutschmann, Joseph 375
Dixon, C.E. 168, 172, 187, 195, 202-203, 218-220, 222, 255, 262, 283
Dockery, Thomas P. 63, 64
Dodd, David Owen 101-102
Dodson, J. 253
Donaghey, George W. 317
Dorrian, C.C. 181, 229, 249, 252-253
Dorsey, Steven 141, 143, 147, 148
Douglas, Stephen 35-36
Drew, Thomas 15
DuBois, W.E.B. xxvii
Dun, R.G. 292

DDunklin, Ann Hendrick "Nancy" Arnold 9
Dunning, William xxvii
Durett, J.W. 65-66
Dwyer, ____ Mr. 251

E

Eakin, John 114
East, John 81
Edwards, George 183-184
Edwards, J.C. 298, 304-305
Elbert (slave) 120
Ellis, Lucy Arnold 336
Erwin, Andrew 329

F

Fagan, James F. 49, 106
Fair, Stephen 50
Falk, Sam 293
Fanner, Levi 69
Few, Zach 249-250
Fishback, William 238-239, 241, 276, 278-279, 281, 307
Flanagin, Harris 71, 98, 112
Fletcher, John Gould 114
Floyd, C.J. 317
Foner, Eric 119
Foreman, Ben 189
Forrest, Nathan Bedford 156
Forster, ____ Mayor 175
Friedell, E.F. 194-195, 253, 264, 296-297, 309, 314-315, 326
Futrell, Junius Marion 332

G

Gantt, Edward W. 111, 128
Gardner, J.W. 239, 245, 246, 250, 256, 275, 291, 301, 304, 308
Garland, Agustus H. 112, 151
Garrison, A.M. 298
Genovese, Eugene D. xix, xxv
God/Lord/Providence xx, xxiii, xxix, 1-2, 3, 4, 5, 14, 22, 42, 78, 82, 95, 98, 103, 104, 115, 119, 137, 151, 172, 196, 222, 226, 260, 301-302, 334, 335, 342
Goff, Hugh 22
Goff, Rebekah 22, 23
Goldberg, Charles 166

Index of People

Gordon, Charlie 153
Gould, George 235, 290
Gould, Jay 177, 228, 235
Grant, Ulysses 54, 59-62, 64-65, 73-75, 76-81, 83, 94, 113, 142-143, 144-145, 146
Gray, Virginia 95, 98, 110
Green, _____ Trainmaster 2300
Griffin, Thomas 2
Grigsby, H.L. 173, 176, 218-219

H

Haile, Jesse 12
Haines, _____ Maj. 201
Hale, Jesse 260-261
Hale, Mrs. Jesse 260-261
Hallum, _____ Mr. 264
Hamby, C.C. 244
Hamilton, W.T. 178, 193
Hanna (slave) 21
Hannibal xxii
Harden, J.W. 65-66
Hardin, _____ Mr. 321, 322
Hardin (Arnold), Lucinda "Lucy" Powell 4-9, 14, 18, 70-71, 89-90, 107-108, 114, 116-117, 234
Hardin, Patrick 219
Harris, Sally Temperance Arnold 89
Harrison, Benjamin 234, 246, 290
Harrison, Isaac 83, 87, 88
Hart, Jesse C. 331
Hartwell, _____ Dr. 26
Hawes, James Morrison 80
Hawthorne, Julian 273
Hays, G.A. 196-197, 210, 218, 233
Hays, G.W. 317
Hays, T.W. 163
Haywood, R.J. 263
Head, James 321, 322
Hedges, Pattie Wright 29
Henderson, _____ Mayor 185, 217
Hendricks, Thomas 233
Henry, John "Father Henry" 8
Hinckley, _____ Mr. 227
Hindman, Thomas 34-35, 37, 47
Hodge, Thomas 253
Hodges, Earl W. 317
Hog, R.J.M. 18
Hogg, James 244
Hollingsworth, S.J. 190
Homer 135
Hood, John B. 108
Horace 135
Houk, John C. 288
Houston, Sam 145
Howells (Jordan), Sallie 97-98
Howells, Lutetia 96-98
Howells, S.J. 96
Hughes, Simon P. 178, 190, 197, 217-218
Humphrey (slave) 21
Hunter, Emilia 42

J

Jackson, Andrew 5
Jackson, J.C. 62
Jackson, L.W. 62
Jacobs, John 4
James (slave) 21
James, _____ Treasurer 176
Jewell, Henry 265-266
Jewell, Horace 13, 37
Jewell, Mrs. Henry 265-267
Joe (slave) 52, 56, 61-62, 64, 66, 74, 102
Johnson, C.E. 332
Johnson, Joseph E. 79
Johnson, J.M. 69
Johnson, Robert "Bob" 25, 37
Johnston, _____ (gambler) 168
Johnston, Albert E. 59
Johnston, Joseph E. 113
Jones, Bill 163
Jones, J.G. 3
Jones, Jim 222-223
Jones, Paul 171, 194, 252
Jones, Sam 308
Jordan, Sallie E. Howells 97-98
Julian, George W. xxvi-xxvii, 128

K

Kelley, William 289-290
Kelso, J.G. 280
Kerrigan, _____ Superintendent 229-230
King, Alphonse 283-284
King, John 262-264
Kirby, Jody "Jo" 202-203, 220
Kirby, John 202-203, 220
Kirby, W.F. 289

Knight, John 62

L

Langford, William 52-53, 66
Larkin (slave) 23
Lary, S.D. 262, 305
Lassiter, J.B. 65
Lee, R.E. 260-261
Lee, Robert E. 79, 84, 112-113
Leverett, Martin 297
Levy, _____ Mrs. 293
Lewis (Arnold), Kate 211, 213, 313, 318, 332, 334
Lewis, Gwyn 333
Lewis, Jerry 190
Lincoln, Abraham 36-37, 39, 43-46, 54, 68-69, 102, 109-110, 111, 113, 275
Littleton, _____ Brother 301
Livy 135
Locke, John xxii
Logan, Mrs. John A. 137
Longinotti, Joe 198
Longstreet, James 188
Lucretius xxii

M

Magruder, John Bankhead 84
Manning, _____ Dr. 127, 154
Marion, Francis "Swamp Fox" 156
Marrable, Thomas 121
Mathews, James 219
Matson, A.B. 219
Maxey, Samuel Bell 216-217, 251
McAdoo, William Gibbs 330
McClellan, George B. 110
McClure, John "Poker Jack" 142
McCollum (Arnold), Mary "Molly" 137
McCollum, James "Jim" 137, 155
McCulloch, Henry E. 80
McCurdy, Ruth Arnold 312, 336
McQueen, John 274
McRae, T.C. 240, 289, 295
Meek, John 24, 27
Miller, _____ Dr. 284
Miller, _____ Parson 6
Miller, C.J. 276
Miller, Mrs. C.J. 276
Miller, William H.H. 246-247

Mills, Thomas 55
Milton, John xxii
Mitchel, C.E. 163-164, 166, 184, 186-187, 190, 195, 197, 201-202, 203, 224, 229
Mitchel, Charles 43
Mitchell, _____ Mr. 324
Mitchell, James 201-202
Moneyhon, Carl H. xxiv, 27-28
Monk, J.R. 72
Moore, Carrie Jane Arnold 155
Moore, Thomas 72
Moose, W.L. 317
Morris, Thomas A. 8
Moses (freedman) 21
Murphy, _____ 148, 149
Murphy, Isaac 47, 111, 112, 127-128
Myers, W.J. 69

N

Napoleon 156
Nelson, A.T. 55
Newton, Isaac xxii

O

Onesimus 2
Ord, E.O.C. 128-129
Orr, Thomas 195, 216
Owen, W.B. 314
Owsley, Frank Lawrence xxiv, 134, 158

P

Pargoud, Frank 73
Parris, T.J. 65
Paul (Apostle) 2
Paxton, William Edwards 64
Perry, Theophilus 72, 78
Pettie, Virgil C. 329
Phebe (slave) 21
Philemon 2
Phillip (slave) 21
Pickett, George E. 156
Pike, Albert 16-17, 98
Plante, Ellen 42, 233
Plato 135
Polybius xxii
Porter, David 86-87
Price, Sterling 69, 98

Index of People

Primm, T.J. 66
Pryor, David 339

R

Ratcliffe, William P. 19
Reagan, John H. 216-217
Rector, Henry Massie 35, 37, 41, 45, 46, 47
Rector, W.H. 320
Reeds, R.E. 105
Reeves, Frederick 29
Regan, Mary Lucy Arnold 34, 58, 126, 127, 155
Reid, ____ Mr. 298
Remmel, H.L. 315-316
Rester, Liberty 62
Reynolds, J.J. 112
Roberts, ____ Mr. 227
Robinson, Joseph T. 317-318, 329, 330, 331
Rogers, John H. 315
Roosevelt, Franklin Delanor 332
Rose, ____ Col. 143-144, 146
Ross (Arnold), Ann H.T. 24, 162
Ross, Caroline M. Arnold 10, 18, 26, 27, 31
Ross, David Carroll 10, 18, 27. 29, 120, 122
Ross, Nancy Peeples Bozeman 14
Ross, Peter 9, 24
Ross, Temperance Arnold 9, 24, 26
Ross, William Brown 14
Runnels, Howell, Jr. 263-264
Rust, Albert 52

S

St. Nicholas 175
Samuels, ____ (pawnbroker) 170
Sanderson, Jeff 288-290
Sarah (slave) 21
Saxon (Arnold), Mary "Polly" 23
Saxon, Charles 23
Saxon, David Park 24-27, 29, 31, 52-53, 141, 145, 146, 148, 152
Saxon, Hugh 21, 23
Saxon, Joshua 23
Saxon, Lewis 162
Scherer, Julius 293
Schicker, E.A. 175, 218-219, 234-235, 298, 304

Scott, Calvin 265-266
Scott, Winfield 16
Shakespeare, William xxii
Shaw, W.W. 254, 288
Sheppard (Arnold), Janet 338
Sheppard, John H. 263, 283
Sheppard, Morris 316, 338
Sherman, William T. 87, 88, 146, 162
Shover, ____ Lt. 17
Simmons, ____ Dr. 305-306
Simpson, Jesse 124
Simpson, Mrs. H.M. 123-124
Simpson, Sarah 124
Sims, Hiram 23
Smead, H.P. 276
Smith, ____ Capt. 85
Smith, A.J. 87-88
Smith, Alfred E. 330
Smith, E.K. 84
Smith, Henry 269-274
Smith, Jody Claypool Arnold 233-234, 336
Smith, Wat 106
Smithers, W.J. 167, 169-171, 188, 202-203
Smoote, George P. 164
Sneed, ____ Judge 275
Snodgrass, Elmira 311
Socrates xxii
Sophocles xxii
Spearman, W.C. 244, 258, 299-300
Speight, Sam 202
Steele, Frederick 71, 98, 104-106
Stephen, "Uncle" (slave) 30
Stephenson, William 8
Stevens, Thaddeus 128
Stevenson, Adlai 244, 248
Stevenson, Tony 253
Stewart, William 287
Strain, Mary 132
Strong, ____ Adj. Gen. 142
Stuart, Jeb 156
Sweeney, ____ (Alderman) 217

T

Tabor, Mrs. M.A. 252-253
Tacitus xxii
Taft, William Howard 315-316, 327
Tatum, Ed 124

Taylor, Charles 317
Taylor, Dick 87
Taylor, Samuel 21
Taylor, Zachary 15-17
Temple, T.L.L. 308
"Thatcher, Lawrence" 32-33
Thomas, Lowell 333
Thurman, Allen G. 233
Totten, James 41
Treher, G.W. 263, 264
Trigg, J.H. 178, 181
Tufts, Mrs. A.A. 102
Turner, P.A. 305

V

Van Dorn, Earl 53
Vance, Henry 269, 272
Vance, Myrtle 269
Vinson, Joe 260
Virgil xxii

W

Walker, David 44, 46-47
Wallace, Minor 248
Ward, Frank 55
Warren, E.A. 164, 166, 172, 173, 183, 184-185, 187, 192, 194, 199, 226, 234, 239
Wasden, John 240
Washington, George 22, 156
Waters, _____ U.S. District Attorney General 247
Webber, _____ Prosecutor, Judge 172, 193, 203
Webber, T.E. 289
Whipple, _____ Col. 239

Whitaker, W.L. 227, 282, 283
White, H. King 144
Whitner, J.C. 293
Whytock, John 142
Wilder, Thornton xx
Williams, _____ Judge 201, 251
Williams, Abner B. 210, 312
Williams, George H. 144, 147
Williams, George W. 282
Williams, Ham 179
Williams, Robert B. 310-312
Willis, Mrs. John M. 97
Wilshire, David 144
Wilson, J.W. 161
Wilson, S.A. 62
Wilson, Woodrow 324, 330
Wolfe, _____ (Evangelist) 183-184
Woodruff, William 261
Woods, _____ Judge 332
Woodward, C. Vann xxv, 168
Wool, John E. 16
Wooten, J.H. 181
Worthington, John T. 316
Wright, Robert R. 341
Wyatt-Brown, Bertram xx-xxi, xxiii, xxv, 260

X

Xenophon xxii

Y

Yarbrough, _____ Mrs. 127
Yarbrough, Will 127
Yell, Archibald 15-17
Youmans, Frank 316

General Index

A

Abolition, abolitionist(s) 13, 32-33, 36, 245
African(s) 81, 267, 268
African American, black 3, 81, 124, 142, 144, 145, 148, 149, 163, 165-166, 167, 180-181, 189, 190, 200, 218, 222, 226, 237, 245-246, 264-265, 269, 270, 274, 279, 283, 289, 292, 301-302, 304, 305-307, 309
American(s) xxvi, xxix, 17, 45, 81, 247, 248, 323, 331, 333, 340
American Bar Association 326
American Law Institute 327
   Committee on the Establishment of a Permanent Organization for the Improvement of the Law 326-327
Ansley Academy 155, 158, 161
Anthony House 142, 144, 149
Aristocracy, aristocrat(s) xxiii-xxiv, 4, 18, 22
Arkansas 68
Arkansas Bar 164, 171, 338
Arkansas Bar Association 313, 319-320
   Special Committee on the New Constitution 320
Arkansas Democrat 320, 322, 323
Arkansas Gazette 17, 320
Arkansas Press Association 308
Arkansas Reports 197
Arkansas Society Sons of the American Revolution 334
Arkansas State Gazette 95
Arkansas, State of
   Archives 98
   Arsenal 142
   Board of Health 243, 244
   Capitol/Statehouse 142-144, 145, 147, 148, 149, 324-325
   Civil War 145
   Constitution 47, 150, 178, 314, 319-325, 339
   Amendments 43, 241, 331
   Constitutional Convention 129, 141, 150, 319-325, 339
   Council for Defense 323
   Donation Law 7
   Eighth Judicial District 338
   Election Commission 129, 140, 141
   Fourth Congressional District 233, 321, 322
   General Assembly/Legislature 37, 41, 67-68, 128-129, 140-141, 144, 145-146, 147, 148, 149-150, 154, 186-187, 314, 315, 319, 320-321, 322, 325, 326, 337
   Confederate 112
   House 139, 141, 148, 150, 186, 320, 324, 325, 337
   Judiciary Committee 337
   Senate 139, 141, 163, 193, 216-217, 314, 319, 320, 326, 337
   Judiciary Committee 337
   Union 111, 112
   Highway Commission 337
   Militia 45, 46, 47, 129, 141, 142, 178
   Ninth Judicial District 164
   Penitentiary 257-258
   Supreme Court 98, 127-128, 140, 142, 144, 148, 164, 182, 195, 221, 300, 321, 325, 331-332, 337-338
   Third Congressional District 144
   Treasury 100
Arkansas True Democrat 95
Army of the Mississippi (CSA) 61, 64-65
Army of North Virginia 217
Army of Tennessee (CSA) 51

Army of Tennessee (USA) 65
Army of Virginia (CSA) 49
Arnold & Arnold (law firm) 294, 313, 326, 336, 337, 339
Arnold & Cook (law firm) 172, 190
Arnold & Hays (law firm) 196-197
Arnold Bill (No. 136, Acts 1925) 337
Arnold Family, The 334
Arnold Law Firm 213, 215
Arnold's Mill 4
Arsenic poisoning 257
Arson 36, 149, 179, 182-183, 221, 298-299
Artesian Church 137
Assassination 113, 276
Associated Press 16
Atheist 184
Atlanta Medical College 49
Australian ballot 240, 246, 248, 251

B

Baptism, baptistry, baptized 2, 4, 8, 14, 30, 85
Baptist(s) 28, 29, 162, 176
Baseball 231-232
Bear Creek Church 127, 132
Bear Creek School 126-127, 132, 136
Beidler Park 231
Belmont College 336
Benefield Hotel 191, 198
Bible 12, 57, 63, 90, 279
  New Testament 2, 77
  Old Testament 236
    Psalms 222
Blackstone's Commentaries 163
Boneset 59
Bourbonism 245
Bourdon's algebra 156
Bowie County, Texas
  Courthouse 184
  Jail 222
Bowie Lumber Co. 226, 281
Bowie Rifles 222
Boycott 181
British 79
Brooks-Baxter War 139-150, 154
Brothels 191, 200, 255
"Brother in Black" 301

Budget Committee of the Judicial Conference (U.S.) 340
Burning/Roasting 33, 124, 264-267, 270, 271, 272-273, 274

C

Cairo Fulton Railroad 225
California Gold Rush 24
Cambridge University 340
  Trinity College 340
Camden Beacon 225
Camden Female College 19, 26
Camp meeting 3, 6, 8, 9, 30, 302
Capitol Hotel 201
Castor-bean 59
Catholic(s) 176, 330
Charm 53
Chemical National Bank 282
Chicken pox 305-306
Childbirth 42, 89, 233
Childhood fever 42
Chillicothe 87
Chitty's Pleadings 163
Chloroform 42
Cholera 67, 226, 242-244, 257
Christian(s) xxi, xxvi, 6, 12, 13, 119, 176, 184, 236
  Evangelical(s) xx, 2, 12
Christmas 100, 137, 157, 175, 293
Citizens Bank 198
Citizens Ticket 218-219, 234-235, 304
City Drug Store 202
Civil Service Commission 288
Civil War xxvi, xxvii, xxix, 41, 44-119, 122, 135-136, 137, 139-140, 141, 145, 151, 152, 156, 157, 158, 159, 166, 168, 174, 186, 277, 278, 281, 303, 310, 311-312, 321
  Battles
  Appomattox 112
  Atlanta 107
  Bull Run 50
  Chickamauga 84
  Gettysburg 84
  Mill Springs 51
  Pea Ridge (Elkhorn) 53
  Shiloh 59-62, 64, 65, 72, 107
  Spotsylvania Courthouse 107
  Wilson's Creek 50

General Index 427

Skirmishes/Action
Bentonville 51
Bushy Creek 51
Campti 87
Goodrich's Landing 80
Hadnot's Plantation 88
Marks Mill 106
Pineville 88
Poison Spring 105-106
Sugar Creek 51
Claiborne Rangers (CSA) 54-55
Classical education xxii, 14, 22, 135-136, 310, 334, 337, 338, 339
Cleveland & Thurman Club 238, 250
Code duello 168, 260
Colonial mercantilism 280-281
Colorado Bar 338
Compromise of 1850 25, 34
Confederacy, CSA, Confederate(s) 41, 42, 44, 45, 47, 50-51, 53-55, 59-65, 68-75, 76-77, 79-88, 95, 96, 98-99, 100-103, 105-106, 109-114, 116, 127-129, 140, 141, 144, 156, 174, 315, 342
    Medical Board 61
    River Defense Fleet 55
Conductors Hall 182, 218
Congress
    CSA 47, 55, 102, 112
    U.S. xxvi, 15, 25, 35, 43, 111, 112, 127-129, 144, 147, 148, 150, 164, 174, 181, 182, 199, 216-217, 223, 225, 240, 245, 246, 254, 277-278, 279, 286-288, 290, 295, 316, 317, 323, 328, 338
        House/Congressman 127, 148, 287, 290
        Senate/Senator 36, 43, 111, 127, 140, 144, 160, 216, 240, 277-287, 290, 292, 303, 316, 328, 326, 369, 383, 385
Conscription Act 55-56, 66, 68, 71, 85, 101
Constitutional Union Party 36
Cook & Arnold (law firm) 197, 240, 294
Cosmopolitan Hotel 208

Cotton Belt Railroad 309
    Depot 238
Coxey's Army 306
Cumberland Presbyterian(s) 12, 29, 166

D

Daily Texarkana Independent 173, 179, 180, 182, 183-184, 187, 188, 190, 191, 200, 203, 216, 218, 219, 220, 226
Daily Texarkanian 300, 301, 303, 317
Daughters of the American Revolution 334
Davies arithmetic 156
Deep South 35, 37, 39, 40, 46, 114
Democrat(s), Democratic Party 15, 16, 35-36, 110, 129, 139, 140, 141, 148, 150-151, 168, 172, 173-175, 176, 186-188, 193-195, 196, 202, 216-217, 218, 219, 229, 234, 237, 238-239, 240-241, 244-250, 251-252, 254, 255, 277-278, 279, 285, 287, 288, 293, 303-305, 310, 312, 314, 315, 316, 317, 320, 322, 328-331, 332, 339
    Arkansas 34, 247, 285, 320
        Central Committee 289, 310, 329, 331, 332
        State Convention 150
    Club 218
    Garland Township Convention 194
    House 287
    Miller County 186-188, 193-195, 201, 216, 238, 248, 287, 288-289, 290
    National conventions 35, 233, 328-329
    Speakings 174, 238, 239, 240, 314
    Texarkana 216-218, 242, 245, 246
    21st District (Arkansas) Senatorial Convention 192-193
Depression 239, 279, 281, 286-287, 291-292, 294, 296
Detroit Evening News 181
Deutschmann Canal 198

Diptheria 62, 257-258, 299
Dixie xxix
"Dixie" 290
Draft 323
Drexel Institute 336
Drought 126, 130, 139
Dynasty 25, 34-35
Dysentry 62

E

East, Eastern 79, 113, 235, 280
Easter 203
East Side (Texarkana, Ark.)
   Board of Health 258, 299-300, 306, 307, 308
   City Council 203, 217, 220-221, 229-230, 234, 238, 244, 296-297, 299
   City Hall 250, 258, 297
   Jail 299
   Police Court 264
   Sanitary Board 306
El Dorado 20, 24, 26, 28, 166, 336
Election(s)
   City 173, 175, 176, 182, 216, 217-220, 234-235, 303-304, 328
   County 193-195
   Presidential 34-37, 102, 109-110, 173-174, 234, 238, 242, 245-249, 251-252, 254, 288, 331
   Special 289, 320-322, 325, 332
   State 35, 41, 47, 51, 127-128, 139-141, 150, 173-174, 193, 238-241, 242, 246, 314-315, 317-318
Electric 191, 192, 197, 236, 237, 243
Emancipate, Emancipation 21, 32, 131, 245, 321
   Day 190
   Proclamation 68-69, 102, 111-112
English xxii, 136, 161, 329, 340
Episcopalian(s) 28, 236
Erskine College 22, 154
European xxiii, 237, 244, 333
Exposition Building 233

F

Factorage system 152

Female suffrage 321, 322, 325
Fifth Louisiana Cavalry (CSA) 86
Fireworks 230-231, 245, 248
First Amendment 340
First Arkansas Infantry, African Descent (Union) 80-81
First Arkansas Regiment (CSA) 49
First Kansas Mounted Infantry (Union) 81
Flood 11, 59, 76, 112, 126, 130, 139, 146, 303, 309, 325
Flu epidemic 325
Flux 62
Force Bill 174, 245, 246, 249
Four-Minute Speaker 323
14th Amendment 128, 129
Fourth Louisiana Cavalry (CSA) 81
Fourth of July/Independence Day 81, 233
Fourth U.S. Military District 128
Freedman (men) 21, 120, 124, 165, 186, 245
Freedman's Bureau 111, 114
French 136
Frisco line 274
Frontier xix, xx, xxv, xxvi, xxix, xxx, 1, 2, 4, 5, 8-9, 11, 17, 18, 20, 23, 24, 25-26, 36, 52, 90, 117, 119, 134, 154, 165, 166-167, 200, 204, 235, 259, 260, 294, 303
Fry's Army 306

G

Gambling, gambler, gaming 8, 130, 168, 183, 191, 199, 200-201, 220, 234, 255-256, 265, 294, 300, 304, 305, 328
Gate City Bank 280, 300
Gate City Club (baseball) 231
Gate City Guards 178-179, 182
Gate City Railroad 292
Gentile 236
German 165, 236-237
Ghio Building 283
Girton School 336
Gospel 2, 4
Great Land Race 294
Great Raft 7
Greek xxii, 136
Greenbacker 387

General Index

H

Hadnot's plantation 88
Hailstorm 285
Hanged, hanging 101, 221-223, 259, 268, 276
Harrison's Brigade (CSA) 83, 85, 86-88
Harvard xxii, 336, 338, 339
Hawthorne place 28, 117
Heaven 89, 107, 301
Hempstead County Bank 311
Henry & Estes (law office) 184
High Holy Days 166
Honor xx-xxi, xxii, xxiii-xxv, xxvi, xxvii-xxviii, xxix, xxx, 19, 45, 52, 72, 77, 85, 95, 99, 100, 125, 135, 159, 168, 177, 226, 259, 260, 261, 268, 274, 285, 311-312, 319, 332-333, 334, 335, 341-342
House of God 301
Huckins House 238-239
Huey gambling house 255

I

Iliad xxii
Inauguration Day 43, 110
Income tax 293
Indiana University 339
Ingram & Bussey Store 121
Inter-State College 264
Interstate Land & Building Co. 281
Inter-State News 262-263, 301, 304
Iron Mountain Railroad 163, 178-179, 180, 181, 182, 199, 228, 266, 281, 306, 309
Iron-weed 59
Italian 329

J

Jeffersonian xix
Jew(ish) 6, 166, 176, 236-237, 299
   Mount Sinai Synagogue 237, 299
   Orthodox 237
   Reformed 237
"Job's Turkey" 70

K

Kansas City, Nevada & Fort Smith Railroad 282, 291
Kansas City, Pittsburgh & Gulf Railroad 291
Knights of Honor 250
Knights of Labor 177-178, 181-182
Know-Nothings 36
Ku Klux Klan 328-331

L

Lady Baxter 143
Latin xxii, 136
Lent 176
Liberty Loan 323
Lightfoot's Drug Store 240
Little Rock Arsenal 41, 143
Little Rock Law Class 171
Little Rock Democrat 201
Little Rock Gazette 187
Lodge National Election Law 245
London Sunday Express 333
Lottery 199-200, 324
Louisville & Nashville Railroad 179
Lumberman's Ball 191
Lynching 264, 265-267, 270, 275, 276

M

Madison Square Garden 329-330
Madison Square Hotel 330
Malaria 5, 49, 60, 62, 107
Manifest destiny 15
Marks' plantation 106
Marquand Hotel 228
Martial law 143
Mason(s), Masonic 31-32, 51-52, 172, 196, 197, 234-235, 250, 296, 310
   Mount Moriah Lodge 31
Mayflower Hotel 327
McGuffey's Eclectic Reader 136
McKillian plantation 8
Measles 56, 62, 233
Memphis and Charleston Railroad 62
Memphis-Little Rock Railroad 33, 53
Methodist(s), Methodism 1-3, 6, 8, 12-14, 19, 20, 29, 30, 37, 57, 129, 162, 176, 236, 301-302, 310, 315
   Arkansas Conference 12
   Colored Methodist Church 301

1844 General Conference 13
Methodist Episcopal
   Extension Society 301
   Fourth Street Church 172, 196, 301
   Northern Conference 13
Mexican(s) 17
Mexican War 15-17, 24, 25, 28, 46
Middle Ages 267
Middle class xix, xxiii, xxiii, xxiv, xxix, 4, 18, 27-28, 29, 118, 126, 131, 134, 200, 230, 310
Midwest 177, 233
Miller County
   Circuit Court 186, 189, 195, 203, 223, 252, 253, 260, 294, 300, 338
   Courthouse 202, 209, 218, 223, 231, 253, 296-297, 313, 323
   Health Board 308
   Highway District (South Miller County) 326
   Jail 253
   Poorhouse 253
Minnesota Law Review 340
Mirror 277
Missouri Car Foundry 181
Missouri, Kansas & Texas Railroad 180
Missouri, Kansas & Texas Trust Co. 283
Missouri-Pacific Railroad 180, 181, 228-229, 290
Mobile and Ohio Railroad 62
Mob law/rule 264-268, 269, 271, 273, 274-276, 277
Monarch Theatre 168
Morse code 101
Mount Holly Academy 18
Mugwumpery 287
Murder, murderer 124, 168, 221, 222, 255, 259, 263, 264-265, 269, 271-272, 276, 292
Mutiny 86

N

National Citizens Rights Association 276
National Conference Commissioners on Uniform State Laws 327

National Republican 245
Native American, Indian(s) 2, 81, 167, 267
Nevada road 282
New Englanders 13
New Falls City 87
New South xxviii-xxix, 311
New Year's 175, 196
   Eve 39, 196
New York Constitution 322
New York Herald 137
New York Sun 115
New York Times 130, 143, 146, 147, 150, 247, 267-268, 322
19th Arkansas Regiment (CSA) 52-54, 61-62, 63-64, 66
North/Northern(ers) xix-xxii, xxiii, xxvi, 13, 18, 25, 32, 34, 36, 37, 45, 49, 51, 54, 61, 70, 83, 96, 98, 100, 101, 102, 110, 112, 113, 115, 125, 128, 129, 134, 135-136, 137, 138, 141, 146, 150, 174, 180, 225-226, 245, 259-260, 267, 268, 273-274, 275, 277, 278, 279, 280, 330
Northeast 17, 70, 233
Northwest 281

O

Oath of Allegiance 114, 115, 127
Occident 302
Old South xxvi, xxvii, xxviii, xxix, 260, 278, 311
Old World xxvi
Opium 221
Orient 302
Oxford 336

P

Panic of 1893 279, 285-293, 294
Park Byrne 239
Partisan rangers 71-74, 80, 81, 83
Paternalism 120
Patronage 129, 140, 141, 174, 254, 287-288
Peabody College 313
Peace Conference 41
Peace movement 102
People's Party 238, 239
Pest house 306, 308
Philadelphia Press 274

General Index

Phillips-Exeter Academy 336, 337, 338, 339, 341
Picayune 239
Pincher 126, 132-133, 137
Pinkerton detectives 180
"Pi-Utes" 267
Pleasant Grove Church 152
Pneumonia 62
Politics xxii
Poll tax 40, 241, 289
Pony Express 16
Poorhouse 168, 253
Populist(s) 303
Poughkeepsie 171
Presbyterian(s) 18, 28, 176
   Cumberland 12, 29, 166
Princeton xxii
Prohibition(ist) 315, 325, 328, 330
Prostitution 234, 304, 328
Protestant 328
Pulaski County Circuit Court 140, 142

Q

"Quaker guns" 65
Quarantine 242, 2243-244, 306-309
Quinine 59

R

Racism, racist 180, 190, 195, 245, 267, 331
Railroad 9 231
Randolph Macon Woman's College 336
Rape, rapist 129, 190, 225, 265-266, 269, 275, 276
Rebel(s) 61, 65, 68, 73, 76, 78, 81, 86-87, 99, 105, 106
Reconstruction xxvi-xxviii, xxix, 128-129, 135, 137, 139, 140-141, 150, 158, 159, 166, 174, 186, 224, 245, 246, 303, 310, 311, 319, 321
   Act 128
   Committee on 128
Redemption xxvii
Republican(s) 129, 139-140, 141-142, 143, 145, 150, 174, 186, 193, 195, 216, 234, 237, 238, 239, 240, 245, 246, 249, 254, 275, 277, 285, 287-288, 303, 304, 315, 316, 322, 328, 329, 331, 340
   Arkansas 315
   Brindletail 139-140
   Minstrel 140, 141
   Mugwumps 287
Revival 3, 85, 183
Revolution/Revolutionary War 13, 15, 50, 156
Rheumatism 176
Rhodes Scholarship 336
Rice University 338
Riggs Law 322
Roosevelt-Garner inauguration 332
Rules of Evidence 163
Rust's Brigade 52

S

St. Louis & Chicago Railroad 227
St. Louis & Colorado Railroad 227
St. Louis, Iron Mountain & Southern Railroad 225, 297
St. Louis Post-Dispatch 245-246
St. Louis Republic 266
Santa Fe Railroad 293
Savoy Hotel 333
Scandinavians 244
Scarlet fever 62
Séance 252
"Seceshes" 61, 96
Secession(ists) 25, 34, 37, 39-41, 43-47, 84, 111, 128, 277
   Convention 41, 43-47
   Referendum, Arkansas 43
Sewers 198, 243, 254, 296
Shepherd Fouke & Co. 240
Sherman Silver Purchase Act 285-287, 290, 292
Shiloh Church 59
Silver Party 287
Slave(s)/slavery xxii-xxiii, xxx, 2-3, 4, 6, 8, 9, 12-13, 18, 20-21, 22, 23, 25, 26, 28, 29, 30, 31, 32-33, 34, 35, 37, 38, 40, 45, 52, 56, 57, 58, 59, 68, 69, 70, 71, 72, 81, 84, 85, 86, 88, 89, 90-92, 93, 96, 97, 98, 102, 106, 110, 111, 112, 114, 116, 118, 119-120, 123, 126, 131, 152, 180, 302

Insurrection, revolt 32-33, 36, 47-48, 69, 180
Smallpox 102, 305-309, 310
Socialism 182
South/Southern xix-xxii, xxiii-xxv, xxvi, xxvii, xxviii, 1, 8, 12, 13, 18, 19, 21, 22, 23, 25, 26, 27, 30, 32-33, 34, 35, 36, 37, 40, 41, 42-43, 44, 45, 46, 47, 49-54, 61, 65, 69, 70, 79, 81, 83, 84, 93, 95-96, 99, 100-101, 102, 104, 105, 109, 110, 112, 113, 114, 115-116, 117, 118, 119, 120, 121-122, 125, 126, 127-128, 129, 130, 134, 135-136, 137-138, 146, 150-151, 152, 156, 158, 159-160, 161, 166, 168, 169, 172, 174, 177, 180, 188, 225-226, 245, 246, 259, 260, 261, 265, 267, 268, 273-276, 277-279, 280-281, 285, 288, 303, 311-312, 319, 322, 332, 334, 335, 341-342

    Character xix, xx, xxvi

    Ideal xix, xxii, xxiii-xxiv, xxv, xxvi, xvii, xxix, xxx, 18, 119, 135, 155, 172, 334, 337, 341-342

Southern Pine Lumber Co. 298
"Southern Yankees" 27
Southwest 197
South Western League (baseball) 231
Spiritualist(s) 252
Squill 157-158
Stanford Law School 339
State National Bank 206, 311
State Line Depot 188
State Savings & Trust Co. 311
Stereopticon 249
Stoic 135
Strike, strikers 177-183, 226
Sub-District of North Louisiana (CSA) 86
Suffrage 150, 321, 322, 325
Sunday blue laws 201, 220, 254, 255-256, 305
Sunday school 236
Supremacist 328
Swedes 244

T

Tariff 174, 225, 233, 239, 246, 249, 277, 279, 280, 285
Teapot Dome scandal 328, 329
Telegraph/wires 16, 33, 41, 46, 101, 110, 178, 181, 224, 227, 238, 244, 247, 249, 307
Telephone 191, 192, 224, 238, 298
Temperance 315
Texarkana & Fort Smith Railroad 282-283, 291
Texarkana Democrat 240, 245, 249, 250, 251, 256, 262, 270, 271, 272, 273, 274, 275, 280, 281, 285, 286, 288, 289, 290-291, 295, 297, 299, 300
Texarkana Federal Building 207, 252, 254
Texarkana Fence Factory 280
Texarkana Furniture Co. 293
Texarkana Furniture Manufacturing Co. 283
Texarkana Gas & Electric Co. 311
Texarkana Hardware Co. 298
Texarkana Ice Co. 192
Texarkana Republican 216
Texarkana Street Railway Co. 281
Texarkana Water Corp. 311
Texas & Pacific Railroad 198, 226, 282-283
Texas & St. Louis Railroad 167
Texas Bar 338
Texas Bar Association 313
Third Louisiana Cavalry (CSA) 73
13th Louisiana (Cavalry) Battalion (CSA) 71-74, 77, 79, 83
Times-Record 321
Transylvania Medical College 9
Treason 140, 148, 149
12th Louisiana Volunteers (CSA) 54-55, 61
Typhoid fever 62

U

"Uncle Sam" 295
Uniform Commercial Code 327
Union(ists) 5, 25, 34, 37, 39, 43, 44, 46-47, 50, 53-54, 55, 57, 59, 61, 64-66, 68, 70-74, 76-77, 80-81, 83, 86-88, 96, 98-99, 100-102,

General Index   433

104-106, 109-112, 116, 123, 128, 129, 130, 278
Navy 54-55, 70, 86
United States (U.S.)
  Army/Troops 17, 41, 44, 124, 143, 145, 147, 148, 149, 311, 323
  Circuit Court of Appeals for the Eighth Circuit 339, 340
  District Court 140, 251, 253
    Eastern and Western District of Arkansas 339
    Eastern District of Arkansas 223
      Texarkana Division (or branch) 197, 210, 223, 254
    Eastern District of Texas 283
    Western District of Arkansas 315, 340
  General Land Office 225
  Marshals 246-248
  Navy 323
  Supreme Court 323, 325, 338, 339
University of Arkansas 171, 339, 340, 341
University of Chicago 336
University of London 339
University of Pennsylvania Law School 339
University of Texas 338
University of the South 337
USS Tucker 41

V

Vaccinations 306, 307, 309
Vassar 336

W

Wah Lee's Chinese Laundry 221
War of 1812 28
Warren & Mitchel (law firm) 163
Washington & Lee University 310
Washington Female Seminary 14

Washington Male Seminary 14
Washington Telegraph 6, 95, 100, 281
Webster's blue speller 136
Weekly Texarkana Independent 173
West 26, 35, 61, 62, 90-91, 125, 167, 246, 278, 279, 281, 285
Western Military Academy 336
Western Union 181, 249
West Publishing 334
West Side
  City Council 184-185, 198, 217, 256
  Sanitation Committee 198-199
Whig(s) 6, 15, 16, 34-36, 310
"While We Go Marching Through Georgia" 329
White Caps/Cappers 279, 292
White House 174, 233, 246, 249, 254, 278
Whitworth mortar-pestle 60
Whooping cough 56
Wilderness 1, 2, 4-5, 7, 8, 10, 11, 24-25, 30, 90, 103
Williams & Arnold (law firm) 310
Wilson Bill 290, 292
Winchester 292
Workers' compensation 321, 325
World's Fair 242, 283
World War (I) xxviii, 323, 324-325, 336, 337
Wright's Saloon 239
Wynne plantation 70

Y

Yale 337, 338, 339
Yankee(s) 41, 64, 68, 69, 70, 72, 75, 78, 79, 81, 83, 86, 87, 88, 89-90, 95, 96, 98, 101, 104, 105, 109, 123, 166
Yellow fever 226
Yeoman xxiii
Yule 175